1984

PRAIRIE
VOICES

PRAIRIE VOICES

*A Literary History of Chicago
from the Frontier to 1893*

Kenny J. Williams

Townsend Press
Nashville, Tennessee

First Printing 1980

Townsend Press
Nashville, Tennessee

ISBN 0-935-99000-3

Library of Congress Catalog Card Number 79-27237

Printed in the United States of America

To My
Parents
MAUDE THELMA and JOSEPH HARRISON JACKSON
whose sustaining love and unwavering faith
are precious gifts

Table of Contents

ILLUSTRATIONS

following page

Introduction

Another "Apologia Pro Vita Sua"

ULTIMATELY EVERY literary critic re-defines both *literature* and *history* partially because he is faced with the task of making readers understand the premises upon which his work is based as well as presenting a justification for "another literary history." Certainly any work dealing with the nation's "second city" may seem to be an exercise in futility. With the proliferation of "Chicago books," readers may feel they know all there is to know about Chicago. And with our current emphasis upon the present, upon the here-and-now, a return to the nineteenth century may seem unwarranted. It may be that *Prairie Voices* begins with two handicaps. It is another Chicago book and another literary history. (And undoubtedly there are those who feel that the world has too many of each.)

It is perhaps an over-simplification to state the obvious, but life *is* a series of choices. And I was perhaps never more aware of "the road not taken" than during the period of working on *Prairie Voices*. Ideally, for example, it might have made everything considerably easier if the book had been divided neatly into categories. While the option of treating each genre separately was present, I dismissed that on the apparent conclusion that literature is not produced so conveniently; hence, several genres frequently appear within a single chapter. Yet, I recognized then—as I do now—that there will be disappointed readers who will search in vain for the chapter on "The Novel" or "Poetry," etc.

From a critical standpoint it might have been well if some of the long quotations had been omitted; yet, in order to give the reader a sense of the times, I chose to let the writers—whenever feasible—speak for themselves. Admittedly the selections are arbitrary. Someone else may have chosen different excerpts or other writers to illustrate the same idea. Furthermore, the various focal points were selected within chapters because they seemed to represent significant steps in the development of the city's literature. It may be that other historians would have chosen another organization or a different set of emphases. The existence of one approach does not rule out the possibility of the existence of many others.

In the final analysis, *Prairie Voices*—like any other book—simply represents the way the author chose to put together the facts of the past. And like Frost in his "The Road Not Taken," I am not prepared to say one road is better than the other. Yet, I have taken the road "less traveled by" for much of the story of Chicago's literature has traditionally been centered on those writers who began their careers in the latter part of the nineteenth century and worked well into the twentieth century. Finley Peter Dunne, Harriet Monroe, Henry Blake Fuller, Robert Herrick, or Theodore Dreiser may not be household words, but certainly their names are more familiar than W.W. Danenhower's, Zebina Eastman's, Benjamin Franklin Taylor's, or other strictly nineteenth-century writers and editors.

The story of Chicago's architecture, a story known throughout the world, is rooted in the nineteenth century. While many of the buildings which had once made Chicago famous are no longer standing, the aficionado of architectural history gains some consolation from knowing that Jenney's Home Insurance Building of 1883 ushered in a new age of American architecture. The same forces which produced the city's distinctive architecture also produced its distinctive literature. Thus to recapture a lost literary past is to help make the present more understandable; however, one must accept the notion that the past of Chicago has something vital and vibrant to give to the present as well as to the future.

Literary histories are frequently attacked by skeptics. Some of them say that literature has no value other than to entertain or to provide necessary information. Others cry that literature must be studied in a vacuum with little or no regard for the time and place of production. They would divorce the writer from his work as they tell the world that the only approach to literary history is to accept the theory of "art-for-art's sake." There are still others who might agree generally with the overall goals of literary history but refuse to accept the validity of regional approaches. To them this represents a provincial, limited, and narrow scope which has little validity in what they vaguely term "the long run." There are some who might agree with a study of Chicago's writing but who are reluctant to deal with the past. They tell us that the past is dead, that there are so many problems today which need our undivided attention, and they list every possible existing social problem. These proclaimers of the theory of relevancy insist that everything be measured in terms of their selfish question: "Is it relevant?" And there are those who view everything in terms of their own restricted definitions of "worth." They are sometimes more unyielding as they insist that everything must meet their standards of *value*. Certainly for them much of nineteenth-century Chicago writing would be dismissed. As they cite the great works of Emerson, Thoreau, Hawthorne, Melville, and Whitman, they note with smugness: "Chicago never produced writers like these."

To dismiss the past as merely what Sandburg called "a bucket full of ashes" might answer the immediate needs of some; but it also dismisses the heritage, the traditions, and the cultural foundations of people, a region, or a nation. To dismiss the study of Chicago writing as something either too new or too provincial for consideration denies not only the contribution which the city's writers have made but also denies the pattern which the city has provided for the analysis of the American character. Chicago as a place, an idea, or an image was rooted in the spirit of expansionism which characterized nineteenth-century America. American art—like American civilization—is composed of the worthy and the unworthy, the classical and the popular, the eastern and the western, the southern and the northern. To negate the worth of writers who do not measure up to some absolute standard of literature is to deny the existence of a host of writers who in a particular place at a particular time gave voice to their concerns as well as their hopes. It is to deprive future generations of the opportunity to make their own assessments regarding the roles of those writers who are not deemed to be "first-rate" by some twentieth-century critics. It is to suggest that "contributions" can come only from critically recognized or acceptable sources. In the long run, of course, only Time—the most impartial of judges—can weigh in the balance the ultimate value of Chicago's nineteenth-century literary history.

Several years ago, when I was working on *In the City of Men*, I was struck by the evolution and development of urban literature as it was being produced in Chicago. At that time, however, I was primarily concerned with the fact that late nineteenth-century architecture and literature sprang from the same impetus in the city. The forces, for example, which produced the architects who were to become known as the Chicago School of Architecture were powerful. Although the architects were certainly artists, they were essentially responding to their environment, their times, and their concerns. That they produced a unique art form that was to become a significant step in the development of American civilization was not their purpose nor their primary object. The same might be said of the development of literature, especially of fiction. The so-called Chicago novel—which has become such an integral part of American literature—was born during the same period, spawned by the same forces.

While much attention has been focused on the latter part of the nineteenth century (and with good reason), I became convinced, while doing my earlier study, that there evolved in the young city a literature—not necessarily of distinction—but one whose themes and concerns frequently foreshadowed the urban literature which was to come. As I turned my attention to those early days and early writers, I realized that the complete history of the region's literature could—perhaps—never be told. There were so many extenuating circumstances that precluded the existence of all of the necessary records. Too often, the researcher who deals with urban history is called upon to make the same kinds of judgments and reach conclusions based upon insufficient data as those ancient historians who try to "piece together" a culture and a people. While nineteenth-century Chicago is not that far away, culturally it seems as removed from us as some ancient community of classical lore. The result is a study which does not pretend to be complete. It is merely a suggestion of what existed in early Chicago as it attempts in some instances to trace the evolution of certain stories—such as the French explorations and the Fort Dearborn legend—through their development into a type of Chicago romance in a city not known for historical fiction. It is a look at some of the ephemeral newspapers and journalists who—perhaps even in spite of themselves—formed a background for the great days of such newspapers as the Chicago *Tribune* and *Daily News*. In short, it is a selective and limited view of the mass of writing which took place in the city during the nineteenth century and traces a few of those themes into the twentieth century.

Perhaps some critics will view *Prairie Voices* as an extension of *In the City of Men*. Certainly the present study fills in some of the gaps of the former work. Others will undoubtedly view it as the first volume of the preceding book. And I agree there is a probable line which one could draw from *In the City of Men* to *Prairie Voices* since both of them are predicated upon the role and the contributions of a city whose image generally does not include the arts. And there will be those who will undoubtedly dismiss *Prairie Voices* as a re-statement of *In the*

City of Men. To them I can only suggest a careful reading of both books.

   In our present-day rush toward discrediting the past, it is easy to forget those who blazed the trails. Certainly the early town of Chicago made no pretenses toward being a cultural mecca. Men and women arrived searching for "success," for a realization of the American Dream. Some were to be sorely disappointed. Yet, within that bustling town one can find planted those literary seeds which blossomed into one of the outstanding regional literatures of the nation. As H.L. Mencken declared in 1917, "all literary movements that have youth in them and a fresh point of view, and the authentic bounce and verve" of the United States emerged from Chicago, "the most civilized city in America." He continued: "Find me a writer who is indubitably American and who has something new and interesting to say, and who says it with an air, and nine times out of ten . . . he has some sort of connection with the abbatoir by the lake—that he was bred there or got his start there, or passed through there during the days when he was tender." To recapture that past is to pay tribute to those writers, publishers, and printers who felt that theirs was a story worth recording as they set about to create a city. But more important, to present some of Chicago's early writers is to suggest that the Chicago of Henry Blake Fuller, Robert Herrick, Theodore Dreiser, or Carl Sandburg had a literary history before Fuller rocked the city and the nation with his *The Cliff-Dwellers* in 1893.

   The story of Chicago's writing in the days prior to 1893 may not rival the genius of the American Transcendental Movement of the 1830's and 1840's nor the great New England writers of the Romantic Age during the 1850's, but it is a story which reflects in miniature some of the problems of the literati in the United States during the century. It shows so clearly that the cultural basis of a literary community cannot be separated into component bins. The interrelationship between literature and culture is so closely interwoven. The popular image of Chicago was established years ago, and it was the result of that group of nineteenth-century writers who unwittingly molded a pattern which remains although many of their names are lost to history. While I am concerned about the literary history of the nineteenth century, I am also concerned about the evolution of that literary image. Hence, the literary history of nineteenth-century Chicago is in part the story of the growth and development of an image which has become an integral part of American civilization. And I dare to predict thousands of years from now, when many of the artifacts from our civilization have crumbled and faded, there will remain that image which will be conjured up whenever the word *CHICAGO* appears. Each generation undoubtedly has contributed to the making of the image and to the evolution of the legend. Many of the prairie men and women who contributed to the making of the image are now buried in obscurity, but at a particular historic moment they lived and wrote of the city which was and captured a sense of what was to be.

PRAIRIE
VOICES

CHAPTER 1

Portrait of a City:
A Literary Model

WHAT IS CHICAGO? La Salle, the French explorer, stood at the Chicago portage before this country was a nation and was impressed by his vision. Later he proclaimed in a letter to a friend in France: "This will be the Gate of an Empire; this will be the seat of commerce." He continued his description: "The typical man who will grow up here must be an enterprising man. Each day, as he rises, he will exclaim, 'I act, I move, I push.' " Little did La Salle realize the exact course of events, but in the seventeenth century he summarized the faith and hope of the French explorers who saw possibilities in the Chicago swamp. La Salle's "gate to an Empire" became the home of Dreiser's titan. For Robert Herrick it was the place where only success matters. Sandburg called it the "city of the big shoulders" and "hog butcher of the world." Algren said it was a "city on the make" and "the hustling town." And somewhere in the folklore of Chicago, it is called the nation's "second city." These are some of the images of Chicago, and these are also images of America.

What R.W.B. Lewis said of the American experience in his *The American Adam* (Chicago, 1955) can well define the Chicagoan and the Chicago experience.

[He is] the image of a radically new personality, the hero of the new adventure: an individual emancipated from history, happily bereft of ancestry, untouched and undefiled by the usual inheritances of family and race; an individual standing alone, self-reliant and self-propelling, ready to confront whatever awaited him with the aid of his own unique and inherent resources (p. 5).

A study of Chicago literature involves understanding "the image of a radically new personality" because the founders of the city were individuals who were indeed "emancipated from history . . . [who were] self-reliant and self-propelling." Eventually, a study of Chicago will lead to an understanding of the nation; for in many ways Chicago has been America in microcosm.

What is a city? Perhaps it is this question which ultimately separates urban records from urban literature. The economist, the historian, the sociologist, the political scientist, and the politician at least pretend to know the answer. But the novelist and the poet are not quite so certain. They know it exists. They agree that the city has mystery and depth, but they have probed those depths only to have the answer elude them.

What is a city? Men and women have written about it, scholars have researched it, scientists have tested it, poets have sung odes to its existence, historians have chronicled the records of it, and artists have tried to capture its spirit on canvas. But for all of this, it is difficult to discover a clear, concise definition of it. One can distinguish some of its characteristics with little or no problem. One can ascertain that it must have a population of a predetermined number. It must have a certain per capita tax. One can describe the collection of buildings or the business structures. One can talk about its entertainment centers or its housing developments. But when that is finished, there still is not a single definition of the city. Instead there exists each person's encounter with a specific urban center. Ultimately, there are as many cities as there are definers of it. Sandburg's Chicago is not the same as Algren's, and both cities differ greatly from that of Fuller or Herrick.

Yet, in spite of the fact that definitions vary greatly, a given city tends to evoke similar mental images. Babylon, Sodom, Paris,

London, Rome, New York, Charleston, Natchez, Chicago. Each name produces an image, and each image has certain dominant characteristics. These images are the result of the historical facts plus the collective use of the city in art. Certainly the historic facts of Babylon are well-known to the historian of ancient cultures. But to those for whom Babylon is simply the name of a city of the long-distant past, it lives again in modern literature. The idea of Babylon is reshaped by the writer who begins with the historic fact of the fallen city and moves to a symbolic inference. The literary city is an image of the real city viewed through the eyes and the impressions of the writer. The literary city is often faithful to the physical actualities which exist and can even be a documentary account of the social, economic, political, and intellectual history of the place. Yet, each literary city is unique because the writer—in effect—creates it for his purpose. Thus, the literary city goes beyond providing a recognizable locale; it becomes a vehicle by which impressions or symbols are transmitted from the creative artist to his audience. To stop merely at the historic fact loses much of the intent of the artist and ignores a difference between history as fact and literature as art.

Today American novelists seem to be essentially urban. The mystery of the city no longer fascinates them as it had intrigued earlier writers, but as the novel was coming to maturity in America there were writers in Chicago who were groping for answers to the questions: What is the city? What is its effect upon mankind? They knew their city was different from those in the tradition-bound East or in the nostalgic South. They knew they had to re-think their own values. They came to the conclusion that the city was not passive, rather it played an active role in the affairs of men. They recognized—unwillingly at first—that the city was a force or a power which guided and controlled the fates of those who lived in it. Therefore, the early Chicago writer (especially the novelist) seldom saw the city simply as a background for an action which could take place anywhere; the city was important to the action. No longer, the novelists concluded, was man a free agent.

No longer could he direct his destiny. The Chicago novel which was developed during the nineteenth century became one of the most explicit statements of the literary city. And it became one of the clearest examples of what a city can do to the creative artist. The naturalistic technique became a fit method for expression.

Thus it was that the Chicago writers created in their city a distinctive urban literature which has since passed beyond the region and has become an integral part of American writing. Consequently, to study what happened in Chicago is not as provincial and parochial as it may appear, for it is to study some of the emerging patterns of American literature as they came face to face with the industrialism and with the materialism of the national life.

Chicago literature frequently comes closer to history than some other urban literatures because almost from the beginning Chicago writers dealt with what they saw rather than with what they wanted to see. Most of them chose to ignore the early history of the region which culminated in the Fort Dearborn Massacre because many of them had rejected an interest in the past. The reality of the city was so powerful that in Chicago it was the writer who came to terms with the fact that an entirely new symbolism would have to be created to explain the American city as it really was. No longer could the romantic approach to literature work for the urban scene. One needs only to compare the type of fiction being produced in the East with that written in Chicago. While there was a plethora of moralistic tales in both sections, eastern fiction remained immune to the urban scene much longer than that of Chicago.

The novelists of Chicago have been—through the years— extremely sensitive to the city and to the need for survival in it. When he told the story of the Chicago Fire in his 1872 novel *Barriers Burned Away*, E.P. Roe suggested that the old Chicago with its growing emphasis upon class and caste had been eliminated, and he felt that a new city would arise. Perhaps he was too idealistic. Perhaps the new was no better than the old. But in 1872 there was the promise of a different lifestyle based not upon a man's New England birth but upon his ability to survive in the city. When Henry Blake Fuller chronicled the history of the city in *With the Procession* of 1895, he was fully aware that the men who had built Chicago had outlived their usefulness; and while he was sorry to see them go down to defeat, he understood that the progress of the city demanded a different type of man. And so it was that his hero, David Marshall, could lament the changes; but the changes were inevitable, and those who survived knew they must deal with them. As Edward Van Harrington, the hero of Robert Herrick's 1905 novel, *The Memoirs of an American Citizen,* indicated time and time again the old men did not understand the new city. Van Harrington learned the lesson which David Marshall could not learn.

Sensitivity to the reality of the city led James T. Farrell, in a later period, to present Studs Lonigan from the life which he knew. He had seen the breakdown of the Irish Catholics as the city forced upon them compromises which were not justified either by what they had learned at church or at home. As Studs and his friends turned against other minority groups in an attempt to salvage what they thought was theirs, they became pathetic examples of those incapable of coping with the city. And no Negro in Chicago can ever forget the loneliness of Bigger Thomas as he crossed that invisible line onto Drexel Boulevard. In that moment of loneliness Wright summarized centuries of separateness. Neither can one forget that bitter irony of Mr. Dalton, the tenement owner, who cared little about the living conditions which he forced upon the Biggers of the city and their families but who donated ping-pong tables to the local Y.M.C.A. so Bigger could have some recreation. Farrell's novels of the Irish Catholic community in Chicago are partial portraits just as Richard Wright's *Native Son* is a story of a segment of the Negro community, but both novelists captured a brutal reality for some Chicagoans.

From Roe to Wright few novelists have pretended to write history, but each in his own way has immortalized a significant historic moment, and each in his own way has been far more conscious of history than those who continue to serve pabulum to

the people. These novelists have understood the city with its dis-
illusionments and broken dreams. They have understood that it
profits a man little to gain the whole world and to lose his soul.
They have understood the city and have recorded honestly the
social structure as well as the moral fiber of Chicago. From them
the reader gains insight into Chicago as a place and gains a sense
of Chicago as an idea.

Trying to establish a relationship between an actual city and its
literary counterpart is not as futile as it may appear because the
separation of history and literature is a fairly recent phenomenon.
The link between history and storytelling is especially evident in
older societies; and the line between history and literature, as we
know them, is frequently non-existent. When one considers the
work of Herodotus (the so-called "father of history") or Thucy-
dides, one has to decide whether these men were historians or
storytellers. And what of the many tribal stories of Africa which
form an outstanding body of oral literature? Do not they record
the history and the important events of the various tribes? And
what of the bards of England or the troubadours of France? For
them the question must be raised (a question which is still valid
today): where does storytelling end and history begin? What would
happen if—in the next two hundred years—all of the histories of
Chicago were destroyed and there remained only the novels of
E.P. Roe, Mary H. Catherwood, Henry Blake Fuller, Robert Herrick, Theodore Dreiser, James T. Farrell, Richard Wright and
Nelson Algren with the poems of Carl Sandburg and Gwendolyn
Brooks? Would later generations be able to construct the events of
the life of the city from the works which survived? The relationship between storytelling and history suggests an age-old philosophical question, and it significantly suggests the value of regional
literature apart from any purely critical theory of 'art for art's
sake."

Admittedly the historian and the storyteller have different goals.
But since both history and fiction employ the narrative method,
the initial reaction is to distinguish between the two by defining

history as a record of something which has happened and by defining fiction as "a story." Within this context history is thought to be a form which concerns itself with real people and the historian as one who deals with the realities implied by a study of the past; whereas the novelist is dismissed as a creator of imaginary people and events.

As one views the beginning of literature in the United States, one notes with interest the excessive number of histories and the almost total absence of fiction. The New England Puritans, for example, rejected fiction but viewed the writing of history as an act ordained by God, an act which permitted them to trace God's will as that will showed itself in their everyday lives. They realized that they were making history and so felt duty-bound to record it. Well into the nineteenth century, the negative attitude toward fiction manifested itself in several ways. Novel reading was considered to be a frivolous activity, and there were those who viewed novelists as workers in the vineyard of Satan. Many of America's early novelists were reluctant to admit their work; hence, they wrote under assumed names or wrote long introductions and prefaces in which they declared that the story which was to follow was really a true story. This practice continued well into the nineteenth century as they defended the "truth" of their work in various ways, but the result was always the same. They were intent upon indicating that they had not been dealing in the realm of the imagination, and they suggested that any reader might get a lesson for life by reading the "true" story. This accounts, at least in part, for the moralistic nature of much of America's early fiction. It also accounts for the inability of some critics to separate novels from "true adventure" stories.

Even as late as 1850 Nathaniel Hawthorne felt compelled in his long introduction to *The Scarlet Letter* to state that he based his work on facts. He noted that he had "allowed [himself] . . . as much license as if the facts had been entirely of [his] own invention," because this was necessary for "the authenticity of the outline." The reader is told that if there should be any who desire to substantiate the materials of the novel, the author has saved all of the historic artifacts—including the scarlet letter—as he had found them in the custom-house. While this is a ruse to get his story started, it is also a means by which he gives authenticity to his tale. Thus, it is true that the introductory statement, "The Custom House" serves many purposes; yet central to its theme is the reinforcement of the "truth" of Hawthorne's narrative.

Unconsciously writers of fiction have added to the dilemma and to the perplexity of trying to separate fiction and history because unwittingly writers of fiction have felt compelled to justify their work by emphasizing what they considered to be the methodology and purpose of history. Perhaps if they had looked more closely and more critically at both history and fiction, those Puritan writers and readers of long ago might have saved themselves and later generations a lot of effort. Even they must have known that the art of story-telling is perhaps as old as man, for even in their own histories and sermons they included short stories or exempla which went beyond merely the recording of history. They must have been aware that one of the functions of literature is to provide—either consciously or unconsciously—order for the chaos in which man finds himself. As an attempt to interpret events, history does tell it the way it was, but literature gives meaning to that reality. Fiction provides a framework which permits the author to present his assessment of the real world. Consequently, the art of storytelling goes deep into the needs of man and provides more than entertainment. As Andrew Greeley stated in "Where are the Story Tellers?" (Chicago *Tribune,* June 17, 1975) when a child pleads for a story "it's a primal religious cry of all humankind . . . the child's longing for a happy ending is really a primal religious hunger for evidence that good conquers evil." Perhaps the adult mind no longer craves for such simplistic answers as "good conquers evil," but we often go to literature in search of explanations, interpretations, and order for life as well as to escape *from* life.

Perhaps if the New England Puritans had addressed themselves to similarities rather than to differences, the course of literature in the United States might have taken another path because both the novelist and historian share certain communal interests. Both of them are concerned with truth, admittedly it is a relative truth, it is a truth as they see it, but truth nonetheless. Within this concern, both attempt to give an order to that truth. This is the point at which imagination and creativity enter. The ancient historians understood this well and saved their work from being a mere recital of names and dates. And some of the outstanding historians of today have understood the need to combine storytelling with their research. Both the novelist and the historian are interested in gathering the facts, whatever those facts might be. And both of them must have a sense of the human condition. History exists because men and women have lived, worked, and died—sometimes for causes, sometimes merely for themselves—but they form the basis of any historic study. It is the rare history which can exist without people. As Emerson in his "Self-Reliance" so aptly noted "A man Caesar is born and for ages afterward we have a Roman Empire." So too fiction exists because men and women have lived, worked, and died. Without belaboring the point of the similarities between history and fiction, suffice it to say that the line is frequently very narrow between them.

Yet while one may list the similarities between history and fiction, there must finally be the recognition that history is not fiction, and fiction is not history. The complexity of a short story or of a novel or of a poem cannot be relegated merely to picking out the historic references and measuring them in terms of how true or how false they may be. Ultimately, one must view urban literature not as the city is recorded with its streets and buildings which can be recognized but as the idea of the city is perceived by the writer. To deal with this perception, then, goes beyond the purely documentary evidence or recognizable facts. In his "Four Preludes on Playthings of the Wind" Carl Sandburg has created an unforgettable portrait of a city which evokes a particular mood. Although the poem does not specify a particular city, one can read in it a powerful warning to Chicago or any other city which believes in its uniqueness and invincibility. Sandburg notes: "It has happened before" and explains that "strong men put up a city and got/a nation together." Afterwards they "paid singers to sing and women/to warble: We are the greatest city,/the greatest nation,/nothing like us ever was." The chant of the singers, however, was heard not only by "the strong men" but also by "rats and lizards." Eventually "the only listeners/ . . . are the rats . . . and the lizards." The rats were not totally idle as Sandburg continues: "The feet of the rats/scribble on the doorsills/the hieroglyphs of the rat footprints . . . ," but "the wind shifts." And he concludes: ". . . even the writing of the rat footprints/tells us nothing, nothing at all/about the greatest city, the greatest nation/where the strong men listened/and the women warbled: Nothing like us ever was." Certainly Sandburg not only faced honestly the rise and fall of a city or nation but also has provided in an impressionistic and symbolic way the history of many cities and civilizations.

The novelist, who is perhaps more realistic than the economist, historian, sociologist, political scientist, and other purveyors of urban knowledge, comes to grips with the effects of the city upon characters and then interprets that fact within an all-encompassing symbol. No one who has read Dreiser's *Sister Carrie* can forget the opening chapter entitled "The Magnet." This is Dreiser's Chicago which Carrie, a young girl from Wisconsin, is entering for the first time. It is a city of mystery, it is a city of power, it is a *magnet* drawing her into its electrifying circle. Neither can one forget Dreiser's later city which is composed of *titans* who answer only the law of themselves.

Throughout the city's literature Chicago is generally described in terms of a single concept which records the effects of the city either upon characters or upon the author himself. Usually the central symbol suggests the power of the "strong men" who "put up" the city and then chanted "we are the greatest city." Out of this symbol of power an image of Chicago has emerged. It is seen early in the histories, magazines, and newspapers of the city. It is also seen in the few attempts to create out of the French explorations, Fort Dearborn Massacre, and Fire of 1871 a romance of Chicago. And it is most clearly seen in the evolution of the business novel for which the city became known.

Literature ultimately tends to define man as he views himself in the universe and in his immediate surroundings. One of the distinguishing features of Chicago literature is the ease with which writers have been able to give meaning to the urban experience even among those who initially tried to create an eastern genteel community in the midwestern town. Somehow they knew from the beginning who they were and where they were. Chicago did not have the Puritan tradition of the seventeenth century; neither was it in sympathy with the English-landholder tradition which came by way of the South; therefore, any attempt to define Chicago in terms of these other cultures met with almost certain failure because it distorted the Chicago experience. The Chicago writer, with few exceptions, generally avoided the situation which had earlier existed on the eastern seaboard as the new American writers at the close of the eighteenth century tried to mold an "American" literature out of a combination of fidelity to the English cultural tradition with "American" subjects. That pervasive sense of inferiority did not afflict the Chicago writer to any great degree until the 1880's. By that time another group of writers had discovered that there was a need to create a new language to describe adquately the evolving urban conditions. A distinct Chicago literature, then, emerged out of those attempts—meager though the first ones were—to define the Chicagoan.

II

The beginnings of any literature are crude, and what occurred in Chicago was no exception. The first group of Chicago writers were a motley crew at best. The city was concerned with the problems of everyday survival, but there were those who were eager to provide an account of daily life in the fast-growing metropolis. Newspapers and journals flourished and contained not only a record of the city in the process of becoming but also the numerous human interest stories which were to serve as a basis for longer and more interpretative works dealing with the effects of the city on its citizens. It is not surprising that the raising of a city did not leave much time for creativity, but there was some interest in what many historians have called "the finer pursuits of life." Eventually a significant group of writers emerged; and the newspapers, especially the *Daily News* and *Tribune*, had provided a training ground for so many of them. By the close of the nineteenth century the city had had a colorful, albeit, short history.

Founded in 1833 as a town in a State that was only fifteen years old, incorporated in 1837 as a city, Chicago had rushed toward its development only to suffer a number of financial panics. By the Civil War the city had become firm in its position as an industrial and financial center. Real estate, transportation, lumber, meat-packing were just a few of the avenues to great personal wealth. In the meantime, as is to be expected during a time of war, there were those who made fortunes out of the misfortunes of others. When the war ended, the move toward the West began in earnest. And there was Chicago standing at the gateway to the West—although that title was eventually bestowed on St. Louis. The tales of easy money had reached both the East and the South. When one said the name, Chicago, one thought immediately of such men as "Long John" Wentworth, Benjamin Hutchinson, Philip Armour, Marshall Field, Gustavus Swift, or George M. Pullman. These men had made a great deal of money in a few years. As people teemed into Chicago, each person saw himself as a millionaire one day because the tales of "easy money in Chicago" were widespread. But some of these people were destined to be disappointed. Among them were those who manned the factories and the industries, who inhabited the tenements, who were broken by the city but upon whose back the giants built their fortunes. The stories of the disillusioned were the daily tragedies in a city where only success counted. These unfortunate ones came with a firm belief in the American Dream; they died after living the American nightmare. But others continued to come, each believing "with me it will be different." And as the city grew, its citizens kept saying to themselves and to their neighbors "we are the greatest. Nothing like us ever was." Then came that dry October, 1871, and one chapter of Chicago's history came to a close.

Perhaps the next phase is best expressed in the words of the real estate agent, S.D. Kerfoot, whose actions the day after the Fire of 1871 have become part of the legend of the city, one which is often repeated. He built a shack and posted the sign: "Open for business—all gone, save wife, children, and energy." Chicago, indeed, was open for business. Within a few years the traces of the great fire had disappeared. Once again the singers had something to celebrate. Once again they could sing: "We are the greatest city . . . nothing like us ever was." But through it all, there was a disturbing element which persisted. Fuller later was to describe the city as the place where all citizens had come to make money. Herrick, a few years later, in *The Gospel of Freedom* (1898) described the city as an "instance of a successful, contemptuous disregard of nature by man." He explained this by comparing Chicago to other outstanding urban centers.

Other great cities have been called gradually into existence about some fine opportunity suggested by nature, at the junction of fertile valleys, or on a loving bend of a broad river, or in the inner recesses of a sea-harbour, where nature has pointed out . . . a spot favourable for life and growth. In the case of Chicago, man has decided to make for himself a city for his artificial necessities in defiance of every indifference displayed by nature . . . Life spins there; man is handling existence as you knead bread in a pan. The city is made of man; that is the last word of it. Brazen, unequal, like all man's work, it stands [as] a stupendous piece of blasphemy against nature. Once within its circle, the heart must forget that the earth is beautiful. 'Go to,' man boasts, 'our fathers lived in fear of nature, *we* will build a city where

men and women in their passions shall be the beginning and the end.
Man is enough for man . . .' (pp. 101-103 *passim.*)

But in spite of the misgivings of Fuller and Herrick, the
effect of the city upon the artist was almost magical. When he
first arrived in Chicago, Louis Sullivan recorded in his *The
Autobiography of an Idea* (New York, 1924) that he was impressed by the "power" of the prairie. He saw Lake Michigan
as "naked power," and the sky was a "vast open power." The
city, to him, was "magnificent and wild: a crude extravaganza:
an intoxicating rawness: a sense of big things to be done. For
'Big' was the word. 'Biggest' was preferred, and the 'biggest in
the world' was the braggart phrase on every tongue . . ." And
Sullivan concluded: "This is the place for me" (pp. 196-197).

Power was the single word which seemed to capture the image
of Chicago. Literally every writer who came into the city—
Hamlin Garland, Robert Herrick, Theodore Dreiser, Carl Sandburg, Edgar Lee Masters, Floyd Dell—commented on the city's
raw power. It was a power which gave them a sense of being in the
midst of great events; it was a power which gave voice to their
creative urges. Although many of them were eventually to leave
the city, they had been "made" by Chicago and in turn had
preserved for posterity an image of Chicago as a representation
of American civilization.

The decade ushered in by 1890 must have been an exciting
period. The city had a "usable past" and a promising future.
The University of Chicago was beginning with a strange amal-
gamation of Rockefeller money and William Rainey Harper
intellectualism. Congregated on the Midway were some of the
outstanding thinkers of America. Many of them were from
Harvard since the University of Chicago could offer more money
than the older prestigious school. They came to work at "Harper's
school" (sometimes called "Harper's Folly") and poked fun at
the materialism of Chicago, but they were grateful to receive
higher salaries in the commercial city and were pleased with the

academic freedom permitted in the newer school. And so they left the notable Harvard University to come to what some of them called "The University in the Mud." Some outstanding academicians came. Robert Morss Lovett, William Vaughn Moody, and Robert Herrick were to make major contributions not only as members of the Department of English but also as writers in the Chicago movement of literature. The University of Chicago became famous for its innovative approach to academic studies. Thorstein Veblen revolutionized the theory of economics with his doctrine of "conspicuous consumption." As he looked around Chicago, he could well document his point of view. John Dewey was to introduce the techniques of modern education. Alice Freeman Palmer made it clear that there were places for women in higher education; Edith Abbott and Grace Lathrop knew that attention would have to be directed toward the immigrant, neglected children, and the tenement dweller. Out of their concern there developed one of the outstanding schools of social work. But all was not to deal with that which was immediately practical. Thomas Goodspeed undertook a translation of biblical literature which put the new college on the map as a center for another movement in theological education and biblical scholarship. In short, the Univeristy of Chicago engendered on the Midway an intellectual ferment that is probably unmatched in the history of higher education.

Close by the University, another event was taking place. The World's Columbian Exposition was to be called the "turning point of American civilization." Perhaps nowhere had this been better expressed than by Henry Adams who—while contemplating the exhibit of the Dynamo in the Electricity Building and the power of the machine—realized that for the first time Chicago was questioning the direction of America.

By the turn of the century the great decade of the 1890's had passed, and Garland's 1894 prediction that Chicago was to be the literary capital and cultural center of the United States appeared to be coming true. The opening years of the twentieth century have variously been called the "renaissance," "the golden age," or the "Chicago years of American literature." There indeed was something "new and fresh" in American literature. H.L. Mencken announced first in the New York *Mail* and later on October 28, 1917, in the Chicago *Tribune* that the city was the literary capital of the United States. Three years later in the London *Nation* (April 17, 1920) he wrote more about the "literary capital" of the United States. And for a time it seemed he might be correct. Every writer of the Midwest was trying to make it to Chicago. Some of them settled on 57th Street in the dilapidated shop buildings left over from the World's Columbian Exposition. They had a camaraderie which was solid as they met with Margery Currey, the estranged wife of Floyd Dell, and spent hours in her studio discussing and reading their works to each other.

While the 57th Street group was getting settled, Harriet Monroe was establishing *Poetry: A Magazine of Verse*, the first magazine devoted totally to poetry. That the magazine became a forum for the new American poetry might have surprised those who remembered Harriet's own stilted, traditional, neoclassical verse. But she recognized that poets should have an opportunity to present their work fairly and securely while being paid for it. She was a member of Chicago's elite and had succeeded in getting one hundred men to pledge $50.00 for five years in order to support her endeavor. These were the same men who gave so much more for the symphony and the Art Institute. Harriet convinced them that poetry was an art form which also demanded their support. *Poetry*—oldest and most famous poetry magazine in the English-speaking world—published the work of most of the giants of modern poetry both here and abroad. Such diverse poets as Ezra Pound, T.S. Eliot, Edwin Arlington Robinson, Vachel Lindsay, Carl Sandburg, Edgar Lee Masters, Amy Lowell, Robert Frost, and Wallace Stevens initially gained an audience through this journal.

By the 1920's the participants in this vital literary movement had moved away. The Chicago literary renaissance was over. There is little evidence that the city knew or cared that they were disappearing to New York and to other eastern points. The writers who had been nurtured and created by Chicago were forced by what they felt was the indifference of the city to leave it and move elsewhere. Somehow they could leave the physical Chicago, but the spiritual Chicago had marked them permanently. As he recalled the city in later years, Floyd Dell maintained that he had been happy in Chicago. Refusing to call it a gray and ugly city, he asserted that he had had enough "beauty" in the city to fill his heart. But the BEAUTY of the later writers was to be the beauty of the "hog butcher of the world" and not that of nineteenth-century gentility.

The spirit of Chicago was not long without other singers to chant of this urban power. James T. Farrell, Nelson Algren, and Richard Wright celebrated the city as a spiritual wasteland. Willard Motley, somewhat later perhaps best voiced and understood the ambiguities of urban life. In the prefatory lines to *Knock On Any Door* (New York, 1947), he observed: "The sparrow sits on a telephone pole in the alley in the city. The city is the world in Microcosm." Recognizing both the beauty and ugliness of the urban experience, he could admit: "There are many doors to the city. Many things hide behind the many doors. More lives than one are lived in the city, more deaths than one are met within the city's gate. The city doesn't change. The people come and go, the visitors. They see the front yard." And he posed the questions: "But what of the city's backyard and the alley? Who knows the lives and minds of the people who live in the alley?" According to Motley, the question would be answered by knocking "on any door down this street, in this alley."

And there are singers today in Chicago who are still defining the urban experience. Saul Bellow, Gwendolyn Brooks, Cyrus Colter, Harry Mark Petrakis, and William Brashler are further evidence of the creative spirit which exists within the city. The shades of Eugene Field have been resurrected in the hard-hitting journalism of Mike Royko. And the multitude of poetry groups all over the city attest to a repetition of Harriet Monroe's faith in the possibility of Chicago as a center for "new poetry."

The Chicago writers, then, have produced an outstanding urban literature which, along with the Chicago skyscraper, was destined to change the course of American art. The architects who were working in the city in the 1880's gave the direction, and certain characteristics of the urban office building are now expected no matter where it is located. In a similar fashion, certain traits are expected of modern urban literature without realizing that a group of writers in Chicago led the way.

III

The study of Chicago literature leads to a portrait of the city which, in turn, leads to an image (or a set of images) of a culture. Confronted by such literary giants as Emerson, Thoreau, and Hawthorne on the east coast in the mid-years of the nineteenth century, one immediately wonders where such Chicago writers as Juliette Kinzie and E.P. Roe of the same period fit into some national schema. It is easy to develop a literary sense of inferiority with such a consideration. But the problem is not with the culture but rather with the comparison. Emerson, Thoreau, and Hawthorne appeared at a time when New England's literary tradition (which was a product of the seventeenth-century Puritan years and the eighteenth-century philosophical, religious, and political revolt) was an accomplished fact. Juliette Kinzie and E.P. Roe, on the other hand, appeared at a time when Chicago was in the process of becoming. They represented, along with the other writers, a starting point for a new American literary tradition, for a new urban culture. So when the purist declares that Chicago has no Emerson, no Thoreau, or no Hawthorne, he should be reminded that Chicago never was Concord nor Salem, Massachusetts. Even though William Bross, an early historian of Chicago, declared in 1876 that Chicago was the "second city," there is no reason to continue unworkable comparisons. The "second city" syndrome might provide entertainment for an intellectual exercise, but it is not compatible with the spirit of Chicago which has been known by various names but which generally can be summarized as "Chicago boosterism." This is the spirit which often makes Chicagoans—when they are away from home—say the name of the city in a tone of defensive pride. It is the same quality which makes a Chicagoan unwittingly respond to the question: "From what State are you?" by simply saying: "Chicago." Fuller knew this inclination well when he described Jessie Bradley, a character in *The Cliff-Dwellers* as being "a true daughter of Chicago; she had the one infallible local trait—she would rather talk to a stranger about her own town than about any other subject" (p. 27). While it has practically produced tons of articles and more than its share of books, Chicago "boosterism" has focused primarily on the bigness and uniqueness of the city.

Although they have frequently contributed to a greater under- standing of this nebulous quality called the "Chicago Spirit," the artists of the city have often suffered undue neglect because of it. Periodically critics of Chicago culture become rather upset over the fact that artists seldom remain in the city for a long time. The rationale for each exodus is generally reduced to the assumption that Chicago is not concerned with art nor with the artist. But, according to Alson J. Smith, artists were "stamped" by Chicago which "brought out the best there was in them, and they never were more creative than when they were working there." But he contended the reasons for leaving Chicago are not complicated. He proposed the answer in his *Chicago's Left Bank* (Chicago, 1953):

Perhaps it really isn't much of a mystery . . . They were set down in the midst of the most cynical and materialistic society on the face of the earth, a proudly idolatrous society that bowed openly before the Golden Calf. Chicago's tremendous energy, vitality and brutality attracted them and held them for a time, but the city was contemp- tuously indifferent to them, even to the ones who sang its praises, and that, in the long run, was unforgivable. Because it was indifferent it forced the writer in upon himself; his loneliness in the midst of so much bustle begat creativity; he wrote and he wrote well, but the city didn't care; only money and power got recognition in Chicago . . .

So Chicago, like a civic devil's advocate, made her writers strong by resisting them. She made most of them rich, too; . . . but man does not live by bread alone, and no amount of success could endear the city to the writers who had suffered spiritually from its indifference . . . But Chicago had scarred them all, and as time went on they were proud of their scars (pp. 19-20).

And as recently as 1975, Nelson Algren said, as he left Chicago for Patterson, New Jersey, that the city he had known and had loved in spite of its unkindness to him had disappeared. He, too, accused the city of indifference.

It is perhaps one of the ironies of the city's history that the artists who have been able to capture all facets of the city's life, who have been able to present the city stripped of any Chamber-of-Commerce glamour, have been the same ones who have frequently suffered most of all from the city's neglect. It is also ironic that the writers who perhaps gave the best expression to the spirit of Chicago in fiction should today be known only by a few specialists, that the surviving elements of the magnificent World's Columbian Exposition of 1893 have all but disappeared, that two of the greatest buildings by Adler and Sullivan should have been destroyed, one for a parking lot, the other for an undistinguished highrise. A few years ago the Italian *Successo*, a business magazine probably comparable to America's *Fortune*, ran a cover story on Chicago (July, 1971) entitled "Chicago: Crossroads of the World." The Italian editors, while attributing the growth and development of the city to the businessmen who "intensely" love their city, were able to pinpoint the basic irony and ambiguity of the Chicago spirit. Citing what it calls the city's "continual, ruthless transformation" the article concludes: " 'Get rid of it' is the spirit of Chicago, [as the city places] its trust in that incredible energy which in just fifty years turned the mud flats with the pungent wild onions into a prototype for industrial cities." The list of ironies can go on *ad infinitum*, but the cultural greatness of Chicago occurred in spite of the city. While all of the Sandburg poem is not applicable, "strong men *did* put up a city" and the artists *did* sing "we are the greatest city . . . nothing like us ever was."

When one looks in retrospect at this period, there is a tendency to put all of the events and names together thereby unwittingly giving the impression that all of these people were working together, consciously, to create a Chicago culture. Whatever reverence one might feel now, however, did not always exist. The fact that there were artists able to capture the urban experience at a crucial moment was frequently lost on their contemporaries who knew little about their work and cared less. They did not always understand each other and frequently misunderstood themselves. When Fuller's *The Cliff-Dwellers* appeared in 1893, much critical comment in the city was positively antagonistic. That he should describe the city stripped of its glamour, that he should claim the city did not mind being dirty if it could only be big, seemed inexcusable as the same moment when the world was glorifying in the World's Columbian Exposition as the city's moment of triumph. Yet, on the other hand, Fuller constantly criticized the new skyscrapers which were bringing fame and visitors to Chicago. He thought they were ugly and tasteless, simply cavernous monsters. In an article which appeared in *The Atlantic Monthly* (July, 1897) Fuller declared:

The associated architecture of the city becomes more hideous and more preposterous with every year, as we continue to straggle farther and farther from anything like the slightest artistic understanding. Nowhere is the naif belief that a man may do as he likes with his own held more contentiously than in our astounding and repelling region of 'skyscrapers,' where the abuse of private initiative, the peculiar evil of the place and time, has reached its most monumental development (p. 541).

Little did he realize that these "hideous" buildings were to become the art of the modern world.

While, for example, Fuller was being attacked for his excessive realistic portrait of the city and while he himself was attacking the architects of the downtown buildings, the men and women of the University of Chicago were holding themselves aloof and had little to do with the others who were working in the city. The newspapermen were divided into many groups. It probably would have been most disturbing to Eugene Field had he known how much he was influencing Theodore Dreiser. In fact, it is reported that Dreiser sent Field some of his first sketches and stories only to have Field never acknowledge having received them. Garland became the gadfly in the city, satirized by many and liked by few. That quite a few of the writers of the city saw each other at the meetings of the Little Room on Friday afternoons following the symphony is true; however, they did not unite deliberately in order to create a Chicago literature. Into the twentieth century the discord between the literati was evident. In its March, 1914, issue *Poetry* printed a series of poems by Carl Sandburg, among them the now-famous "Chicago." *The Dial*, which had been a reluctant supporter of Chicago literature issued a blistering attack. Said *The Dial:*

The typographical arrangement for this jargon ["Chicago"] creates the suspicion that it is to be taken as some form of poetry, and the suspicion is confirmed by the fact that it stands in the forefront of the latest issues of a futile little periodical described as a 'magazine of verse.'

It is perhaps just another ironic footnote to history that *The Dial,* the often conservative literary journal, moved to New York in 1919 and by 1929 had ceased publication while *Poetry,* which it had called a "futile little periodical," has continued to the present time. Perhaps it is not as *avant garde* as it once was, but its very existence is a testimony to the faith and commitment of Harriet Monroe and of those who worked with her.

But no matter what the reaction was then, one can now discover that in Chicago there was created a modern American art which not only captured the essence of the city but also gave voice to the spirit of American civilization. At the same time the distinction between art and history is blurred and becomes practically non-existent as the art of Chicago records the history of the city and of the nation.

Consequently, to pause to pay homage to the past is not really an exercise in provincial self-adoration. Some look toward the past with awe and search for answers to unformed questions. They are aware that probably never before did there gather in one modern American city a more outstanding group of writers. What city could boast of Eugene Field, Herbert Stone, and Hannibal Kimball; of Victor Lawson of the *Daily News* and Joseph Medill of the *Tribune;* of Henry Blake Fuller, Robert Herrick, Theodore Dreiser, George Ade, Finley Peter Dunne, Harriet Monroe, Carl Sandburg, Sherwood Anderson, Edgar Lee Masters, or Floyd Dell? To look backward to understand this evolving urban art form does not mean to escape the present by re-living the past. An understanding of the past often helps one gain greater respect for the present and can lead to a preparation for the future. The past can be an effective teacher. Yet, it may well be that the golden moment of Chicago has passed. It may well be that never again will such a collection of artists ever be assembled on the shores of Lake Michigan. It may well be that Chicago, as a cultural center, has crested. But it is important to understand what did occur in the city which was "put up" by the "strong" and which resulted in the litany: "we are the greatest city, the greatest nation, nothing like us ever was."

Perhaps in the twenty-first century others will stand at the site of Fort Dearborn, to look back and speak of the twentieth century. Perhaps they will say that the twentieth century stood at the cross-roads of American civilization, or perhaps the prophecy of Carl Sandburg will prove to be correct—maybe only the "rats and lizards will be left to listen."

CHAPTER 2

When Chicago was the Frontier (1673-1815) and the Genesis of the Historical Romance

BECAUSE CHICAGO TENDS to be associated with a business culture and the Carl-Sandburg mystique of "hog butcher to the world," one frequently overlooks the historical romance which—in the nineteenth and twentieth centuries—turned attention to the days of fur-trading, Indian warfare, and Fort Dearborn. While it is true that the historical romance of those distant days never became a dominant form of Chicago literature, it is also true that these works give insights into the way certain writers have viewed the past of Chicago. As it is now, they probably have historic interest for those concerned with the role and the importance of the Chicago Portage to the French explorers and subsequently to the British. Yet, they still have another significance for those interested in the development of Chicago's literature. The search for an acceptable past is one of the characteristics of American civilization. From the beginning of our national culture when the Connecticut Wits and others were trying to create an American literature, there has been a search for some past or some tradition which would explain the roots of the community. Later Washington Irving, James Fenimore Cooper, and Nathaniel Hawthorne were obsessed by the same problems as they deplored the lack of native materials. Within Chicago culture there has been a similar search for identity and native materials.

One of the justifiable fallacies of American literature is the idea that it is rooted solely in the tradition of English writing. Since the major thrust toward nationhood was against England, it is not surprising that we associate our cultural life with that of England. Certainly the great writers of this nation—Irving, Cooper, Poe, Thoreau, Emerson, Hawthorne, Melville, Whitman, Twain, Faulkner, Dreiser, Hemingway, *et al.*—are products of the English tradition. So the fallacy has gained acceptance through obvious circumstances. Perhaps, however, the study of American writing —especially that of the colonial period—should not begin on the Atlantic seaboard but should consider the many settlements which stretched the length and width of this continent. Such a study might conceivably alter our understanding of what constitutes American literature without altering the giants who have existed.

Just as it is difficult to locate the various regions of writing on this continent, it is also difficult to define the line of demarcation between a nation's *writing* and a nation's *literature*. There are some areas which are clearer than others. In fact one would not ordinarily say that the average cookbook constituted a part of a nation's *literature* although all would agree that it constituted part of a nation's *writing* and perhaps even a part of the nation's culture. Therefore, it is common to continue to make such distinctions without ever really defining the terms. Some critics and teachers who deal in simplistic theories claim that *writing* differs from *literature* in the sense that writing is designed merely to transmit information whereas literature recreates an experience. What would these same critics do with a cookbook which employed poetic diction and other "literary conventions"? Undoubtedly, the distinction between the two may rest somewhere in the nebulous area of how a reader responds to the written word. At any rate, time has shown that out of a nation's writing there has emerged the nation's literature.

If one is to support the cyclical theory concerning the evolution of a national literature, then one will accept an expanded definition of literature without necessarily resorting to an acceptance of the cookbook-as-literature theory. In his *Cycle of American Literature* Robert Spiller has identified four stages or steps in the development of American literature. The first step, which consists of the work of people who have removed themselves to a new territory, includes their impressions in the forms of reports and chronicles which are designed primarily for the people "back home" (wherever that might be) and are intended to explain, describe, record for posterity, and define the new place. Without specifically saying so, Spiller roots this first stage in regionalism as the chroniclers decide to present the differences between the old place and the recent one. Thus, in order to do this, they frequently resorted to the development of ideas by analogy as they moved from the known to the unknown. The second step or cycle consists of political, social, economic, and theological works which were designed to establish an ordered way of life. Often the writer discovered that the new place demanded a different set of symbols and another approach to life. The former institutions could be adapted but not transferred intact, although many of the failures of colonial settlements resulted because the settlers had not discovered this very obvious fact. Then after the socio-political documents and after the establishment of a workable political and theological state, there was a turn to literature in the sense of *belles lettres.* At this point Spiller found the production of an "imitative literature." Here writers began to produce the kinds of works which they had known or which were acceptable literary forms in the more established cultures. Even though he does not specify any time periods for these various stages, it is clear from his suggestion that the third stage develops only after there is an appreciable reading public who can read for pleasure.

During the imitative period there is a conscious attempt to bring to the new region those works of art which had given pleasure in the old region. Invariably people do not realize at first that each place demands its own literature, and so they attempt to transfer—with little or no success—dominant themes and motifs of the old region. Just as that type of social organization was doomed for failure so also such a literature could be merely a shadow of its original. At this point, one can look with a great deal of interest at the development of American literature to test the validity of the theory thus far. Given the conditions and the unique situation in the colonies just before, during, and after the Revolutionary War, there was no reason for the poets to imitate the work of Alexander Pope with its neoclassical structure and its references to an England with a highly developed leisure class. But that is what they knew, and American literature is replete with a multitude of poems—few of them good—which extoll the virtues of George Washington in the neo-classical heroic couplet. In other words, the poets took the form which was in their remembered experiences and attempted to make it "American" by adding an "American" subject. Or they told the story of the colonial experience in terms of classical mythology. As one thinks about the pioneers in the wilderness of this nation, it is difficult to think of Greek gods and goddesses; but there were writers in those days who did. Even the slave poet, Phillis Wheatley, could produce a long neoclassical work entitled "Niobe in Distress for Her Children Slain by Apollo, from Ovid's Metamorphoses, Book VI, and From a View of the Painting of Mr. Richard Wilson." Nor is this work unusual for her. One can peruse her 1773 volume to see the extent to which she had mastered the neoclassical tradition in terms of both form and subject. Thus to search in her work for some detailed presentation of her condition of her life is to search in vain.

Out of the failures of imitation there develops the fourth stage or cycle which Spiller views as disclosing an emerging distinctive literature which is *of* and *for* that time and place, a literature which captures the uniqueness of human experience. If that work then can become universal in its application, one might go so far as to claim that the point of "absolute creativity" has been reached. It is the work of this fourth step which is generally "studied" in literature courses and which is generally considered when one speaks of a national literature. But Spiller's theory makes it clear that the fourth step is not reached immediately; it does not spring fully developed as a Medusa from the head of Zeus. It is a result of a long, evolutionary process.

Before one dismisses Spiller's *Cycle of American Literature,* one must acknowledge that in its over-all application it is a literary philosophy which explains not only a general interpretation of the East to West movement of American literature (as he used it) but also the possibility of applying it to the development of any regional (as I have applied it to Chicago literature) or national literature. What increases interest in the theory for Americans, of course, is Spiller's assertion that America has undergone a series of cycles rather than a single one. And this too is not only supported by the facts which are presented but also by a view of the literary scene during the nineteenth cntury. Emerson published *Nature,* which was to usher in the Transcendental movement, in 1836 a year before Chicago was incorporated as a city. By 1855, when the city of Chicago was almost twenty years old, Emerson had published *Representative Men* (1850), Hawthorne *The Scarlet Letter* (1850) and *The House of Seven Gables* (1851). Melville had published *Moby Dick* in 1851 and *Pierre* in 1852. Henry David Thoreau had published *Walden* in 1854, and the first edition of Walt Whitman's *Leaves of Grass* was issued in 1855. These five men constitute what has been called the American Renaissance; and while one might object to their eastern association, it is clear that by the 1850's New England—at least—had reached the fourth step in the cycle of American literature. Chicago, on the other hand, was just beginning its evolution toward a distinctive literature. And while it is a matter of record that the city probably passed through all of its stages more quickly than other regions as the city's phenomenal growth defied explanation in the nineteenth century, it is equally true that in the 1850's Chicago had no Emerson, no Hawthorne, no Thoreau, no Melville, and no Whitman. One of the "biggest" names in the city was that of Juliette Kinzie whose work is of historic value as a chronicle of the early days and as a forerunner in the establishment of the Chicago "hero," but certainly no one would confuse her work with a finished literary product.

Furthermore, if one accepts the Spiller theory and admits that these four steps are integral parts of the evolution of a national literature, one must include in the first step *all* reports and *all* chronicles. If this is done, then the origins of American writing go beyond the English tradition and include the Spanish writings of the west coast and the French materials of the Mississippi Valley. It means, then, that in order to begin the history of the Chicago territory one must go beyond John Kinzie. One must even go beyond Jean Pointe DuSable. To do this is to discover that Chicago literature is rooted in an oft-forgotten age.

During the burst of activity in the seventeenth century which led to the great explorations of the New World the place which was to become Chicago, almost two hundred years later, was part of a territory known as New France. Hence, the beginning of the idea of Chicago is rooted in French literature although the area was a familiar one to many North American Indian tribes because by the time of the arrival of the Jesuits in New France, the territory which was to become Chicago was apparently part of a number of Indian trails, the remnants of which exist today. Anyone who has ever traveled in Chicago is first impressed by the fact that most of the streets are laid out in a grid fashion which makes travel and learning the city relatively uncomplicated. At the same time there are a few diagonal streets which are noticeable because there are so few of them. These diagonal streets of modern Chicago are one legacy of numerous Indian tribes to the nation's "second city," and the evidence of these Indian trails culminating in the area of the present downtown Chicago would lead one to believe that the region was important in Indian culture.

According to Dena E. Shapiro in her *Indian Tribes and Trails of the Chicago Region* (Unpublished M.A. thesis, University of Chicago, 1929), there were six significant trails: Portage, Lake, Archer, Green Bay, Berry Point, and Cottage Grove. It is not difficult to trace the present-day existence of these trails. The Portage trail, for example, followed Cicero Avenue and 34th Street to Stewart and Madison Streets roughly parallel to Ogden Avenue. The Lake trail roughly paralleled the present Lake Street and was an east-west trail. The Archer trail followed the same course as the present-day meandering Archer Avenue which was later immortalized by Finley Peter Dunne's Mr. Dooley as "Archy Road." The Green Bay trail began in the north, reached the present-day Robey and Howard Streets, and moved southeast to Foster and Clark where it moved south on Clark to the site of Fort Dearborn. Until the midyears of the nineteenth century North Clark Street was called Green Bay Road because of the trail, and the present Green Bay Road in the suburbs is simply a continuation of the Indian trail. The Berry Point trail moved from Roosevelt Road and Cicero Avenue northward and met the Lake trail near Western Avenue, and the Cottage Grove trail followed the same course as the current Cottage Grove Avenue which, because of the building of Lake Meadows and Prairie Shores housing complexes, has lost some of its character; but it was essentially a trail which followed the shore line of Lake Michigan from Indiana leading into the heart of the modern city. These old, well-worn Indian trails were adopted for use by the new settlers in the 1830's and became their plank roads. The fact that these trails led to the spot where the Chicago River meets Lake Michigan would lead one to conclude that the region was of great importance to the various Indian tribes who coming from East and West, North and South met where Chicago was to arise. Conceivably when more is known about Indian literature of the region, there will undoubtedly be a significant body of work devoted to the region which was the focal point of so many trails.

Probably the Frenchman who did more to describe the region when it was part of New France was Samuel de Champlain who is immortalized today in the city by Champlain Avenue. Although there is no record that he ever got as far West as Chicago, he wrote a series of books from 1613 to 1632 in which he surmised the importance of what is termed the Midwest today. His explorations ended about 1616, but he continued to write of his experiences. Although he preferred the Algonquins to the Iroquois as did many explorers, Champlain demonstrated early that he understood many of the problems of the Indians. As he was achieving success as an explorer and fame as a writer, there were other groups of missionaries who were dealing specifically with what is now called the Great Lakes region. The Jesuit missionaries had the responsibility of reporting on the progress of the work in New France to their superiors "back home." Between 1632 and 1673 there appeared a series of reports or chronicles now known as the *Jesuit Relations.* These works were extremely popular in France and can now be read in the Reuben G. Thwaites' edition *The Jesuit Relations and Allied Documents: Travels and Explorations of the Jesuit Missionaries in New France, 1610-1791* (73 vols.)

Even in translation one gets a sense of the popularity of many of these works. There was enough suspense to satisfy the most adventurous arm-chair explorer. There was enough religious zeal to impress the most dedicated. Simply written they contained a commitment and a devotion to place which convinced the most skeptical. The fact that some of these writer-priests died for their religion in the presence of Indian hostility and unexpected physical hardships did little to dampen the spirit of adventure in New France or in the Old World, and it will never be known how many Frenchmen began the long journey across the Atlantic Ocean because of the adventure promised by the *Jesuit Relations.* These published reports were primarily concerned with the success of spreading the gospel in the New World. They are also well-written documents which record the story of the Indians of the region and present one of the fullest as well as earliest descriptions of the Great Lakes area. These reports were obviously written by men of academic skill, extreme Christian devotion, and great nerve who recognized the significance of what they were seeing and doing. So meticulously did they report their observations for posterity that their works can be viewed not only as a compendium of religious knowledge of the day but also as an encyclopedia of the geographic and physical New World.

While there were undoubtedly many fur traders in the Chicago area, Joliett and Marquette are the first settlers to have left a record of their visit in 1673. Marquette's *Journal* indicates his enthusiasm for the territory which he saw although his first trip was relatively brief. He made friends with the Indians of the Illinois tribe and promised that he would return the following year to preach the gospel. In the meantime he went back to his Wisconsin base via Lake Michigan which he called the "Lake of the Illinois." Trying to fulfill his promise, Marquette made an attempt to return to the land of the Illinois tribe in 1674; however, a bad winter made it necessary to remain in the Chicago area where he said "holy mass every day." It is interesting to speculate upon the possibility that Marquette might have permanently settled in the Chicago area had he not died in 1675. Nonetheless, he has recorded in detail his period in the Chicago region. This record appears as one of the sections of the *Jesuit Relations* and was well known in France.

During the year of 1677-78 Father Allouez replaced Father Marquette, and he was followed by a number of Frenchmen whose devotion to the cause of Christ sometimes became confused with their desire to gain wealth through the cause of fur trading. That a conflict developed is understandable as some settlers in the northern sections of New France accused the Church of using the many missions as trading posts rather than as havens for lost souls. About this time the use of the name *Checagou*, became rather common. In January, 1680, La Salle and his men established Fort Crevé-coeur approximately a hundred miles from Chicago at the site of the present-day Peoria. The Indians called it Checagou which may have been a corruption of Crevécoeur. At the same time La Salle used the name to describe the location of the present-day city; hence, the two distinct references. The records suggest that La Salle and his men did a great deal of traveling on the Chicago River and were relatively familiar with the terrain that became the city.

In fact during the period of 1682-83 it seems fairly certain that they built a "stockade and a cabin" in order to provide a respite for the Jesuit missionaries and traders who traveled the "river Chicaou" [sic].

While the Jesuits were busily engaged in proselytizing, trading, exploring, and recording their individual experiences for the people of France, there was another group of religious leaders trying to gain recognition in the New World. The Franciscans were engaged in similar exploits. They, too, combined religious mission with fur trading and exploration. And they also recorded their adventures as progress reports and chronicles. Thus joining the *Jesuit Relations* was another large body of work known as the *Franciscan Recollects*. Together these documents have been called the "War of the Orders." Of the many works published in France during the seventeenth century probably the one which has the greatest appeal to modern audiences comes from the Franciscan priest, Louis Hennepin, whose *Description of Louisiana* (1683) contains the accounts of his many journeys. It seems likely that he had accompanied La Salle's exploring party through Lake Huron and Lake Michigan in 1679 and had traveled the Illinois River, although it is difficult to separate his experiences from his fantasies. His *Description of Louisiana* pertains primarily to the 1679 expedition and is considered to contain the first description of the buffalo for European readers. Writing definitely for a French audience rather than privately to himself in a journal, Hennepin created suspense and presents excellent as well as graphic accounts of the region. His long passages are still vivid, and he clearly demonstrated a sharp sensitivity to the sights around him. Today his work continues to evoke a sense of immediacy which is so frequently lost when the reader is forced to bridge not only the gap of time but also the chasm of language.

By the end of the seventeenth century it was apparent that the Jesuits and Franciscans had made significant inroads into the new territory although these gains were often negated and offset by internal church conflicts. By 1696 Father Pinet had opened the

Mission of the Guardian Angel a few miles north of the center of present-day Chicago, but it had a precarious existence as a result of the conflict between religious and civil authorities. But in the few years of its existence it apparently was an effective religious mission and educational force among the Indians, and it represented a settlement in the Chicago area. The individual settlements may not matter today; however, of greater significance is the fact that the seventeenth century saw the establishment of the importance of the Chicago territory in the literature of France during the period. The *Jesuit Relations* and *Franciscan Recollects* made this area of the New World familiar to Europe long before there was a United States of America and before the region became a part of American literature. These French documents contributed to the accuracy of the geography of the inland territory. They demonstrated a knowledge of and an interest in the American Indian. In fact the romantic image of the Indian which developed later in world literature stems primarily from these early French writers who were generally better able to understand and accept the cultural differences between their nation and the tribes of North American Indians than were the Spanish or the English. Thus it is not surprising to see the doctrine of the "noble savage" emerging out of French romantic literature.

Although they were essentially reports to the various governing ecclesiastical bodies in France, these works contain certain general characteristics which are also in later writings about the region. First of all, there was a general optimism about the possibilities of the locale as invariably each writer commented on the swampland, the mud, the monotonous sameness of the prairie, and the inhospitable qualities of nature. But they also admitted that it was a place of strange beauty. From the standpoint of later developments in Chicago's literature, it is significant to note that each of these early French writers tended to emphasize that the region was a place of power which demanded strong men. And many agreed with La Salle that this was to become the seat of the

New World. How ironic it is that the Chicago novelist, for example, from E.P. Roe to William Brashler has emphasized this strange power of the region. Each writer tends to explain it in terms of some man-made institution or structure; however, Louis Sullivan—the architect—came closer to the French writers as he rooted the source of power in the prairie. In his *Autobiography of an Idea* (New York, 1924) he vividly records his first sight of the area surrounding Chicago and lyrically reports: "Here was power—power greater than the mountains." Then as he viewed the lake, he exclaimed: "Here again was power, naked power, naked as the prairies, greater than the mountains." Turning his attention toward the "dome of the sky," he noted: "And here again was a power, a vast open power, a power greater than the tiny mountains. Here, in full view, was the light of the world, companion of the earth, a power greater than the lake and the prairie below . . ." (pp. 196-197). Had this territory remained a part of France, obviously the *Jesuit Relations* and the *Franciscan Recollects* would have become a significant part of the evolving literature of the region. As it is now, they are little more than historic curiosities.

During that burst of activity which followed the establishment of the city of Chicago that remote connection to France was all but forgotten. True enough there were some obscure references to it in place names, but for all practical purposes Chicago was content to deal with more immediate issues. Eventually there came the time when the search for a past became a means of establishing urban identity. The city did not have too many "pasts"; hence, the possibility of choices was severely limited. By turning to the materials of the *Jesuit Relations* and *Franciscan Recollects*, Mary Hartwell Catherwood and her followers created one type of Chicago romantic novel. As she looked backward toward the seventeenth century and to the days of New France, Mrs. Catherwood discovered that a gracious culture was finally destroyed through greed for money. Did she mean to imply that such a destruction might serve notice on Chicago? Many of her novels suggest that the modern city's culture could not equal the urbane culture which France had established in the New World. Somehow this past should be remembered.

In a series of short stories and novels Mary Hartwell Catherwood explored the French settlements in the Illinois territory. In *The Romance of Dollard* (1888), written almost two hundred years after the action upon which the story is based, she presented the heroic tale of Dollard who saved, practically by himself, New France from extinction by the Iroquois. The "Preface" to the novel was written by the outstanding historian, Francis Parkman, who attested to the accuracy of historical fact and suggested that the use of romance made history more palatable. Recognizing the possibilities of the French period as a "usable past," Parkman declared: "The author is a pioneer in what may be called a new departure in American fiction" (p. 2). Parkman ranked Catherwood with James Fenimore Cooper and asserted that the life of New France was a natural for romance. He claimed that "the hard and practical features of English colonization seem to frown down on every excursion of fancy as pitilessly as puritanism itself did in its day" (p. 2). Turning his attention to the realistic method which was gaining prominence in literary circles, Parkman concluded his introduction:

The realism of our time has its place and function; but an eternal analysis of the familiar and commonplace is cloying after a while, and one turns with relief and refreshment to such fare as that set before us in Mrs. Catherwood's animated story (p. 3).

The novel oddly has a second preface. Written by Mrs. Catherwood herself, it explains why "the story of Dollard cannot die. It is that picture of stalwart heroism which all nations admire." Continuing her analysis of her own novel, she claims:

It is the possible greatness of man . . . the phase is medieval, is clothed in the garb of religious chivalry; but the spirit is a part of universal man (p. 6).

By implication she suggests that such a spirit could be germane to nineteenth-century Chicago.

In the last paragraph of the novel she returns to the "universal" quality of her tale and at the same time attacks the growing popularity of the realistic method in fiction as had Parkman in his "Preface."

And when we tell our stories, shall we tell them only of the commonplace, the gay, debonair life of this world? Shall the heroes be forgotten? (p. 206)

Essentially, Mrs. Catherwood was convinced that the French settlements of the New World proved that the positive qualities of the medieval world which had been transferred in the New World explorations of the seventeenth century could be transformed, modernized, and romanticized. Her characters are stereotypes and perhaps hold little interest for readers today. The noble characters seem too noble, the women seem too good, the Indians too bad, and the missionaries too pious. But in spite of these faults, she manages to create some memorable situations.

The Romance of Dollard was followed by a series of short stories, sketches, and novels. Perhaps the most notable are *The Story of Tonty* (1890), *The Lady of Fort John* (1891), *Old Kaskaskia* (1893), *The Chase of Saint Castin and Other Stories of the French in the New World* (1894), and *The Spirit of an Illinois Town* (1897). The faults of her first novel are present in all of her works, although she handled the short narrative form more adeptly. Her tales of the French settlements never reached the significance of the use of the French influences in the literature of Louisiana where it formed a distinct genre but neither had the French anything remotely like their New Orleans' culture in the Chicago area. While there was a precedent for Mrs. Catherwood's work in the productions of some writers in France who were trying to project the former glory of France in the New World, the story of the French explorations in the Chicago area were too vague and too remote to cause widespread interest or imitation. The writers who were willing to follow Mrs. Catherwood's lead did so in a search for a "usable past." Thus the obscure French documents, the strange adventurous lives of the coureurs-de-bois, and those oft-forgotten days of La Salle and Tonty have become simply a reminder in Chicago literature that the roots of the past can go back farther than the better known days of Fort Dearborn.

Although her work was very popular as she made New France a part of Chicago's literature, one realizes that her French heroes were not sufficiently strong to become the heroes of a modern city. They could not survive the interest in the more indigenous types of characters, but the search for a glamorous past by Mrs. Catherwood in her romances of Illinois tell much about the desire of the city to find some cultural roots as Chicagoans of the 1880's and 1890's were attempting to codify their definitions of themselves.

This was especially important inasmuch as the World's Columbian Exposition was Chicago's bid to become known as an "international city." Most of the novels during this period demonstrate the concern of the writers to define the city in terms of the urban scene. Some critics have read the romantic novels of Mrs. Catherwood as disguised attempts to deal with urban values. In his *The Rise of Chicago as a Literary Center* . . . (Totowa, N.J., 1964) Hugh D. Duncan assumes that these romances had an "ennobling effect." He continued:

[Mrs. Catherwood] condemned Chicago culture and Chicago's elites because they were concerned with money and material things. She called upon them to return to the aristocratic ideals of the seventeenth century with its emphasis upon action, honor, and dignity, and the life of the mind and spirit (pp. 69-70).

He refused to view her work as "escape" literature because "the assumption . . . is that all literature is a criticism of contem-

porary life, . . . when a writer creates a historical novel
defending certain values in the past, he is also defending them
in the present. The real problem is not what writers are 'escaping'
from but what they are 'escaping' *to*" (p. 70).

Any assessment of Catherwood must acknowledge that she
was not as committed to a re-living of the past as her works
might indicate. Her major concern was extracting those principles
which she thought had been important and suggesting that they
could be applicable to the modern world. What she mistakenly
overlooked, as she viewed the past uncritically, was the type of
greed, pettiness, and acquisitiveness that led to the decline of
New France. The characters were different, the national background was not the same, but she could have produced perhaps
much stronger stories had she selected the negative features which
she decried and shown how they continued as the Chicago
entrepreneurs were making a city to their specifications. Yet she
continued to remain faithful to her belief that the seventeenth
century represented the possibility of the union of Commerce and
the Cross.

II

The seeming unity of the seventeenth century was replaced by
the confusion of the eighteenth century which was a period of
great conflict and change both in the New World and in the Old.
England, France, and Spain were constantly at war. In the New
World the settlements of these major world powers reflected in
minuscule fashion the disorder in Europe as they used the various
Indian tribes to support their causes. Ironically the fortunes of
men and territories are often intricately involved with faraway
events and remote issues. And so it was with the Chicago
territory. During the eighteenth century the territory of Chicago
initially became a pawn between the warring factions of the church
in France—between the Jesuits and the Franciscans. Then it became a prize as the conflict between England and France ripened
into open warfare. Next it figured in the negotiations between

England and the United States after the Revolutionary War. And finally, it was a point of contention between the United States and the Indians. In each case the territory was viewed as La Salle had seen it: "the gate to an Empire." Consequently, each recognized that to hold the Chicago territory meant to hold the power of the interior of the continent.

By virtue of the Treaty of Paris of 1763 France lost much of her New World lands. Canada and Louisiana east of the Mississippi River became English territory, and Louisiana west of the Mississippi River went to Spain. As a result of the close of the Revolutionary War and by the Treaty of 1783 England gave up Louisiana east of the Mississippi and that became additional land for the new United States. Apparently there was some haggling over the Chicago Portage, but the United States finally got it by foregoing the larger territory of Canada. The Treaty itself was vague at many points, and it is clear that the negotiators did not clearly understand the geography of the continent. Perhaps had they read the Jesuit *Relations* they could have been more specific. However, in order to reinforce the Treaty of 1783 there were a number of subsequent Indian treaties which were designed to make clear the provisions regarding the Northwest Territory; but this did not eliminate the British who remained at several posts, including Chicago, ostensibly to protect the Indians. As a result there was a great deal of border fighting. The Treaty of Greenville of 1795 literally ended the sporadic raids which had occurred during the first years of the existence of the United States by establishing the boundaries of the Treaty of Paris of 1783 which required that the Indians give up such places as Detroit and the site of Chicago. With the Treaty of Greenville there was an earnest movement westward, and by 1803 Ohio had been admitted to the union. The story of the Louisiana Purchase, a deal which led to further westward expansion, which also took place in 1803 is complicated; but historians frequently refer to it as "the greatest real estate bargain in history." For $12,000,000 the United States bought the land from the Mississippi River to the Rocky Mountains from France. With this extensive land and in order to solidify the position of the United States in the West as well as to protect the venturous western settlers, the government decided to establish a series of forts.

Among these garrisons was Fort Dearborn established in Illinois in 1803 and named for the Secretary of War, Henry Dearborn. The Illinois fort was considered to be one of the last outposts of civilization. The people stationed at it led an isolated existence and probably would have disappeared into obscurity had it not been for the Fort Dearborn Massacre. Here was a potential subject for later novelists and poets, although the incidents preceding it have been distorted consistently. The War of 1812 had been declared in June of that year, and in July the American general, William Hull, had surrendered his army as well as Detroit and the Michigan Territory to the British. In a memo dated July 29, 1812, he had ordered Fort Dearborn evacuated. Thus was the war brought close to the little group at Fort Dearborn. According to the existing records the order was clear; however later both Lieutenant Helm and Mrs. John H. Kinzie were to claim that the choice to evacuate was conditioned by the phrase "if practicable." The order also commanded that all extra arms and ammunition be destroyed and that the goods which were in the storehouses be divided between those friendly Indians who might serve as their escorts out of the fort and the poor of the region. Mrs. Kinzie, writing almost fifty years after the event and reconstructing her story from hearsay, claimed that the order said to give everything to the Indians.

Apparently the order to Fort Dearborn was accompanied by a message to Fort Wayne indicating that the Chicago territory was considered to be in danger. The famous Indian scout, Captain William Wells, set out for Fort Dearborn with thirty Miami warriors to help in the evacuation. John Kinzie, in the meantime, pleaded against evacuation. And to many later observers it might appear that Commander Heald could have assumed that

General Hull did not really know what conditions existed at Fort Dearborn and might have rejected the idea of evacuating and marching through hostile Indian territory.

There were many logical reasons against evacuation. The fort was well-situated for defense. Furthermore, given the amount of ammunition which was held there and the extent of the fort's provisions, the soldiers might have been able to withstand an Indian attack. It has been reported that the Indians surrounding the garrison outnumbered the settlers ten-to-one, but Milo Quaife has pointed out that success under such odds behind a suitable stockade was not unusual in border warfare because the Indians possessed little taste for attacking a fortified place. Quaife has further noted that if the first assaults were beaten off, there would have been little desire to go on unless the Indians could have been assured that the provisions of the besieged would give out. If fighting occurred, defense behind the walls of the fort would have been more desirable than an outnumbered defense in open country. Undoubtedly, both Governor Ninian Edwards of the Illinois Territory and Governor William Henry Harrison of the Indiana Territory would have sent their militias to help the fort if it had been beseiged. Kinzie, of course, argued that it would be disastrous to his business as a trader as well as damaging to Lee's farming on the Chicago River to abandon the fort. He cited that there would be great danger to the unprotected families of the soldiers and to the civilians clustered about the fort; yet, these people could not be left behind. To take them along with the evacuees meant additional risks. But the reasons against evacuation which were probably apparent to Commander Heald, were inconsequential. As a professional soldier, he believed that obedience to an order was his primary goal. And at all costs he planned to obey.

On August 13, 1812, Captain Wells appeared at Fort Dearborn with his thirty Miamis. There is some indication that a council was held with the Indians at which time Heald told of the evacuation and his intention to distribute the goods. According to Lieutenant Helm, Wells held the council; and since that August of 1812, there have been many blurred accounts of what actually did occur after the arrival of Wells and the departure from the fort. Since the original message had been sent to Commander Heald by an Indian runner, there is a strong indication that the Indians already knew of the contents of the order. On the following day the goods and provisions were distributed with the exception of the liquor and the surplus arms. It was the neglect to give the liquor to the Indians which later reports of the Massacre frequently cite as the cause of the Indians' great displeasure. At this time it also seems that Black Partridge, a Pottawatomie chief from the Illinois River, came to Heald with a belated warning of impending disaster. According to some accounts, he spoke of the "birds" who had been singing in his ears and indicated that this meant care should be taken on the upcoming march away from the fort. As a final gesture, he surrendered a medal which had been given to him by the Americans because he would not be able to restrain the younger warriors who were determined that the group should not reach Fort Wayne. (Interestingly enough, of all of the contemporary accounts of the events of those days, only Lieutenant Helm mentions the surrender of the medal although this act forms a big scene in most novels dealing with the last days of Fort Dearborn.) In all fairness one must note that the warning, if such really did occur, came too late to reverse the plans even if Commander Heald—at this point—had desired to do so.

At 9 a.m. on August 15, 1812, the gates of Fort Dearborn opened, and according to Milo Quaife in his *Chicago and the Old Northwest: 1673-1835* (Chicago, 1913) "there issued forth the saddest procession Michigan Avenue has even known (p. 225)." All accounts agree that the procession consisted of, in the vanguard, part of the Miamis and their leader Captain Wells, the Chicago militia (civilians who had been deputized by Commander Heald), and the remainder of the Miamis. The baggage wagons were guarded by Ensign Ronan, Surgeon Van Voorhis, the soldiers who had families, and the twelve Chicago militia. Less than two miles from the fort this motley crew was ambushed, and sixty-eight Americans had to defend themselves against five hundred Indians. From all sources it seems that John Kinzie, a neutral who had accompanied the group, did not participate in the fighting. When the skirmish was over, fifteen Indians and fifty-three Americans were dead (twenty-six soldiers, twelve militia, Captain Wells, two women, and twelve children). What has been recorded as the Fort Dearborn Massacre had occurred.

History will perhaps never be able to render a final judgment on the Fort Dearborn Massacre. There were so many extenuating circumstances which have subsequently been lost to future generations. Certainly the little band of Americans who were stationed at the "last outpost of civilization" did not view the Indians as the French had done. The spirit of cooperation which prevailed in the French documents seems lacking in those written by the Americans. For example, writing from Fort Dearborn in October of 1811, Surgeon Van Voorhis blamed the British for the troubles with the Indians. At the same time he displayed a less-than-conciliatory attitude toward natives whose land had been purchased often through less-than-honorable means. And so he wrote to a friend:

> I cannot but notice the villainy practiced in the Indian country by British agents and traders; you hear of it at a distance, but we near the scene of action are sensible to it. They labor by every unprincipled means to instigate the Savages against the Americans, to inculcate the idea that we intend to drive the Indians beyond the Mississippi, and that in every purchase of land the Government defrauds them; and their united efforts aim too at the destruction of every trading house and the prevention of the extension of our frontier. Never till a prohibition of the entrance of all foreigners, and especially British subjects, into the Indian Country takes place, will we enjoy a lasting peace with the credulous, deluded, cannibal savages.

The use of the story of Fort Dearborn in Chicago literature has had a complex history. As they searched for a tradition or a "usable past," Chicago writers attempted to reinterpret the past and to create out of it the myths and legends for the present as well as for the future. Since the past of Chicago is essentially limited to the French period of the seventeenth century and the Fort Dearborn Massacre of the early years of the nineteenth, those searching for the city's "usable past" were considerably limited. The eighteenth century has substantially been ignored for obvious reasons. While the various negotiations for the control of the area have political interest, the age does not contain the kind of heroes and drama out of which stories are often made.

The legend of Fort Dearborn with its heroes and villains was established not through the reports which were filed with the United States Department of War but through the work of Juliette Kinzie who got her story from Mrs. Helm and others who were opposed to the actions of Commander Heald. Duncan points out that Juliette Kinzie "who gave the Fort Dearborn legend its accepted form . . . wanted to found a Kinzie dynasty in Chicago." It is true that she was an early nineteenth-century social climber, but there were other reasons for her desire to portray the Massacre as she did. As a Kinzie, she was quite aware of the image which her father-in-law had maintained in the days after the Massacre. The fact that he was not harmed when those with him were either wounded or killed did cause unasked and unanswered questions. Furthermore, the fact that he maintained until his death that the Fort should not have been evacuated led many to feel that he was just selfishly trying to protect his business enterprise which depended upon the presence of the Fort for success. The role of Kinzie was constantly being discussed in the early days of the city. When Judge Brown decided to issue a history of the city based upon the War Department's reports, Mrs. Kinzie took a defensive position which was even more understandable when one considers that her husband had been passed over as the first mayor of the city in favor of William B. Ogden who had recently come on the scene from New York. It was apparently hard for her to imagine that her husband, whose roots had been with the region since pre-Fort Dearborn days, would have been so rejected. But there were those who still whispered about the role of his father in the Fort Dearborn episode, and somehow the Kinzie name evoked memories too unpleasant for the new citizens of an even newer city. There were two products of Mrs. Kinzie's defense. The first, a pamphlet, entitled *Narrative of the Massacre at Chicago, August 15, 1812, and of Some Preceding Events* (1844), was destined to be more important than the document would seem to warrant. While it ostensibly is designed to give the "true" account of the incidents surrounding the Fort Dearborn incident, what it really does is to establish the acceptable story of Fort Dearborn from the Kinzie point of view. Because, undoubtedly, the documents of the War of 1812 did not occasion too many reports of that little band of people on the Chicago River, Mrs. Kinzie's pamphlet gained greater significance as it became one of the few works devoted to that phase of the War of 1812. Getting her story many years after the events from her sister-in-law, Mrs. Helm, Juliette Kinzie added dialogue, romance, and suspense—carefully emphasizing the nobility of her father-in-law. Her work had the added appeal of being based upon an "eye witness" account even though it was thirty-two years after the fact. By the time Joseph Kirkland tried to correct the Kinzie version in his *The Chicago Massacre of 1812 with Illustrations and Historical Documents* of 1893, the damage had been done, and the Kinzie story had become the acceptable story. Thus in the wake of Juliette Kinzie's interpretation of the Fort Dearborn Massacre there appeared a series of fictionalized accounts of that historic moment albeit a moment of defeat for the American forces.

The first writers to discover the fictional possibilities of the Fort Dearborn episode were not part of the Chicago literary tradition, but by virtue of their work they formed an interesting early interlude in the use of "Chicago" materials. They must have realized that the most terrifying aspects of the War of 1812 actually occurred on the western frontier where defenseless settlers were at the mercy of the Indians who had been so "psyched up" by the British that every atrocity imaginable was performed on the hapless and helpless settlers without any possibility of let-up. The officials of the United States, many miles away in Washington, D.C., had their own problems and were convinced they were fighting to protect the right to use the seas; consequently, while they were interested and concerned about events occurring in the Middle West, much of this seemed inconsequential in view of the larger issues. The British had convinced the Indians on the frontier that Americans were weak, and the unfortunate surrender of Hull seemed to support that fact as well as the poorly trained frontier army.

One of the earliest tales to come out of this period was produced by the great American romancer, James Fenimore Cooper. His novel, *Oak Openings; or the Bee Hunter*, appeared in 1848 and contained the episode of Black Partridge returning his American medal because he would not be able to control the younger warriors who were bent upon the destruction of the fort. However, his tale made a major alteration of the facts by having the fort captured rather than evacuated and destroyed. *Oak Openings* also proved to be a vehicle for Cooper's presentation of his idea of frontier democracy although it is one of his weakest novels. None of the freshness of his earlier work is evident here. Instead the reader is faced with impossible dialogue, moralizing Indians, sentimental characters, and dull scenes. While these are usually Cooper characteristics, in many of his works the elements of suspense and adventure seem to overcome these technical deficiencies. Such is not the case in *Oak Openings*.

Appearing originally in a serialized form in *Sairtain's Magazine* in 1850 and subsequently published by the New York firm of Pollard and Moss in 1888 was the first of Major John Richardson's stories on the subject. *Hardscrabble, or the Fall of Chicago* centered around a minor episode which had been recorded by Juliette Kinzie in her pamphlet. Six months before the Massacre, Indians had attacked Lee's farm which was called Hardscrabble. Located just a few miles west of the Fort, this attack and the death of two men served as a warning to those garrisoned at the Fort.

Richardson, faithfully portraying Indian restlessness and warfare, added more scalping incidents than in reality actually occurred. *Hardscrabble*, even today, seems little more than an exercise to prepare him for his second book on the subject which he entitled *Wau-Nan-Gee; or, the Massacre at Chicago: A Romance of the American Revolution.*

The "Prefatory Inscription," dated March 30, 1852, explains the source of his story. As part of "Her Majesty's 41st Regiment, in garrison at Detroit shortly after the occurrences herein detailed . . . in the then Western Wilds of America," Richardson had had an opportunity to meet Mrs. Helm when she arrived as a prisoner of war at Detroit. But he was apparently impressed with all of the women who came from Fort Dearborn and stated:

I inscribe 'WAU-NAN-GEE' to those who were then our enemies, but whose courage and whose sufferings were well known to all, and claimed our deepest sympathy, our respect, and our admiration—none more than the noble Mrs. Heald, and Mrs. Helme [sic], the former the wife of the Commanding Officer, the latter the daughter of the patriarch of Illinois, Mr. Kenzie [sic], some years since gathered to his forefathers.

The novel is extremely faithful to the story which Mrs. Helm had also told to Mrs. Kinzie. Richardson makes much of the trappings of culture and civilization which were to be found at the fort as well as at John Kinzie's house across the river from the fort. The frontier might be barren; but rugs, pianos, and John Kinzie's violin are used to portray the level of culture these early settlers reached as they struggled to maintain a semblance of stability in the wilds of Illinois. As in his former novel, he combines romance and realism in such a way that it is difficult to ascertain where one ends and the other begins. Certainly there is no support for the central love story which forms the basis of the action. Richardson may have been, as he asserted in his "Preface," impressed with the survivors as they were brought to Detroit; but his characters, especially the women, are poorly done. But clearly his sympathies rested with the Kinzie forces as he portrayed Commander Heald variously as an indecisive weakling who could not even maintain discipline at the fort or as an egomaniac. Had it not been for his dedicated officers, according to Richardson, Heald would have créated an even greater fiasco.

Since *Wau-Nan-Gee* was the first fullscale novel devoted to the Fort Dearborn Massacre and since it uses the formula which with little variation was subsequently followed by later novelists, it is interesting to note how well the Mrs. Helm-Mrs. Kinzie version has penetrated the literature on the subject. Under ordinary circumstances an analysis of the novel would be unimportant because it certainly is not one of the "great" novels of the middle border, but it is significant in illustrating how the historical romance manages to weave fact and fiction together to form the mythology of a region.

The novel opens on August 7, 1812, when Winnebag, the confidential Indian messenger of Captain Headley (fictionalized version of Captain Heald) makes his appearance at Fort Dearborn with a message from General Hull. The actual handwritten note was brief and said, according to Milo Quaife in his pioneer study "Some Notes on the Fort Dearborn Massacre" which appeared in the *Proceedings of the Mississippi Valley Historical Association* for 1910-11:

It is with regret I order the evacuation of your post owing to the want of provisions only a neglect of the Commandant of [the next word as recorded by Quaife is illegible but Quaife believes it is the word Detroit and a photocopy of the order would tend to bear this out.]

You will therefore destroy all arms and ammunition, but the goods of the factory you may give to the friendly Indians who may be desirous of escorting you on to Fort Wayne and to the poor and needy of your post. I am informed this day that Mackinac [sic] and the Island of St. Joseph will be evacuated on acct of the scarcity of provision and I hope in my next to give you an acct. of the Surrender of the British at Malden as I expect 600 men here by the beginning of September (p. 138).

That brief and terse note from General Hull to Commander Heald was embroidered into the following long letter by the novelist. This letter is in keeping with what Mrs. Kinzie concluded was the contents of the message.

From the difficulty of access to your post, cut off as is the communication by the numerous bands of hostile Indians whom Tecumseh has risen up in arms aginst us, I take it for granted that you are yet ignorant that war has been declared between Great Britain and the United States. Such, however, is the fact, and in a few days I expect myself to be surrounded by a horde of savages, when my position will indeed be a trying one, not as regards myself, but the hundreds of defenceless women and children whom nothing can preserve from the tomahawk and the scalping knife. I, moreover, fear much for Colonel Cass, who, with a body of five hundred men, is at a short distance from this, and will be cut to pieces the moment an attack is made upon myself. To add to the untowardness of events, I have just received intelligence that the Fort of Mackinaw has been taken by the British and their allies, so that, almost simultaneously with the receipt of this, you in all probability will hear of their advance upon yourself. The result must not be tested, and forthwith you will, *if it be yet practicable* [sic—this appears in italics in the text as Richardson emphasizes the point made by Mrs. Helm and Mrs. Kinzie that Heald had a choice of whether or not to evacuate.] evacuate your post and retire upon Fort Wayne, after having first distributed all public property contained in the fort and factory among the friendly Indians around you. This is most important, for it is necessary that these people should be conciliated, not only with a view to the safe escort of your detachment to Fort Wayne, but in order to their subsequent assistance here. There are, I believe, nearly five hundred Pottowatomies encamped around you, and such a numerous body of Indians would, if left free to act against Tecumseh's warriors, materially lessen the difficulty of my position here. Treat them as if you had the utmost reliance on their fidelity, for any appearance of distrust might only increase the evil we wish to avoid. I rely upon your judgment and discretion, which Colonel Miller assures me are great. I have preferred writing this confidential dispatch with my own hand, in order that, by keeping your exposed condition as secret as possible, no unnecessary alarm may be excited in the inhabitants of this town by a knowledge of the danger that threatens their friends (pp. 5-6).

In addition to the arrival of Winnebag on August 7th, the second event which figures prominently in the novel also occurs. Mrs. Ronayne, the wife of Ensign Ronayne (fictionalized version of Ronan) is allegedly kidnapped when she was out riding near Hardscrabble, which is described in the novel as "about two miles from Fort Dearborn and had been the scene of a recent and bloody tragedy" (p. 18). In April of 1812 Maria Heywood's father (she is Mrs. Ronayne) and a domestic "had been cruelly murdered . . . during a period of profound peace, by a party of Winnebagoes" (p. 19). Subsequently, Maria's mother had died. Since both of her parents were buried at Hardscrabble, her visits there were not unusual. Later she sends a vague letter back to her husband at the fort which partially explains the action. Mrs. Headley helps the Ensign by revealing what she knows, but the entire episode has an air of mystery which is cleared up later in the novel. At any rate, a week before the fateful Fort Dearborn Massacre, Richardson begins the action of his novel.

As soon as Winnebag leaves Captain Headley, he immediately visits Mr. McKenzie (fictionalized version of John Kinzie) and cautions against evacuation and the proposed trip to Fort Wayne. McKenzie agrees that it would be a foolish move and immediately goes to the fort to visit Captain Headley who lets him read the dispatch. After some discussion in which it appeared Headley's mind was set on evacuation even though the note gave him the option through the phrase "if . . . practicable," McKenzie declared:

Captain Headley . . . I have nothing further of advice to offer to one so confident in his own judgment; but bear in mind what I now tell you, that if you follow the letter of these instructions rather than the spirit, you will have cause to repent it. I make not this remark from mere consideration of my own personal interests, which, of course, will be greatly affected by this abandonment of the post, but because I sincerely believe that a defence will entail less disaster than a march through the vast wilderness we shall have to traverse, hampered as we shall be with women, less able to bear up against fatigue, privation, and disaster. . . (p. 51).

Upon leaving this unsatisfactory conference, McKenzie meets his son-in-law, Lieutenant Elmsley (fictionalized version of Helm) and comments to him that Headley "is an obstinate, conceited ramrod" (p. 51).

Headley, on the other hand, could not dismiss what he had read into the General's letter and concluded that evacuation was the only solution, although his wife Ellen, who is presented as a sensible woman, cautions him against his course of action. Headley decided to have a council meeting to share some of his concerns with his men. And so it is scheduled for the 8th of August, the day after the message had been received.

The men, upon being notified, thought initially that the purpose for which they were being summoned to the parade grounds was to search for Maria. Sixty healthy men and fifteen invalids turned out for the parade, certainly not an over-powering force. Instead of suggesting that they organize to search for Ronayne's wife, Headley reads the dispatch from General Hull and shows his nervousness by taking the stripes from Corporal Collins whose offense was "to speak from the ranks" about being willing to search for Maria. Headley then said:

You see, gentlemen and men . . . how intricate is our position, and how little choice there is left to us to decide in the matter. It must be but mere form to ask your opinions on the subject, for the directions of the General are so positive that our duty is implicitly to follow them. Mr. Elmsley, as the oldest officer, what is your opinion? (p.53).

Elmsley shows his displeasure with Headley and at the same time he is presented as a far more rational being than his commanding officer:

My opinion . . . can be of little weight in a matter which you appear to have decided already; however, as it is asked in the presence of the whole garrison, in the presence of the whole garrison will I give it. On no account should we retire from this post. Our force, it is true, is small, but we have stout hearts and willing hands, and, with four good bastions to protect our flanks of defence, we may make a better resistance than it appears they have done at Mackinaw, should the British deem it worth their while to come so far out of their way to attack us. My own impression is that they will not, for there is nothing to be gained by the conquest of a post which commands no channel of communication, and therefore offers no advantage to compensate for the sacrifice of life necessary to take it. Certainly, nothing will be attempted unless Detroit itself shall fall. The British forces will have too much to occupy them there to think of weakening by dividing the troops they have in that quarter. On the other hand, should we undertake a protracted march to Fort Wayne, encumbered as we are with women, and children, and invalids, there is but too great reason to infer that parties of British Indians, apprised of our march, will hasten to the attack, and then our position in the very heart of the woods will be hopeless indeed. These, sir, are my views on the subject, nor can I conceive how a man of common discernment can entertain any other (p. 53).

There is general agreement with Elmsley among the men, and Headley becomes more and more defensive. To make his position still further untenable, while the men are on the parade grounds, some Indians shoot at the flag preceding the council meeting. This should have been an indication to Headley of their intent, but the Commander merely interprets it as an "inconsiderate act of one or two young men [which should not raise] your unfounded and ungenerous suspicions of a whole tribe" (p. 56).

In the meantime, before the council meeting, Ronayne while

looking in the far distance at the horizon thinks he sees his
wife and her horse. Later he receives a note in his wife's hand-
writing which says: "Go not to the council." This increases the
mystery regarding her disappearance and raises the question of
whether or not there is any relationship between her disappearance
and the impending conflict between the garrison and the Indians.
Without telling the source of his information Ronayne conveys
to Elmsley his misgivings concerning a council meeting with the
Indians. The two make some alternate plans since it seems that
Headley is determined to go through with his meeting with
the Indians.

The council meeting is a very austere occasion. There are
approximately four hundred Indian warriors with their leaders.
The chiefs among the Indians are Winnebag, Wau-ban-see,
Black Partridge, To-pee-nee-be, Kee-po-tah, and Pee-to-tum,
"that tall scowling chief that never looks friendly" (p. 61). The
leaders among the Americans are Captain Headley, Dr. Von
Voltenberg (fictionalized version of the surgeon Dr. Van Voorhis),
and Mr. McKenzie. Much to the disgust of the chiefs who are
friendly and to Mr. McKenzie but much to the delight of Pee-to-
tum the Captain promises everything in the storehouse including
the ammunition and the rum. With these provisions committed,
Winnebag and Mr. McKenzie advise leaving the fort immediately so that the Indians will spend time dividing up their loot
and thus give the inmates of the fort ample chance for a headstart
on their trek to Fort Wayne. Headley refuses and sets noon of
the following day as the moment of distribution. Prior to the
Council, some Indians try to storm the fort; but, as a result of the
good thinking of Elmsley and Ronayne, they find the gates barred,
and a gun is fired over their heads.

Because of Richardson's own point of view, it is not surprising
that his opinion of Headley is extremely biased. After the council
meeting Richardson gives one of his most telling portraits of
Headley.

[he] felt ill at ease, for he was conscious that he had irrevocably committed himself; and, what was more mortifying to his pride, he was compelled inwardly to admit that his subalterns, although at the price of disobedience of orders, had, in this instance, evinced far more judgment and prudence than himself. Still the pride of superiority—mayhap of vanity—was in some measure deprived of its humiliation, as he consoled himself with the reflection that their precaution must have been the result of an intimation of some change of feeling on the part of the warriors, whereas he himself had been left wholly in ignorance on the subject, and led to repose confidently on their good faith. Still he shuddered as he thought of those within, at what might have been the turbulence of the young men, evidently encouraged by the dark Pee-to-tum, had they gained admission into the fort (p. 64).

Afterwards Headley is subjected to much concern from his officers, Winnebag, and Mr. McKenzie. They all deplore his lack of judgment in promising the ammunition and the liquor. In fact, Mr. McKenzie calls Headley "a murderer." In the midst of all of this, Mrs. Ellen Headley, the captain's wife, offers a solution. She suggests that they destroy all but one case of powder and one of rum. Then on the following day the Captain would be able to keep his word, but there just wouldn't be much to distribute. Winnebag is asked to call the young men at midnight and to keep them occupied so that they would not know what was happening. During the confiscation period Pee-to-tum manages to get at Ronayne, frequently referred to in the novel as the "Virginian," but Ronayne is saved by Wau-Nan-Gee, the son of Winnebag, who then tells the story of why he has Maria in the Indian camp. He wants to take Ronayne. He has supporting letters which reveal how Wau-nan-gee had been in Detroit and had learned of the possible treachery against the little band of Americans at Fort Dearborn. He hurried back with the information but discovered that British Indians had already transmitted it. Pee-to-tum, who is described by Richardson as "not a full-blooded Pottawatomie, but a sort of mongrel Chippewa" (p. 75), is the only one in favor of the treachery. During the division of the goods, while Pee-to-tum is being as insulting as possible, Black Partridge and the other chiefs return their American medals. When Pee-to-tum returns his with an insult, Captain Headley spits in his face and strikes him with a heavy military glove which put out the Indian's left eye. A fight ensues broken only by the arrival of "five and twenty tall and well-mounted horsemen dressed in the costume of warriors, and headed by a man of great size . . ." (p. 81). Thus Richardson announces the arrival of Captain William Wells and his thirty Miami warriors, which for reasons not made clear Richardson reduces by five.

With the arrival of Captain Wells, the uncle of Mrs. Headley, there is a general state of indecision. Wells apologizes for not getting there sooner before all of the decisions had been made. Even Headley now regrets his decision because he realizes that with the help of Wells they could have held the fort.

At this point Richardson interrupts his action to insert the long and relatively well-done account of William Wells, who became a legend in his own lifetime. But even Wells, the great fighter, recognized the hopelessness of the occasion even though he was willing to fight in spite of his recognition that "the lives of women and helpless children [were] at stake" (p. 88). As the day of the evacuation dawned brightly, Richardson, interrupts his narrative again. This time to present a defense of General Hull, which is rare indeed. Since it comes from the enemy, it is interesting to note what Richardson considers important. He notes that as the little band was getting ready to evacuate Fort Dearborn:

. . . we stood at the battery which vomited destruction into the stronghold of him who had counselled and commanded the advance upon Fort Wayne. It has been a vulgar belief, fostered by his enemies, by those who were desirous of relieving themselves from the odium of participation, and of rising to power and consideration by the condemnation of their chief, that the position of General Hull was one fraught with advantage to himself and of disadvantage to his enemies. Nothing can be more incorrect. The batteries, to which we have alluded, had so completely attained the range of the Fort of Detroit, in the small area of which were cooped up by a force of nearly twenty-five hundred men, that every shot that was fired told with terrible effect, and not less than three officers of the small regular force were killed or mutilated by one ball passing through the very heart of their private apartments, into which it had, as if searchingly and invidiously, found its way. To the left, moreover, was another floating battery of large ships of war, preparing to vomit forth their thunder, and distract the garrison and divide their fire, which could be returned only from their immediate front bearing on the river, that it soon became evident to the besiegers that their enemy had no power to arrest or effectually check the fury of their attack. But not this alone. Thousands of Indians had occupied the ground in the rear, and only waited the advance of the British columns, furnished also with artillery for an assault in another quarter, to rush with the immolating tomahawk upon the defenceless inhabitants of the town, and complete a slaughter to which there would have been no parallel in warfare. They could not have been restrained; their savage appetite for blood must have been appeased, and of this fact General Hull had been apprised. Moreover, five hundred of his force who had been detached under Colonel Cass were at no great distance, and had an effectual resistance been made at Detroit—had blood been, as they would have conceived, wantonly spilt, the exasperation of the Indians would have been such that, in all probability, Colonel Cass would not at the present day be a candidate for presidential honors, nor would any of his force have shared a better fate. All these things we state impartially and without fear of contradiction, because they occurred under our own eyes, and because we believe that the people of the United States do not understand the true difficulties by which General Hull was beset. It may be very well, and is correct enough in the abstract, to say that an officer commanding a post, armed and garrisoned as Detroit was, ought to have annihilated their assailants, but where, in the return of prisoners, is mention made of artillerymen sufficient to serve even half the guns by which the fortress was defended? The fourth Regiment of the line was there, but not the gallant Fourth Artillery, and every soldier knows that that arm is often more injurious to friends than to foes in the hands of men not duly trained to it. With the exception only of the regiment first named, the army of General Hull consisted wholly of raw levies chiefly from Ohio, expert enough at the rifle, but utterly incompetent to serve artillery with effect. Again, the greater the number of men the greater the disadvantage, unless at the moment of assault, for it has already been shown that the British battering guns had obtained the correct range, and half the force had only canvas to cover them.

We pretend not, assume not, to be the panegyrist of General Hull, but we have ever been of the opinion that, as he expressed himself in his official despatch to the commandant at Chicago, his principal anxiety was in regard to the defenceless inhabitants; and that had this been an isolated command, where men and soldiers were only the actors, no consideration would have induced him to lose sight of the order of the Secretary of War—that no post should be surrendered without a battle. If he erred it was from motive of humanity alone (pp. 90-91).

It is interesting to note that the most humane analysis of Hull's surrender of his post should have come from one of the enemy who presented a very judicious portrait of the man who has been tried time and time again by history. It is also ironic that this little interlude precedes the events of August 15, 1812, where women, children, and the "defenseless" were slaughtered.

Richardson notes the day:

As if in mockery of the climax of trial they were to be made to undergo before its close, the 15th of August, 1812, dawned upon the inmates of Fort Dearborn with a brilliancy ever surpassing that of the preceding day (p. 90).

The order of march began with Captain Wells and "his little band of Miamis," thirty men of the detachment, the wagons containing women, children, the sick, supplies, and luggage, and thirty more men of the detachment. In the extreme rear were

Mrs. Headley and Mrs. Elmsley with Ronayne who was wearing the flag. In the midst of the battle which shortly ensued Mrs. Headley and Mrs. Elmsley were hidden in a canoe by Winnebag and Black Partridge. Dr. Van Voltenberg was killed and scalped early when he returned "to the fort for a small flask of brandy which he had forgotten" (p. 99). While there is no truth to the portrait of the surgeon as a ne'er-do-well, it is a picture which follows Mrs. Helm's apparent dislike for the young physician for reasons which have never been made clear. Pee-to-tum, who was wearing the doctor's scalp on his belt, killed Captain Wells and tore out his heart in order to eat it along with the other warriors who wished to share in the dubious "feast." Ronayne became the hero of the day by reaching one of the big guns and shelling the Indians. Eventually he was wounded but not before he had killed the malevolent Pee-to-tum. The Indians, who greatly outnumbered the Americans, gave Headley, through Winnebag their spokesman, a chance to surrender. With twenty-two men left, Headley took a vote. Eleven were for surrender and eleven were against it. Headley, after being assured of Winnebag's good faith, voted in favor of surrender thereby breaking the tie. The conditions of surrender for the defeated were not over-bearing. They asked permission to be allowed to keep the colors wrapped around Ronayne who appeared to be dying, permission to bury their dead, and their surrender to the nearest British post as the earliest opportunity. Elmsley was put in charge of the burials, while Ronayne was captured and taken to Maria who, it is revealed, had herself kidnapped in hopes that her husband would join her and thus they both would have been spared the Indian uprising. Ronayne makes Wau-nan-gee promise to follow and stay with Maria forever and to take the colors and keep them until they can be delivered to an American fort.

As the novel ends, Richardson summarizes the events which immediately followed the Massacre. Once again he praised the American women for their courage, strength, and concern. But he also gives credit to those friendly Indians who were so protective of their charges that they were able to get safely to Detroit. All references to Kinzie are made to suggest that he alone understood the situation and was willing to make necessary sacrifices to save himself and what he owned. Early in the novel Richardson creates the type of image of the cultured man who could cope with the conditions of the frontier. At the same time it was undoubtedly the type of image which Mrs. Helm and Mrs. Kinzie wanted to see promulgated. The following description of Kinzie and his daughter, who became Mrs. Helm, would suggest a level of culture which was not in keeping with the frontier conditions.

On the western bank of the south side of the Chicago River, and opposite Fort Dearborn, stood the only building which, with the exception of the cottage of Mr. Heywood on the opposite shore, and already alluded to, could at all come under the classification of a dwelling house. The owner of this mansion, as it was generally called, which rose near the junction of the river with Lake Michigan, was a gentleman who had been long a resident and trader in the neighborhood, and between whom and the Pottowatomie Indians in particular, a good understanding had always existed. Several voyageurs, consisting of French-Canadians and half-breeds, constituted his establishment, and in the course of his speculations, chiefly in furs, with the several tribes, he had amassed considerable wealth. He was, in fact, the only person of any standing or education outside the wall of the fort itself, and of course the only civilian, beside Mr. Heywood—whom, however, they far less frequently saw—the officers of the garrison could associate with. His house was the abode of hospitality, and as, in his trading capacity, he had opportunities of procuring many even of the luxuries of life from Detroit and Buffalo, which were not within reach of the inmates of the fort, much of the monotony which would have attached to a society purely military, however gifted or sufficient to their mutual happiness, was thus avoided. His library was ample, and there was scarcely an author of celebrity (the world was not overrun with them in those days), either historian, essayist, or novelist, whose works were not to be found on the shelves of his massive black walnut bookcase, made by the hands of his own people from the most gigantic trees of that genus that could be found in Illinois. He had, moreover, for the amusement of the officers of the little garrison, prepared a billiard room, where many a rainy hour was passed, when the sports of the chase and of the prairie were shut out to them, and for those who asked not for either of these amusements, there was a tastefully, but not ostentatiously, furnished drawing-room, with one of the best pianos made in those days, which he had had imported at a great expense from the capital of the western world, and at which his amiable daughter presided.

The "amiable daughter," who was Mrs. Helm, is described as Richardson continues to create the kind of image which was so important to the later Kinzies.

Margaret McKenzie had been born at Chicago, but having lost her mother at an early age, her father, profiting by one of his periodical visits to New York, had taken her with him for the purpose of receiving an education as would enable her not only to grace a drawing-room, and make her a companion to a man of sense and refinement, but to fit her for those more domestic duties which the uncertain character of so secluded a life might occasionally render necessary, and where luxury and education alone were insufficient to a trading husband's view of happiness. After five years' absence, she had returned to Chicago, a girl of strong mind, warm affection, and altogether so adapted in manner and education—for she eminently combined the useful with the ornamental—that her father was delighted with her, not less for the proficiency she had made in all that gives value to society, but because of the utter absence of all appearance of regret in abandoning the gay and enlivening scenes of the fascinating capital, in which she had spent so many years, for the still, dull, monotony of the primeval forest in which her childhood had been passed (pp. 44-45).

Four years after the appearance of *Wau-Nan-Gee,* Juliette Kinzie published *Wau-Bun.* Ostensibly it was a personal narrative of her move to the northwest from the East as the young bride of John H. Kinzie, but it retold again her version of the Fort

Dearborn Massacre and establishes the acceptable story of Fort
Dearborn from the Kinzie point of view. Whether or not she was
familiar with Richardson's work is a moot point. Certainly, his
work seemed to follow the facts as she saw them and related
them in her pamphlet of 1844. But considering he had met
Mrs. Helm who was the source of Mrs. Kinzie's knowledge, the
similarity between Richardson's work and Juliette Kinzie's is
understandable. As she recreated the days of Fort Dearborn, she
took great pains to absolve her father-in-law of any wrongdoing.
And in a Chicago which was becoming more and more suspicious
of the Kinzie role, this was extremely important.

Through the nineteenth century and into the twentieth, the
story of Fort Dearborn as presented originally by Juliette Kinzie
continued to attract the attention of historical romancers. All
of them shared in common the essential story of the weakness
of the Commander, the strength of his lieutenants, the integrity of John Kinzie who tried to prevent the major errors of
Commander Heald, the pioneer women who served as a civilizing
and refining force, the duplicity of the Indians, and the rejection
by Black Partridge of the American forces. Captain William Wells
from Fort Wayne is always pictured as "the noblest of them
all"; thus his death is even more tragic as the price to be paid
for the bumbling "errors" of Heald. In many of these tales a
created hero tries to rescue some "fair maiden" and becomes
involved in the problems of the Indian raids and the subsequent
Massacre.

Of the nineteenth-century tales only John Frost's *Heroes and
Hunters of the West* (1886) seems to deal more with the
reality of Fort Dearborn than with the created Kinzie legend.
Apparently based upon Brown's *History of Illinois*, which was
originally published in 1840 as a lecture given before the Chicago
Lyceum and was subsequently published as a full-scale work,
Frost makes greater use of the documents from the War Department; and these necessarily are more objective than the Kinzie
interpretation.

Commenting on the five romances which appeared between 1900 and 1906 Lennox Bouton Grey, in his perceptive dissertation entitled *Chicago and "The Great American Novel": A Critical Approach to the American Epic* (University of Chicago, 1935), saw them as answers to the growing spirit of realism in Chicago.

These new romances, substituting the garden variety of realism in 1900 for the realities of 1812, [sought] escape from troublesome problems of 1900 into a confident, comfortable, measured scene of the American past, very different from the 1812 awareness of quite another cultural past, from which the frontiersmen had torn themselves to face an immeasurable, uncertain future (p. 95).

Both *The Shadow of Victory* (1903) by Mrytle Reed and *When Wilderness was King* (1904) by Randall Parrish illustrate the strengths and weaknesses of the Fort Dearborn tale as it has come into modern literature. The first novel is set primarily across the river from the fort in John Kinzie's house and has for its hero a fictional character, Robert Forsyth, who is portrayed as Kinzie's nephew, a graduate of Yale. The other uses John Wayland, a young frontiersman, as the hero. There are other alterations mainly around the central female characters, but all of the other ingredients are present. These two, however, use the legend as a basis for providing greater understanding of the city which was to arise on its site. Thus the defeat at Fort Dearborn is simply a step in the ultimate development of Chicago. Evelyn Atkinson's *Hearts Undaunted: A Romance of Four Frontiers* (1917) and *The Fort* one of the four novellas in Mary Hastings Bradley's *Old Chicago* (1930) emphasize John Kinzie and the strong frontier women who suffered so that a continent might be expanded. Atkinson refers to Kinzie as a strong, cultured "man of vision and foresight." Bradley, laudatory though she was, is a bit more faithful to the facts. Her hero, Barry John, "found himself wondering if a soldierly obedience, a fine sense of responsibility were, after all, the right weapons for this wilderness. Perhaps men like Kinzie, shrewd, rough, and ready opportunists, were the only possible survivors. He could never make up his mind about Kinzie; he was likeable and hospitable; he had moods of infectious jollity when he played the fiddle for guests who gathered about his open fire; he was the Indian's friend." At the same time Barry John recognized that Kinzie "was choleric and violent tempered" and noted that "he had stabbed LaLime . . . only a few weeks before . . ." (p. 307).

One of the few novels to question the role and integrity of John Kinzie appeared in 1955. Entitled *Ensign Ronan* (who was one of the key officers at the fort at the time) by Leon Burgoyne, it presents Ronan as being a strong supporter of Commander Heald. However, toward the end of the novel Ronan is injured and is hidden in the region's only safe place: John Kinzie's house. During his convalescence he has time to speculate upon the conflict between Heald and Kinzie. More and more he understands that Heald, who followed his orders as a professional soldier was expected to do, should have had some initiative of his own. Had he done so, he would have seen the folly of the orders. At the same time, he understands the importance of Kinzie who—when he opposed Heald—was acting out his belief in the validity of his cause and like Ronan was convinced the area would become a great city.

The fictional uses of Fort Dearborn have provided a series of juvenile stories which also repeat the traditional legend rather than what actually occurred. *The Sun Maid: A Story of Fort Dearborn* (1900) by Evelyn Hunt Raymond, *A Little Girl of Old Chicago* (1904) by Amanda Douglas, and *Black Partridge, or the Fall of Fort Dearborn* (1906) by H.R. Gordon (pseudonym for Edward Sylvester Ellis) emphasize the strong relationship between the Indians and the frontier children whose survival was assured because the Indians "loved" them. This does not, of course, correspond to the fact that twelve children were wantonly murdered during the Massacre. Bernadine Bailey's *Puckered*

Moccasins (1935) is far more questioning as her young hero, Deave Rogers, goes through a series of improbable episodes. But once again Commander Heald is portrayed as less than honorable, a man so vain that he was willing to sacrifice an entire garrison simply because he had made up his mind to follow a certain course regardless of the lack of logic which his position indicated; however, the Indians are not as stereotyped as is usually the case.

Ultimately, however, one must acknowledge that powerful though Mrs. Kinzie's interpretation might have been in obscuring the facts, it is a matter of record that people seldom create a national or regional literature out of their failures and defeats, unless those defeats and failures can be shown to be the basis of future greatness. The importance of the Fort Dearborn legend is fairly well summarized by Robert Forsyth in *The Shadow of Victory* toward the end of the novel:

'. . . Yesterday a battle was fought, which, in its essence, was for the possession of the frontier. We have surrendered, but we have not given up. If we retreat, it must be fought again. From shore to shore of this great country there must be one flag and one law. Here, where the ashes of the Fort now lie, some day a city must stand' (p. 410).

Mrs. Kinzie merely gave to that horrendous defeat at Fort Dearborn an air of respectability thereby making it usable by subsequent writers.

Perhaps Duncan in his *The Rise of Chicago as a Literary Center* has best summarized the significance of Fort Dearborn not only for Chicago literature but ultimately also for American literature.

The struggle over the symbol of Fort Dearborn was more than an attempt by the Kinzie family to sustain its social status. It was a conflict between status based on the honor of money and the traditional honor of the soldier. . . . The fact that contemporary accounts and later fictional treatments of Kinzie show him to be choleric, violent-tempered, a hard-drinker, an associate of the Indians, and a brawler only indicates the power of the pen, and particularly of Mrs. Kinzie's pen, to give form to the longings of a new business society for heroes drawn from its own ranks. Mrs. Kinzie's transformation of her father-in-law into a 'cultivated trader' and the founder of a dynasty served as a model for all future Chicago 'lady' writers. Martha J. Lamb, Mary Healy Bigot, Margaret Ayer Barnes, Mary Hastings Bradley, Margaret Potter Black, Katherine ·Keith, Marion Strobel, Janet Ayer Fairbanks, and other women of Chicago who produced 'dynastic' novels of generations in which the business hero is a central figure. Soon, as so often happens with tales and legends, the forms of literature became the forms of life. John Kinzie became a Chicago hero not simply in fiction but in history. The 'heroic trader' became the founding father of a great city. Nothing historians can do will desanctify this legend so long as Chicago remains a 'commercial city.'

Duncan continues his discussion by citing Mrs. Kinzie's attempt to give symbolic and social form to a business dynasty actually foreshadowed many of the problems which faced Chicago artists and the elite families as they sought a cultural expression. The artists, the critic maintained, had to deal with a series of questions, such as: What types of characters were the Chicago elites to develop? What was their manner to be. What tone should this new western society assume? On what terms could business be made respectable? What were the roles of men and women in this new elite? Chicago writers were to attempt answers to all of these questions. But these attempts always came back to one central question which dealt with the relationship between business and culture (pp. 1-3).

In the use of the materials of the early days of the Chicago territory, one can repeat the question which was raised earlier: Where does history end and storytelling begin? In some instances, the two are intricately interwoven. Out of the attempts of the past one can see the evolution of the American Dream as well as the basis for the dream of greatness which has permeated the Chicago mystique. When La Salle made his prophetic observation, he could not have known that indeed there would be a place called Chicago which would become the prototype of the modern industrial city, where American literature would have a new beginning. When that lonely soldier from Fort Dearborn, Surgeon Van Voorhis, wrote to his friend in the East in October of 1811, he had no way of knowing that he too would become a part of Chicago's "usable past." Neither did he know that in his letter he would voice the highest ideals not only of the city but also of America. But he saw clearly the possibilities and the probabilities of the twentieth century when he said:

In my solitary walks I contemplate what a great and powerful republic will yet arise in this new world. Here, I say, will be the seat of millions yet unborn; here the asylum of oppressed millions yet to come. How composedly would I die could I be resurrected at that bright era of American greatness—an era which I hope will announce the tidings of death to superstition and dread tyranny.

The days of New France have gone. The Chicago territory which survived eighteenth-century international conflicts has also disappeared. The Chicago of the days of Fort Dearborn with its horrible and useless Massacre has also gone. Today there is a city which has become one of the major urban centers of the world. But what the city became in the nineteenth century and what it is today is based in part on those explorers, travelers, soldiers, and pioneers who had the vision and the faith to believe not only in the New World but also in the move westward. It is true that many of them were not motivated by the highest ideals. It is apparent that so much of what happened represented human error and human weakness with much obeisance being paid to the law of expediency. It is also true that out of the seventeenth and eighteenth centuries there developed a particular way of looking at Chicago, a way which was rooted in worldly materialism. The nineteenth century reinforced the notion that Chicago was to be a city *OF* the present *FOR* the future.

The absence of an extensive body of historical fiction makes clear that the city's writers have not capitalized on looking backward. Certainly by the time the historical romance developed and became popular, Chicago was in the midst of its greatest period of development, and the era covered during the period 1673-1815 was far removed from the vital, vibrant city. Needless to say, in such a city (as is true in some respects in the nation) the historical romance was never to become a dominant literary form; however, its few practitioners offered a view of Chicago which is seldom seen. It was a city tempered by the past and suggestive of a possible future. Mrs. Catherwood and her imitators could romanticize the days when the Chicago territory belonged to France just as some nineteenth-century French writers attempted to do who had never seen the midwestern prairie. Others could lament the days "when wilderness was king," when a handful of brave souls at an isolated U.S. fort were victimized by the lack of understanding between the military forces of the United States and the leaders of the Pottawatomie tribes. But it was not really the Chicago of the fur traders and Indians which captured the imaginations of the largest group of writers, rather it was—as Duncan so aptly notes—the Armours, the Pullmans, and other giants of finance who were to be remembered as "new world explorers." Yet, for those interested in the history and literature of the region, there must be a recognition of the city when Chicago was the frontier.

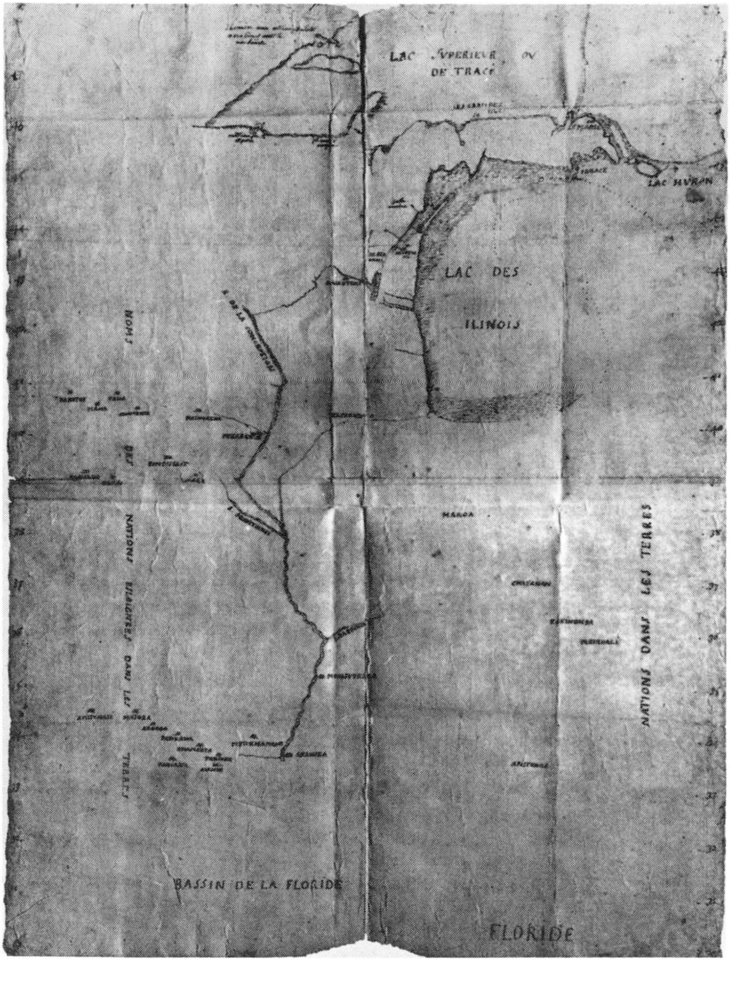

CHICAGO HISTORICAL SOCIETY

ILLUSTRATION 1.—A Detail from Farther Marquette's 1673 Map Pierre Marquette, a Jesuit priest, was an early visitor to the Chicago area. His map furnished a future guide for many of the French expeditions which have been preserved in those important documents known as the *Jesuit Relations.*

OLD FORT DEARBORN.

from *The Artistic Guide to Chicago and the World's Columbian Exposition* (1892)

ILLUSTRATION 2.—Sketch of Fort Dearborn showing the Block-houses.

BLOCKHOUSE OF FORT DEARBORN

THIS BUILDING OCCUPIES THE SITE OF OLD
FORT DEARBORN, WHICH EXTENDED A LITTLE
ACROSS MICH. AVE. AND SOMEWHAT INTO THE
RIVER AS IT NOW IS.
THE FORT WAS BUILT IN 1803 & 4, FORMING
OUR OUTMOST DEFENSE.

ILLUSTRATION 3.—In the vicinity of Michigan Avenue and Wacker Drive there are plaques and brass pavement markers to commemorate the existence of Fort Dearborn. This plaque was given by W.M. Hoyt, the wholesale grocer, in November of 1880 and stands near the site of the blockhouse which was one of the many log buildings which comprised Fort Dearborn.

from *Wau-Bun*

ILLUSTRATION 4.—Juliette Kinzie (1806–1870) gave both form and definition for the "Chicago hero" as she established her version of the Fort Dearborn Massacre.

The Gem of the Prairie.

A Family Newspaper, devoted to Literature, Poetry, Education, the Arts and Sciences, Agriculture, Foreign and Domestic News.

VOL. 8--OLD SERIES. CHICAGO, SATURDAY, AUGUST 21, 1852. NEW SERIES,--VOL 1, NO. 7.

THE EMIGRANTS.

BY ALICE CAREY.

"Don't you remember how oft you have said,
Darling Coralin May,
'When the hawthorns are blossoming we shall be
And then to the prairie away?'
And now, all over the hills they peep
Milk white out of the spray,
And sadly you turn to the past and weep,
Darling Coralin May.

"When the cricket chirped in the hickory blaze,
You cheerily sung, you know—
'O for the sunnier summer days,
And the time when we shall go:'
The corn blades now are unfolding bright,
While busily calls the crow;
And clovers are opening red and white,
And the time has come to go.

"To go to the cabin our love has planned,
On the prairie, green and gay,
In the blushing light of the sunset land,
Darling Coralin May.
'How happy our lives will be,' you said,—
Don't you remember the day?—
When our hands shall be, as our hearts are, wed;"
Darling Coralin May.

"'How sweet,' you said, 'when my work is o'er,
And your axe yet ringing clear,
To sit and watch by the lowly door,
Of our home in the prairie, dear.
The rose is ripe by the window now,
And the cool spring flowing near;
But shadows fall on the heart and brow
From the home we are leaving here.

Incidents of the Battle of the Thames. Who killed Tecumseh?

Gen. Cass, during a discussion in the Senate, on the 5th instant, on the Indian appropriation bill, in advocating the payment of a certain amount of money due the Shawnees, a tribe with which he had had much official intercourse, and of which the celebrated warrior, Tecumseh, was the chief, took occasion to "vindicate the truth of history," as follows:

There are two historical points which have been much debated, about which I wish to say a few words; both are connected with Col. Johnson and these Shawnees. The question has been often mooted as to who was the author of the movement by which the mounted regiment commenced the attack upon the British at the battle of the Thames.

Probably I know as much upon that subject as any other man now living, and the facts are these: Gen. Harrison had prescribed the order of battle, and promulgated it in the usual manner; that order directed that the army should move, infantry in front, with a portion of the force placed at right angles to the main body, to prevent the enemy from turning the flank. The cavalry were to remain in the rear, to follow up all the movements of the infantry. They were posted with the Thames on one flank and an almost impassable marsh on the other. Just as the arrangement was completed, and the British forces were almost in sight, I was sitting on my horse, when General Harrison rode up, and said to me, "I have a great mind to change my order of battle. I feel very strongly inclined to set Colonel Johnson's regiment attack the British line first." I replied, "You have undoubtedly considered the difficulty attending the charge; the mounted men are brave, but undisciplined, and their horses unused to service. If defeated, they may be upon our line, and do us irreparable injury." His answer was, "Col. Johnson says he can break the British line, and I will let him try." Well, the movement was made and was successful; and never, from that day to this, have I had any doubt that Col. Johnson proposed the movement to Gen. Harrison.

Mr. Butler.—Did Col. Johnson's regiment charge the enemy with swords or rifles?

Mr Cass.—The men were all on horseback, armed with rifles; few of them had swords; they rode down the British forces; broke their lines almost without impediment. I saw the whole operaton myself, being there rather as a spectator for I was not in command. I talked about it afterwards with some of the British captured Officers, and having expressed my surprise at the little opposition the movement met with, asked why they allowed their lines to be broken, and their men rode down? They replied that "their men had become alarmed, for they had heard our bugles in the swamp on the left," where they supposed that we had a heavy force of regular cavalry. The *bugles*, Mr. President, were some old tin horns, and we had no force there at all.

I had some conversation on the subject, the other day, at Lexington, with a very intelligent gentleman—Capt. Johnson—a younger brother of Col. Johnson, who was there, and we compared notes, and agreed in our recollections.

Now, as to the other historic but disputed point: Who killed Tecumseh? [Laughter] I will tell you what I know. Tecumseh fell in the battle, as we are all aware; but in the following year the Prophet, Tecumseh's brother, and his son, young Tecumseh, a very intelligent young man, often came to see me, and we had several conversations respecting the series of events in which his father was engaged. The young man was near his father's side in the battle, but his uncle, the Prophet, was in the Creek country. The young man described the battle very graphically—the persons, the parties, present, and the incidents, without hesitation from the beginning to the end, and I have no more doubt from his narration than I have that I am here that Col. Johnson was the person who killed his father. There were three of the Johnsons in the battle, and they were as brave men as ever followed the standard of their country to war.

Gen. Cass continued his remarks, and referred to many incidents to show the services rendered the United States, during the war, by the Shawnees. Gen. Harrison and himself, in 1814, at the direction of the President, held an interview with a large number of them at Greenville, Ohio, when they agreed to join our standard, and subsequently did render to us efficient service. A party of them accompanied Gen. Cass to the northwest frontier, where he had an engagement with hostile Indians, who were urged on by the British, within two miles of Detroit; and in this connection, Gen. Cass referred to the fact that a white man, named Parks, was sitting in the gallery of the Senate, whom he had known since 1814, and who, when a boy, was taken prisoner and brought up among the Wyandots and Shawnees. Parks, at the time of the engagement, although but a boy, and Blackhoof, the principal chief of the tribe, whose son was also in the gallery, with a party of their people came to the rescue, and saved Gen. Cass and his men perhaps from destruction. There being another Shawnee in the gallery, General Cass added:—

"He is the son of a true and brave chief called Captain Tommy, a son of an Indian aid-de-camp to General Harrison, who was with him during his operations in the Northwest, and possessed, as well as merited, our confidence; and, for many years, while they occupied that country, I had relations, political and personal, with the Shawnees, which left a deep impression upon my mind; and whenever they are in any difficulty, I will remember them and their bravery and fidelity, and endeavor to be useful to them."

Louis Napoleon in France.

Extract from the Paris correspondent of the *National Intelligencer*, 22d July.

One of the village correspondents of the *Presse*, however, says that the people are kept so carefully, and at such great distances from the person of the President, by an innumerable soldiery and gendarmery, that no fair estimate can be made of the disposition of the veritable people toward the Prince. The Prince has improved the visit to Strasbourg (this is whispered, indeed, to have been one of the principal objects of his excursion to the Rhine) to visit at Baden his relation, the Grand Duchess STEPHANIE, who, it is said, is negotiating a marriage between her niece, the Princess WASA, and LOUIS NAPOLEON. She was one of the Princesses whose names were connected with the Prince's in the same way some months ago. I think the project now of very probable accomplishment. He will be Emperor as sure as he lives. It is very natural that he should wish to leave his power and crown to a son of his own. This would, moreover, be one of the most certain modes of avoiding the dangers of a disputed succession in his own family, which would probably result in wresting France from the Bonapartes and delivering it up to warring factions. He (the Prince) would like doubtless a more royal and powerful alliance, but recent negotiations with the leading Powers of Europe have satisfied him that, his imperial pretensions being looked upon by them with so little favor, he has no reason to expect that such an alliance would be accorded to him by them. Grand *fetes*, military and civic, have marked the visit of the Prince to Strasbourg. The weather, however, has proved unfavorable. Incessant rains have marred processions and extinguished illuminations, but could have no effect, say the despatches, upon the enthusiasm, affection, and devotion of the people for their beloved Prince whom all tongues hailed as the saviour of France. The illumination of the steeple of the famous Cathedral, the most lofty steeple in Europe, was a complete failure. The same may be said of the striking and curious spectacle of the *Procession of the Village Carts*. National costume is preserved in that portion of France with more fidelity than any where else. The female portion of the population particularly adhere to it with almost undiminished distinctness.

Every village is known by some mark of *coiffure*, or of cut or color of dress; and on Sundays and holidays the various costumes are displayed in all their variety and brilliancy. An interesting part of the programme in honor of the Prince President was the assembling at Strasbourg of all the girls from some one hundred and twenty different villages, and causing them to pass in procession in one hundred and twenty carts, each village represented by its girls in their bravest attire. Each cart was drawn by from four to eight horses. The carts and horses were the same used in the common labors of the field, but the [illegible] selected, and horses and carts were covered, so that their homely proportions were quite concealed, with gay ribands, and green branches, and fresh flowers. The large carts were provided with seats for the accommodation of ten or twelve girls each, the prettiest the villages could afford. The cart of each village was preceded and followed by its young men on horseback, in their respective village costumes, and each village delegation was headed by its mayor. You may imagine the interest and the brilliancy of this procession, which has never been gotten up but upon three or four occasions, and at very distant intervals. But the weather proved adverse, and it is represented to have been really painful to see the drenched and disappointed girls, as they passed with boquets and exclamations of *vive notre sauveur!* in front of the Presidential tent. The military exercises were in better keeping with the weather, and more successful. They represented, in presence of the Swiss and German representatives and officers who were present, a sham-battle, and a forced passage of the Rhine in face of the enemy in a bridge of boats. This exhibition of the skill and ability of the French troops—this passage of the Rhine—must, I think, have suggested some disagreeable reflections to the minds of the spectators from the other side of the river. The President will be back to Paris to-morrow evening.

A Railroad Survey is now being made by W. B. Foster, Esq., of the routes severally proposed for the contemplated Railroad from Philadelphia, by the nearest and most practicable route to the Lehigh river and the Delaware Water Gap.

MORTALITY AMONG PHYSICIANS.—Within a few days past, Drs. Parrish, Stewart and Hunter, well known and highly esteemed physicians of Philadelphia, have died. Their deaths occurred within a day or two of each other.

Rev. Wm. H. Hart, for many years rector of St John's Church, Richmond Hill, Va., died on the 28th of last month, at Shawangunk, Ulster county, New York, after a lingering illness.

A Cunning Dodge.

As soon as it was known that Franklin Pierce was nominated at Baltimore, the liberal minded men of all sects, and particularly the naturalized citizens, declared that unless it could be proved that Franklin Pierce had advocated or favored a repeal of the Catholic disability, they would not vote for him. When Mr. Dallas spoke in Philadelphia, the very next week day evening after the nomination of Mr. Pierce, he could not have seen any public charge made against Mr. Pierce, for neglect of duty in this respect. But as the inspired proverbist informs us, "The wicked flee when no man pursueth." He stated that Franklin Pierce had advocated the repeal of the Anti-Catholic test. On searching the records no speech from Mr. Pierce could be found, but it was decided on that something in the shape of a speech should be, *ex post facto*, put into his mouth. Some dodge must be resorted to, and the leaders seemed to say any dodge, however despicable, will be good enough for the Catholics, who won't know the difference. The telegraph soon informed us that the Washington *Union* would, the next morning, contain the speech of Franklin Pierce on this subject, which he condescended to make, and even descended from the chair to deliver.

Though the speech was just published in the *Washington Union* and copied into the *Ohio Statesman* of June 16, yet the dodge, I believe, was concocted in Concord, and, I cannot help thinking, by the assistance of Franklin Pierce himself. Accordingly the *Concord Patriot*, of June 17th, 1852, contains the speech which was to gull and deceive every liberal minded naturalized citizen, and so far the forgery has succeeded admirably. On referring to the official report of the proceedings in the *Concord Patriot*, I found that Franklin Pierce *had not spoken at all upon the subject*, but on looking further I [illegible] *ished without opposition*, and laid aside as completed, and the *property test* coming up, Franklin Pierce made a speech in favor of striking out the property test, and in that speech the only reference he made to the religious test, was that it had been a "dead letter." And though it had been a "stigma" upon the State, he referred to other parts of the Constitution to *excuse* their fathers' bigotry. Indeed, he contended that the great question of Religious toleration was settled; which, if it meant anything, meant that there was no necessity to bother the Convention about making any alterations on that subject.

When these remarks were made the Religious test *was not* before the Convention. That subject had been *definitely* acted on. (See original report in the *Concord (N. H.) Patriot*, of Nov. 14, 1850, and compare it with June 17, 1852 to see the juggle and trick of a reckless set of partizans.)—*Tribune*.

The Wife.

It needs no guilt to break a husband's heart; the absence of content, the mutterings of spleen, the untidy dress and cheerless home, the forbidding scowl and deserted hearth—these and other nameless neglects, without a crime among them, have harrowed to the quick the heart's core of many a man, and planted there, beyond the reach of cure, the germ of dark despair. Oh! may woman, before that sight arrives, dwell on the recollections of youth, and, cherishing the dear idea of that tuneful time, awake and keep alive the promise she then so kindly gave. And though she may be the injured, not the injuring one, the forgotten, not the forgetful wife, a happy allusion to the hour of peaceful love—a kindly welcome to a comfortable home—a smile of love to banish hostile words—a kiss of peace to pardon all the past, and the hardest heart that ever locked itself within the breast of selfish man will soften to her charms, and bid her live, as she had hoped, her years in matchless bliss, loved, loving and content—the soother of the sorrowing hour, the source of comfort and the spring of joy.

CHICAGO TRIBUNE PHOTOS

ILLUSTRATION 5.—The Gem of the Prairie, an early literary paper, became the weekly edition of the Chicago *Tribune*.

CHAPTER 3

In The Beginning . . . :
The Literature of
Ante-Bellum Chicago

WHEN ONE THINKS of the opening years of the life of the city, one is constantly aware of the emphasis upon commercial pursuits and those wild schemes which did lead to earthly fortunes. Not that everyone had the touch of King Midas, but so much did turn to gold that the name of Chicago, which Henry Blake Fuller was later to call a "shibboleth," early became associated with the titans who were making money as they made the city. The legend is a familiar one and has been repeated often. Many came into the city with little or no money and within a few years had parlayed their funds into thousands—sometimes millions—of dollars. Men were so daring, and the laws were so loose that successive writers have noted the fluidity of the city's morality. Before the fire of 1871 equalized many citizens of Chicago, the fortunes of men such as Gurdon Hubbard, William B. Ogden, John Jones, Marshall Field, Potter Palmer, George M. Pullman, Walter Loomis Newberry, and Philip Armour had been made. (In later years novelists were to draw heavily upon these phenomenal rises to power and wealth as they established the traits of their characters of business.)

In the midst, however, of this commercial activity, there was a search for culture. Art, music, theater, and literature played important roles in the fledgling city. Although much of this activity was supported by those homesick New Englanders who were trying to fashion a Boston Commons in Dearborn Park, representatives from all regions and ethnic groups contributed to the spirit of "cultural uplift." The early biographies of the leaders of the city tend to include the roles played by each in the cultural affairs of the growing metropolis. Some historians have made much of the intricate club structure which existed; however, these clubs served a distinct function. Practically all of them were designed to aid in the elevation of cultural standards, to provide education, and to create social outlets. These early attempts at adult education met with varying degrees of success. Some of the clubs maintained reading rooms. That these were private and for the growing elite did not seem to bother the members who frequently spoke and wrote of the democracy of the West.

Before the incorporation of Chicago as a city in 1837, at least two of these literary, educational clubs had gained prominence not only for their goals but also for their memberships. In 1834 the Chicago Lyceum was formed with William B. Ogden, John Dean Caton, and John Wentworth among the early members. The club was accused of being too exclusive and of "not meeting the adult intellectual needs of the community," but it persisted in its ways until the 1840's. The Chicago Athaeneum, which was similar to the Chicago Polemical Society (1833), was founded in 1836 and sponsored debates and lectures. Among its thirty-eight members were Jean Beaubien and John H. Kinzie, both of whom were descendants of early settlers. By 1841 there had been developed enough interest in literary pursuits to lead to the founding of the Young Men's Association for those who wanted a library and who wanted to read. Although the constitution of this organization proposed a "democratic" membership, such was not the case; and the Young Men's Association, which was destined to play an important role in the development of the Chicago Public Library in later years, remained a relatively exclusive club. In 1842 the Young Men's Junior Lyceum was established followed by the Young Men's Lyceum in 1843. Both groups made literary pretensions and infused new life into the lyceum movement. In fact, the

Junior Lyceum published a journal, *The Stray Leaf*—a semi-
monthly. In terms of the later development of the city's literature
it is significant that these early clubs illustrate that the development and fostering of a literary sensibility came from the efforts
of businessmen in a peculiar marriage of Commerce and Culture.
It appears that by the 1840's and 1850's there had been established a rather substantial reading public in Chicago which
favored the American romantic writers (Washington Irving, James
Fenimore Cooper, William Gilmore Simms, and John Pendleton
Kennedy) and were familiar with the works of Hawthorne, Bryant,
and Whittier through *The Democratic Review*. Early Chicagoans
read the English novelists and poets with emphasis upon Dickens,
Thackeray, and Scott as well as heavier works of theology, history,
and philosophy. Newspapers and magazines from all over the
country were found in the city. Bookstores and publishing companies were being established with an unusual degree of regularity.
This augured well for native writers.

Reconstructing the literature of Chicago in the days before the
Fire is made difficult by the fact that so many records were lost in
that disaster. The Chicago Historical Society, which by 1871 had
become a depository for much of the early literary efforts of the
city, was destroyed. Publishing companies were also destroyed with
their plates and record books. Yet in spite of the irreplaceable
losses, what remains surprises the researcher in its quantity, if
not in its quality.

I

The early literature of Chicago is—in many ways—inseparable
from the development of journalism in the city. The newspapers
deserve some credit for making Chicago such a successful experiment in urban living. As time went on, there were monthly attempts
to introduce new journals with the hope that they would provide a
means to mold and develop public opinion. Frequently, these
journals declared their intentions to support local writing talent.
There was often the strange ambiguity of essentially business-

oriented newspapers and journals calling for local poets and short story writers to augment their pages. Many of these publications failed not because there was a lack of interest but because of that old law of economics which makes it clear that a supply cannot exceed the demand.

Determining the history of newspapers and magazines is often confusing because in addition to the destructiveness of the Fire of 1871, there were so many name changes for a single journal, frequent shifts of editors and proprietors, and the use of a single name for several distinctly unrelated periodicals. For example, there was a Chicago *Commercial Advertiser* from 1836 to 1837 and another journal with the same name from 1847 to 1853. There are instances of a single issue being circulated. One can discover instances of a number of journals being published within a single year never to appear any more. These abortive journalistic attempts proved, however, that there were people who thought newspapers and magazines could succeed in Chicago. In spite of the diversity of types, numbers of issues, lengths of ownership, or duration of the editors, there are certain general characteristics of the city's early journals.

For those familiar with the large impersonal city papers of today, it is sometimes difficult to understand nineteenth-century journalism. At that time the newspapers were not the large corporations of today even though some of them reached relatively large audiences. The publisher or the editor exercised complete control and frequently stamped his personality and prejudices on everything which appeared. Beginning with John Wentworth, the second editor and owner of the Chicago *Democrat*, the editors or proprietors (as they were often called) tended to be strong commanding figures who controlled all aspects of their publications. This was a characteristic which carried over to the early years of the twentieth century. The journalists who came out of this tradition formed a close fraternity from which emerged some names destined to become familiar not only in Chicago but also in America. Franc B. Wilkie, Eugene Field, Theodore Dreiser, George

Ade, Finley Peter Dunne, and Floyd Dell are just a few examples of those writers who came to prominence through journalism. Their stories are relatively familiar. These were the writers—these newspapermen—who were to become part of that great movement which resulted in Chicago being called—for a while—"the literary capital of the United States." Yet, in the 1830's, 1840's, and 1850's there was an equally vocal group of journalists whose work forms a substantial part of the early literature of the city. Many of their names are lost to history, but at a given moment of the city's life they evidenced the same faith in the region as the materialistic builders. Their pride resulted in the repetitive use of the words *Chicago, western,* or *prairie* as identifying labels on the mastheads of these early newspapers and magazines.

As might be expected, the newspapers were concerned about relating the daily events of the new community, but one could gather a great deal about the culture of the city as it emerged through the news, editorials, and advertisements. In addition, nearly all of the newspapers had a "literary" section where appeared the work of homegrown poets, and upon occasion a short story appeared. Although these often served as "fillers," they indicated an acceptance—at least—of literary efforts. The emerging literary journals such as the weekly *Gem of the Prairie* and the monthly *Western Magazine* showed a conscious attempt to establish a native literature. These were predicated upon the supposition that a western literature was possible. Long before the local colorists had become a part of the American literary scene, regional literature was being sponsored, supported, and produced in Chicago. Many of the editors, while displaying a great faith that the region could become a literary and cultural center, were firmly convinced that the power and independence of the city was ultimately connected to the possibility and probability of a distinctive and unique literature. Thus from John Calhoun's Chicago *Democrat* of 1833 the newspapers and magazines formed an important chapter in the development of the city's literature.

Although these early attempts to provide literary journals in the rising marketplace of the West were precarious, the writers followed established patterns. Much of the fiction was confined to the more romantic versions of nature, Indians, border warfare, and to the pioneer's confrontation with these forces. Few of these works really addressed themselves to urban problems. Instead, they were content to provide entertainment for those who were forging a city out of the wilderness. The romantic tradition which was so much a part of American literature during these days found its counterpart in the early fiction written in Chicago. At the same time, writers and editors were trying to prove that the city was "different"; hence, early there appeared that strange ambiguity which characterizes much of the early writing in Chicago.

The following survey of selected titles gives an indication of the nature and the scope of some of the city's early publications. (See Appendix A for a more detailed analysis of nineteenth-century journalism.) The early newspapers and magazines illustrate the sense of region which was so important in the young Chicago. Not only was this evident in the titles but also in the proliferation of local journals. If one should feel that the city in these days was devoid of literary activity and was merely devoted to commercial activity, the list of publications might be impressive. It is important to note, however, that in many instances the journals were designed to support the prevailing business and political structure.

CHICAGO DEMOCRAT (1833-61): When he started the newspaper on November 26, 1833, John Calhoun, the "father of Chicago journalism," had great faith in the newly-incorporated town. When he arrived in the Midwest, he had already achieved a degree of success as a printer in upstate New York. Since small towns needed someone who could produce the necessary broadsides and notices, Calhoun's move to Chicago was a good one. How much of the city's printing was done by him is not totally clear, but he assumed a distinct place in the city's history when he issued from his small print shop the city's first newspaper. Beginning as a weekly, it was essentially a political paper whose motto—("Where Liberty dwells, there is my country")—gives an indication of

Calhoun's independent political philosophy. In addition to national news (or at least his interpretation of it), the paper specialized in local events. The Chicago *Democrat* was to have a long and varied existence; however, Calhoun sold out to the mercurial John Wentworth in 1836, a year before the town was incorporated as a city. Often success in urban communities was measured in terms of those men and women who had the vision to carry on a project rather than with those who began them. And so the name of John Calhoun is almost lost to the city which counts "Long John" Wentworth as one of the important early builders.

CHICAGO AMERICAN (1835-42): It is one of the truisms of journalism that for every one paper, there must be a second. The *American* was started two years after the appearance of the *Democrat*. From 1835 to 1837 this paper which was opposed to everything going on in the nation's capital was guided by its founder, Thomas O. Davis. He was succeeded by the apparently flamboyant William Stuart who directed the paper from 1837 to 1842 while being involved in a number of other journalistic endeavors. Although they disagreed on national political issues, the two newspapers were seemingly in accord on the possibilities of the young city becoming an important area. The *American* had the distinction in 1839 of becoming the first daily paper not only in the city but also in Illinois.

The Democratic and Whig newspapers were soon joined by the *CHICAGO COMMERCIAL-ADVERTISER* (1836-37): This short-lived paper was edited by Hooper Warren, a strong advocate of the anti-slavery cause. Warren, like William Stuart, seemed to be a professional editor for his name reappears with other publications. This first *Commercial-Advertiser* was not successful although the name appears as the title for some subsequent journals in the city.

HARD CIDER PRESS (1840): The "campaign paper" was a common phenomenon in nineteenth-century America, and many of them were established in the early years of Chicago's history. They were devoted to a single cause and soon went out of existence.

The *Hard Cider Press* of 1840, a weekly, was a pro-Whig paper, edited by William Stuart who was also editing the *American* at the same time. Generally the "campaign papers" took the national issues and translated them into regional or local concerns. How successful these publications were is a moot point; however, the accessibility of print shops made them fairly easy to produce.

THE UNION AGRICULTURIST AND WESTERN PRAIRIE FARMER (1841-1905): This journal had a long and distinguished history. In 1843 it became known as the *Prairie Farmer* and continued publication until 1905. After that date its format was considerably altered, but it existed well into the twentieth century. John S. Wright, who wrote an early history of Chicago, prophetically insisted during his two years as editor (1841-43) that the city was destined for greatness. While the weekly *Union Agriculturist and Western Prairie Farmer* was nominally concerned with matters of agriculture, it covered all the news which was of interest to the Midwest; and because Wright was one of the first Chicago "boosters," the paper devoted much attention to developing regional and civic pride. There were many other journals devoted to agriculture during the period, but probably none achieved the success of Wright's publication.

NORTHWESTERN BAPTIST (1842-44): Chicago was to become the home of a large-scale and vital religious press. The first religious publication in the city was the *Northwestern Baptist*, a semi-monthly journal, which was edited by Thomas Powell. Its motto, "Earnestly contend for the faith which was once delivered unto the saints," gives some idea of the dedication of the editorial committee; however, the paper was not able to sustain itself in the city which had more important goals which would bring more immediate results. Hence the journal, like so many others of the 1840's, failed after forty-eight issues; but it had started an interest in a specialized field which was to grow to gigantic proportions.

THE WESTERN CITIZEN (1842-53): While its name might lead one to believe that here is simply another example of a regional paper devoted to boosterism, in reality the paper was one of the strongest reform papers to be established in the area. Devoting itself to the anti-slavery movement as well as to the temperance movement, the *Western Citizen* had a short, albeit distinguished history, primarily because of the men who became associated with it. Initially edited by Zebina Eastman, it was guided by a number of strong anti-slavery advocates including Hooper Warren. Andreas asserted in his *History of Chicago* (Chicago, 1884) that the goal of the paper was "to sow those seeds of emancipation and personal liberty that arrived at their rich fruition in the Emancipation Proclamation of our martyred President in 1863" (I, 383).

Zebina Eastman was tutored by the equally famous Benjamin Lundy who was the editor of the *Genius of Universal Emancipation* when that paper came to Illinois, a fact which helped to put Illinois in the forefront of the anti-slavery movement as the paper became the mouthpiece for the Illinois Anti-Slavery Society. In its first issue published in Illinois (November 8, 1838) the declaration was made that the paper would continue to advocate "free discussion; the total abolition of slavery; and the firm establishment of the constitutional, inalienable, and 'universal' rights of man." As the successor to the *Genius of Universal Emancipation*, the *Western Citizen* had an already-established subscription list which aided its distribution not only in the city but also in the state. Later, in 1853, when it went out of existence, it was absorbed by *Free West*, which existed until 1855, and was avowedly part of the Free Soil movement.

CHICAGO DEMOCRATIC ADVOCATE AND COMMERCIAL ADVERTISER (1844-46): The absence of an editor marked this weekly paper produced by the publishing firm of Ellis and Fergus. Various businessmen in the city supplied editorials. William B. Ogden, the city's first mayor, was instrumental in providing a great deal of material for the paper, but he was not alone. Other businessmen used the paper as a forum for their ideas. Although there was a slight political overtone to the paper, its major impetus came from the business structure. When it lost that support, the paper as constituted could no longer survive. Ellis and Fergus could print the paper, but they did not have the machinery to create a loyal reading public.

GEM OF THE PRAIRIE (1844-52): Perhaps this magazine is best known today because in 1852, when it ceased publication as an independent journal, it became the Sunday edition of the Chicago *Tribune;* yet during its own existence, it was highly successful. In its pages appeared the early work of some of the city's noted writers. It was designed to be a "literary" paper by its editors, Kiler K. Jones and James Beach, and had the distinction of publishing with great frequency the poetry of Benjamin Franklin Taylor. W.H. Bushnell's *Prairie Fire: A Tale of Early Illinois*, often called "the first Chicago novel" was initially issued by this literary miscellany and subsequently by *Sloan's Garden City. Prairie Fire* . . . was apparently successful enough to warrant the many editions of the work which appeared, but it is not in any way an urban work. The *Gem of the Prairie* supported the idea that western materials had literary value although the editors did abstract information and stories from some of the more popular eastern journals. Yet to read its list of editors and contributing writers is to read the list of the local literati. The success of *Gem of the Prairie* inspired a host of imitators who felt that the city could support magazines and papers devoted solely to literature.

ILLINOIS MEDICAL AND SURGICAL JOURNAL (1844-89): This was the first of many medical journals published in Chicago and was edited by the Rush Medical College Faculty with James VanZant Blaney as the supervising editor. Because he was a physician, he was especially sympathetic to the growing problem of health in the over-crowded city. Before it ceased publication, the involvement of Rush College was gradually minimized, but the various journals which emerged were still—in a sense—devoted to the city's first medical school. With the various name changes a reader can note the various shifts of emphases.

CHICAGO DAILY JOURNAL (1844-1929): During its eighty-five year history, the *Daily Journal* underwent numerous name changes and had a multitude of varying political alliances. Its first editors, Richard and Charles Wilson, were devoted to Whig principles and causes. In addition to its political connections, the paper attempted to support the arts and hired Benjamin F. Taylor as its literary editor. George P. Upton, who was to become an important music critic in the city, was the city and commercial editor.

GARLAND OF THE WEST (1845): Apparently trying to capitalize upon the success of *Gem of the Praire*, Robert N. Garrett and Nelson W. Fuller projected *Garland of the West*. Designed as a monthly, it was to be a "western literary" magazine; however, apparently only one issue ever appeared and that was in July of 1845. The editors learned that the success of one paper did not insure that its appeal could necessarily be duplicated.

WESTERN MAGAZINE (1845-46): The short duration of *Western Magazine* belies its importance. Begun by William Rounseville as a literary magazine during a period which was not conducive to this type of publication, it did prove that less than ten years after the incorporation of the city devoted to business pursuits, there was an audience for western literature, even if that audience could not support a journal for a long period. In his own way Rounseville was a Chicago "booster" who made a frank appeal for regional writers and who believed that there was enough literary talent which needed an outlet in the city. In the October (1845) issue, Rounseville declared: "We shall be slow to believe there is not talent enough in the West to maintain a character for a work of this kind." As if in support of the editor's contention, W.H. Bushnell's legend of the upper Mississippi region appeared. Entitled "Ke-O-Saw-Que," it was a typical western story which utilized the culture and the myths of the Indians of the region. Appearing also in this issue was the first installment of a tale, "A Pioneer of the Prairies," by the editor. In the following month's issue (November, 1845) Rounseville observed: "Present indications seem to show that we did not overrate the literary taste of the West when we believed the western people able and willing to support a magazine of their own." Although the monthly literary journal seemed to be operating on a success formula, Rounseville became discouraged and sold the magazine to John J. Moon after ten issues. Moon, in turn, produced the final two issues; and the magazine which had started with a burst of enthusiasm and energy faded out of existence. Rounseville, in the meantime, continued to be associated with Chicago journalism until his death in 1878. In his *History of Chicago* Andreas called Rounseville "a writer of rare and versatile talent. Bits of poetry, charming sketches in prose, historical reminiscences, and well-written fiction, all flowed from his ready pen; and into whatever field he entered, he treated his subject with a grace, vigor, and thoroughness which bespoke the rarest qualities of intellectual strength and culture" (I, 504). While this may have been true, the editor unfortunately was caught up in a surge of failing periodicals from *Better Covenant* of 1844, through *Western Magazine* the following year, to the *Daily Cavalier,* a penny paper of 1846, to the *Morning Mail* of 1847. Given his possible ability, Rounseville is not remembered today as a major force in the development of Chicago writing in spite of *Western Magazine.*

LIBERTY TREE (1846): Its sub-title gives a clearer view of the purpose of the paper: "a monthly publication devoted to the anti-slavery cause." Durings its life Zebina Eastman was the editor. He had been involved during 1845-46 with a short-lived Liberty paper called the Chicago *Daily News,* one of the first daily papers to be issued in the city without a weekly number. Conceivably, *Liberty Tree* was an outgrowth of the former paper.

CHICAGO COMMERCIAL ADVERTISER (1847-53): The editor, Alfred Dutch, was totally committed to the business structure of the city and was thoroughly convinced that the railroads were to be the most important factor in urbanization. He also maintained through his weekly journal that the city as well as the country should be run by businessmen. Through his paper, Alfred Dutch reportedly was instrumental in leading the movement to get large land grants for the Illinois Central Railroad. Long before the twentieth century he was firmly convinced that "the business of America is business" and used his paper to promote his ideas. The irregularity of the appearance of the *Commercial Advertiser* was due to the changes which Dutch made in the frequency of the paper's issues. While it began as a weekly, it went through a period when it was not only a daily but also was issued three times a week.

WESTERN HERALD (1846-47): Actually this paper survived much longer than its dates would indicate because it underwent a number of name changes. Essentially it was a religious paper, but as first established it was only a reform paper devoted to the anti-slavery cause and to temperance. At the same time, it attacked Masonry and asserted that it was following the principles of the Society of Friends. Much of its appeal was derived from the fact that the outstanding Rev. R.W. Patterson, who was for years the pastor of the Second Presbyterian Church, supported the weekly journal. Yet, its eclecticism is demonstrated by the fact that the city's Baptists took a page in order to promote their views on various subjects. In 1847 it became *Herald of the Prairies* with the goal of promoting "practical religion, the maintenance of essential truth, and the advancement of the benevolent enterprises of the age." Two men who figured prominently in the city's business establishment, J. Ambrose Wight and William Bross—the Chicago booster *par excellence*, purchased the journal, its office, and all of its supplies, and changed its name to *Prairie Herald* in 1849, and as such, it became the organ for the doctrines of the New School Presbyterians and the Congregationalists. By 1853 the Congregationalists had assumed control and changed the name to *Congregational Herald* which existed until 1861; consequently, in effect *The Western Herald* of 1846 lasted until the early 1860's. In the late 1850's the

journal called for the establishment of the Chicago Theological
Seminary.
WATCHMAN OF THE PRAIRIES (1847-1920): A religious
journal with specific ties initially to the Baptist church, the *Watchman of the Prairies* followed a checkered career very similar to
that of the *Western Herald*. As the first weekly Baptist paper in
the city, it was strongly anti-slavery. For a time the paper shared
editors with the *Western Herald*, and in 1849 Wight and Bross—
who were also involved with the former paper—became its publishers. The editor-in-chief, Rev. Luther Stone, maintained a degree of continuity in spite of the many organizational changes
going on around him; however, in 1853 he severed his ties with
the weekly journal, and it became the *Christian Times,* and expanded in 1865 by assuming the ownership of *The Witness* published in Indiana and became *Christian Times and Witness*. Then
in 1867 it became the *Standard,* edited by a series of Baptist
clergymen and remained relatively constant until its end.
*THE NORTHWESTERN EDUCATOR AND MAGAZINE OF
LITERATURE AND SCIENCE* (1847-49): The editorial shifts
which were evident in two of the decade's religious journals,
Western Herald and *Watchman of the Prairies,* were absent from
the region's first educational journal. But unlike the other two
papers, *The Northwestern Educator and Magazine of Literature
and Science* was not destined for a long life. The monthly was
edited by James L. Enos whose devotion to educational matters
was total. In the February, 1849, issue he attempted to explain
the goals of the journal:

It was commenced under the most unfavorable circumstances, in a
county where no like publication had ever been circulated, where the
people were comparatively little imbued with a love for education—
or at least, that inculcated by professional teachers—and with the
privations incident to a new country pressing heavily upon them; yet,
notwithstanding these difficulties, the influence of the *EDUCATOR*

has steadily increased, and within the last three months the circulation has nearly doubled.

Yet in spite of his optimism the journal ceased its publication a few months after this. Part of the problem, of course, was related to the distinction which people necessarily made between *education* and *professional education*. In a community where clubs, churches, and newspapers took over part of the educational function, the professional teacher was not deemed to be a necessity. Yet, the fact that the city supported such a journal for a two-year period does indicate something about the nature of the Chicago reading public.

CHICAGO TRIBUNE (1847-   ): The story of the *Tribune* has been retold many times and does not need to be repeated here. Suffice it to say, a Democratic weekly with this name had appeared in the city during the 1840-41 period, but it was sold to an interest in Milwaukee in 1841. From the time of its establishment by a group of businessmen and throughout the nineteenth century, the *Tribune* was a powerful voice in Chicago. Sometimes supportive of the antislavery cause, it was essentially a Republican paper. But more than its affiliation with a political party was its extreme faith in the possibilities of the city. Throughout its early years some of the outstanding men of the city were connected with it; but it started its period of greatest expansion after Joseph Medill, who had come to the city from Cleveland, bought an interest in the paper in 1853. By the twentieth century it had become one of the largest papers in the region and had absorbed many of the short-lived papers; hence, it became an early example of a journalistic conglomerate.

THE LADY'S WESTERN MAGAZINE (1848-49): The success of the *Tribune* was not shared by this journal which was established in order to capitalize on the wide female audience. The East had its share of "ladies' magazines" which were extremely popular, and so there was an attempt to produce a western version. Benjamin

F. Taylor, the Chicago poet, who achieved a degree of fame was selected as the editor, but he had so little regard for matters of business that the magazine, designed as a general and literary monthly, could not survive beyond a few issues.

ILLINOIS STAATS-ZEITUNG (1848-   ): The first German language newspaper in Chicago was the *Chicago Volksfreund* edited by Robert B. Hoeffgen. The weekly began in December of 1845 and existed until the Spring of 1848. At this time the editor began the *Illinois Staats-Zeitung* which was destined to become the most successful German language newspaper in the city. As it began it was strongly attached to the Republican party and was a strong advocate of the anti-slavery cause. The importance of the foreign language press is frequently overlooked. Many of these papers existed in Chicago. For example, there were more than thirty German papers in the city before 1871. All of them served as an important link between the new settlers and their homeland. News from home, significant items about the new land written in the native language, and articles on how to cope with urban living were the bulk of these papers; however, they also furnished writers an outlet for their creativity without making them hurdle the language barrier.

Initially Hoeffgen faced some organizational problems; however, these were finally worked out and the result was an excellent paper. Politically, it also went through some changes. In 1854, when it became the first daily paper to have a Sunday edition—the *Chicago Sonntags-Zeitung*, it was beginning to become more conservative in its political outlook. While it remained kindly disposed toward Abraham Lincoln, the paper deplored not only Andrew Johnson but also the Radical Republicans. In later years, however, it was to become associated with—at least in the minds of non-Germans—those dedicated to political disorder.

THE NORTHWESTERN JOURNAL OF HOMEOPATHIA (1848-52): One of the more unusual journals published in the city was the *Northwestern Journal of Homeopathia* not because it was that influential but because it was one of the first to offer an alternative to traditional medical practices. The monthly was scientific and consisted of many translations from European journals as well as some scholarly papers written by its editor, Dr. George E. Shipman. At the same time, the journal attempted to appeal to popular tastes and so became a pattern for a number of similar journals devoted to homeopathy. The fact that it lasted as long as it did, from October (1848) to September (1852), is a testimony to the fact that there were people in Chicago willing to give an audience to a different approach to medicine. The regular medical establishment was understandably quite antagonistic, and Dr. Shipman undertook to defend Homeopathy. In so doing, he apparently created a relatively large clientele.

THE CHICAGO DOLLAR NEWSPAPER (1849): Another literary weekly which was short-lived, the *Chicago Dollar Newspaper* was devoted to "literature, news, and agriculture." Had editor J.R. Bull been able to consolidate his various interests, the newspaper may have lasted longer; however, Herbert Fleming in his *Magazines of a Market-Metropolis . . .* (Chicago, 1906) referred to it as a "literary journal of merit."

DAILY DEMOCRATIC PRESS (1852-58): One of the many papers absorbed by the Chicago *Tribune* was the *Daily Democratic Press* which was established by John L. Scripps and William Bross, who were early pioneers with the *Tribune*. While the paper is little remembered today, it did make some significant contributions during its own day. It was one of the first general papers to emphasize a commercial department; in this it was following the more avowedly business papers. It was unique in its brand of independence. Without the usual subscription list which formed the backbone of most journals, the *Daily Democratic Press* was committed to an existence based purely upon its merit. As Bross was to say: "It was established in the interest of the city, the State and the great Northwest . . . without any view of making politics the standard of the paper [nor] the advancement of individual politicians the aim of its existence." Its independence is supported by the fact that because of the Democratic stand on the Kansas-Nebraska issue, it

decided to become Republican and made the switch by 1857. The
following year it was absorbed by the *Tribune*.

FRIHED'S BANNERET (1852-53): This was the first Norwegian
paper in Chicago which lasted less than a year, but it established
the pattern which subsequent Norwegian papers followed.

THE CHICAGO LITERARY BUDGET (1852-55): If W.W.
Danenhower had not become so involved with political issues,
there is a strong possibility that the *Chicago Literary Budget* might
have gone down in the city's history as a major literary journal.
It began as a monthly organ for the editor's bookstore with notices
about new books and authors comprising the bulk of its materials.
In 1853 it became a subscription weekly with Benjamin F. Taylor
functioning as an editor and with the ownership still in the hands
of Danenhower who sounded the regional note in the issue of
January 7, 1854, when he declared:

The West should have a marked original literature of its own.
Writers of fiction have used up all the incidents of our glorious revolutionary period. The romantic scenery of the East, too, has been
made to aid in the construction of some of the best romances ever
written. We do not object to this. On the contrary, we rejoice—are
thankful it is so. But a new field is open to authorship. We wish to
present its advantages.

The Great West, in her undulating prairies, deep-wooded highlands,
mighty rivers, and remnants of aboriginal races, presents topics teeming with interest to every reader, and big with beautiful scenes for the
artist's eye. The West is full of subject matter for legend, story, or
history. Sublime scenery to inspire the poet is not wanting. All that is
lacking is a proper channel. This channel we offer. *The Budget* claims
to be a western literary paper, and we invite writers to send us articles
on western subjects, for publication.

Although it had a short duration, the *Literary Budget* was a
factor in the literary life of the city. Not only did Taylor's poem
appear in it, but also in 1854 T. Herbert Whipple's novella,
Ethzelda, or Sunbeams and Shadows, was serialized. The narrative,

which was eventually published separately and which achieved a degree of success among the reading public of Chicago, was called "a tale of the prairie land as it was." Among the innovations instituted by this weekly journal was the printing of the first music from movable type in Chicago. Since the *Literary Budget* expected only western subscribers, the editor called upon "the friends of western literature" to organize clubs for cooperative ventures "in maintenance of a good literary paper in this section of the country."

In 1855 Danenhower, who had become important in the Illinois sections of the "Know Nothing" Party unilaterally closed the magazine and started the *Native Citizen* which was promised to subscribers as a substitute for the former journal. In the last issue of his literary miscellany, Danenhower said:

We hope that our future exertions will be such as to exemplify to the world that the pure fire of American sentiment is sweeping over our vast prairies; that hereafter America shall and must be governed by Americans.

And thus it was that an anti-immigration spirit which would become more and more apparent in the 1860's emerged from a now-obscure literary journal. Yet, as it began it acknowledged that "the West is full of subject matter for legend, story, or history" and promised it would offer a "proper channel" for writers.

WESTERN TABLET (1852-55): This Roman Catholic literary weekly was published and edited by Daniel O'Hara who included a great deal of news about Ireland along with messages about the new land. Its literary emphasis was minimal as it became the forerunner of a number of Roman Catholic papers. Its motto: "Where the spirit of the Lord is, there is Liberty" gives an indication of its religious nature.

CHRISTIAN BANKER (1853): Andreas referred to the *Christian Banker* as a "novelty in literature" (I, 408). It was a utopian monthly journal edited by Seth Paine, who had visions of a perfect world order. Interestingly enough, he believed that utopia would come with a perfection of business techniques. Thus it was that he proposed in his journal the establishment of the Bank of Utopia which would be developed through three evolutionary stages: Bank of Chicago, Bank of the People, and Bank of God. When the paper ceased publication after eight issues, Andreas records that Paine was sent to a lunatic asylum and concludes "how far he was qualified for a residence in that institution during his editorship is unknown" (I, 408). The fact remains that seldom has reform been taken so far.

NORTHWESTERN CHRISTIAN ADVOCATE (1853-1930): Established by the General Conference of the Methodist Episcopal Church, the *Northwestern Christian Advocate* is simply one more example of one of the early journals of Chicago surviving over a long period of time. It became an extremely important paper and influenced a large readership throughout the Midwest, becoming the first religiously-oriented publication to become an eight-paged paper. Initially it was strongly anti-slavery, then it took up other reform movements after the Civil War, eventually settling into a general paper with religious overtones.

SLOAN'S GARDEN CITY (1853-54): In 1853 Walter B. Sloan thought a weekly newspaper might help him distribute his various patent medicines; hence, the establishment of *Sloan's Garden City* which was destined through its few months of existence to become an outstanding literary journal. As an advertising medium Sloan pushed his items, such as "Sloan's Family Ointment," "Sloan's Life Syrup," "Sloan's Instant Relief," and "Sloan's Horse Ointment." As a literary outlet, it provided a forum for such writers of fiction as William H. Bushnell, whose *Prairie Fire* was also serialized here. When Oscar Sloan, Walter's son, took over the paper, there was a conscious search for western literature and western writers. Thus the magazine became a forerunner of the basic philosophy of the local color movement, and was one of the first journals in the country to set forth the importance as well as the methodology of literary regionalism almost twenty years before that movement became a part of American literature. After 1854 it became a part of the Boston *People's Paper* which existed until 1870.

WESTERN GARLAND (1855): Just ten years after the attempt and the failure of *Garland of the West*, *Western Garland* appeared. Whether or not Mrs. Harriet Lindsey knew of the existence of the former journal is a moot point; but like the other journal, *Western Garland* was to be a literary magazine devoted to "polite literature" as well as to such disciplines as art and science with a survey of the news—local, national, and international. This ambitious journal was not only issued at Chicago but at the same time appeared in St. Louis and Louisville. So pretentious a plan would almost demand a dedicated subscription list; yet within the year *Western Garland* had failed like so many of its predecessors.

THE PEN AND PENCIL (1856): Edited by T. R. Dawley, who was very active in journalistic circles in the city during this period, *The Pen and Pencil* was designed to be a story newspaper which would be profusely illustrated. The weekly paper had the advantage of having for one of its major contributors T. Herbert Whipple. But this was not sufficiently attractive to prolong the life of such an aspiring project, and after a few issues it ceased publication.

PRAIRIE LEAF (1856): The D. B. Cooke and Co., which was devoted to bookselling, attempted what so many other bookstores had tried. *The Prairie Leaf* was the monthly advertising paper for the firm, but it also was designed to include some literary articles. While the plan was a good one, journals without a committed list of subscribers found it unnecessarily difficult to survive in the months preceding the great panic of 1857; hence, *The Prairie Leaf* lasted for only a few months.

THE CHICAGO MAGAZINE: THE WEST AS IT IS (1857): Zebina Eastman, who was intricately involved with the anti-slavery movement in Illinois, became the editor of this monthly which had been founded by the Mechanics' Institute as part of the club's on-going process toward self-betterment. The journal was a literary magazine of high quality which included in its issues biographies, historical anecdotes, stories, poems, and excellently executed steel engravings. Unlike some of the literary magazines which were narrowly provincial in interest and subject, the *Chicago Magazine* tried to cover a wide area of tastes while supporting the principle of regionalism. But by limiting himself to Chicago and by being so obviously defensive, Eastman's work on behalf of the Mechanics' Institute was doomed. "We believe failure was never yet wedded to Chicago," declared the editor in his introductory statement which appeared during March, 1857. He continued: "We propose to fill these pages with such matters as will make this publication a Chicago-Western magazine. We shall aim to make it a *vade mecum* between the East and the West—a go-between carrying to the men of the East a true picture of the West which will satisfy their desire for information on the great topics connected with this part of their common country." With a ringing plea for the support of his regional philosophy, he concluded:

We therefore bespeak for our work a place in the eastern market, and some offset there to the competition we must meet with in the circulation of eastern periodicals in the western field. The West will learn to patronize this monthly for the love of its own ideas: the East will read it to get that knowledge of us which they cannot get from any other source.

In the following month's issue the confidence of the editor began to wane as he begged his readers to "buy extra copies to send east." In the August issue, which was the last, there appeared an advertisement addressed to "Men of the West," urging them to purchase extra copies of the magazine, and thereby to aid in establishing a literature of their own, and a monthly magazine also of their own "as good as *Harper's, Putnam's,* or *Godey's.*" Had the economy of the times been better and had the editor been more flexible, the *Chicago Magazine: The West As It Is* might have survived beyond the five monthly issues which appeared in 1857. That Eastman (who was a lawyer, writer, editor, and prominent abolitionist) had high hopes for the magazine was apparent from his efforts, but he was not always realistic. For example, he wanted to publish the magazine without using any advertisements whatsoever; however, by the second issue he admitted: "We respond to the wish of a contemporary that we might be able to dispense with this avenue of public patronage. But at the present the law of necessity must overrule the law of taste." Ultimately, in its few monthly issues the magazine was proof that a concern for literature could be expressed in the midland metropolis without the vulgarity often associated with "western" literature, especially by those in the East. When the magazine failed, one of the potentially best early journals to be produced in Chicago failed.

NORTHWESTERN QUARTERLY (1858): Approximately a year after the failure of the *Chicago Magazine,* James Grant Wilson assumed the editorship of another ambitious literary magazine. It appeared in October, 1858, and carried the following notice written by Rufus Blanchard, its publisher:

On the issue of the pioneer number of this magazine the publisher would beg leave to state that he is well aware that no high pretensions can sustain a feeble attempt, as that a worthy effort would be successful without them. *The Northwestern Quarterly* is now before the tribunal of public opinion to stand or fall as its merits shall determine.

In citing the purposes of the new quarterly, it was noted that the "broad fields of literature" were to be "traversed" and "the progress of the fine arts to be traced"; yet, *The Northwestern Quarterly,* subjected to the "tribunal of public opinion," suspended publication after its initial issue.

BANK NOTE REPORTER AND COUNTERFEIT DETECTOR (1859): Increasingly Chicago saw the publication of highly specialized commercial and banking journals. This was neither the first nor the best; however, it did illustrate the growing concern among bankers with the matter of counterfeiting. The fact that there would be developed a magazine devoted to that interest suggests something of the nature of the problem and suggests that it was perhaps more widespread than many bankers wanted to admit.

As one reviews the journals cited here, it is important to remember that they represent only a small portion of the total number which were produced in the city before the Civil War; however, they do give some indication of the types of concerns with which the early journalists in Chicago dealt. (See Appendix A.) While there was certainly the usual number of politically slanted newspapers, these papers were very early being controlled by the business interests of the city; hence, there are few examples of the "independent" paper. Perhaps the anti-slavery papers and temperance journals were more independent "politically" than most papers, but they were devoted to the cause of reform and did not allow—at least within their pages—any deviation from that. The widespread anti-slavery interests of the 1830's and 1840's seemed to wane during the 1850's in the sense that no new papers were established; and those which survived became less strident as the nation moved closer and closer to the Civil War. In the 1850's there was also a growing spirit of nativism which did not approve of the widespread foreign immigration into the nation or into the city. At the same time, the foreign language newspaper and journals were proliferating. And with each one there was a measure of built-in success because they were limited to those who spoke that particular language. The religious press was not only strong but highly successful as many of the religious papers established during this period survived into the twentieth century. If survival is a measure of success, then the medical journals which began during this period must also be considered, for many of them also lasted into the twentieth century.

Perhaps the biggest success of the period prior to 1860 was the Chicago *Tribune* which, since 1847, has maintained its position as a significant paper not only in Chicago but also in the Midwest. By 1860 it had grown to gigantic proportions by absorbing so many of the less successful and poorly-managed newspapers. And for

whatever it is worth, it is significant to note that this first con-
tinuously successful paper was begun by a group of businessmen
who were committed not only to the growth of the city but also
to the maintenance of the business interests.

The most ephemeral journals were often started with high ideals
and low budgets. The number of journals which lasted for a single
issue is not as high as one would imagine, but there were enough
attempts to suggest that the reading public of Chicago may have
been more selective than one would ordinarily think. Among the
short-lived journals were many of those devoted primarily to literary interests. It is not surprising that many of them did not survive over a number of years. What is astonishing is the fact that
so many of them should have been started during the days when
Chicago's interests definitely were not "literary." That some of
these editors recognized that there needed to be outlets for "western voices" long before the local color movement swept the country
is a testimony to their literary astuteness even if they could not
always recognize their goals. Yet, out of these literary journals
there did emerge some names, such as Benjamin Franklin Taylor,
T. Herbert Whipple, and William Bushnell, who were forerunners
in the early Chicago's initial efforts toward producing its own
literature.

Through all of these journals there seemed to be a conscious
effort to identify with the region. Consequently, even special interest magazines, such as those devoted to agriculture or to medicine, took great care to use some word in the title which would
relate it either to the Northwest, to the Prairie, or to the city. This
regional interest did much toward creating an atmosphere not only
for a growing literary sensibility but also for a sense of place which
was to become one of the dominating characteristics of Chicago
literature. Ultimately, as one notes this period and its journalistic
offerings, one must consider not only the successes but also the
failures. Together they form one of the great chapters in the development of writing in a city more committed to action than to
contemplation. Thus with the advent of the golden age of Chicago

writing during the latter part of the nineteenth century and into the twentieth century, there was a firm foundation upon which later writers could build.

II

From the very beginning of the city's existence the residents of the new, bustling urban center displayed a keen interest in what they were doing. They seemed to feel that they were creating a city of promise, of worth, and of distinction. Hence, just as newspapers and magazines have been a distinct element of the city's early writing so also has history been a significant genre. Needless to say, some of the first histories of the city appeared in the journals of the period. By far the most common type of historical writing has been geared to a sense of "manifest destiny" designed for popular consumption. Beginning with the early booster documents and culminating in the rash of popular pictorial histories which still seem to appear with a degree of regularity, Chicago history has emphasized the phenomenal growth patterns which have occurred. Some of these histories have been interpretive and have tried to portray the city in terms of dominant themes. Some few have actually achieved that objectivity that loosely is called "scientific" history. But no matter what type it has been, each history has attempted to recapture the spirit and mood of the city. That most of these were and have been written by Chicagoans does—as one might suspect—limit the seriousness with which they have been taken. But once again, one can see in miniature the story of American culture told and re-told in terms of a minuscule part of the totality of the national civilization.

Before Chicago was a city, the organization which was to become most supportive of the city's first budding historians was established. When it was founded in 1834, the Chicago Lyceum was designed as a social club with intellectual pursuits; however, it soon became a forum for a number of lectures—many of which dealt with the history of the region. As it was proposed, the membership consisted of the outstanding men of Chicago.

Andreas includes in his pioneer work the reminiscences of the
Honorable Thomas Hoyne, one of the popular lawyers of the city,
who was secretary of the Lyceum in 1840.

'[The Lyceum] was the foremost institution in the city, when I
came . . . in 1837. At the time I became a member not a man of note,
not a man in the city of any trade of profession, who had any taste
for intellectual and social enjoyment, who loved books, conversation
and debate, but who belonged to the Lyceum. . . . When I came here
the society had, for those days, an excellent library, consisting of, as I
remember, over 300 volumes. . . . We ran along until 1843 or 1844.
The city was then entering upon its career of rapid growth and development, which has since astonished the world, and which about
that time absorbed the interests of the citizens so much that the
Lyceum meetings began to be poorly attended and finally, as an institution, it died from sheer neglect' (I, 522).

Before that "sheer neglect" took place, the Lyceum was the place
which provided an outlet for some of the earliest histories of the
region.

Ascertaining the first historian is risky at best. Much depends
upon not only one's definition of history but also one's opinion
concerning the form—written or oral—that history must take.
However, for all intents and purposes, it appears that the first
history was produced in 1840, just three years after the city's incorporation. It appeared first as a lecture before the Lyceum then
as a pamphlet that same year, still later (1876) it appeared as
the first in the now-distinguished series of historical works published by the Fergus Printing Company. The author was Joseph
N. Balestier, a Vermont lawyer who arrived in Chicago in 1835.
By 1836 he had joined forces with another lawyer and had opened
an office dealing mainly in real estate, land titles, and money lend-
ing. On January 21, 1840, he delivered a lecture entitled "The
Annals of Chicago," which was subsequently published that same
year "by demand." He attempted to show how in such a short time
Chicago had emerged as a center of great growth. Laudatory

though he is at many points, he is essentially objective in his ability
to isolate the various contributing factors which led to the widespread view of Chicago as a place of great opportunity. Of possible interest to modern audiences is his perception of the real estate
"deals" which made fortunes for so many unsuspecting candidates.
He presented his information clearly and in a style which one
ordinarily would not associate with the frontier community. If the
myth of Chicago is as real as later historians like to believe, it
seems fairly certain that Balestier must be credited—at least in
part—with giving that myth a tangible definition as well as presentation. The following passage illustrates the basis for the myth
in terms of real estate transactions:

The year 1835 found us just awakened to a sense of our own importance. A short time before, the price of the best lots did not exceed two or three hundred dollars; and the rise had been so rapid, that
property could not, from the nature of things, have acquired an as-
certained value. In our case, therefore the inducements to speculation
were particularly strong; and as no fixed value could be assigned to
property, so no price could, by any established standard, be deemed
extravagant. Moreover, nearly all who came to the place expected to
amass fortunes by speculating. The wonder then is, not that we specu-
lated so much, but rather that we did not rush more madly into the
vortex of ruin. Well indeed would it have been had our wild speculations been confined to Chicago; here, at least, there was *something*
received in exchange for the money of the purchaser. But the few
miles that composed Chicago formed but a small item among the
subjects of speculation. So utterly reckless had the community grown,
that they chased every bubble which floated in the speculative atmosphere; madness increased in proportion to the foulness of its aliment;
the more absurd the project, the more remote the object, the more
madly were they pursued. The prairies of Illinois, the forests of Wisconsin and the sand-hills of Michigan, presented a chain almost un-
broken of suppositious villages and cities. The whole land seemed
staked out and peopled on paper. If a man were reputed to be fortunate, his touch, like that of Midas, was supposed to turn everything

into gold, and the crowd entered blindly into every project he might
originate. These worthies would besiege the land offices and purchase
town sites at a dollar and a quarter per acre, which in a few days
appeared on paper, laid out in the most approved rectangular fashion,
emblazoned in glaring colors, and exhibiting the public spirit of the
proprietor in the multitude of their public squares, church lots, and
school lot reservations. Often was a fictitious streamlet seen to wind
its romantic course through the heart of an ideal city, thus creating
water lots and water privileges. But where a *real* stream, however
diminutive, did find its way to the shore of the lake—no matter what
was the character of the surrounding country—some wary operator
would ride night and day until the place was secured at the Government price. Then the miserable waste of sand and fens which lay
unconscious of its glory on the shore of the lake, was suddenly elevated into a mighty city, with a projected harbor and light-house,
railroads and canals, and in a short time the circumjacent lands were
sold in lots, fifty by one hundred feet under the name of 'additions.'
Not the puniest brook on the shore of Lake Michigan was suffered to
remain without a city at its mouth, and whoever will travel around
that lake shall find many a mighty mart staked out in spots suitable
only for the habitations of wild beasts.

No Chicago novelist has done a better job in describing the type of
land speculation which was the forerunner of so many Chicago
fortunes. The vividness of Balestier's description reveals elements
of humor which may have been intentional or which may have
been simply a result of his ability to portray graphically the situation as it existed in a day when so many wild schemes actually did
work. The fact that he was a lawyer who specialized primarily in
real estate and title work does lead one to suspect—on occasion—
his motives. But his facts can be documented.

   Balestier was not so naive as to assume that what was taking
place in Chicago was a local phenomenon. Rather he saw it as a
part of the general "land fever" which was sweeping the country
and was aware that people were beginning to understand the kinds
of profits which could be made from real estate. In fact the more

speculative ventures which he found to be an "unwholesome spirit" were permeating all classes of society:

It extended into every walk of life. The farmer forsook the plow and became a speculator upon the soil instead of a producer from beneath the sod. The mechanic laid aside his tools and resolved to grow rich without labor. The lawyer sold his books and invested the proceeds in land. The physician 'threw physic to the dogs,' and wrote promissory notes instead of prescriptions. Even the day laborer became learned in the mysteries of quit-claim and warranty, and calculated his fortune by the thousands.

He noted that this did not augur well for a community and asserted:

When the mass of the community thus abandoned or neglected their proper pursuits, it may readily be assumed that the ignoble few who were willing to work received an ample reward for their pains. The price of labor was exorbitant; the simplest service was purchased at a dear rate. Even the barbers, who, since the days of Abraham, had shaved for sixpence, discovered that they had been working at half price.

As he viewed it, "the great increase of consumers and the proportionate decrease of producers rendered the price of provisions enormous." This also meant "credit, reckless and indiscriminate, was the master principle of those wild and maddening days." He recognized that the banks had not only "greatly multiplied at this period" but also that they had "issued sufficient paper promises to create a spirit of wild extravagance." As a result, "the property of the country rose too rapidly to be represented by an inflated banknote circulation. Individuals, in humble imitation of the banks, issued their notes without stint or limit." He concluded that if "old established communities were thus frightened from their propriety, it can scarcely be supposed that the rising village of Chicago should escape the contagion" which was sweeping the country. But as various panics settled across the country, Chicago was spared some of their more devastating effects.

In a perceptive and objective way, Balestier looked closely at the operation as well as the effects of speculation.

If a man were so fortunate as to have a disputed title, it made no great difference where the land lay, or how slender was his claim, his fortune was made; for the very insecurity of the purchase made it desirable in the eyes of the venturous. A powerful auxiliary to the speculative spirit was the sale of lands by auction. When bodies of men, actuated by a common motive, assemble together for a common object, zeal is apt to run into enthusiasm; when the common passion is artfully inflamed by a skilled orator, enthusiasm becomes fanaticism, and fanaticism, madness. Men who wish to be persuaded are already more than half won over, and an excited imagination will produce almost any anticipated result. Popular delusions have carried away millions at a time; mental epidemics have raged at every period of the world's history, and conviction has been ever potent to work miracles. Now the speculating mania was an epidemic of the mind, and every chord struck by the chief performers produced endless vibrations, until the countless tones of the full diapason broke forth in maddening strains of fascination. The auctioneers were the high-priests who sacrificed in the Temple of Fortune; through them the speculators spread abroad their specious representations. Like the Sibyls and Flamens of old they delivered false oracles, and made a juggle of omens and auguries.

Balestier was well aware of the results of this fanatical behavior, and he continued by showing what happened to the young city.

But the day of retribution was at hand; the reaction came—and the professional speculator and his victims were swallowed up in one common ruin. Trusting to the large sums due to him, the land operator involved himself more and more deeply, until his fate was more pitiable than that of his defrauded dupes.

The year 1837 will ever be remembered as the era of protested notes; it was the harvest to the notary and the lawyer—the years of wrath to the mercantile, producing, and laboring interests. Misery inscribed its name on many a face but lately radiant with high hopes; despair was stamped on many a countenance which was wont to be 'wreathed in smiles.' Broken fortunes, blasted hopes, aye, and blighted characters: these were the legitimate offspring of those pestilent times. The land resounded with the groans of ruined men, and the sobs of defrauded women, who had entrusted their all to greedy speculators. Political events, which had hitherto favored these wild chimeras, now conspired to hasten and aggravate the impending downfall. It was a scene of woe and desolation. Temporary relief came in the shape of Michigan money—but like all empty expedients, it, in the end, aggravated the disease it pretended to cure—it seemed a sovereign panacea, but it proved a quack specific. Let us turn from this sickening spectacle of disaster and ruin. Made as her citizens had been, Chicago *was* Chicago still. Artificial enterprises had failed, but nature was still the same. There stood Chicago 'in her place of pride'—unmoved and immovable. Though mourning and desolate, she could still sustain an active population. Need I add that SHE HAS DONE IT?

The note of civic pride and regional patriotism upon which this passage ends is a typical one to be found in Chicago histories which emphasize not only the greatness of the city but also the city's ability to "bounce back" after any disaster. A survey of the histories written especially after each major catastrophe will reveal the "I-Will" spirit being exemplified. As he dispels a sense of pessimism, Balestier concludes that Chicago will continue to prevail. Recognizing that "Chicago has sprung, as it were, from the very mire, and assumed the aspect of a populous city" he noted, "Well may we rejoice in a result so glorious." With the prospects of its phenomenal growth practically assured, it is no wonder that the citizens of the midland metropolis were beginning to take the new settlers crowding into their city with a rather sanguine air. "No curiosity is excited by the advent of a schooner, and even the vapor-driven monsters which frequent our harbors have ceased to call forth our wonder."

The survival of this piece from the ravages of the Fire of 1871 is an interesting coincidence not merely because of what happened to it specifically, but in a general way it illustrates one method by which Chicago materials held by those outside of the city were returned in order to help Chicago retrieve its past and replace lost documents. According to a report from the Chicago *Tribune* (November 25, 1872), Balestier's work was found in the Wisconsin State Library. It seems that after the work was published as a pamphlet by Edward Rudd, Printer, in 1840, the author autographed a copy and sent it to an acquaintance in New York with an inscription. It was this copy which found its way to Wisconsin. Subsequently, it was issued as the first document in Fergus' Historical Series. Thus it still survives as the first attempt at a published history of Chicago. The emphasis which he placed upon land speculation as both a means of ruin and a way to great fortune has been noted by later historians. In fact, there are many who support the idea that it was the nineteenth-century land speculation which was a major factor in Chicago's growth.

In December of 1840 William H. Brown, who had moved to Kaskaskia from the East in 1817, delivered his lecture entitled "Early History of Illinois" before the Lyceum. He was ably suited to deal with the subject because he had spent much time traveling throughout the State displaying a genuine curiosity about the various towns. In addition to his work as a lawyer, he was also involved in the publication of the Illinois *Intelligencer*, the first newspaper established in the area. In the 1820's Brown and his partner became embroiled in the question of whether or not slavery should be permitted in the State. Brown was opposed to it; and rather than permitting the paper to suffer because of their feud, he relinquished his share. However, he worked throughout the State to defeat the possibility of slavery being brought into Illinois and is credited with being largely responsible for a reversal of attitudes. When the State Bank decided to open a branch in Chicago in 1835, Brown was sent to the city to become the cashier; hence, he had been a vocal and active citizen of Illinois before taking up residency in Chicago. From that time on, he was most active in financial circles and held a number of significant posts within the city, but probably he did his most good as the fiscal agent for the school system. Like many others in the city, he became extremely wealthy through his early involvement with the railroads, and before his death was considered one of the richest men in the city. His interest in history was not unusual. Many of the early histories were produced by businessmen who were not only aware of the commercial nature of the city but also who were determined that the influence of business should be clearly understood by those who were about the business of building a city.

While many of the lectures delivered before the Lyceum found their ways into print, these pamphlets were ephemeral at best. Often printed on inexpensive paper by harried jobbers, they were not considered "books" although certainly they were publications. Needless to say, after the Fire, it was more and more difficult to find these publications. The ones which came back to Chicago often had been inadvertently saved by someone out of the city. Because they were designed for such temporary use, their plates would not have been saved at any event; and certainly most plates were lost during the Fire. The first detailed historic work—not a pamphlet—was written by Judge Henry Brown who had moved to Chicago in 1836 from New York State. Published by a New York firm in 1844, *The History of Illinois* was the first to deal at great lengths not only with the State but also traced the development of the Northwest Territory. Erroneously called *The History of Chicago* by some critics, undoubtedly because he does deal at great lengths with the Chicago territory, his work is well-done. One of his major contributions was his attempt to establish the actual events of Fort Dearborn and to view judiciously the actions of Commander Heald and the other men at the garrison. Underlying his objectivity is the expected civic pride which is manifest in his prediction of the expected greatness of the region. From a local point of view the work is highly successful in the sense that it does trace the major influences and concerns of the area. Yet the work which is significant for dealing with a seldomly treated facet of

American history might appear to be too provincial and limited. Writing about Brown's work many years after its publication, Andreas, who is not always the paragon of accuracy, noted:

> Not that the history does not, in the light of subsequent research, contain many errors, both as to dates and in the correctness of its subject matter, yet no one would be warranted in the assertion that Judge Brown did not make best use of all available means to secure accuracy.

Andreas continued by crediting the book with fulfilling a valuable necd.

> . . . he did the work at a time when it was needed; and, with whatever imperfections it may have possessed, it met the popular want, was appreciated by those who read it, and it still lives a modest but enduring memento to the memory of its author, who was an able lawyer, a just Judge, and an impartial historian (I, 502).

Perhaps ultimately Brown's importance will rest with his method rather than with his production. Relying heavily on diaries, journals, and memories of earlier settlers, his chronicle of the history of the region is based largely upon the immediacy of the documents which provided source materials for him. That this early work was issued by an eastern firm was evidence—at least to some—that Chicago history had become part of the national scene by 1844.

The credit for the preservation of much of Chicago's early writing must go to William Ellis and Robert Fergus who organized a printing firm. Many of the city's printers were attached to various newspapers although they often did "outside" jobs; however, there were some independent printers such as the firm of Ellis and Fergus. The first work of history published by that firm was destined to become more important than its thirty-four pages might have indicated at the time. In 1844 there appeared Juliette Kinzie's pamphlet *The Massacre at Chicago, August 15, 1812, and Some Preceding Events* which launchcd Ellis and Fergus as a major outlet for regional lore. (Later Robert Fergus was to initiate the now-famous series which preserved many of the documents, reminiscences, and speeches of early Chicago, many of which were delivered either before the Chicago Lyceum or the Chicago Historical Society.)

When there was some question about the dating of Mrs. Kinzie's work, Robert Fergus attached a note to it explaining that the work was done in 1844 rather than in 1836, as Mrs. Kinzie later claimed. It was "from manuscript written and furnished by Mrs. John H. Kinzie, contained in a small letter-page half-bound blankbook. I set the type for the first edition of this pamphlet in 1844. The presswork was done by my partner, the late William Ellis. Mrs. Kinzie read, revised, and approved the proofs. It had not been printed prior to that date."

In a prefatory advertsiement which appeared at the beginning of the first edition and which has been reprinted in subsequent editions Mrs. Kinzie explained her reasons for writing what was to become, unknown to her at the time, an important document of the Fort Dearborn period.

This little record . . . from the lips of those who had been eyewitnesses of the events described, was not designed for publication. It was made simply for the purpose of preserving to the children of the writer, a faithful picture of the perilous scenes through which those near and dear to them had been called to pass. This will excuse many personal and family details which it contains.

At the solicitation of many friends, and to avoid the possibility of its unauthorized appearance in print, the writer has consented to its publication in its original form.

In 1911 when George Fergus, Robert's oldest son, decided to re-issue Mrs. Kinzie's work, he added a note of his own which was designed to explain the significance of the work:

Subsequently, it was inserted, substantially, by Judge Henry Brown in his 'History of Illinois,' New York, 1844; it also appeared in the three editions of 'Annals of the West,' Cincinnati, O., 1846; St. Louis, Mo., 1850; and Pittsburgh, Pa., 1856, by James Handyside Perkins. Major Richardson made use of it in two of his tales, 'Hardscrabble' and 'Wau-nan-gee,' Mrs. Kinzie reproduced it as Chapters XVIII and XIX in her 'Wau-Bun, the Early Day in the Northwest,' New York, 1856.

Because they were either written or commisioned by businessmen, the early chronicles naturally emphasized the commercial growth and mercantile possibilities of Chicago. Furthermore, they naturally highlighted the role of business in the evolution of the city. Thus, long before the novelists had created the businessman as the cultural hero of the city, the historians had already done it. Understandably the major period of writing history followed the Fire of 1871 when concerned men and women attempted to re-create and recapture the story of the phenomenal growth of the city up to the time of its destruction; however, the first histories— which began just three years after the city was established—were prophetic in their insistence that the growth of the city's business life was the significant factor in the development of the city. Coupled with this, of course, was the suggestion that the men and women who cast their fortunes with the city were "different."

Perhaps this first stage of historical writing culminated with three works, all of which were published by Chicago firms: W. Thorn and Co., *Chicago in 1860; a Glance at Its Business Houses* (Thompson and Day, 1860); Isaac D. Guyer, *History of Chicago: Its Commercial and Manufacturing Interests and Industries* (Goodman and Cushing, 1862), and John S. Wright, *Chicago: Past, Present, and Future* (Horton and Leonard, 1868). These works clearly demonstrate the dominant traits of many of the city's early histories with their emphasis upon a business orientation, the staggering growth, the commitment of the citizens to the "Chicago spirit," and the destiny of the city to become one of the outstanding urban centers not only of the United States but also of the world. Thus these early historians were highly optimistic about the future of the city as they constantly reechoed a sense of the manifest destiny of the young city. In their conviction that Chicago was to become great, they offered little of the negative or suggested that the urban patterns being established were defective. Problems were dismissed either as not existing or as being the fault of those who did not understand the great—and almost pre-ordained—mission. Thus their presentation of the facts was limited to some degree by their apparent roles as spokesmen for the prevailing business structure. This is not meant to suggest that the works have no value. Certainly any community which takes as much effort to record its past for posterity has answered some of the needs of that posterity.

Of the three works cited, Guyer's book is rather typical of the type of comprehensive histories which were so popular during the period. It used a format which compilers of large biographical collections frequently employed. The *History of Chicago . . .* attempted to relate the story of the city through specific firms; thus it did not allow for any contingencies or events outside of its proscribed limitations. As was frequently the case in these so-called comprehensive works and gigantic literary undertakings, Guyer— the stated author—was not the writer. He financed part of the project and through subscriptions from firms which wanted to be "written up" he managed to collect enough money to make the venture worthwhile. He then hired George S. Phillips, an unemployed journalist, to do the actual work. Phillips may well have remained an unknown, as is true of most ghost-writers, had it not been for Francis Fisher Cook who—in his memoirs *Bygone Days in Chicago: Recollections of the "Garden City" of the Sixties* (Chicago, 1910)—had bemoaned his tragic death as an alcoholic (p. 103). Guyer, then, was the supervisor rather than the author. Phillips was apparently a master of that hyperbolic prose which seems so characteristic of certain types of works produced during this period. The cynic might well question whether the extent of the laudatory prose was in any way connected to the size of the donation. The description of the bookstore of S. C. Griggs is an example of the use of over-statement:

One of the most encouraging and significant signs of progress of learning on this continent—in this great centralization focus of the Valley of the Mississippi, where are culminating the arts, commerce, and political power of this nation—where the eye of the scholar, or the man of science, whose sympathies are with the progress of light and learning, turns with the most interest and encouragement, is the Publishing House of S.C. Griggs & Co. . . .

The building is described as "a massive edifice, with an ornate iron front elevation" which would be typical of many pre-fire business structures; however, the fact that deliveries are made to the rear (not necessarily an outstanding characteristic) is noted:

There is little pomp or parade to attract the eye of one who passes by, for all the goods of this vast concern are received and shipped from the rear entrance; but compared with any other place in this Western World, it is to the scholar what the Parthenon was to the Athenian which stood on the summit of the Acropolis, and was dedicated to the Goddess of Wisdom . . . .

Once inside the store, the writer observes:

One cannot pass through this store without being impressed with the thought that the genius of all ages presides here, from Moses to Hallam, each one having made contributions. Greece with all its classics; Rome and the historians of her eternal annals; modern Europe from the revival of learning to the startling revelations of Layard—the lights of a thousand guiding, shaping intellects of the world . . .

And he concludes with the importance of S. C. Griggs and Company for Chicago life:

It is this aspect then, as the medium through which we derive this ceaseless and exhaustless stream of light, we see in the firm we are speaking of, who are the gleaners of this intellectual wealth, something more than merchants and salesmen. They are doing for us, in this first florid period of the cultivation of letters, what the Medici did for the Florentine Republic, after the fall of Constantinople. It is time for our eagle, that has spread his pinions over such vast territories of the earth's surface, to begin to wing his flight into the Empyrium, where he will achieve conquests in the empire of learning, more lasting than the sceptre of the Caesars. Crowns, thrones, presidencies vanish, and are lost in the midst of the ages as they sweep on, but science is eternal (pp. 240-41).

With this type of prose in circulation it is no wonder that Chicagoans began to believe in their uniqueness.

III

Ultimately the history of a city can be viewed as a composite narrative of the men and women who forged into the unknown to create a settlement. As Ruth Russell noted on the dedicatory page of her 1931 novel *Lakefront:* "Since this is the story of a city, truth to the lives of individuals has been subordinated to truth to the life of the city." The lives of the men and women who founded the city were intricately interwoven with the story of the city. The history of Chicago from the Fort Dearborn Massacre of 1812 to the incorporation of the village in 1833 at the Sauganash Hotel is a chronicle of those families who in the midst of the wilderness had the faith to believe that they could create a civilization in the wilderness. These were years of privation and settlement.

Unfortunately much of the region's writing seems to ignore these years. It was the day of men whose names were to become associated with the establishment of the city: Mark Beaubien, John Kinzie, who left the legacy of his name and drive to his son, John H. Kinzie. (Many of these names live today as the names of minor streets.) It was the day of Gurdon Hubbard who worked for the American Fur Company in Illinois, one of America's most clearly-defined monopolies' and whose personal narrative is the best portrait of the period and which established the fact that in the Illinois territory Commerce could—and would—exist without the Cross. The years between 1812 and 1833 are replete with tales of frontier adventure in a territory which led a precarious existence. It is the story of a struggle for survival and of the gradual subjugation of the Indians by men who were not necessarily smarter but who perhaps were more determined.

In an attempt to maintain its territorial rights in the West by neutralizing the British control over trading and the Indians, the government of the United States authorized the building of a new Fort Dearborn in 1815. The old settlers then returned. In 1818 Illinois was admitted to the Union, and in 1825 the opening of the Erie Canal made travel to this part of the country convenient but not necessarily comfortable. More settlers arrived. Some of them were destined to become the giants of commerce and the captains of finance. They early learned to speculate not only in land and lumber but also in life itself as they created some of the great fortunes of nineteenth-century America. In the language of the space age—"all systems were go" for the settlement and establishment of the city, the city of Chicago.

The personal narratives and autobiographies produced in Chicago have been—at times—difficult to separate from the histories written about the region. These autobiographical works shared at least one characteristic in common with those written by the seventeenth-century New England Puritans. They were products of a people who believed that they were participating in a noble experiment. They were convinced that their lives might serve as examples or at least explanations. As might be expected, the genre's value as history is directly related to how much the subjects chose to remember about the past or how they viewed their places in the evolution of the city. What often strikes the reader is the absence of certain kinds of materials and the remembered perception about events which occurred in the city. They frequently seemed to forget some of the more significant details which would have given greater meaning to their recital of their experiences. Yet what they chose to tell is revealing and is often done either apologetically or defensively.

Perhaps nowhere is this dilemma more clearly shown than in Robert Herrick's use of the autobiographical form in his 1905 novel *The Memoirs of an American Citizen*. Edward Van Harrington, the hero, muses as he looks over Chicago:

> I, too, was part of this. The thought of my brain, the labor of my body, the will within me, had gone to the making of this world. There were my plants, my car line, my railroads, my elevators, my lands— all good tools in the infinite work [of the] world. Conceived for good or for ill, brought into being by fraud or daring—what man could judge *their* worth? There they were, a part of God's great world. They were done; and mine was the hand. Let another, more perfect, turn them to a larger use; nevertheless, on my labor, on me, he must build (p. 266).

And this is essentially the philosophy underlying the bulk of the personal narratives and autobiographical works produced in the city during the nineteenth century.

This era may not have caught the fancies of modern poets and novelists, but it has produced a representative number of works by those who participated in the Chicago experiment and who felt the necessity to record their experiences. Often their narratives match later works in excitement and suspense. It is unfortunate that in the search for "literature" the wealth of information and the untapped resources of personal narratives and other autobiographical works are frequently overlooked. Yet much of what later generations learned about Puritan New England and other colonial settlements came from personal narratives, diaries, and journals. Consequently, this genre cannot be underestimated when one attempts to reconstruct the early period of Chicago. These autobiographical records chronicle a significant part of the story of the American frontier. Like the

Puritans, these settlers believed that autobiographical writing was a method by which they could preserve for future generations the story of those periods of great change in which they had participated. There is a vast collection of material which provides an accurate portrait of the lives of those pioneer men and women who willingly gave up whatever security they had earned "back home" in order to pursue their version of the American Dream in early Chicago.

One of the best sources for a reconstruction of the Chicago territory from the time of the second Fort Dearborn to the city of the 1830's is *The Autobiography of Gurdon Saltonstall Hubbard*. The subsequent importance of Hubbard as one of the founders of the city lends additional importance to his work which ends rather abruptly at 1830. It was apparently widely read in manuscript during Hubbard's lifetime; and two years after his death his nephew, Henry E. Hamilton, had the work published as *Incidents and Events in the Life of Gurdon Saltonstall Hubbard*. When it appeared, the work gained even wider circulation not only because the subject had been instrumental in developing so many facets of the city's life but also because it became apparent that the work was a storehouse of information concerning the seldomly treated period of transition. It told of the adventure with the Indians, of the pioneer's confrontation with nature, and of the development of the American Fur Company in Illinois. In 1911 it was selected by the Lakeside Press as one of the books in its famous series known as the "Lakeside Classics" and was subsequently re-issued from time to time by various other publishers.

Hubbard records his decision to leave the security of his Vermont home and to become apprenticed to the American Fur Company at the age of sixteen. He soon displayed an acumen for business and was elevated to positions of authority with the company in Illinois. It was not long before he envisioned the possibility of that little settlement huddled about Fort Dearborn, and he records his first visit to Chicago:

We started at dawn. The morning was calm and bright, and we, in our holiday attire, with flags flying, completed the last twelve miles of our lake voyage. Arriving at Douglas Grove, where the prairie could be seen through the oak woods, I landed, and climbing a tree, gazed in admiration on the first prairie I had ever seen. The waving grass, intermingling with a rich profusion of wild flowers, was the most beautiful sight I had ever gazed upon. . . .

Looking north, I saw the whitewashed buildings of Fort Dearborn sparkling in the sunshine . . . I was spell-bound and amazed at the beautiful scene before me. I took the trail leading to the fort, and, on my arrival, found our party camped on the north side of the river, near what is now State street. A soldier ferried me across the river in a canoe, and thus I made my first entry into Chicago, October 1, 1818 (pp. 32-33).

History has drawn a portrait of Hubbard as a midwestern hero of superhuman strength and has recorded his rise as an early businessman who recognized the needs of the community. His autobiography is reminiscent, however, of the early life of Cooper's Natty Bumppo, and the excitement of his narrative seems similar to the Cooper tradition. Hubbard, like Natty, knew the frontier well; and he was not afraid of the challenges of the wilderness. He understood the role of the fur trader and realized the era would not last forever. Considering the later significance of the businessman in Chicago's culture and literature, the fur trader of the Midwest represented the first of a long line of those entrepreneurs who by sheer force of will balanced by tangible accomplishments became the Chicago hero.

Of the works which were not only written but also published during the early period of Chicago's life perhaps none became as famous as Juliette Kinzie's *Wau-Bun* of 1856 which covered a slightly later period than Hubbard's *Autobiography* and which is concerned with a more distant view of the days of the fur traders and Indian agents. Whereas Hubbard literally "became" an Indian even to the point of assuming an Indian wife, John H. Kinzie remained the "great white father" although his wife insisted that his love and respect for the Indians were intense. *Wau-Bun, or the Early Day in the Northwest* is the story of pioneering to be sure, but it is also pioneering with the trappings and attitude of cultured life "back East," the former home of Mrs. Kinzie who came as a bride to the wilds of the West. Whether or not Mrs. Kinzie did what she says or whether life was made more comfortable as she brought to the wilderness, first of Prairie du Chien then Chicago, her determination to live genteelly might raise questions in the minds of modern readers. Certainly she gives a different view of "civilization in the Midwest. As has already been mentioned, she incorporated into her memoir the story of Fort Dearborn and its massacre as she had heard it from her sister-in-law, Mrs. Helm, and from her mother-in-law, Mrs. Kinzie. Thus in Chapters XVIII and XIX she interrupts her own action to include the "hear-say" story of the Massacre which had already been published as a pamphlet in 1844. Her reason for doing so may well have been her attempt to vindicate the Kinzie name at a time when questions were being raised concerning her father-in-law's role. At the same time she does chronicle the growth of Chicago from just a mere military garrison to an outstanding city. By the time that she died in 1870, Chicago had fulfilled the dreams of the city's greatness which she had had in those first days of 1834 during her residency in the small village on Lake Michigan at the mouth of the Chicago River. She lived long enough to see the north side of the city develop into one of the outstanding communities and to see the property of the Kinzie family become worth millions and millions of dollars. That the Fire was to destroy much of it the year after her death was a catastrophe which she was spared.

Later critics, such as Duncan in his *The Rise of Chicago as a Literary Center*, were to refer to *Wau-Bun* as an early Chicago novel. Andreas, who must have imagined how later historians might view the work, refutes the possibilities of the charge that *Wau-Bun* is a novel. Speaking of Mrs. Kinzie and her work, he said:

Herself one of the early pioneers of the West, a woman who had the historical distinction of living in the first house built in Chicago, of remaining here until she saw the fort and its few straggling houses grow to a thrifty little town, and, later, of witnessing its rapid and truly marvelous strides as a city, she was eminently well qualified in her later years to put into narrative form her personal reminiscences of early life in this region. But what enhances more than anything else the value of the book, is its importance as a faithful history of persons and things as they were in Chicago a half century ago. True, to the citizen of today, it reads like romance, and to those who have never experienced 'life on the frontier,' it seems hard to realize that the story of Wau-bun is not a tale of fiction, rather than an authentic account of life, and in those times. But the well-known character of the author, and her connection with the oldest family in Chicago, aside from her own early residence here, leaves no more room for doubting the truthfulness of the narrative than for disputing the authenticity of the book itself. Indeed, neither has ever been questioned; but after reading its interesting pages, one lays the book down with the thought almost involuntarily expressed, 'it is true; and verily truth is stranger than fiction.'

One of the most interesting aftermaths of Mrs. Kinzie's book was played out against the background of assumed propriety and personality conflicts. Although he had implicitly raised questions concerning her conclusions in his *Chicago Massacre of 1812* (Chicago, 1893) by presenting sources which had been previously ignored, Joseph Kirkland did not suggest that Mrs. Kinzie had deliberately falsified her record. Milo Quaife, on the other hand, denounced her in an essay which was published as part of the *Proceedings of the Mississippi Valley Historical Association* (1910-11). The paper which he had presented formed the basis for a portion of his outstanding study *Chicago and the Old Northwest. 1673—1835* (Chicago, 1913). What Quaife had to say might have gone unnoticed by the general public if the Chicago *Tribune* (August 16, 1912) had not headlined the refusal of the Chicago Historical Society to publish his book. "Massacre Story Stirs His-

torians," "Chicago Society Decides Not to Publish Fort Dearborn
History of Professor Quaife," and "[He] Assails Mrs. Kinzie's
Book" were the opening captions of the *Tribune* story which
pointed out that the city's Establishment feared the impact of
the corrected version of Fort Dearborn on the Kinzie descendants.
The work, however, was published by the University of Chicago.
In view of these events, Quaife's introduction to the Lakeside
Press edition of *Wau-Bun* might have created a furor; but he
demonstrated that he had mastered the technique of understate-
ment and wry humor. Although he had been accused of being
tactless by some of his contemporaries, he exhibited a rare diplo-
macy when he wrote:

For Chicago readers, her book has a particular significance not shared
by those alien to the Windy City. So thoroughly has her narrative
permeated the local mind, that not all the efforts of all the historians,
probably, will ever succeed in replacing it with a more correct and
judicial concept. Through her literary exploit, John Kinzie has become
the Captain John Smith of Chicago history.

He continued by citing some of the problems inherent in her version and then proceeded to evaluate her story.

In appraising *Wau-Bun* the reader should regard her as a literary
artist, whose primary ambition was to produce an entertaining narrative. . . . The scenes as depicted by her have commonly a certain
factual basis, but into the recital of them much imaginative fiction is
woven. Accuracy of statement is clearly not her forte, while to the
objective detachment of the historian she is a complete stranger. Yet
she succeeds well in creating a life-like picture of the current scene
of her daily activities and experiences. Her ardent love of nature, and
her sympathetic appreciation of her husband's native wards in a day
when the terrible motto that the only good Indian was a dead one
still held almost universal sway over the minds of her contemporaries,
are both deserving of warmest praise.

Certainly a reader who is in search of history would doubt the work of a writer who is oblivious to "accuracy of statement" as well as being a "complete stranger" to "objective detachment." But the survival of *Wau-Bun* might serve as further testimony that the pen can be mightier than the sword.

One will never be able to ascertain with clarity the extent of the destruction of early diaries and journals occasioned by the destruction of the Chicago Historical Society in the fires of 1871 and 1874. After the first devastating fire, however, Robert Fergus did undertake to print those documents which he could find, among which were several "reminiscences" of old settlers. Foremost of this group is *Early Chicago Reminiscences* by Charles Cleaver, which covers the days of the 1830's, 1840's, and 1850's in Chicago. Especially good is his story of the development of the railroad in the city.

Although Hubbard's book was printed long after it was written, it has a sense of immediacy which is so unlike those autobiographies which in their backward glances frequently become another way of looking at the "good old days" with rose-tinted glasses. This is in contrast to most of the memoirs which appear after the subjects had become older and more subject to forgetfulness. Although they cover the beginning years of the city, both Isaac Arnold's *William B. Ogden and Early Days in Chicago* (1882) and Edwin Gale's *Reminiscences of Early Chicago and Vicinity* (1902) were written years after the action covered by the books. There is a distorted view of history occasioned by the nostalgia of old-timers. Yet, all of these works make it extremely clear that the businessman was early the region's cultural hero and celebrate the ingenuity of the Chicago businessman as they pay homage to the business structure of the city.

Among the publishers who did much to resurrect the "old" Chicago was the Lakeside Press which, in instituting its series of Christmas books, reprinted memoirs of early visitors and early settlers. For a view of the early years, two collections are invaluable, both of which were edited by Mabel McIlvaine. *Reminis-*

cences of Chicago during the Forties and Fifties contains selections
from William Bross' lecture, "What I Remember of Early Chicago," first delivered in 1876; from Cleaver's reminiscences, and
from Joseph Jefferson's *Autobiography*, as well as a selection
from Andreas' *History* on the early railroads. The following year
the Lakeside Press issued, as a means of showing its continuing
interest in Chicago history, *Reminiscences of Chicago during the
Civil War* also a collection of a number of previously printed
selections. Included in the volume are such diverse pieces as:
Francis Cook's memories of the city during the days of conflict
which first appeared in his *Bygone Days in Chicago,* a report
from a military outfit and from the 1860 Republican convention, discussion of how troops were raised in Illinois and the
same period covered from a woman's point of view in Mary A.
Livermore's *The Story of My Life* which covers a section on "War
Excitement in Chicago." Of great interest is probably William
Bross' 1878 lecture on the "History of Camp Douglas." While
each one of the selections could be read elsewhere, the Lakeside
Classics did serve the function of making an exposure to the early
records readily accessible to more people. And in that they served
a necessary function.

As one attempts to reconstruct the early years of Chicago the
many collective biographies which appeared during the latter part
of the century and into the twentieth place emphasis upon the
history of the city as it can be told through the lives and actions of
the early settlers. Such collections as *Biographical Sketches of
Leading Men of Chicago* (1868), which defined the city essentially
in terms of the businessmen along with some of the more prominent
lawyers and clergymen added, and Josiah Seymour Currey's five-
volumed work *Chicago: Its History and Its Builders, a Century of
Marvelous Growth* are examples of this type of biographical study.
Most of these are so laudatory that they cease to be of value for
someone looking for a more balanced approach, but they do have
the advantage of providing a survey of the men and women who
made the city and whose names might have been subsequently lost

to history. Such collections make it clear that in the days before the great fire a magnificent city arose because there were dedicated men and women who believed not only in the locale but also in themselves. Ultimately, it is through such biographical studies that one can view a version of history.

Perhaps nowhere is this made clearer than in Andreas' *History of Chicago* and Hurlbut's *Chicago Antiquities*. At each step in the development of the city there are a number of autobiographical studies which interpret in terms of the personal the significance of a particular stage of the city's growth. Conceivably one could read the story of the city through these works. Yet few of them actually do recount—as did Hubbard—a little-known era of the region's growth. Certainly the use of biographical works culminated with Andreas' three-volumed work. Admittedly deficient in some areas, admittedly unfinished in others, the Andreas history was a gigantic undertaking of the post-Civil War period. His reliability is fairly trustworthy (although he is sometimes given to great moralistic judgments frequently common in nineteenth century history), but even more important is the fact that he came at a period of transition. Many of the people who had "made" history were still alive, and so his work combines the personal narrative within the larger framework of his volumes. And on Andreas subsequent historians have had to build.

IV

Within a two-year period two books of poetry were published in Chicago. The first, by Horatio Cooke, was published in 1843 by the firm of Ellis and Fergus. In his "Preface" dated May 5, 1843, Cooke declared that poetry came to him late in life and that he did it "merely for amusement" because he was "in a strange part of the country, entirely amongst strangers, and almost un-educated" (p. iii). Claiming that he had been writing poetry only "four or five years," he felt it important to publish his work because "it may serve as a gentle hint that man is never too old to learn; that man is never too old to attempt self-improvement; that man is

at all times a learner, and should ever consider himself as such"
(p. iv). With such disclaimers one is hardly prepared for the first
long poem in his *Gleanings of Thought* which is entitled "A Voice
from the Dead." Consisting of 142 iambic pentameter quatrains
the poem employs some elements of the graveyard school, some
metaphysical elements, and over the entire work there is the aura
of romanticism. Moving from a pessimistic attitude to a final vic-
torious acceptance of death, there is nothing about the poem which
would lead one to believe that it was produced in a Chicago as
vibrant and as bustling as the city of the 1840's. Following this
long poem are a series of others, some long and some short, which
give evidence of Cooke's wide reading and which are essentially
imitative. The only poem which might remotely be called urban is
the one entitled "An Extract from one of my Old Poems" which,
as he explains in the headnote, consists of "scenes in London"
which are in reality "reflections on that metropolis, and my feelings on human life at that period" which were made when he was
between twenty and twenty-five. The poem consists of twenty-six
stanzas. It begins with descriptions of some of the more familiar
scenes: the Tower, Westminster Abbey, St. Paul's, the theater
district, St. James, and on to Kensington Palace. Here, as he con-
templates nature, he realizes that it is a fitting contrast to the
crowded city:

> Oh! here, within the precincts of the foul
> Contaminated crowd, and city noise,
> Contemplation can refresh her soul,
> And feel allied to tranquil rustic joys,
> Forgetting in her bliss all worldly toys,
> Flown away as 'twere from gross distraction,
> Reveling upon the scene that never cloys
> The taste that finds in nature satisfaction,
> Here every step with such is more than blissful action.

The poems in this collection range from Homeric imitations to
lines written after a contemplation of Alexander Pope to a series of

sonnets and shorter poems. Singularly absent, except for the reference in the "Preface," is an indication that these poems were
composed in the midland metropolis of Chicago. Either consciously or unconsciously, Cooke seemed determined that his place
of residence was not going to control his subject matter.

One of the few poems in his work which seems to relate to his
immediate surroundings and to suggest his awareness of the situation of man in the world is his "A Few Stanzas on a Subject Much
Talked Of." In the midst of the many nature and philosophical
poems, it is strange to read:

> The world shall smile when tyrant force shall fall,
> And shall it not? who, will dare gainsay
> The wish of freemen? Slaves! whate'er your thrall,
> Strike at its root, the glorious call obey;
> Bend with the might of unity, A day
> All lucidness, shall quickly, surely beam;
> And Joy shall sing a glorying roundelay.
> Startling the phantom Tyranny, to seem—
> Nay, be—a shadeless ghost, in Freedom's vivid gleam.

> O nurse of Hope, and only guide to bliss,
> Liberty! of light the brightest ever past
> Through the fertile mind's expansive abyss,
> By all good men for ever justly class'd
> The only wealth fitly to be amass'd,
> In pond'rous bulk to feed the hungry herd
> Who, screw'd and shackled 'neath oppression vast,
> Can scarcely whisper out the giant word,
> Which clanking chains would burst were it but loudly heard.

> Heaven defend the right! But where is right—
> Amidst this world of sore oppressive wrong?
> Seek for the mind a clear transparent light,
> And generate it widely forth among,
> For e'er; no matter, let it blaze, and strong,
> So that its influence may well be felt,
> Raising itself alike a sainted song,

Which, in the souls of millions rapt shall melt,
Becoming ambient as atmospheric belt.

Nations, arise, and burst your clanking chains,
Awaking from your sombrous sleep, arise;
Extend the soul's imperial domains,
Clearing the mist which flits before its eyes,
Impeding the fair prospect which wide lies
Beyond the darkening influence and glows,
Ready to strike the senses with surprize [sic],
Whene'er the cleared atmosphere reflows
To genialize whate'er in its embrace grows.

Welcome the soul of Freedom to each dwelling;
Seat it on high, alike a household god,
Submit to nought that seeming threats a quelling
Unto the goodly sign that man hath trod
At last on reason's verge—steadily plod,
Clear sighted, rapid, surely becoming,
Bend to the right, but snatch the adverse rod
Quickly away from Tyranny presuming,
To sing a funeral dirge o'er Liberty's entombing.

Arise, ye nations, from your deep dark sleep;
Avail yourselves of strength from its repose;
Awake, arise! the glorious harvest reap;
Spread o'er the champaigne [sic] mentally uprose,
In just perspective, to attract the throes
Of just perception to a steady gaze,
That she may gleam a lesson ere she close
Her aching eyes before the glorious rays,
Which, flung by childling Truth, his manhood there portrays.

When shall he rise? when shall great Truth unfold
His giant wings, spread out in manly prime?
Not till mankind, inspired in virtue bold,
Shall dare Perfection's tranquil height to climb,
And there look back upon the waste of time
So full of blots, spread out beneath the feet,
Like a broad mass of reddish color'd slime,

Ting'd by the clotted blood, which, in retreat,
Earth's pilgrims, lash'd by care, hath shed to mark their beat.

Yes, e'en perfection may be sought by mortals,
And reach'd by application of deep thought,
For lo! the glorious angel opes her portals,
As if all anxious by them to be sought,
The circling light above by her is taught
To flow untrammel'd by untimely blight,
With beauteous imagery transparent, fraught
In semblant modesty it streameth bright,
And shapes itself in words—LIBERTY IS LIGHT!

In still another poem "The Imprisoned Rose," Cooke once again writes of freedom. His central image describes a rose which has been placed in a room and indicates that this is an unnatural state for such a beautiful manifestation of nature.

A beauteous rose within a room did blow,
And feebly there around did fragrance throw,
It droop'd it's [sic] head, and seem'd to tell of woe,
    And loss of Liberty;
It spake a language which most prison'd know—
    "Would I were free!"

While it is apparent that the rose can never again be attached to its bush, the poet asserts that "a lady," who was very kind, opened a window; and so the rose felt the breezes.

It cheer'd itself, and lifted up its head,
Its color came, and full its flower spread,
A beaming smile, it seem'd from heaven sped,
    To bless that kind hand,
Which, lifting up the sash, it nourished,
    Its fate to withstand.

In a poem strangely prophetic of Whitman's famous "A child

asks: 'What is grass?' " Cooke penned a sonnet entitled "A Blade
of Grass."

> What worlds are hid within thee, blade of grass?
>   An infinity's within thy tranquil green,
> And busy nations to and from thee pass,
>   Although by heedless men but seldom seen;
> E'en buzzing myriads on thee convene,
>   And live in unity and love and die.
> A season passes; why know thou hast been?
>   But yet another doth thy place supply,
> And smiles a grace beneath the canopy
>   Of the arch'd heaven, and from it doth claim
> A patronage its power will ne'er deny,
>   If ask'd with humbleness and honest aim.
> The power supernatural judges aye the same
> Upon the lowest thing and of the highest name.

In the midst of the seriousness and the didacticism of much of
his verse, Horatio Cooke did have some time for elements of
humor. In "A Nondescript Ode" he demonstrates his ability to use
a well-established form for purposes of jesting.

> Hail, well made pen, and flowing ink!
> Hail, power gain'd to deeply think!
> Hail, to a sheer white sheet of paper!
> Hail, to the sun light, or the taper!
> Hail, to the subject that is novel,
> Whether a palace or a hovel!
> Or Monarch, reigning freely o'er
> A barren or a fertile shore;
> Or a people forever loud
> In boast that they're a free born crowd!
> It matters little what it is,
> So it will stand the critic's quiz,
> So it be with ardor written,
> As if the poet might be bitten

By a mad dog just passing by,
That wouldn't stop to tell him why.
Therefore, the poet, short of whying,
Stupid reason ne'er thought of trying;
Just as if a rhyming noodle
Had intellectual food to codle,
And so for want of fuel spoiling,
That which, if it had more boiling,
Might a gracious savor render,
Or feel unto the feeling tender.
So sent abroad, a pretty gem,
Quite satisfactory to them
Who think that excellence in rhyming
Consists in length of line and chiming.
And so, in these days, 'tis the fashion,
Instead of imagery and passion,
To send abroad the poet's lay
Without a solitary ray
Of aught but that which such folks tingle;
A pun or two, with a neat jingle.

The reception of Cooke's poetry seems to be lost to history. Andreas does not mention his work; neither did Robert Fergus, in resurrecting much of the early work of the firm of Ellis and Fergus, deem it necessary to republish *Gleanings of Thought; in a Series of Poems.* Cooke himself, while he asserts that poetry became a way by which he had entertained himself in a new city, does not in any way suggest that his poetry is to be measured against the great poetry of the world. In fact, the title page carries a poetic admonition by him.

I hate the rule that, measuring a word,
Shackles the mind, and renders thought absurd:
Therefore, your prejudices please discard,
If for a foot, my muse should take a yard;
Nay, if necessity my thought should pinch,
Excuse me, pray, if I should fall an inch.

Cooke, who is listed in the 1844 Directory as a turner, used poetry to occupy himself because he had been "used to active employment; but in this city, at that time, I had not much work at my trade, consequently my mind was thrown into a sort of corrosive fermentation." He continues:

Thought would have its sway, either for weal or woe; and as I had nothing definite to cast it on, at times ran wild, and then sinking to a state of sullen gloom, seemed to gnaw itself for want of other food. Fortunately, I was attracted to poetry. I commenced writing, and every day my mind found solace in the consciousness of growing power, and in the anticipation of future pleasure and usefulness (p. iv).

From this evidence one is led to believe that Cooke must have arrived in Chicago around 1837 or 1838; and from the eternal evidence, it seems safe to assume that he was at this time approaching middle-age. There is, however, no evidence that he became attached to the growing "literary" circles which were budding in the 1840's. This undoubtedly was due in part to the fact that these societies, except for those involved in the issuance of the newspapers, were primarily designed for the elite, and an artisan would not have been welcomed—if indeed he was even aware of them. Needless to say, Cooke's verse does show signs of his "unlettered" state; but as the first book of poetry published in Chicago—six years after the incorporation of the city—one might view it as an interesting historical curiosity.

Although much of Chicago's early writing was essentially utilitarian, there were poets and writers of fiction who contributed to another phase of Chicago's literary history. Thus, one might explain the work of Horatio Cooke, done first for his own enjoyment. While books of poetry may seem a "bit odd" in early mercantile Chicago, one can find from the very inception of Chicago's newspaper history the offerings of some of the city's versifiers tucked between the columns of stock and grain quotations. Poetry served in the early periodicals as "fillers." There was small chance that a great poet would appear, but the very use of verse does illustrate an awareness of poetry.

One of the early poets who achieved a degree of fame was William Asbury Kenyon (1817-1862), who referred to himself as "a humble artisan." In 1845 his *Miscellaneous Poems, to which are added writings in prose on various subjects* was printed in Chicago by James Campbell and Company. The volume was sold by— according to the note on the title page—Brautigan and Keen, S. F. Gale and Company, W. W. Barlow and Co., and Comstock and Ackley. In his "Preface" Kenyon echoed his faith in the city and noted that there would soon be a flood of literary offerings springing from Chicago; however, he believed his work—though early —had merit. If he knew about the work of Cooke published two years earlier, he did not mention it. "As a whole," he said, "the collection has been designed for this community. The specimens here presented have spontaneiously [sic] sprung and blossomed upon the prairie, and, it is hoped, if they possess either beauty or fragrance, [they] will not, like the flowers which spring to greet us, become extinct by the hoofs of rudeness." While the Preface is dated "Chicago, 1845," his poems are not urban in the sense that they deal specifically with the growth of the new city. In fact many of them are totally unrelated to the Midwest as a region. After his long and detailed "Preface," "Uses of Poetry Exemplified" is the lead poem in the collection. In this rather long patriotic poem, Kenyon emphasizes the beauty of nature which had become so apparent to him as he traveled westward. And he utters the hope that the nation will not be involved with those things which will take away from Art. "An Address to My Native Village" is another combination of love of nature and love of country. In the opening lines he asserts: "I love thee Hingham" and states four reasons: " . . . for thy hills and plains," "neighboring ocean wide," "notes of industry," and "for thy many rural seats". Emphasizing the age of Hingham, which was settled in the seventeenth century by men who were interested in freedom, he noted that many of those con-

nected with the War for Independence were from this community.
To compare Kenyon's ode to his native city with that by Cooke
entitled "To My Native City" is to note one of the essential differences between the two poets. Cooke begins in a similar fashion
with "Sweet Worcester! city where my life began" and continues
to recall the pleasantries of his past. But instead of looking forward
to a possibly great future, he continues to look backward and
laments that he cannot recapture the past. He misses his family
and friends and declares that they have joined "To rein my wand'r-
ing thought from seeking distant lands." But no matter how he
might dream and long for the past "stern reality . . . doth stamp
as nought/those scenes of bliss . . ." and he concludes that "the
backward gaze" results in the "present pain" and he realizes "That
youth's bright sun hath sunk no more again to rise."

While Cooke does not present any patriotic poems addressed to
his adopted land, Kenyon is very fond of this theme. Of his patriotic
poems, "The Eagle" is probably the most effective. A prophetic
poem which equates the eagle's possible power with the emerging
power of the nation, Kenyon decries the ruthlessness of the eagle
and concludes his poem:

> O, Liberty! thy emblem this? Union of pride,
> Of noble pride, and tyranny! Oh, mayest thou ne'er
> —thy heaven born power, with unenlightened sway
> But soar, unsullied, in the majesty divine,
> Blessing all nations with just clemency and peace.

There are the usual romantic and didactic poems such as "The
Mocking Bird," "To the Baltimore Oriole," "May Song," "Encouragement," or "Be Cheerful." By far, however, the most significant poems in the collection are those which are directly related
to the Midwest. In his "Prairie Song," for example, he says:

> Oh, some may choose the forest glade,
> And some may love the sea,

> Others may seek the city's din:
> But none of these for me.
> No hermit's cave, no crowded hive,
> No storm-tossed prison lone;
> But life at ease, in joys own breeze,
> A prairie cot my own.

In another poetic effort entitled "Sleigh Ride" he demonstrates not only his love of nature but also indicates his capacity for a more sustained poetic technique, including internal rhyme.

> Come! The moonbeams are glancing; with ready steeds prancing,
> The land-shallop waits, at the door,
> Hearts akin to the lark, let us gaily embark;
> Heed Winter's keen pinching no more:

The next stanza indicates a change of pace with shorter lines, with only one line of internal rhyme, and an end rhyme which differs from the preceding stanza:

> In Winter 'tis time to be gay;
> Love glows with its quickening ray;
> For the fresher the air, the more bright is the glare
> All ready;—now swiftly away.

"Sleigh Ride," in spite of its obvious shortcomings, does recreate in poetic form the joys of a winter's sport (which could of course take place anywhere) and the beauty of the snow-covered prairie (which is highly localized). The grandeur of nature impressed Kenyon as he contemplated the smallness of man in the midst of such awe-inspiring scenes.

To spend a winter on the prairie is an unforgettable experience. And as many writers were to do later, Kenyon captured the spirit of the prairie in "A Winter Morning on the Prairie."

> The storm has ceased! All nature hushed and still,
> Enshrouded in one sheet of chrystal [sic] lies.

Now forth walks, joyous, with industrious eyes,
The early poet, musing fancy's fill.
Yes! this is nature's magic! this the skill
Her hand evinces, through the varied year!
What sweet enchantment reigns in every scene!
In spring, from earth uprising, all is green;
In summer fields of white and gold appear;
In autumn party-colored woods are sere;
In each stream's murmur, zephyrs, softly bland,
Wave o'er the lawn, and sway the forest's tops,
Birds choir, flowers breathe, or withered verdue drops;
Now, stark, and motionless, each twig must stand,
Streams bound, birds mute, flowers dead; fast, by her potent
   wand.

As thus the bard, in audible delight,
Day's blazing monarch, ushered by the morn,
Glances, with majesty, wide o'er the lawn,
And all, erst swaddled in transparent white,
With dazzling lustre overcomes the sight.
The spriggy tree tops, fiercely sparkling, seem
Vast branching pearls, with glittering pendants hung,
On high, by glassy, huge Briarci swung.
The scattered cottages, with many a gleam,
Far flashing, broad effulgence stream;
Heaped cones of plenty all a blaze are seen,
Bright zig zag fences teem with shreds of glass;
The bristled stubble fields a glowing mass;
Each upright blade a staff, and the whole scene,
Groves, farm yards, streams, and plain, one glaring waste of
   sheen.

Kenyon's description of the midwestern locale followed many
of the romantic conventions of the 1830's and 1840's; however,
there is infused in his work a sense of the reality of the locale. In
"A Prairie Song," "Àn Address to the River La Fox," and "Song
of the Prairie Warbler" he captures the spirit of the Midwest.
His "Address to the Mississippi . . ." opens with "Hail monarch

river, flowing sublime in majesty . . ." and proceeds to herald the
Mississippi River as the French explorers had done centuries before him and as Mark Twain was to do so well afterward. The
"Epistle of a Prairie Poet to his Cousin in the East" displays
Kenyon's ability to describe minutiae at the same time that he
suggests the region has literary possibilities even though he clearly
notes it is an area remote from the East both in actual mileage as
well as in speech and customs. A different place demanded a different man.

Dear cousin; since I last disturbed your repose,
With such dull dissertations as die in my prose,
I had almost resolved on resigning my pen,
Ere you should receive its inflictions again;
But, intolerable urged by that prurient fire
Imputed to all by de Coverly's sire,
And assured this invention would soften the crime,
I have yielded once more, to address you in rhyme.
    Now, methinks at that word you will start, and exclaim
"What!—in rhyme?—sure he's mad! has he, too, caught the flame?
I thought he was wiser! but, I know it. I know it!
"The soil is prolific; a spontaneious [sic] poet!—
    Expressions like these, poets all are aware,
From the facts of the case, cannot be very spare;
And, perhaps, did you know, you would be filled with wonder
I was not overwhelmed with Olympian thunder,
While engaged in the act, for presuming to write,
With language, and every thing, in such plight,
All dialects, here, that were ever heard,
At courts, and elections, together are stirred,
Like potions, at druggists shops, only, the lees
Are chiefly made use of, in compounding these.
Through this odious mixture must Pegasus steer,
And, although other perils we scarcely hope to clear,
As quotations aid brevity, beauty and rhyme,
We may try a few samples by way of sublime.
If these, haplessly, "*snag*" you, imagine them in latin;

But in case it shall prove an anomalous thing,
Neither fit for the table, nor musical ring,
It will serve to exhibit the folly of man,
In attempting a work, with no specified plan.
That same folly was mine, and, for fear of the worst,
I will stick in some feathers collected at first.
    "*I allowed*" I would mention we think "*in these parts*"
Constitutions of nations are government charts,
To be used for conducting their vessels of state,
At the speediest, safest, and easiest rate:
That the crew, and the passengers, ever should know
What course they are shaping, how fast, how slow,
And that officers, wanting, should speedily be
Thrown, like Jonah the obstinate, into the sea.
It is very repugnant however to mix
The sweet charms of poesie, with politics;
And I, therefore, will, only refer to some names
Concerned in directing political games,
Without once attempting the task, to decide
Which part of the board is thus stoutly belied.
There is not much to choose, in a general way,
Do, like judges at races, I'll see there's fair play.
    Perhaps 'tis antique, among you of the east,
But here it is fashion (with great folks at least,
Who seldom have anything better to do)
To play "*poker*," for apples, and "*sixpenny loo*."
I was offered a hand once, and winked at, to save
The "*rascal*"; said they "every Jack is a knave"!
Which I afterwards thought could be no such a thing,
Since a Jack was, at times, just as good as a King.
The same holds in our country's political pack,
From which (one half red, the other half black)
I have drawn four face cards, each well known as a John,
(Or Jack, if you like it; I favor the ton,)
That show the conclusion is perfectly just;
Jacks may be the best cards, as well as the worst.
Observe them, with care, as I call them to view;
This formerly served under Tippecanoe,

Esteemed as an officer, loved as a friend,
Who, though he had faults, would, undoubtedly mend;
But, being quite early advanced, he was seen
To loose, on a sudden, his generous mien.
If he is now truly our national head,
I should say the corporal soon must be dead,
For never before did a rack-tortured nation
So patiently wait its own decapitation.
The second appears as with sapience crowned,
All glistening and beaming effulgence around:
About him the youthful wise eagerly crowd,
While judges, and rulers, before him are bowed;
Minds rev'rence his vastly superior mind,
And men deem him sprung of a mightier kind.
Alone, in his might as a barrier, he stood,
Repelling the waves of a strand eating flood,
And conquered thus guarding the cause of his sire,
To meet whose approval, he soon must retire.
As nightly tossed mariners, on the wide waste,
View a long lighting star to the dark waters haste;
As gloom overshadows their fear stricken hearts,
When day's brilliant orb, in his glory departs;

When he contemplated the nature of man, Kenyon was not always impressed that man reached his highest potential. In "About
Our Late Indian Hunt" he questioned the validity of and the
necessity for the Black Hawk War. In this early poem of social
protest Kenyon suggested that the cause of his people had not been
a just one because the Indians had already been cornered and
defeated.

Say! Did you hear of Black Hawk's war,
Where nature's own was struggled for?
Terror struck all the country through,
Raised by aggressors bugaboo!
A few poor Indians cornered up,
Saw, day by day, the Whites usurp

Their last game grounds, their childhood homes,
And even profane their father's tombs.
They saw, they wept with deep still grief;
Hope held no prospect of relief;
"Farther, yet farther we must go:
Swim to new wilds, like buffalo!"
They bore in silence, 'till their wives,
"Whippled like the dogs, we loathe our lives"
'Till from their mouths was snatched their bread;
'Till the last star of peace had sped.
Then roused they pride's expiring ray,
Their thickening deaths to hold at bay:
They roused for home, they stood for life;
Peace heaped them wrongs; wrongs called for strife.
Blow came for blow; the cry was raised,
"Behold the savage fury blazed,
The frontier wide in ruin lies!"
"Death to the race!"—the aggressor cries—
Death to the race! Yes, when no more
They turned the cheek, as heretofore,
'Tis "savage fury" prompts the stand,
On the last hold of childhood's land!
　Take back the term! The wildman's heart
Abhors the deeds of savage art!
Expiring, starved, they fled like dear [sic];
Still, still the gorgeless hounds pressed near.
　Wiskenan, and the Broad-Axe tell
Tales which your final dirge may knell!
A war! Alas! a ruthless chase,
For famished remnants of a murdered race.

In 1851 *Poetry of Observation and Other Poems* appeared and contained a "Preface" dated "August 1st at Hingham." The majority of the lyrics are general nature poems or elegies; however, in "Thoughts While Beholding the Mississippi River for the First Time" he sees the river as an example of a strong power from the "Great Source" and sees its didactic role "teaching all things for good." With some slight variation "The Sleigh Ride" appears again in this volume. Two years later *The Poetry of Observation, Part Second; and Other Poems* by Kenyon who styled himself "a Massachusetts mechanic" was issued at Hingham. In the dedication the poet makes clear that his latest collection of over twenty poems was intended "like its preceding counterpart [for] the laboring population of New England by one of their own number." These poems "by a humble artisan" once again emphasize the relationship of God and nature to man.

Certainly his production while he was in Chicago was not "urban" in the modern sense, but it does have more than a passing historical significance. As an indicator of the poetic tastes of the city which was less than ten years old, the volume published in Chicago had the prospects of a sufficient readership so that it was sold by the five bookstores which were in existence by 1841. Stephen F. Gale had also organized a circulating library in 1838. The *Daily Chicago American* noted in its August 5th (1841) edition "Mr Gale has provided his library with all the light literature of the day, and every new book worth reading is at once placed on his shelves." That Kenyon's work was "worth reading" in those days might be assumed on the basis of his use of familiar subjects and his use of a simple form. But the mechanical aspects of his work were not always simplistic. He had the ability to use complicated forms and images.

In the meantime, Kenyon was simply one among several poets who found in their sojourns on the prairie a source of literary inspiration. Had Kenyon remained in the Chicago area his poetry might have become more "urban"; however, he returned to his home in Hingham and continued to write poems in the romantic tradition until his death in 1862. By that time the nation, and certainly Chicago, had changed from the days when his *Miscellaneous Poems To which are Added Writings in Prose, On Various Subjects* was sold widely.

The poets were not the only "creative" artists in the city. Much of Chicago's early fiction appeared in the journals of the day, and some of it was even being issued as independent publications. One of the most prolific writers of fiction was a civil engineer in Chicago during the 1850's. William Bushnell delighted in Indian lore and legends. He used them freely in a series of stories and sketches. One of his most popular works was *Prairie Fire: A Tale of Early Illinois,* which first appeared as a serial and was subsequently published by Sloan of *Sloan's Garden City* in 1855 with Robert Fergus as the printer. For several years thereafter new editions of *Prairie Fire . . .* appeared. While his earlier "Ke-O-Sau-Que: Legend of the Upper Mississippi"—which appeared in Rounseville's *Western Magazine* of 1845—did not achieve the same popularity, Bushnell was very much in demand. In 1867 his *Ah-Meek, The Beaver; or the Copper-Hunters of Lake Superior* was published in New York by the American News Company. In that same year his *The Pearl of Panama; or, The Spaniard's Vengeance* was issued by the Boston house of Elliot, Thomas, and Talbot. He contributed stories to the *Gem of the Prairie,* the *Literary Budget,* and the *Sunday Leader* where he served as one of the editors. Andreas claimed that there had been "no equal" to Bushnell "since Cooper" (I, 503). Yet calling him the equal of Cooper does seem to tax one's critical judgment, although both writers suffered from some of the same problems in the creation of character. In spite of his popularity in the city with the various regional literary magazines, he returned to New York in the 1860's.

The career of T. Herbert Whipple was full and varied. As a child, he had been taken to Illinois where he lived with his family; and in 1854 he was in Chicago to work for two years as the editor of the *Literary Budget.* While serving in this capacity, he published in the *Budget* his adventure story entitled "Ethzelda, or Sunbeams and Shadows: A Tale of the Prairie Land as it Was." Soon thereafter, the work appeared as a separate work from the publisher, Rufus Blanchard. Had Danenhower, the owner of the *Budget,* not become so involved with his Native American Party, it is conceivable that Whipple would have done some truly distinguished regional stories; however, he left his post in 1856. The following year he was in Chicago working with several papers until 1861 when he became a war correspondent for the Chicago *Tribune*. His articles from the "front" had all of the excitment that his prairie tales contained; and because he had done such a spectacular job, he accepted the job of city editor with the *Herald* of New York. But the pull of Chicago was great, and once again he returned to the city. By this time he had become quite involved with several detective agencies and gradually ceased writing. His interest in western literature perhaps came too early.

The city's first two "novels" raise a series of questions concerning the form as well as the authors. To call *The Banditti of the Prairies, or the Murderer's Doom! A Tale of the Mississippi Valley* a "novel" truly taxes the definition of the genre. The author's introduction assures the reader of the authenticity of the "thrilling adventures of the western country." The work is a product of that extremely lawless period on the Illinois frontier in the 1840's and was supposedly designed to vindicate Edward Bonney's role as a bounty-hunter. Even today there still remains some controversy about the authorship of the narrative. When it appeared, the work was said to have been written by Edward Bonney; many bibliographies carry Bonney's name for it. According to Andreas, however, it was discovered that Henry A. Clark had written the book which had such "an immense sale [which] at once took its place among the popular romances of the day" (I, 503). Phillip D. Jordan, in his introduction to the University of Oklahoma Press edition of *The Banditti of the Prairies* (Norman, 1963), attempts to present the background of Bonney and unilaterally rejects the notion that Clark was the author, although he accepts the idea that it "is possible that Clark or some other person assisted Bonney in editing the manuscript" (p. xx). Clark, on the other hand, is the accepted author of *The War Scout of Eighteen Hundred Twelve*. There was much difference between the two men. Bonney was the unpolished frontiersman who spent most of his time tracking down criminals for a fee; Clark, on the other hand, was the polished, urbane city lawyer who had migrated to Chicago in

1848, two years before his work was published by W.W. Danenhower who also issued *The Banditti of the Prairies*. Both books
appeared in 1850 although Jordan notes that the "first printing"
of Bonney's book "was deposited for copyright by James R. Bull
as proprietor on September 10, 1849" (p. xviii). If this is so, then
this work would be the "first novel" rather than *The War Scout
of Eighteen Hundred Twelve* as is usually supposed.

Of the two works, *The Banditti of the Prairies* was apparently
more popular. It had a checkered publication record although the
frequency of its re-issue by different companies between 1850 and
1900 suggests its popularity with a reading public eager for the
cheap thrills provided by the sensationalism of the murder tale. It
did much toward creating that image of the lawlessness of the
Midwest, but in keeping with the moralistic overtones of so much
of nineteenth-century fiction, Bonney, in the chapter entitled
"Concluding Remarks," said:

. . . I commend the book to the attention of the reading community, not for any brilliancy in style or beauty in sentiment, but
simply as a record of true events occurring in our own day and in
our own midst. I have not sought to make myself the hero of a story,
and I claim no credit for my successful crusade against the band of
robbers and murderers, except that of having done my duty to community. In looking back over the transactions connected with the
pursuit and capture of these men, I can recall no one act which I
regret, for I believe that circumstances justified the deceit which I
adopted to accomplish their detection.

After a support of the "deceit" which he used, he turned his
attention to the reality of life in the West.

. . . I believe that it presents true and faithful pictures, confined
it is true . . . to a class of the community whose characters develop
only the worst aspects of human nature. Such delineations . . . cannot but have their interest even to the fair and gentle reader who may
chance to peruse these pages—a fearful and abhorrent interest it is

true, but no less absorbing than the fanciful crimes which fill the pages of poetry and romance, adorned though they may be by the master skill of genius.

The chapter finally concludes with the promise: "And now reader, gentle or ungentle, farewell! We shall never meet again upon the literary field. This is my first and last book. . ."(pp. 260-61).

The fiction which appeared during the 1840's and 1850's, tended to be romances in the Cooper tradition. Full of adventure, with many Indians and border skirmishes, they utilized the locale to produce exciting stories, There were few attempts made to deal with the city as an urban locale. Notable exceptions to this, however, were the tales and sketches which appeared in *Chicago Magazine*. Here writers were often interested in establishing the new city as a place for the pursuit and fulfillment of the American Dream of success. For example, in the April (1857) issue there appeared a story entitled "The Stern Chase," which presents the story of one John Smith who found it impossible to progress in his native Vermont. Seizing the opportunity to move westward, he finds that it is possible to succeed in the growing city. Eventually he returns to his native home, impresses everyone with his "rise in fortune," marries his hometown dream girl, and returns to the West. The tale is romantic, but the underlying philosophy of it is similar to that of the urban fiction of the latter part of the nineteenth century. The newspapers were filled with human interest stories dealing with the methods by which people learned to cope with the city, but few of these tales became part of the early fiction.

The early romance of Chicago business and its commercial growth was a story repeated constantly in the histories of the community; but writers were slow to discover the fictional possibilities of the subject. No matter how exciting the beginning of Chicago might appear to the present, it must be remembered that the 1840's and 1850's were strong periods of literary romanticism. Writers in Chicago followed the current literary trends and interests. In so doing, they overlooked the greatest romance around them: the settlement and growth of the city. It was left to later writers to fathom out the great impact of the urban community upon character. The early writers told entertaining stories based upon some regional lore. While they may not have made a lasting impression upon American literary historians, they did develop a substantial school of local color long before that became a movement in the nation's literature. In this, the early Chicago novelists and short story writers made a significant contribution.

V

By 1860 there had been a call for western literature, and there had been produced a substantial body of poetry and fiction which today seems distinguished by its provincialism. For those who found Nature important and who wanted a distinctly regional flavor, the prairie furnished adequate subject matter for all types of contemplation. At the same time it emphasized the uniqueness of the Chicago terrain. Even William Cullen Bryant, after a visit to his brother, wrote a poem on the prairie. The literary productions in the early Chicago were often crude and hastily written. Much of it is difficult to find because so much of it is tucked away in now-obscure—and in many cases nonexistent—journals. Yet the authors shared a strong belief in the literary possibilities of the region. Through personal narratives, biographies, histories, news-paper accounts, as well as in poetry and fiction, the reader becomes quite aware of LOCALE as a determining factor. The non-fiction of the period presents a detailed portrait of the early businessmen whose importance for the growth of the city was made clear to all who read about Chicago. These portraits, of course, often described men committed to a "business morality'" which did not always agree with traditional ethical concerns. If a conflict arose between the two, it was the Chicago "business morality" which prevailed. Thus from the beginning of the city there was the acceptance of a new American hero—the businessman, who by his acumen was forging a city in an inhospitable wilderness. At the same time there was also a toleration for the application of a "different" set of standards in life and art. The rules which had governed the lives of men and women in the more traditional communities of the East and of the South were no longer applicable.

In spite of the popularity of the Indian legends and stories of the prairie, the existing written records show that there was—in this new midwestern community—generally a rejection of the past. This may well have been the reason that the popular romantic writers could not sustain protracted careers with their stories. Exciting as was the tale of the settlers' victory over the Indians and over nature, the major business of the community was getting on with the present. The literature of Chicago up to 1860 reflects not only a turning away from the past but also a rejection of those symbols which might be associated with a yesterday as each settler looked forward to a tomorrow when his dreams would be fulfilled. Consequently, the themes and motifs which were to become important in Chicago literature are evident from the beginning, in the production of a prose and poetry for a new city.

CHAPTER 4

Printing the News and Raising Hell: From the Civil War to the Fire of 1871

"It is a newspaper's duty to
print the news and raise hell"
—Wilbur Storey, 1861

BY 1860 CHICAGO was beginning to recover from the Panic of 1857. The type of faith and optimism which had characterized the city through its first decades had not diminished. Hence, by 1860 there was a complacency in the city which defies explanation. Many Chicagoans were convinced that theirs was the best of all possible worlds; and for those who did not believe in the efficacy of the city, there was always the option of "moving on." To say that the city was provincial is simply to describe its rural nature and self-centeredness. It was—or so it thought—"the Garden City"; and in spite of its pretensions to bigness, there was a small-town quality still hovering about. By now the three divisions of the city—West, South, and North—were firmly established in the minds of the citizens; and those who lived, for example, in the West Division viewed their community as someone else might view his town. In his *Walks About Chicago* (1869) Franc B. Wilkie, popular journalist for Wilbur Storey's Chicago *Times*, described the western section of the city with a type of humor infrequently displayed by those who took the city seriously.

Any person who has ever traveled much, or who has studied physical geography, must have visited, or must have seen, a place known as Westside. It is one of the largest places of its size, and the most singular in respect to its singularity, in the world.

To get to Westside, the traveler provides himself with a waterproof suit of clothing, an umbrella, a life preserver, and a box of troches. He then enters an immense hole under ground which leads mainly westward in one direction, and eastward in another.

This subterranean entrance to Westside was constructed for a double purpose. One of these purposes was to prevent anybody who lives on Westside from leaving. The other was because there is a river which nobody can cross, owing to its exhalations. The subterranean entrance runs under this river.

Going through this hole is a work of immense difficulty and danger. The best way to get through in winter is to skate through. In summer, for a few days, in dog days, there is good boating. The innumerable cascades, cataracts, pitfalls, and the intense darkness make its navigation a work of great risk. Like the entrance to Rasselas' Happy Valley, it is constructed to keep people in, who are once in, and to discourage the coming in of those who are out.

Once in Westside the traveler finds himself on an enormous plain sparsely covered with houses. Westside extends from the river to a park somewhere on its limits to the westward. Just where this park is, nobody knows. The boundaries of Westside are as limitless and indefinite as the interval from the Gulf of Mexico to the present time.

The architecture of Westside is fine and peculiar. A residence with a marble front always has a butcher's shop on one side, and a beer saloon on the other. The people who live in Westside are as diversified as their architecture.

Westside has streetcars which are sometimes visible when a rain has laid the dust. One conductor on one of these streetcars washed his hands one spring. At least it was said he did. . . .

When ever a man in Westside builds a house and puts up a fence in front of it, he immediately calls the space in front of his lot an avenue. Almost every Westsider lives on an avenue. Sometimes a Westside avenue is as much as two hundred or three hundred feet long.

Every other shop in Westside is owned by a butcher, who has always a bloody and half-skinned calf hanging up in his door for a cheerful sign. The thing is so agreeable to Westsiders, that on every pleasant afternoon, the ladies take their knitting work and go and sit in front of the butcher's shop.

Westside is the residence of a good many notable, strongminded women. These strong-minded women all have virtuous and docile husbands, who are further characterized by their sweetness, and their retiring dispositions. Whenever a Westside woman gets to weigh 270 pounds, she immediately starts out in favor of woman's rights. In this way, she is able to afford great weight to the cause which she advocates.

Every woman in Westside once lived on The Avenue of a place known as Southside. Whenever she goes downtown, she goes to visit a friend on The Avenue. Whenever she has been downtown, she has been to call on a friend who lives on The Avenue. A good many ladies who live in Westside carry the idea, in the cars, that they live in Southside, on The Avenue, and are only in Westside for a visit. The uncle, aunt, cousin, grandmother, brother-in-law, step-sister, half-uncle, and godfather of everybody in Westside lives on The Avenue in Southside. No young lady in Westside will receive permanent attention from a young man unless he lives on The Avenue in Southside. When a Westsider of the female persuasion dies, her spirit immediately wings its way to the blissful and ecstatic realms of The Avenue on Southside.

The railway companies in Westside never water their track. They do their stock. The result, in both cases, is to throw dirt in the eyes of the public.

There are no carriages in Westside. It is so dusty there, that a vehicle which does not run on rails can never find its way from one point to another. When it is not dusty it is muddy. The dust has no top, and the mud no bottom. In either case, locomotion, except on tracks, is impossible.

Westside has no newspapers. It likewise has no opera house . . .
Its principal local amusements consist, among the men, in chewing
tobacco, and among the women, in going to church. Whenever there
is a corner in Westside not occupied as a drugstore, it is occupied
by a church.

All the churches in Westside have something going on in them
every evening, and seven afternoons in every week, and four times
every Sunday. Whenever there is anything going on in any church,
they toll the bell for an hour and a quarter before it commences, and
at intervals during the performance. The result is, that every man in
Westside hears from one to eleven bells tolling cheerfully three-fifths
of his time.

A stranger in Westside would conclude that the whole town was
dead, or that ten or fifteen melancholy funerals were in progress in
every neighborhood. There is one church, on the corner of Washington . . . Robey [Avenues], that has been tolling its bell without
cessation for two years. When there isn't a prayer meeting, or somebody dead, they toll it for somebody who is going to die. They use
up a sexton there every thirteen days. When there is no prayer meeting, or anything else, or anybody dead, or anybody who is going to
die, then the bell tolls for the last deceased sexton.

Westside is immensely philanthropic. It has an asylum for inebriates
from Southside, and other places. The asylum has often as many as
from one to two inebriates who are undergoing treatment. The treatment consists in leaning against the fence, when tight, and in stepping
over the way to a saloon and getting tight, when sober. The asylum
is a very cheerful building, with enormous windows of four-by-six
glass. Some of the rooms are fine and airy, and would answer for
dog kennels if enlarged and properly ventilated.

There are a good many other peculiar things in Westside, which
can be better understood by being seen than by being heard of. Anybody who dares to face the dangers and darkness of the hole in the
ground by which one reaches Westside, will be well repaid for his
visit.

While Wilkie delightfully poked fun at the pretensions of the

"Westsiders" and at their impossible tunnel, all of the guide books of the period noted the beauty of the boulevards and the sense of community which existed. Hobart C. Chatfield-Taylor, one of the active writers in the city during the latter part of the nineteenth century, grew up on the West Side. He recalled in his *Chicago* (1917) that this section was "so reminiscent of our strait-laced past . . . where scarcely more than a generation ago the customs, speech, and traditions of New England were so firmly planted that they seemed ineradicable"; yet, he noted that "we of West Washington Street felt ourselves to be socially a little superior to our friends in other divisions" (pp. 49-62 *passim.*)

To go to any other division—even for a visit—demanded thought and time; furthermore, one generally did not have friends who lived outside of one's own community. As late as 1893 Henry Blake Fuller observed in *The Cliff-Dwellers* that one of the first bits of advice which George Ogden received after moving to Chicago related to his choice of residence. He is told that the North Side is "better" than the West. As his informant notes: "This is a big town and awfully cut up. A man has to pick out his own quarter and stick to it. If you move from one side of the river to another, you bid good-by to all your old friends; you never see them again" (p. 12). Perhaps the situation was not quite so final as Walworth made it as he tried to convince George to move; but suffice it to say, the "sides" of Chicago were a serious reality for the nineteenth-century city, and writers of fiction frequently alluded to it.

The sections, virtually small towns, were held together by a downtown business area which was the magnet that had drawn most of the people to Chicago in the first place. Here in the heart of the city commerce and trade were plodding along in 1860, surprised and delighted with their progress. Those who might have longed for another way of doing things had to admit that the businessmen were succeeding beyond anyone's wildest dreams—so perhaps all was right considering the progress that had been made. One of the best portraits of Chicago in the early years of the 1860's was written by Frederick Cook in his *Bygone Days in Chicago*. Having arrived in the city in 1862, when it was recovering from the panic and was succumbing to the beginning war fever, Cook describes in detail the physical and spiritual Chicago. Yet this description can be multiplied many times: bold images of the growing city, excessive construction with no consideration of building codes or building materials, emphasis upon bigness in everything, an energetic people with complete faith in the future. This was Chicago in the 1860's.

The optimism expressed by many Chicagoans was repeated in the *London Illustrated News* (August 22, 1863):

Extraordinary as has been the growth of many . . . cities of the United States as Philadelphia in the east and Cincinnati in the west, yet all are eclipsed by the rapidity with which the great city of Chicago . . . has risen up. Thirty years ago the site of this fine city was almost a wilderness—not more than half a dozen cottages occupied the flat prairie lands where now is a magnificent city containing one hundred and twenty thousand inhabitants. Chicago is not composed of all kinds of buildings, good, bad, and indifferent, as many American cities are, but is beautifully built of brick and stone. The public buildings are very fine, the streets wide and well paved. In fact, the city has as noble and stately an appearance as any city of its kind in the Old World. The shops and stores are of the first class and the hotels on the largest scale, offering the best accommodation . . .

The geographical position of Chicago is, perhaps, the very finest that exists on the American continent. It is situated on the southwest angle of Lake Michigan, quite in the 'far west' of the continent, more than a thousand miles from the Atlantic Ocean. Yet vessels which shipped their cargoes in the docks of Liverpool may often be seen discharging them beside her quays; and many a cargo of corn, beef, and pork shipped in this great prairie capital finds its ways to Bristish ports without ever being transshipped; for between Chicago and the Atlantic the water communication is complete for seagoing ships of considerable burden, by the Welland Canal, which passes them from

Lake Erie to Lake Ontario, missing the great Falls, and by the canals of the St. Lawrence, which avoid the rapids of that river. Chicago is also connected with New York by a grand system of canals; in fact, New York is the true port of the prairie country.

From Chicago in every direction branches a system of railways of the most complete kind. . . .

It is impossible to contemplate the future of the North American States without seeing that the city of Chicago must occupy the most prominent position in it, standing as it does at the head of inland navigation, and at the head also of those great alluvial tracts of rich prairie lands, which even now are scarely touched, lands where soil, climate, and all desirable things . . . invite men to settle upon them and progress. . . . The greatest nation the world has even seen will be that which will one day inhabit the plains of Illinois: Chicago will be its capital, and New York its seaport.

Faith in the region was accompanied by a strong desire to eliminate the ills of urbanization. A few months after the *London Illustrated News* article appeared, the Chicago *Tribune* (November 15, 1863)—under the caption "Array of Horrors"—listed a series of crimes which had recently taken place in the city. The despondency which was partially a result of the Civil War and the type of degeneracy commonly seen about town caused some concern in the city. There were efforts made to remind Chicagoans of their potential greatness. In this the *Tribune* played a significant role.

The literary scene was essentially dominated by the newspapers which provided an outlet as well as employment for all budding writers. There were many papers and magazines. Those which survived the Panic of 1857 were joined by new journals almost daily. Each one was designed to capture the reading market of the city without realizing that there were limits to the number of papers which could command the attention of a people actively engaged in carving out of the Midwest a city destined to become that region's major metropolis. These new journals were often intended as general papers, but there were specialized ones such as the religious press (which seemed to grow stronger daily), the foreign language interests, and those few which were devoted to "culture." Like the journals of an earlier age, these were also devoted to a promotion of the West. Thus, while Chicago journalism was evolving into a modern super-structure, two catastrophes—one destined to result in an even more phenomenal growth and the other to destroy all that there was—occurred. The Civil War and the Fire of 1871 produced a body of essentially occasional literature. Yet, these two events were in the future when Chicago was the site of the Republican National Convention in 1860.

The almost unanimous excitement in the city over the establishment of the new party and the nomination of a native son, Abraham Lincoln as the standard bearer, was soon replaced by a divided city. Even though there were always those who were supportive of Lincoln because he was viewed as one of their own in spite of the fact that he had spent little time in Chicago, there were still many others who were not so certain about the impending conflict. When the Civil War began, the advocates and the opponents of it waged a battle of words in the city. William Bross later suggested in his lecture before the Chicago Historical Society in 1878 that there was a great sense of patriotism in Chicago.

From that quiet sabbath morning, when the news flashed through the streets that the rebels had fired upon Fort Sumter at 4 o'clock on Friday afternoon, April 12, 1861, and the people left their churches, with the organ pealing out the 'Star Spangled Banner,' till treason was stamped out . . . , a very large majority of them seemd deeply imbued with the same spirit that inspired their fathers when 'they pledged their lives, their fortunes, and their sacred honor,' to preserve the integrity, and to establish the liberty of their country.

While there may have been a pervasive sense of patriotism, the reality of the situation pointed to the fact that there were many in Chicago who were not certain at all about their feelings on the matter. This, then, was a period of pamphlets and other ephemeral work created by those who thought their ideas should be given some permanent form. The term "author" was indeed loosely used. Many of the issues were significant but the expression was essentially amateurish and merely designed for conditions of that present. The openness of the city resulted in it being not only the scene of much patriotic activity conducted by those who were attempting to maintain the ideals of the Union but also the center for a great many southern sympathizers. Eventually these groups conflicted, and there arose one of the questions of the Civil War: Shall the rights of free speech be maintained? The question—which centered around the activities of Wilbur Storey and his newspaper, the Chicago *Times*—was answered in Chicago.

I

In 1861 Wilbur F. Storey started his editorship of the weak and almost defunct Chicago *Times,* a daily paper which had had a checkered career. Started as a politically independent daily on November 16, 1853, with William Duane Wilson as editor, later called the Chicago *Courant,* the newspaper soon faced both financial and editorial difficulties. It was hard to retain an aura of independence when there were so many vital political, economic, and social issues which needed either commitment or rejection. In 1854 Isaac Cook, Daniel Cameron and J.W. Patterson bought the paper, changed its name to *Young America* and its allegiance to the Democratic Party; and the first issue appeared prophetically enough on July 4th. This daily and weekly paper lasted almost two months when, on August 20, 1854, it reappeared as the Chicago *Daily Times.* Two of the founders, Isaac Cook and Daniel Cameron were from *Young America,* and they were joined by James W. Sheahan, who had been active in the Chicago newspaper world. The paper was a strong supporter of Senator Stephen Douglas and adopted his point of view on all major political issues. As a result, the paper supported Douglas in his senatorial campaign of 1858 against Abraham Lincoln. In 1858 another paper was established which ultimately was to figure in the early history of the *Times*.

Isaac Cook had become increasingly disenchanted with the editorial policies of the paper which he had helped to establish, and—with the aid of Charles N. Pine—founded the *Herald* as a paper supportive of the President, James Buchanan, in opposition to the *Times*. Such a restrictive goal was not an avenue of success, and in 1859 the *Herald* was sold to businessman Cyrus H. McCormick, who continually made efforts toward newspaper ownership. Like many businessmen before and after him, McCormick felt the need to "control" at least one segment of the press. Thus it was that in the following year he bought the now-floundering *Times* with the intention of combining his two papers. The philosophy of the proposed merger was clearly stated in the advertisement which appeared in the *Herald*. The reader was advised that as "an organ of Democratic thought and an exponent of constitutional principles," the new paper would "advocate the equal rights of the people and the fraternal union of the States." With the motto, "Principles, not Men," the newspaper would be "a commercial, mechanical, literary, and moral" journal which would "be inferior to none in the West. Nothing will be allowed in its columns that will cause a blush to the most rigidly pure."

On September 8, 1860, the *Times and Herald* appeared, owned by Cyrus McCormick and edited by his good friend and fellow Virginian, E.W. McComas. Throughout the year it was a strong supporter of the theory of states' rights and necessarily an opponent of Lincoln. Since there were so many other more powerful papers, among them the very vocal Chicago *Tribune*, which were advocates of Lincoln and the new Republican Party, the fact that the *Times and Herald* supported southern doctrine and ideology seemed harmless enough at first. But this was destined to change. By 1861 the *Times and Herald* had become the *Times,* and Wilbur Storey had come from the Detroit *Free Press* to take over the editorial responsibilities. This move was to be a significant event not only for the development of journalism in Chicago but also in the nation. Undoubtedly, many of the changes wrought by Storey would have been made eventually by someone somewhere, for him it was a matter of expediency which was of greatest concern and not making newspaper history. Some of the changes had little lasting value, but all of them supported his contention that the role of a newspaper was "to print the news and raise hell."

In many ways the development of the *Times* from a small-town news-sheet to a major post-Fire paper paralleled what had occurred in the city. The Chicago of 1860 was vastly different from the city of 1880. Seldom have such phenomenal changes been recorded in urban development. In less than twenty years the city had emerged from a frontier town with pretensions of culture to a modern urban area whose culture was being noticed by other sections of the nation and by those world travelers who reported on the strange growth which they found in the midland of the United States. In spite of the nightmares of the Civil War and the devastating Fire of 1871, Chicago proved to the nation that it was an unconquerable force, and the literature of the period recorded this sense of invincibility. In other words, in that twenty-year period Chicago writing—led by the journalists—came of age. But such accomplishments are not made without struggles and sacrifices.

When Storey took over the *Times*, the paper—under various ownerships and with different editors as well as political alliances—was seven years old and struggling against the popularity of the older, more prestigious, and more successful *Tribune*. In a period when Lincoln, the man from Illinois, was gaining national prominence, the Democratic *Times* was a voice truly crying in the wilderness while the Republican *Tribune* could rejoice in being on the winning political side. The city had always had newspapers of varying opinions and persuasions, but for the first time in the city's history this was beginning to make a difference.

While in Detroit, Wilbur Storey had been a strong opponent of the Abolition movement. His view of the Negro was unreasoned and venomous. Once he became the editor of the *Times* he had a platform, but he was able to see the larger view of the need to

preserve the Union. For that reason Storey was supportive of the
Civil War in its early stages not as a Democratic partisan but as
an American citizen. When many of the northern Republican
papers turned against Lincoln and his method of prosecuting the
war, the President had the support of Wilbur Storey and the
Times. Many did not understand the fiery editor's approach, but
he explained in one of his masterful editorials (June 22, 1861)
that while he felt it to be "the duty of every citizen to serve his
country in the manner which his conscience directs," he also
thought people should be aware that "insurrection exists in the
land [and] the laws of the Union are set to defiance." The alternative to insurrection, as he saw it, was "government or no government." And he called upon American citizens to support the
government of the Union. He further noted:

Mr. Lincoln is the head of the government, and upon him, as such,
devolves the duty of meeting the insurrection and suppressing it if he
can. If he hesitated to do this he would live forever a man of infamy,
and imbecility. He has no option. It is his duty to his country, to
democrats as well as republicans, to North as well as South, to all
parties, to all sections, to all ages of time. He stands in the breach and
must defend it. He cannot, he must not let the light of American
liberty stand in the darkness. If then it is his duty to defend the
government, it is our duty to sustain him in all proper efforts to that
end. It is true that tomorrow we could not vote for him if he was a
candidate for the Presidency,—that we deem the party he belongs to
mischievous in their principles, and that we will, whenever he ex-
ceeds his powers . . . hang about him and attack him with all the
power God has given us. But our duty to our government, to American institutions, is above all jealousies and party advantages.

Certainly one could not ask for greater commitment from one who
had been so vehemently opposed to the legislation and the
abolitionist forces which brought—as he viewed it—the nation
to the brink of ruin. Throughout the remainder of that first year

of war, Storey's was a strong voice in support of President Lincoln. At the same time he continued to be unilaterally opposed to the doctrines of abolition. This was not an uncommon dilemma for there were many in Chicago—as elsewhere—who viewed the war and the abolition of slavery as two distinctly separate subjects and could support the war while rejecting abolition. By the end of 1861 Storey was aware that the Chicago *Times* was basically Lincoln's only support in the city where just a year before he had been hailed as the new political voice by Republicans throughout the Midwest.

In 1862, as the war progressed feebly for the northern forces, Lincoln began to consider the possibilities of a limited emancipation of some of the slaves, and Storey became vocally concerned. At the same time, the attacks upon Storey by the Chicago *Tribune* were intensified despite the fact that during this same period the *Tribune* opposed Lincoln strongly because there had NOT been an order to emancipate the slaves. Eventually that order came—and not without some trepidation on the part of the man who was later to be remembered and honored as "the Great Emancipator." For Storey it represented a time of great decision. Earlier he had indicated his belief in free speech as he castigated those liberals and abolitionists who believed that they alone had the right to freedom of speech. Said he in the September 17, 1862, issue of the *Times*:

> Instead of meeting argument with argument, and manfully attacking a theory or a policy which is believed to be erroneous, the radical attacks the man who upholds the opposing theory, denouncing him as a criminal, and attempts to destroy the force of his arguments by destroying him or his reputation.

Thus committed to free speech and to a Union without emancipated slaves, Storey saw nothing wrong with the publication on election day, November 4, 1862, of a parody of "We Are Coming Father Abraham."

Song of Democracy

Selected for the Chicago Times

We are coming Father Abraham, Three Hundred Thousand Strong.
To save you from the clutches of the abolition throng.
You've heard from Pennsylvania and from Indiana, too,
And Ohio has been speaking through her ballot box to you!
The sturdy men of iron, from the Furnace and the Mine,
With the Hoosiers and the Buckeye boys are swinging into line!
They are marching to the music of the Union as of yore,
And Illinois is coming after them, Three Hundred Thousand more.

We are marching, Father Abraham, to that familiar tune
With which, so often, in former years we've reared the same old coon!
Once more from hill and valley, it rings forth with cheering sound,
To gladden every household where a loyal heart is found.
See! Every star is blazoned with the banner we unfold;
For the Union that our Jackson saved, our SHERMAN will uphold!
To scatter all the nation's foes—the Union to restore.
We're coming Father Abraham, Three Hundred Thousand More.

We are coming Father Abraham, and as we march along,
We'll relieve you of the 'pressure' of the abolition throng!
You told them that you couldn't make a pig's leg of its tail,
And that against the comet papal bulls would not avail.
They wouldn't heed your anecdotes or listen to your pleas,
They swore that white men should be slaves and niggers should be free.
But you need not mind their ravings now, nor trouble at their roar,
For we're coming Father Abraham, Three Hundred Thousand more.

We are coming Father Abraham, to cast away your fears,
Tis the democratic 'slogan' that is ringing in your ears!
They pretend to call us traitors! But we point you to the blood
That soaks into Virginia's soil, or—that dyes Potomac's flood—
That stains the hills of Maryland, the Plains of Tennessee—
Such 'traitors,' Father Abraham, the Union loves to see.
It's a growing 'traitor' army that is thundering at your door,
And Illinois'll swell the columns by Three Hundred Thousand more.
We are coming Father Abraham, to vindicate the laws,

To hold the Starry Banner up—to guard the Nation's cause;
Our motto is "The White Man's Rights"—For this we've battled long—
For this we'll fight with sinewy arms, with earnest hearts and strong—
For this we'll burst Fort Warren's bars, and crumble Lafayette—
For we'll crush the Nation's foes and save the Union yet.
Thus speaks the North! Oh, Abraham, you'll heed its mighty roar,
When Illinois shall swell the chorus by Three Hundred Thousand
more.

How much influence this parody had on the outcome of the election in the Chicago area is a moot point; however, the Democrats won substantially, and Storey knew that he had supporters, that he was not alone in his anti-Negro attitude—an attitude shared by many northerners, Republican and Democrat alike. What he did not realize was that freedom of speech is so relative and that there were forces in Chicago "after" him at all costs.

Storey, however, refused to be intimidated. Having instituted the use of the sensational headline, he now employed that technique to capitalize on what he viewed as a sympathetic reading public. "Shall Illinois be Africanized" and "Negro Civilization: Its Bestiality and Degradation—Incompetency of the Negro Race to Observe the Laws of Society" are two examples of the Storey headline. Not only did he begin a direct and forceful attack on Negroes but also he ridiculed the war effort in such columns as "Outrages by Federal Soldiers." Perhaps in retrospect one might say that Storey was fighting on too many fronts; however, the impetus for his displeasure was made clear in his statement on January 3, 1863, as he lambasted the Emancipation Proclamation which had taken effect two days earlier.

The deed is done—the deed which unites the people of the South forever in their rebellion; which converts the war from a constitutional contest for the integrity of the Union to an unconstitutional crusade for the liberation of three millions of negro barbarians; which destroys the last hope of the preservation of the old government and inaugurates a future dark, uncertain and dreary—the deed is done.

The Chicago *Tribune* and other anti-Storey forces began to inten-
sify and to consolidate their attacks upon the *Times* which was
clearly providing an outlet for the northerners who were not
totally committed to the impending results of the Civil War.
Many people who subscribed to the concept of the preservation
of the Union did so fully intending that the the Negro "should be
kept in his place." They were not willing to extend their beliefs in
freedom nor the franchise to those who had been enslaved. Storey's
newspaper became the spokesman for this group which seemed to
be growing larger every day. These divisions which plagued the
North were not making life any simpler for those responsible for
the prosecution of the war. While many believed as Storey,
there were those who recognized that his approach was "bad for
business." Certainly, he was not helping Chicago where war profits
were widespread. Furthermore, the city had prided itself as being
a bastion of freedom, and the civic leaders did not want that image
tarnished. Both the Galena and Chicago Union Railroad as well
as the Chicago Board of Trade banned the *Times* from their
premises not totally because of their patriotism; they did not want
any business repercussions from this flagrant opposition to what
some had come to view as "a noble cause." Anything slightly
detrimental to business could not—and would not—be tolerated
by either the railroads or the Board of Trade.

Just when the accusation against Storey moved from a charge
of imprudence to the possibility of treason is not clear. By April
of 1863, General Ambrose Burnside (whose territory covered
parts of northern Kentucky, Ohio, Indiana, and Illinois) had issued
"General Order Number Thirty-Eight" designed to silence for all
time the opposition to the Union forces. The order provided that
any overt or covert activity which might be deemed supportive or
in collaboration with the Confederacy and its principles would be
deemed a criminal offense and "those who commit acts for the
benefit of our enemies will be tried as traitors and spies." No
longer, continued the order, would "the habit of declaring
sympathy for the enemy . . . be tolerated." Anyone so accused

under this order would be subjected not only to arrest but also to a trial conducted by military rather than civil authorities. Shortly after the order, a case occurred in Ohio where Burnside executed the order much to the regret of those who were fearful that freedom of speech was being abridged. In times of national crises it is always difficult to draw the line between freedom of speech and treason; and so it was during those days.

In view of the events, it would have been wise had Storey exercised more caution; however, he did not stop his venomous attacks which now included Burnside as well as the restrictive military order. As a result, the General summarily notified the commander at Camp Douglas, General Sweet, to close the *Times*. That specific order stated: "On account of the repeated expression of the disloyal and incendiary statements, the publication known as THE CHICAGO TIMES is hereby suppressed." According to Francis Cook in *Bygone Days in Chicago*:

To call this order a blunder is the mildest characterization that can be applied to it. The unthinking mass of Republicans hailed it with delight, and gave it stout support. But the more sober-minded leaders of the party fully appreciated its menace, not only to civil liberty, but to law and order. Perhaps the one personally least concerned in this crisis was the owner and editor of the *Times*, Wilbur F. Storey. It required no prophet to predict that the order would not stand; and in the meantime it gave the paper a country-wide notoriety, while the act served only to give color to the often reiterated charge (that for which the paper was suppressed), namely, that 'the war, as waged by military satraps of the administration, was a subversion of the Constitution and the people's rights under the law.'

Cook further describes what the order to suppress the newspaper meant in Chicago:

To the Copperhead leaders the order came as a godsend. Through an irresponsible military zealot they had at one bound been fixed in the saddle, booted and spurred, with the hated 'abolition' enemy divided, distracted, and on the run. Let it be remembered that Chicago was in fact a Democratic city; that it had a Democratic mayor and council; and that the *Times* was the municipality's official organ (pp. 151-52).

Because of the nature of Burnside's order the city of Chicago was subject to being placed under a state of seige. Those who supported Storey were just as vocal as those who had opposed him, and the prospects of street battles grew hourly as crowds gathered, Much of this, needless to say, was part of the general phenomenon of war hysteria; but anyone who has attempted to reason with a mob recognizes the futility of the attempt. As Cook noted:

> The order [to suppress the *Times*] was in effect a declaration of martial law. Only by a military force could it be carried out and maintained, for the entire civil machinery, including the United States court, was opposed to it. Another step, and the city, the State, and wide areas beyond might be in the throes of a civil war within a civil war. As soon as the news of what was to happen spread among the people, the strain between the opposing sides became threateningly tense, and with 'Copperheadism' most resolutely to the fore; while on every side one heard the threat, which grew with each hour, 'If the *Times* is not allowed to publish, there will be no *Tribune*' (p. 152).

The tension in the city had reached a critical moment; and it was only through the intervention of such influential Republicans as Wirt Dexter that a potentially dangerous situation was defused. Lincoln was petitioned to revoke the military order, and on June 5, 1863, the *Times* reappeared, just two days after it had been suppressed by a military force. President Lincoln, understanding the constitutional arguments involved, upheld the right of Storey to publish his paper. Franc B. Wilkie, certainly not a strong supporter nor admirer of Storey (although he was associated with the *Times* for a long period), wrote several years later in his *Personal Reminisicences of Thirty-Five Years in Journalism* (Chicago, 1891) that the suppression of the *Times* "was an immeasurable benefit to the financial interests of the journal." He noted that the circulation of the *Times* "bounded upward in unprecedented fashion" (p. 101).

Storey's brand of journalism was inflamatory and incendiary, to be sure; but there were those in his own day who defended his right to speak. Yet, the question of whether or not his rights should have gone as far as he took them remains one of the unsolved riddles of the Civil War era and remains at the core of the issue of the responsibilities of the press in a free society. His support in Chicago tells a great deal about attitudes during the war in that city in spite of the many patriotic efforts which were executed during the 1861-65 period. Thus the widespread popularity of the *Times* not only in Chicago but throughout the northern states was due in part to its appeal to certain points of view. Especially is this true after the Emancipation Proclamation went into effect. But perhaps more important was the fact that Storey believed that no expense should be spared in order to get the war news as quickly as possible. So it really was the *Times* which had enough men on the various fronts and which used telegraph services fully in order to get the news to the subscribers. Wilkie asserts in his memoirs that upon joining the staff of the *Times* Storey had said to him: "Telegraph fully all news, and when there is no news, send rumors" (p. 85).

Storey's full use of rumor and innuendo did not endear him to dedicated journalists of integrity, but it did sell papers. And that— after all—was the whole purpose of any journalistic effort. Yet, the bitterness and rancor which he directed against Lincoln became more and more intense in 1864. In fact on March 2, 1864, Storey made a pronouncement concerning the possibility of Lincoln's re-election which he was later to regret—that is, as much as he was able to regret any of his actions or statements. At that time he said: "Should [Mr. Lincoln] not be elected, he goes to his political funeral when he leaves the White House, and should he have another term, there will be a national funeral."

Judgments on Wilbur Storey have been mixed concerning his

behavior during the Civil War. Called a traitor by many, seen as
a brave soul by others, Storey did test—either consciously or
unconsciously—the nation's commitment to free speech. And
whether for good or for ill, he won the right to be heard. In his
Reminiscences . . . Wilkie recalled Storey as being "insolent,
audacious, defiant . . . in war matters, his paper became equally
noted for another quality in its post-war existence. This feature
was its glaring indecency." Wilkie continued by defining this "indecency" as something "which reeked, seethed like a hell's broth
in the *Times* cauldrons and made a stench in the nostrils of decent
people" (p. 130). That Storey relied heavily on sensationalism,
often bordering on the obscene, is well-known. However, he introduced many innovations as an editor which eventually led to the
Chicago *Times* becoming not only an outstanding and popular
paper but also one which spared no expense in getting the news
to its readers. Storey continued to be a mean, vicious, vituperative
man who fought against friend and foe alike; but more than anyone
else, he singly raised western journalism to a peak where it was
able to compete favorably with the eastern press.

Truly as he ended his life—a man broken both in mind and
body—Wilbur F. Storey had done what he had said a newspaper
should do. He really had printed the news—sometimes biased,
frequently slanted, but no paper had had such a reverence for
foreign news, for the need to have special correspondents, and for
the importance of the Sunday paper with special features. Yet,
through all of his contributions—positive and negative—the *Times*
had followed the prescription of its mercurial editor and had
"raised hell." But it had also spawned a generation of journalists
who were to influence the outcome of Chicago writing.

Prior to 1871 there was a great proliferation of newspapers.
Anybody with a proposal for one could generally find the capital
and available printers. Frequently, the investment meant little more
than the funds to rent the printing facilities and the energy to
promote the new adventure. Some attempts were so specialized
that they lasted less than a year. Many were quite good, but the

basic law of supply and demand curtailed excessive circulation. Most of the newspapers, as well as the magazines, were edited by a strong dictatorial journalist whose commitment to the city was often just as pronounced as that of the businessmen. As the period of the 1860's opened, the newspapers, which were essentially "small-town sheets," were little more than functional utilitarian papers designed to give the local news from whatever editorial or political bias existed. There was, of course, that evident pride in the development of the city.

The role of the Chicago *Tribune,* the newspaper which conflicted more than the others with the *Times,* cannot be minimized during this period. The *Tribune* was a major force during the war years as it tacitly adopted the Storey-formula of "printing the news and raising hell." It had long been a supporter of the cause of abolition and saw in Lincoln's election as well as in the establishment of the Republican Party a chance to effect some major social changes not only in the city but also in the nation. Part of that newspaper's editorial disenchantment with Lincoln during the time was predicated upon his refusal to emancipate all slaves immediately. Through its mergers and absorptions of lesser-known papers, the *Tribune* had become not only the leading paper in the city but also the one which employed the greatest number of journalists. Standards were high, the writing consistently good, and the flamboyance of a Wilbur Storey was absent. But nonetheless, there were readers just as devoted to the *Tribune,* as there were those committed to the *Times.* Among the outstanding *Tribune* journalists were William Bross, Horace White, George P. Upton, and Elias Colbert who—during the Civil War period and in the days before the Fire of 1871—were active in the newspaper world as well as in various civic and community organizations. All of them arrived in Chicago between 1848 and 1857 with the belief that success in journalism was possible in the fast-growing city. Of the four, Bross was the only one who parlayed his career in journalism into an active political life.

William Bross, sometimes called the "original" Chicago booster, was associated with the Republican party from its inception in 1854 and with the *Tribune* from 1858 when he and John Scripps merged their paper, *Democratic Press*, with the larger paper. The *Press* had switched its political affiliation after the Democratic stand upon the Kansas-Nebraska question with which Scripps and Bross could not agree. Bross was an ardent supporter of the Union and a firm believer in Chicago. From the time of his arrival in the city in 1848 he was totally convinced that business, commercial ventures, and industry would make the city an outstanding urban center. And it was he who insisted that a city such as Chicago should emphasize commercial journalism and declared that this would help illustrate the potentialities of the city to other people and regions. His career in journalism was augmented by his involvement with a number of cultural institutions, and he became identified with several organizations dedicated to cultural uplift and literary interests, among them the Mechanics' Institute, the Chicago Library Association, and the Chicago Academy of Science. During the Civil War he was active in relief organizations, recruiting, and in anything devoted to the preservation of the Union. He discovered the plan of the Chicago Conspiracy of 1864 and is credited with alerting officials at Camp Douglas in time for the plot to be circumvented. In that same year he was elected lieutenant governor of the State. Yet, through all of these activities, he spent much time in lecturing and writing. His 1878 lecture before the Chicago Historical Society on the history of Camp Douglas is still, partisan though it is, one of the best and most readable contemporary accounts of Camp Douglas which was not only a Union training base but also a Confederate prison. In his own day the lecture was reprinted and distributed widely.

Horace White arrived in Chicago during 1854, a year after he had graduated from Beloit College. By 1857 he was on the *Tribune* staff and became its editor-in-chief in 1865, a position which he held until he retired in 1874. White had neither the flamboyance nor the same decision-making power as Wilbur Storey; but when he became associated with the *Tribune*, the paper was probably the most outstanding paper west of the Allegheny Mountains. Through his careful manipulation of men and materials, he maintained its high quality during this period, a difficult task because of the conflict with the *Times* which often seemed about to border on violence. As an active community leader and a staunch supporter of Lincoln, White was pleased when the issue of Secession was solved by South Carolina. He felt that when the southern states had taken this stand, it would be easier to crush the rebellion "once and for all." At all costs he was convinced—as were other Republican newspapermen of the period—that the Union must be preserved. Speaking of White, Andreas noted:

> Mr. White is a gentleman of comprehensive education and fine literary ability which his studious habits and varied reading have enlarged and perfected. His jurisdiction in the editorial room of the Tribune resulted in an elegance of literary style that is rarely equaled, while his painstaking attention to detail maintained and perpetuated the accuracy which the paper had previously acquired, and which have given and preserved its prestige and influence (II, 494).

As a graduate of Brown University, George Putnam Upton early decided that he wanted a career in writing, and he started contributing articles and sketches to various publications in New England before traveling westward in 1855 to try his luck in Chicago. While a journalist for the Chicago *Evening Journal* he wrote a very successful series of essays entitled "Gunnybag Papers," and antedated the work of such later essayists as Eugene Field, Finley Peter Dunne, and George Ade. In 1861 he went to the *Tribune* where he remained for fifty-seven years. After his stint in 1862 as a war correspondent where he reported some of the outcomes of major battles such as Fort Pillow, he devoted the rest of his career to what he liked best: the arts, and he became noted as the music critic for the *Tribune*. Using the pseudonym Peregrine Pickle he wrote a series of essay on manners, customs, art, music, drama, and other cultural offerings of the city. *Letters of Peregrine Pickle* appeared in 1869. Finally, he produced a study of Theodore Thomas (1905) in two volumes which still remains one of the primary documents on that great nineteenth-century musician.

Elias Colbert shared the interests of Bross and also emphasized the importance of commerce for a growing city. He moved to Chicago from England in 1857 and began his journalistic career under the sponsorship of Alfred Dutch who with his *Daily News* spent much time trying to show that business—especially the railroads—would be the most important factor in the growth of the city. From working with Dutch, Colbert moved to the *Times* briefly, and then became associated with the *Tribune* in 1863. By 1866 he had become its commercial editor and had instituted annual reviews of trade and commerce which became the bases for the work of many later historians. Following Bross' interest in history, Colbert also began to investigate the role of the developing city and eventually produced two of the outstanding histories of the nineteenth century. One dealt with the history of Chicago up to 1868 and provided much material which was used by later statisticians and the other, *Chicago and the Great Conflagration,* was the first book of the Chicago Fire published shortly after that devastating event of 1871. But his interests also extended to science, and he produced some outstanding pioneer work on astronomy. His *Astronomy with the Telescope* appeared in 1869. In his histories he tended to focus on aspects of the subject which ordinarily seemed too mundane to warrant investigation. For example, he placed a great deal of emphasis upon recruiting procedures and the formation of various companies within the city during the Civil War. This military history which might seem dull at best is made lively and vibrant through Colbert's writing technique. In the same manner, his essay on "The Science of the Fire" explains the progress of the fire in scientific rather than emotional terms but does not in any way lessen the drama of the situation. In the final analysis, he investigated his materials well and wrote with a flourish.

The major *Tribune* journalists during this period were well-trained, dedicated men with a variety of interests outside of their newspaper work. While they did not join in the defensive talk of Chicago as a cultural center, through their work they proved that there was indeed a cultural life in the city. Of course, no one was permitted to forget the paper's business or political orientation; yet there was an interest in the development of cultural institutions in the city. Thus the newspaper which was one of the first to support the idea of emancipation for the slaves was also the one to support the idea of an orchestra for the city. During this same period the writers on the staff of the *Tribune* were not only excellent stylists but also extremely realistic. The type of laudatory excesses which were so common in the journalism of the period were limited. Instead it was not unusual to read articles on the filth of the city or the crime rate or the less-than-honorable business practices. Underlying these well-executed articles, however, was the ultimate belief that urban perfection was possible. The *Tribune* shared that same sense of manifest destiny which often characterized a great deal of the non-fiction written about the city.

In addition to the *Tribune* and *Times*, there were other political papers which rose to prominence during this period. Generally they adopted a rather strict party line; however, many of them had the problem of trying to decide editorially—especially after 1863—how to reconcile their views on the war with their attitudes toward the newly-emancipated. As far as the newspapers were concerned the end of the Civil War followed so quickly by the assassination of President Lincoln brought to a close one era of journalism in the city. Perhaps the editorial from the Chicago *Tribune* of May 2, 1865, summarized the city's interest in Lincoln. His body had arrived in the city on May 1st. Lying in state at the court house for two days Lincoln's body was viewed by thousands. The *Tribune* thus noted:

The solemn pageant of yesterday, and the final ceremonies today, are mournfully appropriate. In Chicago he first laid deep and broad the foundation of his legal attainments. In the courts of Chicago he gathered that distinction which made him peer among the ablest counsellors of the land. In that remarkable debate with the lamented Douglas, Chicago, more than any other city, aided to give his immortal utterances a widespread circulation throughout the land, and thus brought prominently before the country this hard working toiler, this acute thinker and logical reasoner, this unflinching and unyielding patriot. Chicago first summoned from his comparative obscurity, in a political sense at least, this man of men, and demanded that the country should recognize in him, one fit to stand in high places—a safe counsellor in danger, a wise and prudent ruler in crises. And when, as the clouds were gathering thickly, and the mutterings of the approaching tempest were heard on the southern horizon, the servants of the people gathered together in this city to select the pilot who should stand at the helm, Chicago firmly demanded that that pilot should be Abraham Lincoln. His abilities had been tested in the wrestle with the most able and cunning debater in the land, and his sagacity and honesty and purity no man could question. The convention nominated him, and the announcement that he was to be our standard bearer was received by the people of Chicago with glad shouts of jubilation, and, in the November succeeding that nomination, they rallied in their might at the polls as they had never rallied before. Chicago honored his call for troops at the very outset of the war, and before an army was organized, sent her sons to the field to do battle for the immortal principles of which he was the exponent and representative, and never, from that day to the day of his unnatural murder, has she dishonored his calls. The loyal men of Chicago loved him and he loved them. They of the East admired and respected him as they saw his innate nature illustrated in his deeds; they of the South hated him as vice always hates virtue; we of the West loved him as a friend and neighbor who had grown up amongst us, whose every trait and habit were as familiar to us as household words, and that love he returned. His calm, sad face was ever turned westward, and already he had determined that, when he had fulfilled his glorious mission, full of honors, his course as rounded and complete as the orbit of a planet, *pater republicae*, then laying aside the reins of government, and sheathing the sword of justice, he would come to Chicago to spend the remainder of his days in the enjoyment of that ease he had so deservedly won, and go down to the grave in the quiet of home, peacefully and serenely. By the mysterious and inscrutable providence of Almighty God, that near desire of his heart was denied him. The grieving widow and afflicted sons follow the path he would have trod, and hence forth Chicago will delight to honor them and extend to them the warm grasp of sympathy and friendship, in memory of the great dead and in token of the love it bore him.

At that moment the *Tribune* editors, as well as others, forgot that they had fought him whenever his plans did not seem to coincide with their newspaper's philosophy. And thus it was that the end of the Civil War—which should have been a period of great rejoicing—soon became a sad occasion. Whatever role the newspapers may have played in making Lincoln's Presidency difficult was soon forgotten in the midst of the multitude of eulogies and panegyrics, but Wilbur Storey and the Chicago *Times* remained as the sole perpetrators of the anti-Lincoln myth. Certainly Carl Sandburg was serious in his *Abraham Lincoln: The War Years* (New York, 1939) when he said "Had Booth merely permitted himself to be led by such newspapers as the . . . *Chicago Times* then he would have felt himself correct and justified to go forth with a brass pocket pistol . . ." (IV,340). But if there is to be blame placed upon the media, all journals who opposed so vehemently the prosecution of the war must share Storey's responsibility. He was merely putting into operation his philosophy of journalism which unfortunately did not include a recognition of that fine line between prudence and imprudence.

During the years of the Civil War quite a few magazines were founded in the city. Many of these, despite their pronounced aims and goals, were soon caught up in the war fever; and some of them may have sounded their own death knells. For example, when she began the *National Banner* (1862) Mrs. Delphine Baker had an excellent idea. Designed as an outlet for articles on art, music, and literature, it was to be national in intent although she provided for the publication of "western" literature. In the

early issues there appeared a series entitled "Olula: A Romance
of the West" which included all of the conventions of the early
romantic tale of the West with border skirmishes, Indians, settlers,
and the ever-present magnificence of the prairie. Yet, in order to
appeal to the ever-present war hysteria, Mrs. Baker announced
that the purpose of the magazine was "first to create a patriotic
fund for the relief of disabled soldiers and their families"; thus
she informed her readers that part of their payment for subscriptions would go for "patriotic causes." Her second purpose was
"to diffuse a high-toned moral literature throughout the land,"
and finally, she ended with her third purpose, "to bind with the
golden chain of love all hearts together in one grand, glorious
national cause." After seven issues of the magazine which started
as a monthly in Chicago, Mrs. Baker found it necessary to move
her journal to Washington, D.C.; hence, the "literary" magazine
did not have an opportunity to affect the development of Chicago
writing at all.

As committed as the *National Banner* to a cause was another
journal which appeared in Chicago during the war years. *The
Workingman's Advocate* began in 1864 and was to become a
major force in supporting the idea of labor unionism. *The Advocate* was as vociferous in its demands and positions as any
other journal which had been established. Bessie Pierce in her
A History of Chicago . . . 1848-1871 (New York, 1940) referred
to it as "the exponent of radical labor" and asserted that "it
lashed into fury by its venomous attacks on capital all readers
inclined to accept its interpretation of the relationship between
employer and employee" (II, 420). Lasting until 1879, it was
responsible—if a single journal can be considered so influential—
with establishing Labor as a power which would gain importance
in American life.

In 1865 the first major children's magazine appeared in the
city; and although it did not last very long, it was destined to
establish not only a pattern for juvenile journals but also a cult
of "little corporals." In 1865 the Reverend Alfred Sewell founded

the *Little Corporal* whose motto was "Fighting Against Wrong, and for the Good and the True and the Beautiful." Through the children and through a series of highly moralistic tales Sewell preached the cause of the Union Army. He also devised a scheme which was to become even more popular in the twentieth century whereby children could be enlisted to perform certain tasks in order to become "little corporals." Undoubtedly, parents who could not get a child to follow home rules could threaten —with success—by suggesting that membership as a "little corporal" was in jeopardy. Although the magazine had a tremendous circulation, it had difficulty raising the necessary funds for all of its programs and counter-attacking its many imitators. The magazine ceased publication in 1875, a victim of its own success. By that time, however, it had accomplished many of its goals.

While these three journals were not the only ones founded in the city during the war years (See Appendix A), they give some indication of the diversity of interests exhibited by the magazines of the period. Yet, it was not unusual to find references in the support of the war effort by reminding people of the need to preserve the unity and integrity of the nation. Even *The Workingman's Advocate*, which strongly supported the rights of labor against the Establishment recognized that a fragmented nation was of no advantage to any group.

II

While the newspapers seemed to dominate the Civil War scene, the magazines enjoyed a degree of popularity—albeit limited circulation at times—as they frequently addressed themselves to the national crisis. At the same time there were other literary efforts made in response to the war. Much of it was in favor of the preservation of the Union and therefore supported a militant patriotism. George F. Root and Henry Clay Work became nationally known. Such songs as "Lay Me Down and Save the Flag," "Just Before the Battle, Mother," and "Tramp, Tramp, Tramp" were stirring calls by Root to continue the war and were sung wherever Union soldiers marched. Work's "The Battle Cry of Freedom" was equally as popular. According to Andreas who remembered those days well:

The Chicago war-songs, for sudden popular effect, were equal to those produced in any other part of the country, and those published by Messrs. Root & Cady did much toward keeping alive the enthusiasm which ultimately crushed the Rebellion. Many a soldier has been nerved to duty by the chorus of "Marching Through Georgia"; many a man has gone into battle, whose soul had just been cheered for the fray by the strains of the "Battle Cry of Freedom"; and when not shouting "Tramp, Tramp, Tramp, the Boys are Marching," many a soldier, thinking of home, has found the asperities of camp-life softened by George F. Root's song of the "Vacant Chair." The songs of a nation are sometimes more potent than battalions, and Chicago, by her martial songs, must have been worth to the Union cause many a veteran brigade (II, 484).

The Civil War also produced its share of literary curiosities in Chicago. One of them was written by Mrs. Delphine Baker, a well-known journalist. In 1862 S.P. Rounds, the book and job printer, offered for sale the thin volume entitled *Solon, or the Rebellion of '61* "by Delphine." The allegorical story has two main characters: Solon (the South) and Nora (the North). According to the tale, Solon and Nora have been married for a few years, but their fathers are having a serious disagreement. (In an explanatory list of characters "Delphine" explains that the father of Solon is Jefferson Davis, "leader of the Rebellion"; and Abraham Lincoln, "the leader of the Federal Army," is the father of Nora.) The story is told in terms of a broken marriage.

The extremely sentimental tale begins as the two discuss their problems. Solon is unyielding; and Nora equates slave-holding with drunkenness, both of which are mortal sins in her view. When Solon's father enters the action, he declares that it is all right for the young couple to separate although Solon has strong misgivings about the course of action because he recognizes the sanctity of the vows of marriage will be abridged. Much of this, however, is contingent upon whether or not Nora's father becomes the head of government. When Lincoln—who is presented as a gracious and noble man—is inaugurated, the fate of Nora and Solon is sealed. Nora and her father are extremely sad, but Mrs. Baker decrees that Heaven is with them; whereas, Solon and his people are traitors who are destined for failure. Eventually the battle between the two forces begins. Solon predicts that it will be bloody and "the most fearful contest the world has ever known" (p. 48). Although he is committed to his cause, he misses Nora and realizes that her force has been felt throughout the world. Solon's father chastises him for showing signs of weakness.

Compressed in a few paragraphs are the battles which have been fought and the major Confederate leaders who have fallen during the initial phases of the war. As Mrs. Baker projects the continued war, Nora maintains that they will eventually succeed because "the God of battle is our God" (p. 53). Then Nora notes that her side must win "or we shall be blotted out of the great book of nations . . ." (p. 54). At this point the author projects all of the hopes of those who longed to keep the nation together and predicts the North will win. When this does occur, the characters on Nora's side feel certain that not only has God saved the Union but also "we have subdued the Cotton King in his glory" (p. 55). Nora's father is willing to forgive in order to re-unite Solon and his daughter, but he has difficulty trying to decide what to do with the "rebel traitors." But they must be severely punished. At the end of the tale, in a brief chapter entitled "The Vision," Solon and Nora dream of the future as they try to put the past behind them, feeling certain that the "Almighty Architect" will help them restructure their broken world. The tale ends with the author making the following observation:

Thus, dear reader, we will leave them, hoping that no domestic storm may ever again darken their horizon, or o'ercloud their happiness. Praying, too, that King Cotton will never more enkindle in the home circle the fire of Disunion, or seek to break those bonds which God has joined together, commanding: 'Let no man put asunder' (p. 74).

In spite of the obvious didacticism of the tale and the wooden, unbelievable characters, the author captured the sense of sadness and alienation which swept the country at the beginning of the Civil War. The vehemence with which both Solon and Nora supported their positions eventually gave way to a spirit of compromise which was a portent of the healing which was to come. How comforting Mrs. Baker's story was to a North facing the crises of 1862 is not known, but her prediction of ultimate victory must have been satisfying.

Although the collected edition of H.C. Ballard's poems appeared in 1870, many of his verses are dated from the late 1850's and the 1860's. In addition to the inevitable poems of nature (staple fare among the Chicago poets of the period), there are a number of works which present a romanticized version of brotherhood and deal with various aspects of the Civil War. In "Richmond— April 3, 1865" he expressed great joy at the fall of that city. The poem begins:

> What joyous tumult none may drown
> Is heard in every Northern town!
> What clamor rises, wild and free,
> And fills the land from sea to sea!
> What countless banners fleck the sky,
> All hearts are glad, all hopes are high,
> For Union men march up and down
> The haughty streets of Richmond town!

Each subsequent stanza ends with a reference to the southern city with "the haughty streets." At one point the poet counsels:

> First drag the rebel ensign down,
> And plant our flag in Richmond town!

The wild acclaim continues as

> The rebel flag comes sweeping down,
> And Union blue fills Richmond town . . .

And he concludes the last stanza with the observation:

> And Union songs ring up and down
> The busy marts of Richmond town.

While a patriotic verse flourished in the city, there was serious concern about the so-called "Chicago conspiracy." Whether it was real or imagined is difficult to discern now, but there were those who were absolutely convinced that there was a plot to take over Chicago. It was believed that the Confederate forces would be joined by the prisoners at Camp Douglas as well as the southern sympathizers within the city. There was a reason for real fear because the plot could have been executed with little or no difficulty given the general conditions of the city at the time. This fear resulted in producing some exposures of the scheme. The anonymous report from the 1864 Democratic National Convention, which was held in Chicago, was designed to stir the citizens out of their complacency. The work carried the following title: *Spirit of the Chicago convention. Extracts from all the Notable Speeches Delivered in and out of the National "Democratic" Convention. A Surrender to the Rebels Advocated—A Disgraceful and Pusillanimous Peace Demanded—The Federal Government Savagely Denounced and Shamefully Villified, and Not a Word said Against the Crime of Treason and Rebellion.* It did a great deal to alert the city to the possibilities of violent dissent and may have been one of the deterrents against the planned raid. The author of the document was apparently trying to counteract any influence Wilbur Storey's *Times* may have had as well as attempting to stem the growth of the Democratic party in the city. During the same year John Walsh, sometime publisher and bookseller, issued two more works which indicate some of the concerns of 1864. One work, entitled *The Copperhead's Prayer*, carried the following subtitle: "Containing remarkable confessions; by a degenerate Yankee. (This singular document was found in the 'Democratic Wigwam,' after the adjournment of the national convention. It is supposed to have been accidently [sic] dropped by a delagate [sic] from some one of the New England states. It was doubtless unintended for publication and is therefore presented without comment." The second work was written by I. Winslow Ayer, M.D. and was *The Great Northwestern Conspiracy*. The reader was promised to get "all its startling details" which included "the plot to plunder and burn Chicago, release all rebel prisoners, seizure of arsenals, raids from Canada, plot to burn New York, piracy on the lakes, parts for the Sons of Liberty, trial of Chicago conspirators, inside views of the temples of the Sons of Liberty," along with "names of prominent members." The title page also noted, in the third edition of 1865, that it was illustrated "with portraits of leading characters," and "that it was for sale by all booksellers and periodical dealers in every city and town in the Union."

Opinion was divided on such matters as Emancipation and on the growing number of refugees—black and white—who were flooding into the city. The franchise had not been extended to all in Chicago, and the city in its attitude toward Negroes differed little from major southern cities. There were certain opportunities in Chicago which were not open to those Negroes who were still in the South, but many civil rights were seriously curtailed by the Black Laws which were still in operation in Illinois. One of the least-known documents of freedom was written by a Chicago businessman. Entitled *The Black Laws of Illinois and a Few Reasons Why They Should Be Repealed*, it was written by John Jones and published by the *Tribune* Book and Job Office—a subsidiary of the *Tribune*—in 1864. Jones had come to Chicago in 1845, practically a penniless tailor. Having been born free in the South, he had traveled to Alton, Illinois, and then on to Chicago looking for that freedom which he had been told existed in the North. What he did find in Chicago was the opportunity to develop his own business. And by 1864 he was not only wealthy but also a highly respected member of the community. His pamphlet has the ring of the "Declaration of Independence" as he notes:

Now it may be said by our enemies, that we are not citizens, and therefore have no rights . . . . If being natives, and born on the soil, of parents belonging to no other nation or tribe, does not constitute a citizen in this country, under the theory and genius of our government, I am at a loss to know in what manner citizenship is acquired by birth. Fellow Citizens, I declare unto you, view it as you may, we are American citizens; by the principles of the Declaration of Independence, we are American citizens; within the meaning of the United States Constitution, we are American citizens; by the facts of history, and the admissions of American statesmen, we are American citizens; by the hardships and trials endured; by the courage and fidelity displayed by our ancestors in defending the liberties and in achieving the independence of our land, we are American citizens . . .

Seldom is a single work successful in achieving a desired goal; but the Black Laws were repealed, and John Jones was given the credit.

If one discounts William J. Anderson, John Jones would be the first Negro writer of any note in the city, and his reputation rests upon a single work. Anderson's work, in the meantime, had appeared in 1857 and was also from the *Tribune* Book and Job Office, a firm which issued a number of works dealing with racial matters. Using the nationally popular form of the slave narrative, Anderson's title indicates the amount of material which he covered in a work of less than one hundred pages: *Life and Narrative of William J. Anderson, twenty-four years a slave; sold eight times! in jail sixty times!! whipped three hundred times!!! or the Dark Deeds of American Slavery Revealed. Containing Scriptural Views of the Origin of the Black and White Man. Also, a simple and easy plan to abolish slavery in the United States, together with an account of the services of colored men in the Revolutionary War, day and date, and interesting facts.* As was frequently the case with the genre of the slave narrative, the title page assures the reader that the work was "written by himself." In view of the extensive publication of these narratives up to the 1860's and considering the number of publishers in Chicago, it is interesting to note that this is probably the only slave narrative issued in the city.

The spirit of patriotism had reached a fever pitch by 1864 and the early years of 1865. Emotionalism ruled on both sides, and it was—perhaps—the assassination of Lincoln which sobered people throughout the nation. Lincoln's death resulted in an untold number of literary efforts; however, nothing produced in Chicago reached the majesty of Whitman's work. In 1866 the poet George P. Carr issued his highly patriotic *The Contest* in four cantos. It is extremely antagonistic toward the South which he said was "full of treason." His inflammatory approach was cooled to some degree by his excessive use of classical poetic devices. The martyred President was the object of his admiration:

> I sing the man, who, in this latter time,
> Rivalled the virtues of an earlier age:
>   Abraham Lincoln, and his deeds sublime,
>   Shall stand emblazoned upon history's page,
>   With earth's most mighty heroes.

Most of the poems about Lincoln which were produced in Chicago tended to be extremely maudlin. Undoubtedly he gained more in death than he would have in life. Among the prose works, the most ambitious one was produced by Isaac Arnold, the lawyer-politician who served the city well as a member of the U.S. House of Representatives, whose *The History of Abraham Lincoln and the Overthrow of Slavery* (1866) was one of the first extensive studies of the role of Lincoln. Arnold, who believed that the course of history was often the result of the actions of specific men at specific times, did much toward creating the larger-than-life image of Lincoln which has become part of the folklore of American culture. The period between the close of the Civil War and the Fire of 1871 saw the beginning of the Lincoln legend in Chicago writing. For many "the man from Springfield" became the symbol of the frontier qualities of the Midwest. His humor, his low-keyed speeches, his paternalism were some of the qualities which writers found appealing as they tried to establish the relationship between Chicago and Lincoln. The fact that he had spent little time in the city made little difference as the legend grew rapidly. The postbellum days in northern citics were full of activity, and Chicago prospered in this boom period. Literary evidence of this growth is most obviously seen in the proliferation once again of newspapers and magazines. Whereas the early 1860's had witnessed the development of the polemical and religious journals, those from the mid-years of the 1860's quite frankly devoted themselves to "literature." Some of the magazines were destined to achieve a degree of fame; but many were never seen again after the Fire of 1871. There was also the beginning version of a literature of social protest.

In 1866 J.E. Chamberlain's novel appeared anonymously and is one of the longest works of fiction to come out of this era. Entitled *Cotton Stealing*, it carries on its title page the admonition: "Who riches gains by wrong, is but a thief." The preface makes clear that the incidents are true, but names and places have been changed "to prevent identification." Yet the author wisely notes some important aspects of fiction.

'Truth is stranger than fiction.' Although every incident set forward is believed to be true, still, as fiction, the work must either stand or fall. . . . Although founded on fact, and built of materials furnished by actual experience of the cotton trade, the novel is witness rather than judge—written by no believer in the doctrine of human perfection, nor the possible power of any individual to remodel the age, nor the probability of a single work reaching the moral heart of the nation.

He continues by identifying his purpose:

> [The novel] has been written by a Western man as a contemporaneous novel, to stand the test of to-day—by a Western man whose whole nature revolts against the attempts to deify the participants of war, by magnifying virtues and extenuating faults, in some cases ignoring them entirely. There is one tribunal among a free people which no wrong-doer can escape—enlightened public opinion. At its bar let friends and neighbors try every officer or soldier who comes home rich beyond his monthly pay. Wealth greater than this must be explained to the home tribunal, which alone can inflict the punishment of public condemnation. Will they do it? Keeping this in mind whenever the "I" appears, and any shall ask—Who is this "I"? this is the answer: I am a Western man with a story to tell. Will any one read—will any one hear it? (pp. iii-iv)

What follows is an unusually realistic story about the intrigue which centered around cotton speculation. True to his prefatory word, Chamberlain does not praise nor condemn unilaterally. His characters are true-to-life and the episodes selected are presented stripped of any emotional overtones; however, his reliance upon "enlightened public opinion" colors his view of life, and as the novel ends, the character who serves throughout most of the novel as the author's spokesman says:

> . . . You will fail because God has ordained your failure. Free institutions and a free people will rule not only in this land, but in the world. I grant you that an ignorant, unenlightened, unchristian people are subjects of an aristocratic government; but knowledge, education, and christian principles. are capable of self-government. And the time is coming when the world shall be educated, for God has promised that all men shall know Him from the least to the greatest, and the world shall be full of His knowledge and His glory. What that means absolutely, I cannot tell; but it does mean that white men

and black men shall be honest men, pure men, good men, doing as they would others shall do to them: that there shall be universal equality, a universal ballot, equal rights of personal liberty, personal security, and personal property: that free men shall bind themselves to no party, nor to any set of party principles, but the truth; so that the only question before the world shall be, What is truth?—Now, I do not expect this in one day, nor will the great result be obtained without contest, defeat and victory. You throw yourself on one side, and will in the end fail; because your cause is the cause of despotism, ignorance, and evil. I put myself on the other, and shall succeed, because mine is the cause of education, of progress, of liberty, of universal, human brotherhood, and it is the cause of God! (pp. 486-87)

Chamberlain understood well the type of graft which was rampant during the Civil War. He recognized that great fortunes were made by capitalizing on the misery of others; yet, he fully believed that the day would come when universal brotherhood would be buttressed by universal education. The optimism of the closing scene of *Cotton Stealing* is matched by the pessimism of the satirical *Age of Humbug* (1869), which also appeared anonymously. The brief work recognized the use of devious means frequently employed in various types of investment schemes. This particular work addresses itself to telegraph stocks and claims that there is little anyone can do about "humbug." In fact, the author ironically begins the work with "Vive L'Humbug" and asserts that "humbug and success go very often hand in hand . . . (p. 3). Brief though it is, the *Age of Humbug* represents the type of work which many have come to associate with the post-war period.

Chicago writers customarily viewed all of the problems of the period, but with Shane's long, didactic poem, *Social Evils: Their Cause and Cure: A Poem for the Times* (1868), there was the attempt to treat the problems together. Alcoholism, slavery, prostitution—for example—were thought to be the result of the same causes. The poet maintained that Christians had a responsibility not only to help the poor and destitute but also to rid each community of anything which contributed to the poverty of the spirit. He blamed newspapers for the perpetuation of many of society's ills claiming that in their desire to "publish verbatim crimes," they were operating "for the sake of filthy gain" (p. 42). He continued by calling upon Christians to spurn such "sickly journals" and upon the wealthy to assume gainful roles in the eradication of economic problems. He supported the theory that the safety of the city was in jeopardy until men and women assumed a greater sense of civic responsibility. While he has little trouble identifying the "social evils" of his period, and is remarkably frank in many instances, his panaceas resorted to stock solutions for multi-faceted problems.

While some Chicagoans may have found solace in Edgar L. Wakeman's *Winter-Freed: A Summer Idyl* (1866) or in the posthumously published metaphysical poems of Alfred W. Arrington, others were still reliving the past conflict. William Sumner Dodge provided a series of personalized accounts of soldiers and regiments. *A Waif of the War; or The History of the Seventy-Fifth Illinois Infantry, Embracing the Entire Campaign of the Army of the Cumberland* (1866) and *Roger Henry Hendershot; or, The Brave Drummer Boy of the Rappahannock* (1867) were both issued in Chicago by the firm of Church and Goodman. They combined the narratives with enough historic information to be considered "factual"; yet, they included the sensational adventure which has become so much a part of war fiction. Returning soldiers found a ready audience for their "stories," and for a number of years the various Sunday supplements used these as staple fare.

The 1860's saw the publication of a group of plays by William Bush, a local phenomenon who is justly unknown. Whether his plays were performed seems to be lost to history. If these records were among those lost in the Fire of 1871, it is probably just as well. He was a prolific writer who in 1869, for example, seems to have had at least five of his works published. Both *Prometheus; or Mephistopheles Gets His Fill*, "an original ethical dramatic extravaganza, in five acts" and *Claudius the Fickle, or Fickleness,*

Thy Name is Man—Not Woman . . . were issued by G.S. Utter and Co. The others were privately printed. There seems to be no record of either sales nor reception, but he "ground out" these works which can be called "dramas" primarily because that is the way he identified them. While the existing theaters tended to rely upon the standard playwrights performed by visiting companies, there were some skits and performances put on by local talent. It was not, however, until the Little Theater Movement that there was a viable dramatic literature being introduced into the city, and it was primarily derivative.

While much of the work of the 1860's either dealt with the issues of concern to the nation or to a body of work which was not identifiable according to time or place, there did emerge during the decade a particular type of "Chicago book" which defies definition. While not categorized as fiction, it did—and still does—frequently embroider the facts in order to make the subject more enticing. Guidebooks became unique literary products in Chicago. They were designed to display proudly the accomplishments of the young city and to point out those sites which had to be seen by both visitors and natives alike. These were often produced by the so-called boosters whose love of the city was evident, often hiding their inability to see the city as it actually existed. From the standpoint of reconstructing the pre-fire city, many of these guide books play an important role. Yet, from the inception of the city, the guide book was a significant type. Beginning as a product of real estate developers and designed to point out the most desirable parcels of land, they evolved into laudatory reports of the young city.

If "pride goeth before a fall" is a truism of human existence, Chicagoans had every right to be concerned at the end of the 1860's because the "instant historians" of the city had concluded that the city was "the best" and "the most beautiful" in the nation. There was nothing that Chicago could not do, and they used the city's phenomenal growth as evidence. Such books as *A Strangers' and Tourists' Guide to the City of Chicago* (1866), *A Guide to the*

City of Chicago: Its Public Buildings, Places of Amusement, Commercial, Benevolent, and Religious Institutions; Churches, Hotels, Railroads, Etc., Etc., With a Map of the City, and Numerous Illustrations of the Principal Buildings (1868), Rufus Blanchard's *Citizen's Guide for the City of Chicago* . . . (1868), and *Chicago: A Handbook for Strangers and Tourists* . . . *Containing Historical Retrospect; an Account of the Rise and Progress of the City; Descriptions of the Public Buildings, Churches, Institutions, and Objects of Interest* . . . *A Book Indispensable to Strangers and Visitors* (1869) achieved a great deal of popularity, each one trying to include information which could not be found elsewhere. For that reason, the titles tended to be descriptive presentations of the contents. There was even issued in 1869 *Chicago After Dark; A "Flea in the Ear" of Strangers Visiting Chicago, and A Word of Advice to Persons Going Out After Dark*, a type of guide book which modern readers still find fascinating. Designed to show the seamier side of urban life, these "after dark" guide books titillate the reader with promises—many of which are undelivered. As a literary type, the guide books tend to cover essentially the same material and found favor not only with visitors but also with Chicagoans who were ever eager to read about their city. Probably the form came closest to being "literature" in the following decade when Everett Chamberlin issued his *Chicago and Its Suburbs* (1874) which is still considered to be a classic. But it was the period of the World's Columbian Exposition which produced the greatest number of these boastful guides to the city.

As the decade of the 1860's came to a close, the writers—with the exception of those employed by major newspapers—did not form a cohesive group, and even the journalists did not always recognize their similarities. Yet, there was a spirit of optimism which pervaded so much of the work of the period. The writers had unwittingly—in spite of their great diversity—adopted the viewpoint that a perfect society could be formed on earth, a spirit which they would need more than ever after the Fire of 1871. And for those wedded to a sense of regionalism, what better place than

Chicago could the nation offer, they seemed to ask. The fortunes which were made during the Civil War era were just a portent of what could be. Thus even the so-called literature of social protest ended lamely with visions of an earthly paradise. In another place and at another time this might have produced an outstanding utopian literature; instead, it merely produced a group of second-rate didactic works, ridden with maudlin sentimentality which somehow failed—in most instances—to come to terms with the reality of the city. Essentially the most creative writing of the era —with few exceptions—was produced by the newspapers; and because they were so torn by partisan loyalties, they often failed to rise to the task that the Chicago boosters had set before them.

III

On September 10, 1871, less than a month before the Great Fire, a *Tribune* editorial castigated the level of building and construction in the city. In a fashion—reminiscent of the Chicago booster—the *Tribune* called for a return to the spirit which had made Chicago great. The editorial analyzed quite clearly some of the concerns which were common in the pre-Fire days.

Chicago, as we are all persuaded in our secret hearts and as we sometimes venture to hint in our more confidential moods, has something to be proud of. So conscious are we of our merits, and so confident of our superiority over all other places, both in the Old World and the New, that we can estimate at their true value the carping criticism and envious jibes of peripatetic letter-writers, who profess to find in us something of the spirit of self-glorification and something of that overweening sense of our own excellence, which assumed that we have nothing to learn from the experience and the ways of older communities. It is well enough for them whose growth has been slow, and whose development gradual to talk of *ars longa*; it is only for us to remember the other half of the rusty old adage, that life is short, and to do what we do quickly, persuaded that, if only a thing is done at all, it is necessarily done well because we do it. If our buildings sometimes tumble down over our heads, because we run up walls, a hundred feet or more in height, of a single brick's thickness; if our magnificent cornices sometimes come rattling down into the street in a high wind, because their seemingly beautiful stone carvings are only ingeniously molded and skillfully painted sheet-iron; if our stately Gothic church-towers sometimes topple over, or depart from the perpendicular, because they are tin only, and not the massive stone they are meant to represent; if our marble fronts are sometimes only thin veneers, so chamfered as to cheat the eye into believing that they rest upon solid blocks; if on these fronts we stick figure heads of stucco, or soft stone, in places where, neither in the heavens above nor in the earth beneath, there can be found any reason for putting them at all, or any reason whatever even for the existence of such effigies; if we mix up Ionic and Corinthian, Renaissance and Elizabethan, in inextricable confusion, their lines of beauty and strength preserved in everlasting pine and shingle-nail and putty—in doing these and a hundred other things like them quite as shocking, when judged by a true standard in art or science, we hug ourselves with a comfortable feeling of self-complaisance, and rejoice, and possibly boast, that if we have not got the real thing itself—if we are sure we know what that is—we have got, at least, the semblance of it. And the worst of it is, we are growing content with that semblance. The dispensation of veneering, of sheet-iron, of pine planks, of stucco, of the meretricious in architecture and the false in art, seems of late to be becoming the established order, and if so be that we can achieve the outside appearance of some respectable reality, we are quite indifferent to the fact that the thing itself is only a sham and a cheat, a snare and a lie. Whether it is that sudden prosperity has debauched us, this is not the spirit that distinguished the Chicago of a few years ago. But where is that spirit now? Has it all run to sham and shingles?

Then that October night arrived in 1871 when the city which had shocked the nation with its phenomenal growth, the city whose writers were consumed by the spirit of commercial expansion, the city which the *Tribune* had cautioned a month earlier about its "sham" buildings with "tacked on" ornament, was destroyed by fire and reduced to ashes. While catastrophes have become such common occurrences in the twentieth century that the modern mind has become almost immune to them, the Fire of 1871 still seemed such a harsh judgment on a city which had been growing at such an unbelievable speed. The days after the fire inspired the legend of the invincibility of the city which could be destroyed materially but not spiritually. The last ember had barely died when those who intended to rebuild began to talk about the kind of city they wanted. It was generally believed that a dream city was possible, and the pattern was to be Boston or some other eastern city. Out of this emerged the great conflict between two great traditions, one devoted to the spirit of gentility with which they thought the East was imbued, and the other the raw, frontier spirit of the West. It was this conflict which ultimately was to condition the literature of the city for almost thirty years.

Before, however, this took place, there were some immediate literary results of the fire. Probably no event in Chicago's history has equalled the Fire in producing so many "instant writers." Generally, these works recount the terror of the nights when the fire raged, show a regard for the need to record actualities for later historians, and have a sense of immediacy because these stories were told by those who were there. Because the authors tended to tell their own stories, the fire narratives became in essence a form of the personal narrative. Most of these works are extremely optimistic and maintain Chicago will rise again.

Of the many fire narratives which have survived, some are negative. Because modern readers are so attuned to think only of the heroic in times of crises and disasters, the narratives of the terror of the night display fascinating elements. There are existing records, many of which were quite well done, which tell the tales of men and women who were less than heroic. Many of these works have escaped the attention of history. Andreas recreated some of the horrors of the events and scenes from Chicago's North Side:

. . . The sweep of the flames across the region east of Clark Street drove the people living in that section to the lake; but they soon found

that they were between two deaths—the burning city on the one side
and the lake upon the other. The intense heat from the west forced
the sufferers into the water, where many perished; others, stronger
and more self-possessed, bowed their heads close to the watery surface, thus escaping the gusts of gas and smoke that rushed past them.
These hot tempests of poisonous vapor rendered life almost unen-
durable; but no avenues of escape existed, and nothing was left for
the victims but to patiently endure, or die.

Vividly as many writers have described the scenes upon this stretch
of sandy purgatory, they paused abashed and heart-sick at the awful
task before the worst was told. Nor will the pen of man ever dare to
lay before a reader's eyes the truth in literal nakedness. No publisher
would be permitted to preserve in types—no man of moral consciousness would place before his family—the volume that told what
there transpired. The tragedies upon the Sands differed from those
whose broader limits marked the encampment of the victims of the
fire. The prairie seemed to give relief to pent-up agonies, and nerve
the soul to silent endurance; even the park and grave-yard, bleak and
somber as they were, seemed to impart an atmosphere of personal
security that was not possible upon the Sands. There, on the scorching
earth, that held the heat and sent a shimmering, ceaseless wave of
blasting air and sand from underneath the feet, parching the flesh
and drying up the fountains of blood and life, the spirit of infernal
revelry prevailed. As in the region of the damned, told of by Dante,
the evil nature of mankind glared forth to vex the tender souls of
those whom fate had sent into their presence.

Imagine the scene of the horrible drama. No possibility of escape—
a raging fury at the rear, a pitiless expanse of lake in front—a small
area filled with human creatures, maddened animals, delicate and refined women, pure and innocent children; the aged, the infirm, the
weak, the dying, the despairing young girls, whose artless lives were
unfamiliar with even the name of crime; men of well-ordered lives
and Christian minds; brutes in human form, who were not only ready
to do acts of crime, but whose polluting wickedness was rank and
cast off prison-fumes upon the air. All kinds and conditions and
grades of life—all forms of death, from calm and peaceful passing
to a welcome rest to that which follows in the train of vicious deeds.
Here, huddled close and helpless, the purest girlhood was forced to

endure the leering of the vile; and, if a chance protector spoke in her defense, the wicked laughed and jeered and cursed, until the stoutest heart grew faint with apprehension. Women, whose claim to woman-hood was long since lost, took fiendish delight in adding undefinable shame and terror to the misery of those who shrank from crime. Think what it would be to place a loved one in the lowest haunts of vice, and there bend over the death-bed of that failing friend, while all about the din of wickedness was sounding in the ear. Increase the circumstance of grim necessity, and add the consciousness that home, treasures, everything was gone, and this the only, the enforced sport, where death must meet the loved father, mother, sister, friend. Could all the powers of hell itself devise a keener form of anguish? Yet, these lines are drawn from actual knowledge; and the shudder awakened at the recollection of sights stays the pen, for what was seen can never be spoken to public ears. The creatures who there tortured the helpless were no longer human—vice had dulled their moral instincts, and despair had transformed them, for the moment, into demons. Their orgies were born in malice, they delighted in their sins; they shrieked aloud with glee to see the innocent rush from them, and plunge into the lake, that, for the instant, the sight might be shut out. The dying were not always comforted with the caress of love. Upon a burned and blackened blanket lay the dead body of one poor woman, whose babe lay by her side, crying in shrill alarm. The crowd about this type of life and death gave no more heed than if it was the natural order of events. All night the corpse lay there untouched. If fate preserved the babe, the writer does not know of the fact. Above the terror of the fire—for that emotion grew pangless as the hours progress; above the loss of worldly riches; above the grief of death—for death seemed then the only mercy-bringing power; above all the conditions of the scene that added elements of horror,—the mingling of the two extremes of vice and virtue, and the momentary triumph of the bad, in their malicious show of wickedness, seemed the most appalling quality of this immediate spot (II,754-755).

Andreas concludes his recitation of the horrors of the night by predicting:

> In thousands of homes today are felt the consequential effects of those fateful hours. Shattered nerves, premature age, disordered minds,

still cast a baleful influence over our lives that, up to then, were vigorous, healthful and sound. If no one can portray the scenes for fear of shocking public taste, at this remote time, what may not the student of heredity find, as food for thought, in this grave subject? The results of the fire upon the minds of those who suffered and still lived can never be fully written (II,755-756).

While the eye-witness accounts published in Andreas' monumental study of Chicago are graphic and extensive, these were not the first records of the Fire. The first book on the fire was issued in November of 1871. Entitled *Chicago and the Great Conflagration* by Elias Colbert and Everett Chamberlain, the first part of the book is a detailed history of the city from an analysis of its geography and the fur traders up to 1871; the second part addresses itself specifically to matters of the fire. In retrospect, it is not only the first but also the most complete book on the Fire of 1871. In an interesting appendix Colbert and Chamberlain include editorials and articles from newspapers from around the world on the significance and the meaning of the fire. Almost without exception, the articles state "Chicago will rise again." But there were other views of the calamity. Needless to say, there were some clergymen who used the fire as an example that God's retribution was still operative. Chicago had been a sinful city; hence, it was made to suffer. This type of argument was to be expected, but in the Rushville (Indiana) *American* there appeared the following article which Colbert and Chamberlin included in their book:

Why She Was Burned—A Rebel View

Near one-half the city has been laid in ashes, and a hundred and fifty thousand people rendered homeless.

The announcement, at first, seemed incredible. When the telegraph confirmed the facts, a thrill of horror and sympathy pervaded the universal heart. This fact presents a palliative for many of the outrages and cruelties of the past ten years, and shows that human nature has, after all, some redeeming traits. It was far different when Sherman's army desolated and destroyed the fairest region of the South, robbing and plundering, and burning as they went, leaving the people to starve; or, when Sheridan, a monster of cruelty, overran and destroyed the valley of Virginia, afterward boasting that a crow would have to carry its provisions under its wings, if it should attempt to fly over it; and thus he brought starvation on old men, women, and children of that region, so that thousands perished of famine. More property and more lives were destroyed in these raids than all Chicago put together, and what was the sentiment of the North? One of exultation and rejoicing. These acts of vandalism were paraded as victories, and the heroes were met on their return with ovations of men and oblations of kisses from many of the gentle damsels of the North, carried away by the military glory that settled around the heads of these vandal chiefs, that was degrading, sickening, disgusting! What cared these women for the homeless, houseless, starving mothers and children of the South? Nothing, They exulted in their sufferings; laughed at the story of the ravishment of the daughters of the South, the burning and robberies of their dwellings, and slaughter of her strong men; shouted hosannahs and threw from the tips of their fingers kisses to the perpetrators of these acts of vandalism.

That was then! Now, that which is not half so horrible, thrills their bosom with sympathy, and their hand is quick and liberal to the relief of the sufferers. These things prove that man is a good deal lower than the angels, and sometimes, at least, a little higher than the devils. Chicago has lost, perhaps, three hundred million dollars by the fire. The property destroyed in the South is estimated at over one thousand millions. The fire in Chicago was the result of accident. The destruction of property in the South was done purposely, by Northern soldiers, and compares exactly with the acts of the Goths and Vandals, savages that overran and subjugated the Roman Empire. But we are living under a higher civilization. Chicago did her full share in the destruction of the South. God adjusts the balance. Maybe with Chicago the books are now squared.

Perhaps the clearest answer to those critics of Chicago who saw the Fire as some kind of judgment designed to punish the city for its sins was delivered by the Reverend Robert Collyer on the Sunday

after the disaster. Standing among the ruins of his Unity Church as
he preached to a crowd, he said:

I have heard not a little speculation about the moral significance of
our great calamity, and men who meant better have unwittingly
accused God of a great wickedness, when they have intimated that it
was a judgment of Heaven because of the ungodliness of our city.
First of all, judgments of Heaven are not retrospective, but always
prospective; that is, they are never of the backward glance, but always
of the forward . . . God's way is otherwise. He disciplines without
destroying, and builds up without pulling down. No such punishment
could possibly do any good if it were only received as a wilful infliction
of the rod of Heaven. Second. Then there was no reason why Chicago
should have been made an example for the rest of the world. Of
course, we were a people of great worldliness and selfishness, of great
boasting and parade; but certainly no city in the Christian world has
ever done more, according to its means, for schools, churches, and
charities . . . Third. We have been strikingly short sighted in the
boundaries of our fire limits, in permitting so many, or any, wooden
buildings within the limits of the city, and today the fire limits should
be the city limits. We have given full sway to drinking, gambling, and
licentious houses, and have, by our moral laxity, invited to the city,
and harbored in it, a criminal population almost equal to that of
London, which is the worst on the face of the earth. We have done less
to reform this very population, when in our power, than almost any
other city. . . . We have drifted, too, into the hands of a set of tricky
politicians, . . . and the only recognized aristocracy of the city is a
set of ignorant and recently enriched social swells and snobs.

. . . What is lost? First. Our homes. Thousands of families are
homeless and penniless. Second. Our business. This is temporary.
Third. Our money. This is a great misfortune, but one which we can
repair. We have not lost. First. Our geography. Nature called the
lakes, the forest, the prairies together in convention long before we
were born, and they decided that on this spot a great city should be
built—the railroads and the energetic men have aided to fulfill the
prophecy. Second. We have not lost our men—noble, generous, and
of genius. Third. We have not lost our hope. The city is to be at once

rebuilt, and 'the glory of the latter house shall be greater than that of the former' (quoted by Andreas, III,57).

In addition to the histories, narratives, editorials, and sermons written about the fire, the disaster also inspired the production of poetry and fiction. Fire poetry actually came from all over the country. Chicago poets did not deal with the subject until some years after the event, but the notable John Greenleaf Whittier was inspired almost immediately after the event to write:

> Men said at vespers: All is well!
> In one wild night the city fell;
> Fell shrines of prayer and marts of grain
> Before the fiery hurricane.

> On threescore spires had sunset shone,
> Where ghastly sunrise looked on none;
> Men clasped each other's hands and said:
> The City of the West is dead!

> Brave hearts who fought, in slow retreat,
> The fiends of fire from street to street,
> Turned, powerless, to the blinding glare,
> The dumb defiance of despair.

> A sudden impulse thrilled each wire
> That signalled round that sea of fire;
> Swift words of cheer, warm heart-throbs came;
> In tears of pity died the flame!

> From East, from West, from South, from North,
> The messages of hope shot forth,
> And, underneath the severing wave,
> The world, full-handed, reached to save.

> Fair seemed the old; but fairer still
> The new the dreary void shall fill,
> With dearer homes than those o'erthrown,
> For love shall lay each corner-stone.

Rise, stricken city!—from thee throw
The ashen sackcloth of thy woe;
And build, as Thebes to Amphion's strain,
To songs of cheer thy walls again!

How shrivelled, in thy hot distress,
The primal sin of selfishness!
How instant rose, to take thy part,
The angel in the human heart!

Ah! not in vain the flames that tossed
Above thy dreadful holocaust;
The Christ again has preached through thee
The gospel of humanity!

Then lift once more thy towers on high,
And fret with spires the Western sky,
To tell that God is yet with us,
And love is still miraculous!

Like most occasional verse, Whittier's poem is not representative of the best of his own work. Neither is the poem by Bret Harte at all indicative of his better work. The poem, "Chicago: October 10, 1871," appeared in the Presbyterian weekly newspaper, *The Interior,* for November 9, 1871.

Blackened and bleeding, helpless, panting, prone,
On the charred fragments of her shattered throne
Lies she who stood but yesterday alone.

Queen of the West! by some enchanter taught
To life the glory of Aladdin's court,
Then lose the spell that all that wonder wrought.

Like her own prairies by some chance seed sown,
Like her own prairies in one brief day grown,
Like her own prairies in one fierce night mown,

She lifts her voice, and in her pleading call
We hear the cry of Macedon to Paul—
The cry for help that makes her kin to all.

> But haply with wan fingers may she feel
> The silver cup hid in the proffered meal—
> The gifts her kinship and our loves reveal.

Both poems, however, are typical of the spirit which prevailed after the catastrophe as they salute the invincibility of the city. As 1871 ended, the stories of the fire were increasing. The newspapers and the magazines which resumed publication kept their audiences informed of the "latest" fire stories. Although the eye-witness accounts can not be surpassed with their emphasis upon the "I-was-there" approach, stories of the Great Chicago Fire still evoke a certain sense of adventure in modern-day readers. What is perhaps most impressive about all of these accounts when one considers them as a collective body of literature is the general sense of optimism which pervades so many of them. The "I-Will" spirit was manifest everywhere. As Andreas so aptly notes about those days:

> . . . it was not the fact of necessity alone that aroused the ener-getic people of Chicago for their great task. They were inspired by a large hope for the future greatness of their city. In the midst of their present desolation and distress, they saw that in the larger view of things these calamities, however discouraging, were but passing inci-dents in its larger life; that the 'great fire' would soon become a thing of the past, whilst the rebuilt city must be the glory of the future. And as hope and courage revived, the new Chicago rose in beauty to the imagination while yet only the black and smoking ruins marked the site of the old. Led on by such visions, speculations and reasonings as to the possible future of such a city were heard on every hand (III,54).

And he continues prophetically in a vein which was so common among nineteenth-century Chicago historians:

> . . . the rebuilt Chicago will stand as a monument, not alone of the courage, the energy, the strength, the acquisiveness and world-wisdom

of the men and women who in three years accomplished that almost incredible task, but a monument also of their intelligence and morality and all the noble sentiments by which they were inspired in so great a work (III,56).

Thus before all of the fire debris had been cleared away and defying all of the outside prophets of doom, Chicago began a task which was destined to capture the imaginations of people all over the world. The events of 1871 gave Chicago an opportunity to create a new city on the ruins of the old.

ILLUSTRATION 6.—William Bross (1813–1890), often called the original "Chicago Booster," was extremely active in the world of journalism. He did much toward insisting that the business community was the foundation of the growing city. He served a term as the Lieutenant Governor of Illinois and became an outstanding historian.

ILLUSTRATION 7.—S.C. Griggs (1819–1897) was an early book-seller and publisher who did much toward making Chicago a nineteenth-century book center.

ILLUSTRATION 8.—Benjamin Franklin Taylor (1819–1887) was a popular editor who also became one of the first nationally recognized Chicago writers. Although he devoted much time to the writing of poetry, his prose pieces frequently appeared in eastern journals.

ILLUSTRATION 9.—S.C. Griggs and Co., Bookseller, occupied part of the ground floor of Burch's Building in 1866 when Lake Street was the bustling center for the city's business activity. The photograph is taken from a Jevne and Almini lithograph.

ILLUSTRATION 10.—The new Tribune Building of 1869, which was located at the corner of Dearborn and Madison Streets, was destroyed in the Fire of 1871.

ILLUSTRATION 11.—Horace White (1834–1916) edited the Chicago *Tribune* from 1864 to 1874. During that time he did much toward making it a prestigious journal. Although he was a firm supporter of Abraham Lincoln, his political commitment did not interfere with the strong beliefs that a newspaper should be a forum for good writers.

ILLUSTRATION 12.—Wilbur F. Storey (1819–1884) moved to Chicago in 1861 when he assumed a controlling interest in the Chicago *Times*. He became the editor and remained in that post until 1878. His methods were often questioned by his colleagues, his loyalty was debated during the Civil War, but no one could deny his commitment to the *Times*.

Courtesy of R.R. Donnelley & Sons Company, Chicago, Ill.

ILLUSTRATION 13.—Richard Robert Donnelley (1836–1899) arrived in Chicago in 1864. From the time of his association with the firm of Church and Goodman, Donnelley proved himself to be an excellent businessman and a perceptive book publisher. After the Fire of 1871 his faith and work led to the establishment of R.R. Donnelley, Steam Printer, and eventually to the firm which still bears his name.

ILLUSTRATION 14.—Church Goodman, and Donnelley (located at 108–110 Dearborn Street) was formed when Richard R. Donnelley became a partner in the firm of Church and Goodman. The three men had an active and successful business which became the forerunner of the Lakeside Publishing and Printing Company and eventually of R.R. Donnelley and Sons.

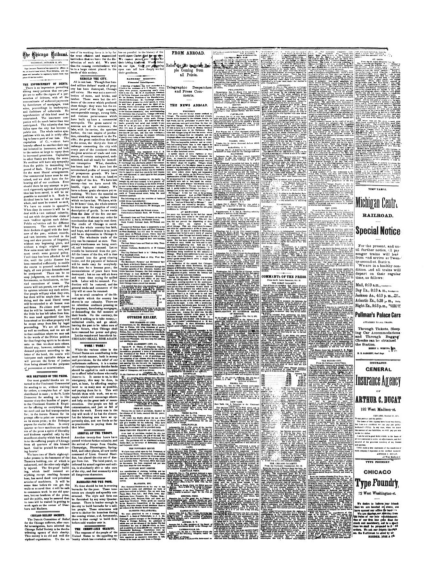

CHICAGO TRIBUNE PHOTOS

ILLUSTRATION 15.—On Thursday (October 12, 1871) the *Tribune*, which had resumed publication, issued the editorial "Rebuild the City." The concluding statement "CHICAGO SHALL RISE AGAIN" became the city's unofficial motto during the days of rebuilding.

Courtesy of R.R. Donnelley & Sons Company, Chicago, Ill.

ILLUSTRATION 16.—The ruins of the new building for the Lakeside Publishing and Printing Company which was under construction at Clark and Adams Streets at the time of the Fire of 1871.

ILLUSTRATION 17.—By June of 1873 the building of the Lakeside Publishing and Printing Company had been completed on the site of the ruins of the former unfinished structure.

CHAPTER 5

The Rise and Fall
of Publishing Houses
in the "New City"

PIONEER LIFE WAS accustomed to stories of disasters and heroic feats, and life on the midwestern frontier was noted for each even after Chicago had been founded. There had been panics in 1837 and 1857 which had rocked the newly-established city by wiping out many quickly-gained fortunes. Even fires were relatively familiar. Among all of the early fires, there had been the devastating ones of 1839 and 1857, both of which ironically also occurred in October. And the Civil War, which had meant financial gain for the meat packers and the grain operators, had left so many others broken. The city had been flooded with war refugees at a time when the city could not cope with them. Yet, in spite of the many problems, the city somehow managed to survive. But it was the fire of October 8-10, 1871, which totally destroyed one era of Chicago's life and provides the dividing line for much of the city's history. *Before the Fire/After the Fire* is an epochal division which everyone dealing with Chicago seems to understand. And seldom is the question raised: Which fire? It is always assumed the *Before* and *After* refer to the Fire of 1871 and not to the fires of 1839, 1857, or 1874. The destroyed city was replaced by another one which was as man-made as the one which had been leveled, and in some ways the differences between the two were practically imperceptible and so subtle that only the experienced could discern

197

one city from the other. Yet, everybody "knew" that the pre-fire Chicago could never exist again.

Hugh Duncan in his *The Rise of Chicago as a Literary Center* (Totowa, N.J., 1964) maintained that the development of the city as one of culture actually grew out of the catastrophic fire.

> The destruction of property has been described often enough, but when we consider that 'property' included books, manuscripts, libraries and a whole range of art products, we begin to understand what the fire meant to the cultural life of the city. The continuity of cultural traditions, as well as the material base established through nearly a half century of effort, was destroyed in the holocaust. The share of psychic energy not used in making a living was drawn on for the difficult task of rebuilding institutions which provide a necessary base for community life. Chicago needed all the help she could get. If she was to survive the competition of nearby cities, if she was to rise again out of her ashes, the spirit of the city which had put Lincoln in the presidency, and given so generously of its blood and treasure in the Civil War, must inspire its people to a new burst of energy (p. 1).

The "new burst of energy" was seen throughout the city. Although the giants of finance were able to recoup their fortunes within a few years, the wild gambling spirit of the frontier town was accompanied—and sometimes replaced—by a more determined desire to create an ordered society. The ante-fire Chicago had been marked by a great sense of self-reliance and individualism. A person, for example, could build on his property as he saw fit. There were few—if any—building codes which had to be observed. And perhaps because of the initial speed of much of the building, there was a temporary quality to much of the city, in spite of the glowing reports of the guide books of the 1860's. Rebuilding the city forced an adoption of building codes and suggested that there should be the attempt to rebuild "for all time."

It was especially common during 1872 for the city's journals to chart the progress of the rebuilding efforts. Perhaps no one journal combined hyperbolic writing with a concern for the city more than the *Landowner,* which had been started in 1869 by the publishing firm of J.M. Wing and Co. as a monthly and which—according to its purpose—was devoted "exclusively to the landed interests of the country." In January, J.M. Wing, the editor, published an illustration of the now-famous Kerfoot Real Estate "office," the first building to appear while the city was still smoldering. The picture was accompanied by an editorial comment:

> We give this as an illustration of the remarkable elasticity with which our citizens have rebounded from the great blow. It is the same indomitable and unconquerable spirit that built Chicago on the site of the swamp. It is able to rebuild it, and it will. There are no grumblers or fault finders here except in the one instance of disappointment and chagrin at the knavish doings of the insurance companies. Everybody, and especially our real estate men, wear a cheerful face, and have gone to work to rear again their fortunes, this time on a surer basis, profiting by the sad experience of the past.

In the following month's issue, Wing declared:

> What made Chicago? What caused this great city to leap, as it were, into existence, and in the short space of forty years to assume a prominent position among the marts of the world?
>
> The answer to this conundrum is that Chicago is the epitome—the concentrated type of the Great West. Illinois, Iowa, Minnesota, Nebraska—all the Northwestern States speak to the world through Chicago. The products of these great States, each capable of producing more food for man than all New England, with New York and Pennsylvania annexed, needed an outlet, and responsive to that need, Chicago, with its elevators, its stockyards, its packing houses, its countless shipping, stepped forth with 'Here am I.' The lands of the West are the magician whose work has astonished the world, and because these lands still exist, Chicago can never be destroyed, but must rise again.

Throughout the year Wing continued to praise the "spirit" of Chicago which would create a "new city" with "all deliberate speed." Truly he was describing a "new burst of energy." In October of 1872, Wing celebrated the first anniversary of the Fire by promising his readers that he would stop giving the monthly reports; however, he noted:

There has been but one parallel to the mighty creation recorded in Genesis, and that parallel is the rebuilding of Chicago in twelve months. That God made the world in six days, by the divine exercise of power, is no greater a marvel than that men have erected 3,000 brick and stone structures—a majority of them as costly and massive buildings as the world can boast—in three hundred working days . . .

After recounting some of the buildings which had been completed, the editor concluded his article, "The Marvels of the Year," by observing:

And now we enter upon the second year. The work has not stopped. Still 100,000 skillful workmen ply the hammer and trowel, and still the work of building goes on. Where and when will it stop?" When the old city is replaced? No, for that is almost done now. There are stores and offices and warehouses and hotels to build for ONE Million people. Not until then will the work slacken. Not until then will the demand be supplied.

This is just one example of the belief that the city would be greater than before. A desire for permanence supplanted the more narrow vision of the past. Instead of a group of special interests each going various ways in a mass display of self-reliance, there was an evolving spirit of community. The partisan separation between the North, West, and South Divisions did not disappear; but people began to think beyond their Divisions. There was a greater desire to maintain standards of taste, to produce not only a magnificent physical city but to create one of culture. This commitment had existed before, but then it was more local; now it encompassed the entire city.

Chicago, of course, had lived through a terrifying experience.

Wealthy and poor alike were brought together because the fire had had no respect for money, power, or social status. For at least a short period E.P. Roe's conclusion that the fire had burned all barriers away seemed to be correct. One of the manifestations of the determination to establish a city of *culture* with *standards of taste* (terms which meant different things to different people) can be seen in the rather elaborate club structure which developed during the post-fire period. There was, of course, an equally complicated club life prior to the fire, and many of them continued with their emphasis upon education for their members into the 1890's. Others were simply replaced by other organizations. As in the case of such groups similar to the Chicago Lyceum of the 1840's, there was a desire to provide intellectual and literary outlets for the elite who viewed themselves as the tastemakers for the city. Just as many of the societies formed in the 1830's and 1840's were designed—peripherally at least—to serve as "civilizing elements" in the wilderness so also did those clubs formed during the 1850's and 1860's.

Before-the-fire clubs tended to be centered around neighborhoods, churches, or business associations, with some using places of origin as a membership requirement. While they were inclined to be far more cosmopolitan as they united for their purposes of "uplift," the post-fire clubs based membership on some of the same conditions, although they often were more restrictive. The "democracy" of the city was perhaps more evident before 1871—and even then it was often times difficult to find. After 1871, however, the various clubs and societies assumed an even greater importance than they had had earlier.

The clubs which were established during the 1870's had as their goal to make certain that the continuity of life was not disturbed by the catastrophic fire. Therefore, it is not unusual to note that some of these clubs—such as the Sons of Vermont of 1877—based their memberships upon the former home states of the members. The Illinois Club of 1878 was formed by a group of westside businessmen for "the cultivation and promotion of literature and social life." While its contributions to literature were minimal, it was highly active as a social group which provided hours of enjoyment for its members. Many of the eastern and southern states had similar clubs. Most of these made pretenses at being "literary" societies. This generally meant that the members read and discussed essays written by each other. Seldom were actual writers—especially journalists and those connected with the book trade—invited to join these pseudo-literary clubs which in reality were organizations of the business and social elites.

There were, of course, some organizations which made a greater display of their "literary" inclinations. For example, both the Chicago Philosophical Society and the Fortnightly Club were organized in 1873. The former was designed to permit both men and women to gather together for mutual benefit. While there was some display toward concerning themselves with the "less fortunate," they seriously considered weighty questions for lectures and discussion. The Fortnightly was perhaps more oriented toward "the society lady." As a women's club, it drew its membership from the wives and daughters of the businessmen of the city. Together they studied art, music, literature, and history with great emphasis upon the classical periods of the arts. In both groups the members wrote papers which they delivered before each other. Thus these clubs provided not only social outlets but also intellectual stimulation for their members.

The same goal was achieved by the Chicago Literary Club which was formed in 1874 and which had a singularly distinctive membership. Gookin in his history of the organization, *The Chicago Literary Club: Its First Fifty Years, 1874-1924* (Chicago, 1924) has reported the aims and goals of the club as summarized by Robert Collyer—noted clergyman—at the first annual dinner.

[It] was the result of a feeling those who became members of it had in common before they came together, that the time had fully come when all true lovers of books in our city should enter into a league through which whatever each man had of special worth to his fellows should be brought to the exchange, so that there might be a common wealth of culture which had come to any ripeness, together with a company of men eager and anxious to welcome every new sign of such culture either among those of their own community or those who might come to us from otherwheres (pp. 20-21).

Composed of the outstanding men of the city, the club could also be characterized by its general lack of writers. This is not to suggest that there were no writers among them Its first president, Reverend Robert Collyer, considered himself a writer as did some other members; but the newspapermen of the period who were doing so much to define the city in literary terms were not asked to join. Yet, as in the case with other clubs of its type, the men wrote essays and read them before the membership.

The year 1876 saw the establishment of three women's clubs which more or less were committed to literary endeavors. The Saracen, which eventually took men into its membership, was concerned about the intellectual quality of life in the city; and by devoting themselves to reading and the discussion of books, this exclusive club had notions of effecting some changes in the city. The Women's Christian Association turned its attention to the elevation of others. It had as its purpose the promotion of "moral, religious, intellectual welfare . . . [of] working women." To this end at the boarding house which the organization sponsored copies of "good" literature were made available in order to edify the residents who would in turn—it was imagined— be uplifted. The Women's Christian Association did not permit maids to board with the working women. Thus, the "whosoever- will" spirit of Christianity did not extend to all working women as far as the organization was concerned. The Women's Club also directed its attention to the cultural uplift of others. It was designed to promote artistic and literary activities which would benefit the city and provide patterns for living. Of the three groups, the Women's Club eventually turned into a reform organization, but by the 1890's it had discovered that cultural uplift meant little in a corrupt city.

In addition to the more elitist groups, there were some clubs which claimed—at least—an open membership policy. Among those of the 1870's there was frequently the tendency to combine an altruistic purpose with a social one. The variety as well as the diversity of the urban club structure is supported by the following organizations of the 1870's: Chicago Relief and Aid Society (1871), Apollo Music Club (1872), Beethoven Society (1872), Commercial Club (1877), Society of Decorative Arts (1877) which provided art instruction for those who could not pay and became the nucleus for the formation of the city's Art Institute, Calumet Club (1878) which started the Old Settlers' Receptions in 1879 and made a great deal of the social distinctions determined by who was present in the city prior to 1840, Union Club (1878), and the Union League Club (1879). All of these clubs shared in common the idea that they could be instruments to aid in the elevation of standards during the trying days of the rebuilding of the city. Many of them, modeled after Boston clubs, were convinced that there had to be more "culture" in the new city.

I

While the elite men and women of society were busily creating their worlds out of the fragmented surviving pieces of the pre-fire days, what was the status of literature in the city? The fire with its destruction of plants and materials had brought Chicago journalism temporarily to a halt. Of the pre-fire periodicals and newspapers, some survived, some merged with other publications, and some simply gave up. The task of restoration proved to be costly in time, money, and energy. Just two years before the fire, the *Tribune* had erected an expensive structure. After the fire all that remained was a vault and some walls. According to reports of the period, the vault contained a safe, a linen coat, and a box of matches! Yet, with makeshift facilities the *Tribune* issued an edition on October 11, 1871, with the tacit understanding that "Chicago Shall Rise Again." Wilbur Storey, on the other hand, felt the depression of the moment and believed all was lost. But he was prevailed upon to begin again. Consequently, surviving the effects of the fire became for some a matter of determination over the physical facts of disaster. The importance of the city's "I-Will" attitude is demonstrated by the subsequent growth of the *Tribune* as well as of the *Times*.

By 1874 it was clear that some papers were in trouble but not the *Tribune*. With Joseph Medill having assumed the controlling interest in the newspaper, more outstanding writers were hired, and the *Tribune* continued to grow. The *Times,* with Storey at its helm, also entered its best period where it had a great influence upon the newspaper world. While many people tend to remember him for the depths to which the paper would go, Storey managed to alter several journalistic techniques including the excessive usage of clips from New York and other eastern papers. He was willing to spend a great deal of money for news and pioneered in practically every phase of modern journalism. Thus both the *Tribune* and the *Times* began periods of great activity and growth. It was the post-fire city which provided the setting for the rise of the popular columnist. Franc B. Wilkie of the *Times* and G.P. Upton of the *Tribune* became two of the first to benefit from the use of the by-line.

Among the newspapers founded in the 1870's three are significant. *The Inter-Ocean* of 1872 had its inception in *The Republican* (1865-1871) which had been started by a group of rather influential men in Illinois who had become disenchanted with the *Tribune* and its political stand on many issues. Among the Chicagoàns who backed the paper were John Farwell and J. Young Scammon. Charles A. Dana was the editor; however, in spite of his reputation, the paper had considerable problems. When The *Republican* was destroyed, Scammon bought out the other men and continued the paper without a great deal of success. *The Inter-Ocean*, established by Scammon, had a much more successful history and continued into the twentieth century as one of the important papers of the city. It also has some historical interest because in 1897, following the procedure of many businessmen, Charles T. Yerkes bought the controlling interest. Hence, for a time, *The Inter-Ocean* was one of the few papers in Chicago to support Yerkes and the Gray Wolves and had as its motto: "Republican in all things; independent in nothing."

Then there was the *Saturday Evening Herald* a weekly newspaper which began in 1874 and also survived into the twentieth century. Originally it was intended to combine news of literature with some original stories and poems, news of the fine arts, and news of the socially elite. Its pretensions to culture soon disappeared, and the paper simply became the news outlet for the activities of the wealthy. It was one of the curiosities in a city which constantly maintained that it had no class system for the *Saturday Evening Herald*, which was based on the assumption that such a class did exist in the city, to last as long as it did.

By far the most outstanding journal to be established during the decade of the 1870's was the Chicago *Daily News* which became one of the outstanding newspapers of the Midwest. When it appeared rather inconspicuously on Christmas day, 1875, there was nothing particularly unusual about it. There had been other papers in the city called *Daily News,* and there had been other papers which sold for a penny or for two cents. On the surface, there was nothing extraordinary about the three men who established it—Melville Stone, Percy Meggy, and William Dougherty—to suggest that their newspaper was destined for a significant place in Chicago history. In fact, the last two made their contribution by becoming discouraged rather early and selling out to Stone. In 1876 Victor E. Lawson purchased the former shares of Meggy and Dougherty; and the winning combination of Stone and Lawson was launched. The two men were admirably suited to one another. Stone handled the editorial duties and Lawson the business matters.

During the 1870's the *Daily News* had to struggle to meet the competition of so many other existing newspapers. The task was made even more difficult because most of the other papers were members of a national news service; hence, they had little difficulty getting national and international news. The *News,* on the other hand, was not a subscriber. Its biggest rival was the afternoon *Evening Post,* a newspaper which had had a stormy history. Andreas has recorded a story which partially explains the quick and successful rise of the *Daily News* (III,700). It seems that the *Evening Post* was managed by the McMullens who were often accused of being unscrupulous. The *Daily News* charged that the *Post* was stealing its material. Charges and counter-charges were hurled between the two newspapers. *The Daily News* ultimately devised a scheme which proved to be the undoing of the *Post.* As the story goes, during the Turco-Russian War the *News* issued a special edition with a special dispatch ostensibly from Bulgaria. The dispatch began with ERUS SIHT LAETS LLIW SNELLUM MC EHT and was followed by an alleged translation. The next edition of the *Post* appeared carrying the same heading with its subsequent translation. The *Daily News* then issued its story which noted that the headline simply said: "The McMullens Will Steal This Sure" with each word being spelled backward. The *News* gained an immediate notoriety which increased its circulation; and the *Post* went into a decline from which it never recovered. The final blow to the *Post* came in 1878 when it was purchased by the *Daily News.* Thus began a series of mergers which would make the *Daily News* a rival to the *Tribune,* a newspaper which in earlier years had grown in the same fashion. While its greatest period of literary activity was to come in the 1880's and 1890's, the *Daily News*—by the end of the 1870's—had established itself as a leading and popular newspaper which maintained the highest degree of excellence in reporting and which gathered together a group of writers who were to become pace-setters in the field of journalism. Three distinct types of journals emerged, although each one had predecessors in ante-fire publications. First of all, the 1870's saw the development of an ephemeral literature destined for commercial success. The city as well as its enterprises needed money; hence, there was not much emphasis upon the "art-for-art's sake" approach. To be considered worthwhile was to make money. And this attitude permeated many of the literary productions of the period. The type of experimentation which one can see in an earlier period with the various and sundry attempts to produce non-paying literary magazines could no longer be supported. There was no room for failure in the new city. Admirably suited to the times and out of this emphasis upon immediate success there developed a magazine or paper sometimes referred to as "family story" magazines. They relied heavily upon short fiction which appealed to a wide audience. One of the first of this type to appear was the weekly *Chicago Ledger* of 1872 which in reality capitalized upon the form made popular by the *New York Ledger* of 1851. As it began its career in the still distraught city, the *Chicago Ledger* offered popular entertainment for the entire family. Stories were romantic and idealistic, but they provided a respite from the realities of everyday. Essentially the stories were well-written. By 1875, however, the *Ledger* was forced to compete with the Lakeside Library which had begun to issue cheap reprints of so-called standard fiction at ten cents a copy. This dime series, established by Donnelley and Loyd, produced three such books a month, and the Press was able to increase its assets tremendously with very little output. The *Ledger* then began to issue the kind of thrillers which were the fare of the Lakeside Library. While the stories were sensational, they were still designed for family reading.

Capitalizing upon the popularity of the *Chicago Ledger* were such imitations as *Our Fireside Friend* (1872), *Cottage Monthly*

(1873), *Turner's Minaret* (1873), *Western Home* (1874), *Old Oaken Bucket* (1876), and *Sunset Chimes* (1876). As Chicago publications all of them were singularly unique in their lack of emphasis upon the urban experience. Their stories, instead, tended to deal with modern fairy tales with a great deal of western local color to appeal to those who did not live in the city. None of them ever attained the initial literary standards of the *Ledger,* but they shared the extensive market for the family-story type journals. Of these periodicals only *Western Home* antedated the fire. Appearing in 1868 as *Chicago Western Home* it had such contributors as Harriet Beecher Stowe. It was a family magazine, but its emphasis upon the popular story as a means of entertainment was developed more after it resumed publication in 1874.

While they were popular literature, the family-story magazines did not deal with serious subjects nor present provocative essays; however, the 1870's did see the establishment of some journals which were designed for more than popular entertainment and which met varying degrees of success. One of the most significant of these journals (in terms of influence) did not last long, but its short existence belies its importance. The roots of the *Lakeside Monthly* (1871-1874) were to be found in H.V. Reed's *Western Monthly* which had been started in 1869 as "an institution of the West" which would "explore the fields of literature" and would use "pioneer talent." Reed was as committed as anyone to the notion that a western literature could exist and would survive. In this literary faith he was joined by Francis Fisher Browne, who became an editor *par excellence* in the western city. Reed, however, in spite of his faith found it difficult to execute the journal; and Browne, his associate, became the editor. One of the first changes he made was to assure the subscribers that the journal would be "literary" in the broadest sense. And in order to guarantee its acceptance by a wider range, Browne changed the name of the journal to *Lakeside Monthly* in January, 1871.

The relationship between the magazine and the establishment of the Lakeside Press as a subsidiary of the printing and publishing firm of Church, Goodman, and Donnelley is a complicated one, but the journal did much toward expressing the philosophy of the company which supported it. Its success as a "western" journal was judged in part by its influence upon eastern writers and publishers. They began to see that there indeed was a fertile field in western subjects and writers. In his *Magazines of a Market-Metropolis,* Herbert Fleming correctly assessed the value of the *Lakeside Monthly.*

With the advent of [the magazine] *Scribner's Monthly,* the forerunner of the present *Century,* began to give attention to western subjects, and to seek the work of western writers. During the years of the *Lakeside's* growth other eastern publishers began to glean in Mid-West fields, and the competition among them for the virile western productions, which has since become so keen, was fairly on by the time the magazine had reached the zenith of its career (p. 402).

In many ways the *Lakeside Monthly* was the culmination of that type of "local color" literature which Chicago magazines had talked about since the early days of the city. By the time the movement had reached national proportions in the post-Civil War days, at least one journal in Chicago had perfected the form well enough to serve as a model for others. Unfortunately, Browne's health and financial problems combined; and as 1874 opened, he found it necessary to cease the publication of the journal. He spurned the opportunity to have it merged with *Scribner's Monthly.* Hence the *Lakeside Monthly* ended as it had begun—in Chicago.

While the *Lakeside Monthly* was in existence, another journal was founded. Its purpose was noble, but the unusual magazine could not sustain itself. *The Alliance,* established in 1873 by liberal clergymen who were devoted to the principles of ecumenical approaches to religion, was a non-sectarian weekly which was designed to broaden the scope of the religious press by including representatives from the major religious groups in the city. There had been a strong religious press prior to the fire, but it was a press which generally followed the lines of denominational concerns. Such men as Professor David Swing of the Presbyterian Church, Professor William Mathews of the Baptist Church, and the Reverend Robert Collyer of the Unitarian Church were among the founders along with other outstanding clergymen, and—as originally planned—all of these ministers were to form the editorial board of the journal. Either Chicago was not ready for such an enterprise or the ministers had too many other demands on their time, but for one reason or another Professor David Swing was editorially in charge of the journal and used it to promote his move toward an independent church. As the chief contributor, his sermons appeared weekly. During his heresy trial before the Presbytery, his writings in the *Alliance* were frequently quoted by the prosecution.

The paper underwent numerous editorial shifts and changes; however, in 1877 Francis Fisher Browne became the literary editor and gave new life to the journal. The religious emphasis gave way to one of a literary nature; but in spite of its popularity and success, the magazine had financial problems. Its consolidation with *Western Magazine* in 1879 added some life. Although *Western Magazine* had been founded in Omaha, Nebraska, in 1876, it decided to take advantage of the Chicago market and move eastward to the larger city. Mrs. Helen Elkin Starrett became the editor and developed a first-rate literary journal in the city, one which paid great attention to the major literatures of the world but one which at the same time dealt with the immediate economic and social issues of the city. The merger of the two journals took place in 1882, and as the *Weekly Magazine* it issued its first number on May 6. At that time Mrs. Starrett declared:

We have believed from the first that there is need and a demand for a low-priced periodical to supply a kind of reading differing like the magazine from the newspaper in its greater deliberateness and earnestness, and yet without those qualities of cumbrousness and extensiveness common to the magazines.

With contributors of the stature of David Swing one would have imagined that the success of the *Weekly Magazine* would have been assured. But it was plagued by poor business management as had been the *Alliance* and soon was forced into bankruptcy. In the same year that the clergymen had such high hopes for the journal which they were launching in Chicago, there appeared another magazine which in its own way marked a milestone in the development of literature in the city. In 1873 Charles H. Harris began *Carl Pretzel's Magazine Pook,* the first magazine devoted exclusively to humor. It was written in a distorted German-American dialect; and in a city which had so many German immigrants, it became quite successful as Harris dealt with local scenes and issues. Capitalizing on its success, Harris decided to expand into a more national publication; hence the beginning of *Carl Pretzel's National Weekly* in 1874 was made to interest a larger audience with more emphasis upon national events and situations. Slowly it became political in nature although "Carl Pretzel" still remained the central figure and elements of humor still pervaded its pages. Harris became more interested in political matters, and the magazine soon developed into the mouthpiece for some of the political secret societies of the period. Such men as Robert Ingersoll and John A. Logan were frequent contributors. Before it folded in 1893, it began an extensive use of cartoons and added the word *Illustrated* to its title. Had Harris not become so imbued with his own success, conceivably *Carl Pretzel's Magazine Pook* could have become not only a forerunner of Mr. Dooley in Chicago but could have been as well known because initially Carl Pretzel was as clearly defined as Dooley. Yet the later humorists such as Ade, Field, and Dunne were preceded by Charles Harris who was just as perceptive about the city and the times and who could laugh at both.

In the midst of all of this activity it is not surprising that there were some attempts to continue purely literary magazines, but they were meager indeed. William Frederick Poole edited *The Owl* which was published by the publishing firm of W.B. Keen, Cooke,

& Company. While Poole maintained that the newly-established Chicago Public Library should include good fiction since that was an important part of the literary heritage of the nations, *The Owl* was more concerned with publishing the advertisements for the company which owned it. Poole's essays, of course, were of a high quality; but they were primarily concerned with the public library which he was heading. *The Owl*, which was established in 1874, apparently took over some of the functions performed by the *Chicago Librarian* which had existed from 1872 to 1873. The earlier journal was also a monthly, and it was devoted exclusively to the new library. Like *The Owl* it also stressed new books and printed the list of books which were received within any given month. But, unlike *The Owl* it did not have the benefits of Poole's editorial supervision and actually lasted less than a year.

Both *The Chicago Librarian* and *The Owl* gained some support because of the interest in the formation of the Chicago Public Library. Oddly enough, in spite of all of the books and book readers in the city, Chicago did not have a public library in the truest sense of the term. Certainly many of the clubs and organizations had libraries which sponsored a limited circulation, and many of the club houses had reading rooms, but it took the Chicago Fire of 1871 and the efforts of England's Queen Victoria to establish a city library.

The world of journalism was far more diversified than one might imagine. The daily and weekly newspapers had their publics just as did the family-story, serious, and "literary" journals. When one actually surveys examples of the various types of journals which were existing in the city, one questions how a nineteenth-century community could have supported so many. It is important to recognize that the political nature of the early newspapers cannot be minimized neither can their affiliations with big business be ignored. The 1870's made it clear that money was a controlling factor and could shape public opinion through the ownership of periodicals. Even the so-called *independent* publications were free primarily in the sense that they felt they were able to

choose one side or the other in political issues and were not bound
by party loyalties. By far, however, the most significant trait of the
journals of the 1870's was their attempt to imitate older and more
established publications of the East as well as their desire to create
general works which would appeal to a mass audience. Time would
prove that the small, restricted journal with a limited circulation
had no place in the new Chicago.

The decade of the 1870's saw a fewer number of journals beginning; yet, it was a period which produced some works which
were to have a lasting effect. Although the family-story magazines
did not specialize in "great literature"; they at least provided entertainment for a large number of people. The newspapers were entering into their period of the strong dictatorial editor whose
personality was literally stamped upon every article. In a city of so
many periodicals, only the best could survive. The day for mere
existence was over as the newspapers resumed the kind of local
pride which had been a strong characteristic of the journals of the
ante-fire days. For many the decade was simply a prelude to their
later periods of greatness. "Survival of the fittest" was the unspoken watchword in the world of journalism during the 1870's in
Chicago.

II

With the growing importance of Chicago newspapers as the
"voice" of the West and with the evolving national interest in
Chicago-based magazines, the publishers of the city had an opportunity to capitalize on the attention which was centering on the
Midwest. Book publishing continued to prosper after 1871, but
there was a considerable reduction in the number of firms operating in the city. With few exception all of them had been destroyed, and starting over was not as simple as it might have
been in an earlier day. Until the establishment of Stone and Kimball in 1893, however, books publishers in Chicago are frequently
ignored although many of them made some outstanding contributions to the development of the city as a literary center. That

Chicago was to emerge as a printing center could have been predicted as many publishers turned their attentions solely to printing. But before that occurred, the city had achieved importance as a publishing center. In fact, John Tebbel observed in his *A History of Book Publishing in the United States* (New York, 1975) that the city "had become the largest publishing center . . . outside the East Coast" by 1883 (II, 427). He continued:

> The rise of the trade in Chicago had been startling. It was grossing only a few hundred dollars in annual sales in 1834, but the total was more than $9,000,000 by 1884. The big subscription houses alone had annual sales ranging from $250,000 to nearly a million each, and did business in the eastern as well as the western states. The leading eastern schoolbook houses had branches in Chicago to introduce their books into western schools . . . (II, 428).

Publishing, as it is understood today, did not exist in nineteenth-century Chicago. The earliest publishing was in actuality conducted by printers, most of whom were hired to do specific jobs. The printers who had the best access to machines and materials were those connected with either a newspaper or a magazine; hence, it is not surprising to note during the 1830's through the 1850's that much "publishing" was issued from the offices of such papers as the Chicago *Democrat* and Chicago *American*. By the 1860's the Chicago *Tribune* Book and Job department issued a substantial number of books and pamphlets. Thus, when one thinks of a publisher during this period, one must think in very general terms. As a result, it is impossible in many cases to trace completely the scope of the publishing industry in Chicago prior to the Civil War. With rare exceptions, the relationship between book dealers or sellers, printers, and publishers was so closely interwoven that it was not uncommon for a publisher to be a job printer or to have a book store attached to his place of business. Thus, for the early Chicago imprints, it is a frequent notation to see a printer as well as a bookseller noted on the title page. For example, the title page of Kenyon's *Poems* . . . issued in 1845 records the following information: "Printed by James Campbell and Co., Sold by Brautigam & Keen, S.F. Gale and Co., W.W. Barlow & Co., and Comstock and Ackley." Yet both Barlow and Gale also did some "publishing." The roots, therefore, of the major publishing companies are frequently connected with early printing firms and booksellers in that "before-the-fire" period.

Two post-fire activities occurred which were apparently unrelated but which were destined to influence—if not alter—the course of the city's publishing activities. One resulted in the growth of subscription houses, and the other—an immediate event—produced the "instant" works of the post-fire period. That many of the publishers were also booksellers should not cloud the fact that they issued both specialized and general books not only for the city but also for national distribution. The subscription book companies flourished in Chicago, partially because of the city's central location and the availability of rail distribution. Furthermore, in a day when the motto seemed to be "anything goes," it is not surprising to see money being made with practically any enterprise. Some of the larger houses grossed a million dollars annually.

When it began in 1869, the city's first subscription firm—Haywood and Crean—literally had a clear market. With little capital invested, the firm displayed the possibilities of such a venture. By the 1880's many companies existed and had agents in all parts of the country. Bibles, encyclopedias, European classics, and popular American novels were the core of subscription offerings. In most instances these firms built their inventories on reprints rather than on original works. In addition to Haywood and Crean, there were other large houses capitalizing on the sucess of both installment and instant cash sales. Such firms as Baird and Dillon, Western Publishing House, A.L. Coburn, J.M. Wing and Co., Standard Book Company, Elder Publishing Co., and G.W. Borland and Co. had such fantastic sales that there were undoubtedly many who agreed with the publisher, A.P.T. Elder who claimed that the day would arrive when all books would be sold by subscription. It is perhaps difficult today to realize the extent of the success enjoyed by the city's subscription houses. These firms sent dealers to all parts of the country and eventually some of these houses established outlets in other regions. Frequently, the editors of these firms put together their own special volumes, highly illustrated, to add to their lists of available books. Hence, L.W. Yaggy, the owner of Western Publishing House (which had handled the works of T.S. Arthur who become famous with his *Ten Nights in a Bar Room*) put together such picture-book anthologies as *Our Home Counsellor, The Royal Path of Life, The Museum of Antiquity, Wit and Humor of the Age,* and *Practical Home Physician,* all of which indicate the diversity of his offerings. The firm which had begun in 1874 had sales of more than a million dollars in less than ten years. And this success story could be repeated with many of these companies. For example., A.L. Coburn made his firm with two history books, *The Two Americas* (1877) and *America* (1881). A.P.T. Elder's *Lives and Graves of Our Presidents* became a staple offering of his firm as did *The Manual of Social and Business Forms* of Thomas E. Hill, the owner of the Standard Book Company. The list could go on; but suffice it to say, no discussion of the publishing situation in Chicago will be complete until there is a thorough study of these subscription houses which parlayed a few dollars' worth of initial capital investment and merchandise into a multi-million dollar business.

In the period immediately following the disaster of 1871 the publishers of the city had a ready-market for one type of book— the "fire story." In addition to the multitude of such books which continued throughout the 1870's (most of which were issued by firms in the city), there was a wide interest in the production of historical accounts of the city. These were designed to preserve and pay homage to a great past with the intention of replacing the lost records. Many of these histories had the advantage of having been written by people who had participated in the action, and thus they were able to transmit a sense of immediacy. While these served as a substitute for the records which had been destroyed, they had the disadvantage of being produced by men who were able in effect to re-write history by their selections and eliminations of certain details. Interestingly enough, all of these histories have certain characteristics which tend to help mark them as post-fire documents. The most obvious, of course, is the initial reference to *The Fire*. Then there is the insistence upon the manifest destiny of the city which in many ways is quite similar to the Puritan concept of history. Through a recital of past events which took place in the face of adversity the "historians" insisted that the fire is simply to be viewed as a means of making Chicago greater than she was before. Almost without exception, these histories were commissioned —if not written—by the businessmen of the community. Part of their interest was in seeing to it that the life of the community was recorded for posterity, but obviously they also used these histories as a mean by which they could convince businessmen in other parts of the nation that the city had a chance to redeem herself and that there had been no break in continuity. Some businessmen, such as William Bross, even traveled to the East to speak personally with the business establishment there. Foremost among the post-fire histories was Bross' *History of Chicago* which was comprised of "Historical and Commercial Statistics, Sketches, Facts and Figures, Republished from the 'Daily Democractic Press' " and "What I Remember of Early Chicago; a lecture, delivered at McCormick's Hall, January 23, 1876." This work appeared in 1876, and while some readers may deplore its lack of organization, no one can deny that Bross includes all of the facts of the city.

While there is much merit in the work of Bross and in the historical series issued by the Fergus Printing Company beginning with 1876, the popularity of these works tended to establish the patterns for Chicago history which have not totally been overcome as yet. These histories emphasize the greatness and the power of what Bross was pleased at one time to call the nation's "Second

City." Even those urban histories which purport to "expose" the city and its wickedness do so with an aura of respect and delight in the mythical city. Thus the nineteenth-century histories defined for all times the legend of Chicago; and it has become increasingly difficult to separate the legend from the reality. One of the tragedies of this kind of story is the fact that the nameless thousands upon whom the city was built never have gotten into the history books. Their names, which may have been preserved in some of the earlier records, were never recalled. Thus the philosophy of Chicago historical writing has been one predicated upon the city's successes. And in a city where only Success mattered, perhaps this is to be expected. Consequently, the adage, "if you have read one, you have read them all," is applicable to much of the city's history books. The fact that this pattern can be discerned before the fire is understandable when one considers the youth of the city. Conceivably had the fire not occurred, there would have been the possibility of more realistic approaches as the city grew older. But the fire, by consuming the records, made it possible for a selective replacement. Furthermore, since most of the history had to be reconstructed from what people remembered, it is not unusual that they tended to remember only the positive and the outstanding.

The apparent cooperative ventures between the city's publishers and historians (whose work perhaps rivalled that of the fire narrators in volume), did not extend to all literary endeavors. Yet, if any city's publishers are to become important, they must obviously be concerned about more than purely local matters. At the same time, any concern for the writers of a region must include a recognition of the publishers of that locale. In Chicago the publishers were just as concerned as the writers about the image of the city, and they were just as committed to the idea of the importance of Chicago as they sought to extend their imprints to all sections of the country. One might expect that these two forces would have united, but the writers unwittingly shared with the publishers a mutual distrust of each other. There was a tacit belief among the poets and the novelists that the local firms were too provincial and would not give them the greatest exposure. Many of the writers felt that they could get better national circulation if they used eastern firms, and many of the publishers were convinced—or so it seemed —that the home-grown talent would have no appeal for a national audience nor would they command national attention. They sought to issue the works of popular writers from other regions. Hence, both publishers and writers—especially the novelists—suffered from the same response as they attempted to avoid restrictive local identification.

This sense of regional inferiority became an unspoken factor in the relationship between Chicago's writers and the city's publishers. This is not meant to suggest that none of the city's firms issued local work, but even among those firms committed to the idea of "western" literature, there was a tendency to produce the works of popular authors who would—in turn—guarantee large sales. An underlying motivation which cannot be ignored of both writers and publishers was the desire to make as much money as possible. Some of the more experimental companies or the most successful could risk printing the work of an unknown Chicago writer, but it was not until the advent of Stone and Kimball and Way and Williams in the 1890's that there was a concerted effort made to establish a close working relationship between the city's writers and their publishers. Thus to study these two groups in the city is to consider men and women who were committed to the idea that their city could become an important literary center but who were not thoroughly convinced that they could achieve these goals together. This mutual distrust had historic precedents. Wright's *History* of 1844 and Mrs. Kinzie's *Wau-Bun* of 1856 were both initially published elsewhere.

While there were a number of printers and publishers in Chicago prior to the Civil War as attested to by the proliferation of newspapers and magazines during the period, Chicago did not become a center for publishing activities until after the Fire of 1871 when restoration activities saw the reactivation, consolidation, and the beginning of those firms which were to become important. If one assumes that the existence of a literary center is dependent upon the accessibility of publishing facilities, then one must take into account the fact that from the beginning of apparent literary interests in the city, there were printers willing to issue the works. Chicago printers, of course, were handicapped by their frequent inability to penetrate the eastern market and by the reluctance of some writers to place their works with a local house, but in spite of this the Chicago firms managed to produce enough to become a factor in the publishing history not only of the city but also of the nation.

Independent though the writers and publishers were from each other, both groups made significant contributions to the urban literary scene. When one speaks of a city's literature, there is a tendency to view only the writers and pay little attention to the publishers. Yet, just as the writers did much to call attention to Chicago so also did the publishers do much toward making the nation aware of the activity taking place in Chicago. Walter Sutton, however, rejects the importance of Chicago. In his *The Western Book Trade: Cincinnati as a Nineteenth-Century Publishing and Book-Trade Center* (Columbus, 1961), he agreed that Chicago became important as a center of book distribution because of the railroads, but "it never became a great regional publishing center" (p. 285). Yet, between 1871 and 1893 Chicago firms not only made some notable contributions to the national scene but they also issued some outstanding books. Much of this activity reached its zenith in the 1890's with the establishment of Stone and Kimball as well as Way and Williams. The same spirit which had motivated so many of the city's other business also operated with many of the publishers who were willing "to take a chance" in the city. They were instrumental in developing techniques and introducing some writers to the national scene; as a result, these publishers actively influenced the course of American literature although they did not do as much for Chicago writing as they might have done.

Initially magazine and newspaper publishers were more than willing to gamble with local writers. Certainly this is understandable in view of the local nature of these more ephemeral publications. Yet, curiously many of these early writers sought eastern publishers for their books. As fiction appeared independent of the journalistic world, writers searched for publishers who could command the widest audience. At the same time, printers and publishers, becoming more confident of a possible audience, became more interested in issuing from their firms works of fiction. A survey of much of this early fiction by Chicago authors reveals that it can be characterized generally by a singular absence of the gloomy fiction which was flooding the East. Up to 1850 a great deal of eastern fiction dealt with the evils and the temptations of the city. Clearly within the genre of sentimental tear-jerkers and the sentimental novel as practiced by William Hill Brown in *The Power of Sympathy* (1789) or Susannah Rowson in *Charlotte Temple* (1791), these novelists felt moved to discuss the "mysteries," "the pitfalls," and the "dangers"—even the possible degradation which faced young men and women who moved to the city looking for the nebulous realization of a still more frothy dream. Americans talked about *SUCCESS,* Americans believed in it, Americans searched for it. The city came to represent the possibility of the dream of success being realized.

As the nation's mobility increased, as more and more people moved from the country to the city, self-appointed moralists were quick to point out that the city was little more than a dungeon or a trap waiting to snare the innocent and lead each one into a life of sin. This became a story repeated constantly from the pulpit or from the homes of those country girls and boys who were planning to go to the closest big city. The popular novelists—sometimes searching for a moralistic tale which contained enough pornography to make their stories "exciting"—recorded all of this. That these tales are called romances is understandable in terms of the limitations of the genre, but they were "realistic" in their portrayals of current attitudes toward urban communities.

While Cooper was continuing his fictional move westward with his Leatherstocking series and tales which analyzed some of the social issues of his day, while Emerson and Thoreau were contemplating the significance of Nature and the relevance of self-reliance, and while Hawthorne and Melville were musing upon the dark inner recesses of man's mind, writers such as Fanny Fern were pouring out tales and novels for popular consumption which were warnings against the possible damnation which would come when people were "roped in" by the glitter, glamour, and promises of the city. Emphasis upon crime, poverty, diseases—both spiritual and physical—were just a few of the problems with which the urban dweller had to deal.

The fiction of Philadelphia, Boston, or New York can be characterized by the proliferation of these moralistic tales which in their sensationalism and subtle pornography represent the urban fiction of the major cities in a formative period of the nation's history. Some of this popular fiction pointing out the vicissitudes of urban life found its way westward, but interestingly enough little of it was written about Chicago although Chicago publishers issued the tales about other cities. One of the few exceptions is *Lakeville* (Appleton, 1873) by the Chicago author, Mary Healy Bigot, which portrays the city as it actually was in those days; however, an early reviewer whose work was reported by W.M. Griswold in his *Descriptive Lists of American, International, Romantic, and British Novels* (Cambridge, 1891) claimed the book pictured a "reckless, comfortless existence of a community made in the pursuit of sudden wealth" and concluded that the book had a "bald, hard, almost dreary aspect [with a] narrow range of feeling." Yet, all of this produced "a coarse excitement and . . . indescribable vulgarity" (p. 83).

As evidenced by the popularity of the family-story magazines as well as the availability of long and short fiction issued by the various publishing companies, it was apparent that the post-fire period witnessed an intensified interest in fiction. It is true that a great deal of the novels being read were the standard popular ones from the East or from England. Much of the "native" fiction consisted of the short stories and tales which appeared in the magazines. There were, however, some few pioneers who were addressing themselves to the cityscape. Although devoted to the romantic tradition, some of these sentimental tales might have been highly moralistic, but they were beginning to show an understanding of the problems of the city. Other stories followed a pre-fire technique and used the prairie as a setting for tales based upon the inevitable conflicts between Indians and settlers.

While the fiction being produced in Chicago generally was not primarily concerned with urban problems or issues, Chicago publishers did issue a large number of novels and short story collections, designed to capture audiences beyond the city's limits. (See Appendix B.) Truly before H.L. Mencken observed that there were interesting events taking place in that "abbatoir by the lake," many firms had sprung up, and many had gone out of existence. In fact, the printing and the distribution of books was a "big business" in the nineteenth-century city. Their lists of publications might not be impressive individually, but collectively they suggest that the city which was often concerned with the purely materialistic was in part a city of books. By the end of the 1880's the great work of Stone and Kimball and Way and Williams was yet to come. Perhaps no two firms accomplished so much in so little time. Both firms, especially the former, brought attention to the city not only as a publishing center but also as a place where outstanding and innovative techniques could be tolerated. Certainly, Stone and Kimball's *Chap-Book* ushered in a period for little magazines which has not been equaled in quite the same way that this little journal from Chicago struck the American reading public. For those who had come to expect something "western" from Chicago, there was little preparation for the elegant journal which seemed so "eastern" to supporters.

The story of publishing in Chicago is further complicated by the fact that few of the major nineteenth-century firms survived into the twentieth century, and those that did appeared in a greatly altered form. Four of the major companies antedated the fire; those which survived did their most creative work after 1871 as these companies assumed some of the characteristics which are more familiar to modern audiences. Among the many nineteenth-century job printers who became publishers, some have achieved a significance based not only upon their output but also upon their contribution to the city during its period of growth. Among these important firms, some will undoubtedly seem strange.

For example, to the twentieth-century reader the firm of Ellis and Fergus probably means little, but its work cannot be minimized. The fact that this company published the city's first book of poetry in 1843 and the first directory the following year might be overlooked, but it was this firm which also published in 1844 the city's first work of history, the pamphlet by Juliette Kinzie, *Narrative of the Massacre at Chicago, August 15, 1812*.

Robert Fergus, a printer in Scotland, had heard the success stories which were commonly told about America and decided—as did many others in the opening years of the nineteenth century—to cast his fortune with America. Once in the country, he selected the Midwest which seemed—after the opening of the Erie Canal in 1825—to be the place of greatest activity and arrived in Chicago a scant two years after the city's incorporation. William Ellis, on the other hand, arrived in Chicago from Canada in 1840 and went to work immediately as a printer for the *Press and Tribune*, a place where many subsequent publishers began their work in the city. In 1841 the two men decided to combine their fortunes into a publishing and printing venture. Much of the young firm's work before the Chicago fire was confined to the annual publication of Norris' edition of the *City Directory* and to other miscellaneous pieces since customarily people who needed the services of printers tended to use the resources of the newspapers. The publication, then, of the poetry of Horatio Cooke and the narrative of Juliette Kinzie were isolated titles which initially did not have overwhelming sales but are two examples of the pioneering of the firm whose works included *The Rosarist's Companion* (1845), the first Roman Catholic book issued in the city.

The major contribution of the firm which became known as the Fergus Printing Company came after the fire and after the death of Ellis in 1873. It was in 1876 that Robert Fergus began the historical series which bears his name. It was his attempt to rescue for posterity the city's historical documents, many of which had been destroyed—except for one or two copies which were frequently found in the unlikeliest places. Fergus believed that the city ought to have a real sense of its past, and how else—he reasoned—could this occur than through a thorough knowledge of the days of the "long ago and far away." He contended that the city's importance could be maintained if the records could be saved and if the men and women who "made" Chicago could "speak" again to the city. While there was some passing interest in the collection of pamphlets issued by Fergus, there is no indication that a great number of Chicagoans understood the service which he was rendering to the city. Between 1876 and 1897 approximately thirty-four appeared (with the last one in the series being issued in 1903). After the death of Robert in 1897, his son attempted to continue the series; but George Fergus was not as successful as his father had been.

It is of some interest to note that of the first thirty-four works in the series, more than ten consisted of lectures read before the Chicago Historical Society. The role of the Society cannot be minimized as it faced the task of replacing documents after the fires of 1871 and 1874. Founded in 1856 for the exclusive purpose "of providing at Chicago a Documentary Library of the most comprehensive character," many of the losses occasioned by the fire were irreplaceable, but the Society started over again. In spite of those two disasters, it amassed more material; and today is one of the outstanding repositories of Chicago-related documents.

The items in the Fergus Historical Series initially ranged in price from twenty-five cents to a little more than a dollar. While they are presently worth a fortune, in his own time they apparently meant little even as the city was intent upon preserving its history. It is, therefore, not surprising that a few years after the death of Fergus, the firm—which had not been able to compete with those of the latter part of the nineteenth century—should be declared bankrupt even though it did manage to limp into the twentieth century. Yet, much of the knowledge which present historians have about the city is based upon the work of this particular firm.

When S.C. Griggs arrived in Chicago in 1848, Ellis and Fergus had already been established. Griggs, a twenty-nine-year old man from Connecticut by way of New York, was destined to become known as the first general publisher in Chicago. Like others of his day, he was convinced that Chicago was the place to be and had agreed to establish a publishing outlet for the New York firm of Mark Newman. His bookstore of 1848, according to a note in the Summer, 1963, issue of *Chicago History* did a business of $23,000 during the first year. Twenty years later, in 1868 sales "approached $1,000,000" (p. 379). After meeting Chicago's original booster— William Bross—the two men formed the firm of Griggs, Bross, and Co. That firm did not last long, and during the following year, S.C. Griggs and Company was started. In a city full of fledgling firms and optimistic people, the 1849 establishment of the new publishing company went unnoticed, but it was not long before the firm began to issue textbooks thereby hitting a sure market. Until 1858, when Griggs took complete personal control, the company had had a tenuous connection with the small New York firm of Ivison and Phinney, but from the beginning it was the Chicago imprint which was most prominent.

The firm was not reluctant to issue the work of local talent and managed to do quite well with some of it. Among the authors cited by Maurice Thompson in his list of "Some Successful Books by Chicago Authors" in the March 26, 1891, issue of *America* was Dr. Nathan S. Davis, an early outstanding physician and medical-school advocate in the city who found time to produce some notable books. In 1851 the S.C. Griggs & Co. began its independent publishing history with Davis's *History of Medical Education and Institutions in the United States*. Three years later the firm's "best seller" was *History of Illinois* by Governor Thomas Ford. According to local reports, it averaged sales of 1,000 copies per month for over five months. During this early period, however, the bulk of the company's offerings consisted in the production of lectures in pamphlet form. These ephemeral paperbound booklets had immediate local audiences which seldom extended beyond the city. Griggs published anything which had a potential market including religious and medical books. As was the custom in those days, the publishers were also distributors; and the location of Chicago was admirably suited to such activites. According to Tebbel in his *A History of Book Publishing in the United States,* Griggs "soon became the largest agent for domestic books in the Midwest, and for a time was one of the largest importers of foreign books in the country" (I, 493). Calling his business on Lake Street "Literary Emporium of the Prairies," Griggs was also the foremost publishing house and bookseller, well-known throughout the entire Northwest during the pre-fire days in Chicago. Part of this early sucess was based upon the company's ability to issue previously-published titles with the Griggs imprint. This eliminated the need for a large editorial staff and permitted issuing not only more books in a given year but also books whose success had been proved.

Within less than ten years three disasters struck the company, any one of which would have closed a lesser firm. While the Civil War resulted in a period of polemical prose, money was tight, and people were not spending as much on printed materials, with the exception of newspapers which gave daily news of the battlefronts. Book publishers—including Griggs—faced uncertain days. Three years after the close of the War—as the firm was recouping from the effects of those days and was beginning to regain its public, a fire struck and destroyed the company on January 28, 1868. Then came the destruction of the Great Fire of 1871, which destroyed the city. Tebbel has recorded the story that in the ashes from S.C. Griggs and Company, which by this time had done well and had become a part of the famed Booksellers' Row of Chicago, the only remains from the fire consisted of "a single leaf from a Bible . . . on which all that could be read were the words of Jeremiah: *'How doth the city sit solitary, that was full of people! how is she become as a widow!* ... *She weepeth sore in the night, and her tears are on her cheeks'* " (II, 294). This undoubtedly is perhaps just one more of the many apocryphal stories that came from the fire and the days which immediately followed it; yet, it partially describes those days of utter desolation which followed the fire.

In spite of the disasters which the company faced and in spite of the fact that book publishing was not as important as the firm's commitment to bookselling and book-distributing, Griggs issued almost a dozen books between the opening of the Civil War and the fire of 1871. In 1862, for example, Mrs. Mary Ashton Rice Livermore's *Pen Pictures; or, Sketches from Domestic Life* appeared. And seven years later in 1869 the firm published *The Mississippi Valley* by John Wells Foster. Both works, while totally different, were destined to achieve a degree of success.

Recouping losses from the fire of 1871 was difficult, a man with less stamina than Griggs may have given up; but Griggs realized that the city with which he had cast his fortunes in 1848 was far from finished, and he reasoned—as did those book publishers who were brave enough to begin again—that there would be an even greater need for books. There would be a need for cheap reprints to help replace the many personal libraries which had been destroyed, there would be a need for texts and medical books, and there would be a need to publish the multitude of "fire stories" which were bound to be written. In fact, just nineteenth days after the Fire, the firm issued the first book on the subject, written by Colbert and Chamberlain, who used the popular "I-was-there" formula which was to become an integral part of all fire stories.

S.C. Griggs joined other publishers in the task of rebuilding. One of the biggest decisions that he made in the post-fire period was to limit himself exclusively to book publishing and to sell out his claim as a bookseller. As a result of this decision in 1872 S.C. Griggs became "the first general publisher" in Chicago and as Tebbel has recorded members of the Chicago book trade believed "if anyone could make the city a publishing center to rival those in the East, Griggs was the man who could initiate the process" (II, 295).

Practically alone, Griggs began with the publication of much-needed textbooks; but ever-aware of the popular market, he published in 1872 *Getting On In the World,* one of the "success formula" books in the tradition of Franklin's *Autobiography,* by William Mathews, a professor from the University of Chicago. The book went through many printings and became one of the firm's early best sellers. Other books by William Mathews also sold well. By 1874 Griggs had built a solid business relying on scholarly as well as popular titles and upon authors who could appeal to varying tastes within the city, but the often-ignored fire of 1874 struck his firm. So once again Griggs was forced to begin again. The year of his latest disaster was also the year of his greatest success. Few people today are unaware of *Robert's Rules of Order.* It was Griggs who saw the merit in this handbook of parliamentary usage written by an obscure army major, Henry M. Robert. It was this book which was destined to remain a best seller long after the name of S.C. Griggs ceased to be an active part of the Chicago literary scene. And that book remains—even today—a popular and often used volume. In 1875 Griggs published fiction for the first time and issued two novels: *The Mishaps of Ezekiel Pelter* and Reverend J.A. Smith's *Patmos; or, The Kingdom and the Patience.* For the next twenty years Griggs dominated much of the publishing scene and the market of Chicago, defying those who maintained that a publisher should concentrate on a particular type of book. Not only did Griggs diversify his offerings, but he was catholic enough to include among his authors not only local talent but also writers of other sections of the country. When it became apparent that Griggs's health had failed completely, the newly-organized firm of Scott, Foresman bought part of his stock including *Robert's Rules of Order* and the textbook market. (And that firm is still one of the major publishers of elementary and secondary textbooks.) Thus the spirit—if not the name—of

S.C. Griggs of Chicago remains a part of the book industry. Perhaps Griggs did not foster an emphasis upon midwestern literature as such, but he made it plain that publishing activities did not have to be limited to the East to be successful, and the Griggs' imprint from Chicago helped to lay the foundation for a renewed interest in the city.

While much of the business activity in Chicago seems characterized by a gambling spirit with frequent overtones of "shady operations," the firm of Rand, McNally was marked by an intense, over-cautious spirit in its pioneer days. Beginning as a printing company, the pioneer firm did not enter book publishing until 1877 and did so then only because all signs seemed "ripe" for the venture. William H. Rand, a Bostonian who arrived in Chicago in 1856 with the notion that there was a totally new world in the West, met Andrew McNally, a Scotsman who had succumbed to the "promise" of America, in 1858. The two printers worked together on various jobs and eventually became incorporated in 1873 as a firm which issued materials which were relevant and of interest to railroad travelers. Capitalizing on the location of the city, the firm soon became the foremost railroad printers in the country. After issuing some business reports, the two men began to publish guide books, atlases, and maps for which they designed special printing techniques. Ever mindful of the importance of the business structure and its role in the city, the firm issued the *Bankers Directory of the United States and Canada* in 1876, the first such directory to be published in the country. Because of these early successes, the firm's name has been consistently associated with business documents or with maps; however, after 1877 the firm was an important outlet not only for Chicago authors but also for European writers. The firm issued the works of Charles Dickens (as did most American companies). At various times the works of Rudyard Kipling, A. Conan Doyle, Robert Louis Stevenson, and Henry Makepeace Thackeray also proved to be popular favorites. In fact, few of the outstanding writers of Victorian England escaped the Rand, McNally imprint. At the same time that the firm considered itself to be issuing the "best" of popular British literature, it also published a great deal of material dealing with the American West. Among its early publications which sold widely were several cowboy narratives such as Charles A. Siringo's *A Texas Cowboy, or Fifteen Years on the Hurricane Deck of a Spanish Pony* (1886) and stories about William Cody, better known then as "Buffalo Bill." Included among these were *Buffalo Bill: From Prairie to Palace* by "Arizona John" and *Seventy Years on the Frontier* by Alexander Majors. The popularity of the western tales led the firm to initiate a number of "series" which were sold in railroad stations. The firms ultimate appeal to the railroad traveler was made with the publication of much of the work of Opie Read, whose *Arkansaw Traveler* had made him popular with the "railroad crowd."

While the core of these paperback series consisted of tales of western adventure and western lore, a number of sentimental novels of the "true romance" variety appeared. Thus, the staid firm of Rand, McNally and Co. included among its titles such works as *She Fell in Love With Her Husband* and *For Another's Sins.* Tebbel has noted, for example, that the "Globe" series—just one of several which the firm issued and which included such names as "Alpha," "Antique," "Atlantic," "Rialto," "Oriental," and "Twentieth Century"—"had 398 titles, covering a wide range of subjects, with some particularly mild erotica and titilating titles" (II,292). Distinctions between the series could be made by noting where the books were sold and the type of paper used. The books of the "Globe Library" were frequently sold at newsstands or to travelers. Generally priced at twenty-five cents, they provided reading for a mass audience. The "Rialto Series," on the other hand, was printed on better paper and was designed for a "better class" of readers.

Until it ceased the publication of adult fiction in 1914 Rand, McNally made an appeal to a popular level of the reading public with a group of ephemeral sentimental novels. While few of these were "great"—or even "good"—literature, they were popular enough to maintain a successful line for the company. Covering a wide range of settings and locales these works were seldom "Chicago" novels in the restricted sense; hence, early the firm disavowed a purely regional approach in its publication of fiction. On the other hand, like many of the publishers of the period, the firm was aware of the interest in Chicago work and published *Suppressed Sensations; or Leaves from the Notebook of a Chicago Reporter* (1879). This thriller, whose authorship was later attributed to James Maitland, was of a genre devoted to exposing the ills of the city and was based upon "fact." A few years later, in 1885, Mrs. A. A. Wellington's *By A Way That They Knew Not* appeared, a novel of manners using Chicago society. The influence of the railroads can be seen in James Daly's *The Little Blind God on Rails: A Romaunt of the Gold Northwest* (1888), a story which recounts a long trip on the Chicago and Northwestern railroad. Later than most publishers, Rand, McNally cashed in on the Chicago fire with John McGovern's *Daniel Trentworthy: A Tale of the Chicago Fire* (1889). Of this group of writers, John McGovern was perhaps best known in the circle of Chicago literati.

The firm of R.R. Donnelley and Sons Co., another early company, survived the vicissitudes of the times and is still considered a Chicago landmark although its days as a publishing company of distinctive books has long since passed. Like other companies, its founder began as a printer. The firm, which started as a printing company and became a publisher of books, has returned to its initial purpose. In 1864 there was nothing unusual about the formation of Church, Goodman, and Donnelley to suggest that this was the beginning of a dynasty that would extend to the present time. Edward Goodman and Leroy Church had been in Chicago for some time but felt that they would do better if they had a partner who could oversee the printing phase of the business, and Richard Donnelley was invited to join them. In a series of successful moves, the firm became a major force in Chicago's publishing world—and later remained one of the nation's outstanding printing companies.

By 1870 the young firm had achieved a degree of success. It had done some excellent work, and some significant books had been issued from its presses. In order to diversify its offerings and to capture the growing market for fiction, the firm approved the establishment of the Lakeside Publishing and Printing Company. Had it not been for the foresight of Richard Donnelley the new company, incorporated in 1870, may not have become so important during the 1870's as a producer of a great many of the cheap paperbacks of the period. Specifically, the Lakeside Library of 1875—the firm's major asset—produced standard (and not so standard) works of fiction which were sold in inexpensive paper editions. Shove has noted in his *Cheap Book Production in the United States, 1870 to 1891* (Urbana, Ill., 1937) "the role of the Lakeside Library in popularizing the accessibility of 'good' literature cannot be minimized" (p. 74). By so doing, the firm made available to the general public the works of major American and European writers. But Richard Donnelley and Alex Loyd had no way of knowing that 1870 was not a good year to begin a new endeavor such as the Lakeside Publishing and Printing company. The destructive fire was followed two years later by the Panic of 1873 which ushered in a nation-wide Depression.

By 1877 the Lakeside Press was forced by the circumstances of the times to close; but before it ceased its operations, its famous Lakeside Library had issued over 250 titles. The following year, Norman T. Gasselte joined Donnelley and Loyd to form a short-lived company which was also primarily concerned with appealing to the market for cheap paper editions. In 1879 Donnelley got the control of the firm, and in 1883 R.R. Donnelley and Sons began. He was one of the first city printers not only to recognize the difference between publishing and printing but also to do something about it. Thus, from 1864 and the days of Church and Goodman to 1883—through a number of combinations and subsidiaries—Richard Donnelley was the dominant figure. Long after his other partners have been forgotten, he remained one of the stalwart figures in the city's printing and publishing history.

Strongly committed to the city, Donnelley was willing to take some risks as he asserted that the role of the city could become a major factor in the country. While book publishing as such represented a small segment of the firm's history, those books published became significant examples of what could be done. In 1903 the firm instituted a series known as the *Lakeside Classics*. These books, which appeared annually at Christmas, were designed originally to give apprentice printers an opportunity to work on all phases of book production; but they also reprinted some outstanding works in western Americana.

Like many other book publishers of the period in the city, Alexander McClurg became a legend in his own lifetime; and the two companies with which he was associated made significant contributions to the art of publishing as well as to Chicago literature. The Civil War interrupted his work as a bookseller in 1862 when the Crosby Guards, which he had organized, became Company H of the 88th Illinois Volunteer Infantry. From the standpoint of the State's participation in that war if McClurg had done nothing else he would have made a significant contribution. Beginning as a Captain at Camp Douglas, he quickly rose in military rank as he participated in some of the important campaigns of the war including the famed Sherman's March to the Sea. Perhaps another man would have remained in the military where such advancement had come so rapidly, but McClurg was a "bookman" who felt that he wanted to spend his life in the book trade; hence, in 1865 he resumed his civilian life although he affectionately was called "General" by his friends. Returning to S.C. Griggs and Co., where his career had begun, McClurg found two men who shared his love for books in E.L. Jansen and F.B. Smith. Together they decided to buy out Griggs bookselling business when Griggs decided after the Fire of 1871 that he wished to devote himself to publishing alone. Thus it was that Jansen, McClurg, and Co. began on April 1, 1872. The booksellers began with a series of popular books and continued a successful operation. In 1873 the firm issued only one book, but that was *Landscape Architecture* by Horace W.S. Cleveland. And had Chicago followed Cleveland's suggestions, the post-fire restoration might have led to a planned city which would have eliminated many subsequent problems of the urban community; however, the work was popular in its own day and has become a classic at the present time. In 1874 the firm issued one of its few new offerings, the sermon collection by Reverend David Swing entitled *Truths for Today*. This book became central in the controversy between Swing and the Chicago Presbytery; it was also a central exhibit in Swing's famous heresy trial. When the trial was over and Swing had been exonerated, the firm—recognizing the popular interest in the matter—issued a transcript of the trial which had captured so much popular interest. This in two years, with a limited output, the firm had been perceptive enough to issue some works which were destined to become important in the annals of Chicago culture. This was just the beginning of a close relationship between the city's cultural/literary establishment and McClurg.

Throughout the 1870's, however, the firm continued to emphasize bookselling and distribution although the textbook trade was diminishing because specialized textbook publishers were localizing the distribution of schoolbooks as these publishers became more and more common. Yet during this period the firm published two apparently disparate types of books which merely represented another testimony to McClurg's "book sense." First in 1875 the firm issued two sentimental novels which captured the attention of a public addicted to these cheap romances. Then beginning in 1877 it issued *Catalogue of Standard Library and Illustrated Books in Fine Bindings*, a project which was continued almost until the end of the century, which reflected McClurg's interest in "fine" books, and which appealed to bibliophiles all over the country.

By the end of the 1870's both Jansen who had started in the book business in 1848 and McClurg who had entered it in 1859 could count their successes. The 1880's, however, represented a period of reorganization. First of all, Lucien Mitchell who had been a part of the firm of Mitchell and Hataway, religious book dealers, joined Jansen and McClurg in 1880 as the more specialized firm went out of existence. In the following year Edward Cook, who had worked in the city for a New York firm, also joined the firm for a three-year period. The two new partners added strength to the young firm which as one of the outstanding booksellers in the city had become known for its rare book section affectionately known as the "Saints and Sinners Corner," where such writers as Eugene Field could be found almost daily. Perhaps at no other time in the city's history has a bookstore been such an integral part of the city's literary life. That Jansen, McClurg, and Co. did not take more chances publishing the works of these midwestern writers is interesting, but the firm did issue a representative number of Chicago writers. Thus some of the works of Hobart Chatfield Chatfield-Taylor, Mary H. Catherwood, and Mary Abbott carried the Jansen and McClurg imprint or that of its successor, A.C. McClurg Co. Perhaps of greater importance was the firm's apparent commitment to the fledgling local color movement. Even some of Joaquin Miller's stories of the Sierras were published by Jansen, McClurg and Co. in the 1880's; however, the firm issued a substantial number of novels dealing with the South. Perhaps this interest in the South as a locale was a reflection of McClurg's participation in the War or perhaps it was a recognition that sectional divisions would have to disappear as quickly as possible if the wounds from the War were to heal.

By the end of the decade Jansen who had to retire for health reasons in 1886 was no longer part of the firm. McClurg, then, reorganized under his own name, and the firm of A.C. McClurg and Co. was brought into existence, a new legal entity but one run by a man with years of successful experience. Jansen had been a cautious publisher, and the firm's output had mirrored this in the issuance of few titles; however, for the first time A.C. McClurg could control this aspect of the firm, and he marked the new independence by issuing the works of the *Tribune*'s music critic, George P. Upton, *Women in Music* (1886).

In the following year A.C. McClurg and Co. issued seventeen

new books, and—as in the past—the popular and ephemeral were combined with reference books which had built-in audiences. Such titles as *The Standard Oratorios* by George P. Upton and *Home Life of Great Authors* by Hattie Tyng Griswold enjoyed wider circulation. The publication in 1891 of the two-volumed medieval romance by the Chicago clergyman, Frank W. Gunsaulus, signaled the firm's interest in historical romances. Such works as *Monk and Knight: An Historical Study in Fiction* might not have told readers much about their Chicago, but it opened the door to that "escape" literature which has always been popular with readers. Into the twentieth century A.C. McClurg remained both a visible and viable force in the cultural as well as literary life of the city.

The custom of issuing the works of other publishing firms under his own imprint was a common practice of S.C. Griggs; yet, many firms in the city followed this practice, some with more success than others. Among historians of the book trade, the memory of the Chicago-based firm of Belford, Clarke and Co. remains an enigma as some of the company's maneuvers are still condemned. It must be said, however, that some of the firm's devious devices— according to the nineteenth-century code—have become accepted practices in twentieth-century bookselling. While the manipulations, price-cuttings, and publishing tactics of the firm might have helped the modernization of the book trade, they also caused some concern to those who were interested in the city's reputation. Yet, many of the activities of Belford and Clarke were in keeping with the money-grubbing image associated with Chicago.

The Belford brothers (Alexander, Charles, and Robert) along with James Clarke had become successful in Canada before Alexander and Clarke joined the post-fire search for fortune in the rising Chicago. Arriving in 1875, incorporating themselves in 1879, they immediately became involved in the printing of cheap reprints of standard authors. They flooded the city with underpriced—and often poorly done—editions of some of the major British and Continental writers. Their use of the discount method met disfavor with other publishing houses; however their reprints of the works of such giants as Henry Thackeray, George Eliot, John Ruskin, and Sir Walter Scott sold widely. For example, they produced a fifteen-volume edition of the works of Charles Dickens which in 1885 had a run of more than 75,000 subscribers. Soon they had developed other means to increase their fortunes. Tebbel has cited a group of Canadian printers who used the same techniques, but he also carefully noted:

It was no more than coincidence that these notorious reprinters began their careers in Canada and came down to make fortunes in the United States. If they had anything else in common, it was their instant ability to make money, usually by methods not approved in the book business. In the case of Belford and Clarke, they were making a million dollars a year in Chicago before long, in ways that outraged the retail trade. [Alexander] was the innovator and chief entrepreneur of these methods. If a bookseller refused to handle a firm's line of undercut standard sets, for example, he would approach the nearest clothing store and install a supply of the firm's books at its own risk. This method not only sold books but the resulting controversy produced a good deal of free advertising.

Belford also opened book stalls in most department stores and elsewhere until there was scarcely a major city . . . which did not have such a Belford retail department, all of them selling books at cut rates. . . . Other publishers had tried to employ Belford's methods, but had failed because there was not enough of a market to carry the capital tied up in plates. Belford overcame this obstacle not only by establishing the department store book stalls but by opening temporary stores in small towns—'hippodroming,' as he called it, selling 'tail-ends' and 'plugs' (II, 445).

This questionable behavior—which did have a positive effect by sponsoring book departments in already-established stores—was ultimately unnecessary because Belford apparently had a fine "book sense." Tebbel, for example, duly reported that before Belford was thirteen years old, he had entered the publishing business and had become one of the managers for the Toronto *Evening Telegraph*. Furthermore, he was perceptive enough to see the merit in Fitzgerald's edition of *The Rubaiyat of Omar Khayyam* and issued the "first reprint" of it in the United States (II, 444). Discerning that there was a fortune to be made in the tales written by the Wisconsin governor, George Peck, for the Milwaukee *Sentinel*, Belford—for an outrageously low price—bought the rights for the sketches and essays. Thus it was that *Peck's Bad Boy* became staple reading fare for generations. The firm's activities in Chicago may have done little to enhance the literary image of the city, but from Chicago Belford and Clarke achieved the publishing coup of the century when they received permission to issue the *Encyclopedia Britannica* in America. The permission was really gratuitous because they had been reprinting the mammoth reference work; but when official permission was negotiated, the firm— as the American agent—made *Britannica* accessible to ordinary people and made the English owners richer than they had been with their own restricted edition. Of course, none of these activities advanced Chicago literature as such, but the city became better known in publishing circles because of them.

With branches in New York and San Francisco, the firm overextended itself and eventually ran into serious financial problems. In the late 1880's it went through a series of re-organizations but was forced out of business in the 1890's. Before this occurred, however, the firm began an ambitious periodical in 1888 which was dated from Chicago as well as from New York and San Francisco. It is important to remember that Belford was not totally estranged from the Chicago power structure, for he had a close friendship with Lyman Gage—an unlikely friend in view of Belford's dubious financial ability. Gage, a Chicago booster and a banker with a "sterling" reputation, helped Belford solve many of his problems. And until the last financial crisis, it was Gage who quietly supported many of the schemes attempted by Belford, and his support lent a degree of respectability to Belford's operations. Ultimately, the style of Belford and Co. was seriously questioned.

The various legal maneuvers initiated by the firm could not salvage what had been a successful and flamboyant business.

Little has ever been discovered about William Henry Lee who apparently arrived in Chicago sometime during the 1880's. It appears he may have been born in Philadelphia, although he served as a valet for a Confederate officer during the Civil War. Tebbel has noted that it was "whispered in Chicago that he was a Negro, but this was never proved" (II, 453). He was "obviously a well-educated man who spoke several languages and had the air of a gentleman [who] discouraged inquiries about his background, but did let it be known that he had been a waiter . . . , a clerk, a book agent, and a commercial traveler" (II, 453). The records seem just as cloudy about Laird, but from 1883 to 1893 Laird and Lee were associated in a relatively successful publishing venture based upon an initial outlay of $2,000. By 1893 Lee bought out his partner for $60,000 and for some reason continued to operate under the firm's original name. His continued success might be noted as the firm soon moved from Lake and South Water Streets. Eventually Lee settled at 263-265 S. Wabash Avenue for nineteen years before going to 1732 Michigan Avenue.

Lee apparently was fascinated by fine bindings and ornate type faces. He issued a Zola novel and impressed his public with its format and his advertising techniques. Among the best sellers issued by the firm were some sure winners including Conklin's *Handy Manual* (2,000,000 copies sold), *Uncle Jeremiah and His Family* (400,000 copies sold), *World's Fair View* (300,000 copies sold), and William T. Stead's *If Christ Came to Chicago* (300,000 copies sold).

Just as mysteriously as Laird and Lee came upon the publishing scene in Chicago did they disappear, but for a time the firm joined others in issuing a great share of the popular sentimental fiction of the day. Working in Chicago during the period of the World's Fair, the firm also issued its share of "Exposition" books. Yet, its publishing coup was the production of Stead's expose about what he found in the city. The book was destined to rock Chicago and the rest of the nation as it made clear what the Civic Federation had been claiming in less spectacular ways. Chicago was a crime-ridden city where prostitution had become too acceptable. That the English clergyman should have been concerned about it was no less disturbing to those self-appointed souls who had decided to "clean up" the city. At the same time *If Christ Came to Chicago* contained enough sensationalism to please those readers who were not as committed to reform. Through the years the book continued to sell, and long after the firm of Laird and Lee had been forgotten, it remained as a silent testimony to the firm's existence. Less spectacular but no less important for the firm were the *Annuals* issued by the firm and which had a guaranteed sale of nearly a half million copies. Lee's specialty, however, was in the production of dictionaries. And Tebbel has noted that upon the death of Lee on June 30, 1913 "he possessed what was probably the finest set of plates for dictionaries of all sizes, to be used in public schools, ever gathered together" (II, 453).

In a city accustomed to remembering only the successes, the career of Frank Tennyson Neely, who did not remain in Chicago, is interesting. *Publishers' Weekly* (October 28, 1899) ran a story about his firm entitled "A Successful Business," which described in detail the so-called "Neely System." Ironically, a few days after the article's appearance Neely, who had moved to New York City in 1891, declared bankruptcy. Referred to as a "surprising failure" by *Publishers' Weekly* (November 15, 1899), Neely seemed initially to be destined for a quick rise in fortune.

He is still a puzzle, and it is difficult to determine exactly what it was that he was trying to do with his publishing firm. His imprint appears with a degree of frequency in the latter part of the nineteenth century; yet, the firm remains clouded by a lack of information. Unlike some firms whose initial entry into the publishing business was well-publicized and often heralded as a "new star," Neely arrived in Chicago around 1879 and seemed to "slip" into the business around 1888; yet by the early 1890's he was the publisher of some of the most popular writers of the period. Western writers such as Bill Nye and James Whitcomb Riley, prolific easterners such as Richard Henry Savage and Charles King (who wrote *A Tame Surrender: A Story of the Chicago Strike*) are examples of writers whose work carried the Neely imprint. Although he was not interested in single titles or individual writers, his Chicago days were successful. Capitalizing on the subscription books which had become the mainstay of the cheap, paper editions of books, Neely developed a company whose success was unbelievable. At one time his firm was published over six million copies of his collective titles.

While his books have been forgotten, Neely is still remembered for the landmark case of Savage v. Neely which culminated in 1896 in a decision by the Appellate Division of the New York Supreme Court in favor of Colonel Richard Henry Savage whose fictional thrillers were extremely popular. At issue was essentially an ethical question which—of course—was rooted in business practices. There had been general dissatisfaction among American authors about the financial arrangements which seemed to result from inconclusive contracts. Frequently publishing firms promised one royalty rate and eventually paid another. Authors were often helpless in the face of such duplicity. Ultimately the suit was settled but not before the ruling had been made which gave authors who were receiving royalties the right to seek and to obtain verification of sales. The implication was far-reaching, and it affected the kinds of author-publisher relationships which currently exist. The fact that it was a second-rate Chicago publisher and an equally second-rate—albeit popular— novelist involved in the case does not in any way diminish its significance to the course of publishing in the United States.

Among the phenomenal success stories in Chicago publishing history is the legend of Francis J. Schulte, a German immigrant, who had arrived in America in 1866 as a child of seven. The family of some means had migrated to St. Louis where there was a large German community; however, the family "fortune" was soon lost, and Francis found work at the St. Louis *Post-Dispatch*. After learn-

244 Prairie Voices

ing as much as possible about the newspaper business, including the printing trade, he moved to Chicago in 1883 where success stories were common in spite of the strong anti-German sentiment in the city at this time. After working in the city for six years, he opened his own company. The F.J. Schulte Co. actually "struck gold." From his work in Chicago subscription houses he was aware of the tremendous market for encyclopedias; hence, he compiled, editied, and published as his first venture *The Little Giant Cyclopedia*, which profited from the ready market for such work. After such a sure winner he willingly took the chance on Ignatius Donnelly's novel which had been rejected by some major firms because of its socialistic nature. *Caesar's Column* (1890) sold over a million copies. Limited though his offerings were, Schulte was producing one success after another. In 1890 Opie Read's *The Kentucky Colonel* appeared, and the Read enthusiasts eagerly purchased the work of the man who had done so much for popular literature in the Midwest. Unlike some publishers who longed to rise above region, Schulte saw merit in a devotion to locale and believed firmly in the development of a western literature and probably did more than any other small publishing house toward promoting western Americana. At the same time, he had become accustomed to predictable success, something not always possible with new or unknown writers. He then decided upon a technique which was to further advance his company. Taking the unknown work of major writers or those works which had gone out of print early in a book's history, he instituted a plan to re-issue these works in cheap editions and captured a market which had probably been untouched by the first edition. Thus through various means he got the works of some major authors published under his imprint. For example, it was F.J. Schulte who issued Howells' *A Modern Instance* after it had practically failed in its 1872 edition. By capitalizing on the subsequent reputation of Howells, he was able to make a successful venture out of one of Howells' initially little-known works.

In the early years of the 1890's Schulte captured the right to publish two novels by Edgar Fawcett, the popular and prolific writer who dealt with New York society. He was not well-liked in his city but, nevertheless, produced one best seller after another. Both *American Push* and *An Heir to Millions* were published in 1892 with a Schulte imprint. During that same year Schulte issued Stanley Waterloo's story of the Wisconsin frontier, *A Man and a Woman*. After the publication of *A Kentucky Colonel* three more Opie Read works were published: *Emmet Bonlore* (1891) *Selected Stories* (1891) and *The Colossus* (1893), which did early for Chicago what Dreiser's *The Titan* (1914) was to do in a much later period. Hamlin Garland, an early enthusiast for the development of Chicago as a literary center, placed many of his works with midwestern publishers. To Schulte went the privilege of publishing *A Member of the Third House: A Dramatic Story* (1892) and *Prairie Folks* (1893).

Unfortunately, the phenomenal rise of F.J. Schulte and Co. was matched by an equally fast decline, which was the result of a bad personal investment rather than a business problem. As his company suffered, so also did the cause of western literature. Had Schulte been able to survive his own personal financial crisis, undoubtedly his company would have remained in the forefront of those publishers who were willing to cooperate with western writers.

Before the World's Columbian Exposition, the firms of Ellis and Fergus, S.C. Griggs, Rand and McNally, R.R. Donnelley, A.C. McClurg, Belford and Clarke, Laird and Lee, F.T. Neely, and F.J. Schulte had proved that a large and successful publishing center could exist in Chicago. Diverse though these companies were, committed to paying literary ventures rather than to experimenting with unknown writers and questionable subjects, they were nonetheless proud of the imprimatur of Chicago. And they were not alone. There were some smaller and more experimental firms which also flourished. In the late 1880's the George W. Ogilvie Co. achieved a degree of fame albeit some of it was negative. After an 1885 incorporation, the firm capitalized upon the growing interest in "detective" and "mystery" fiction, a literary genre which had a rather large audience. In the 1890's Charles H. Kerr became known as a publisher who would issue rejects from other houses. He was especially interested—as was Francis J. Schulte—in books with a socialistic angle and published a number of utopian novels.

Among the distinguishing characteristics shared in common by most of the city's publishers was their willingness to gamble on techniques if not on authors. Sometimes this was expressed in their defensive pride, other times in their courage to "take on" the so-called Eastern Establishment. They generally believed that they had a right as well as an obligation to make the inaccessible convenient for the average reader. This attitude in part accounted for the controversy between George Ogilvie and the Merriam Company. The argument revolved around Ogilvie's publication of *Webster's Imperial Dictionary* which Merriam sold for $10.00 and which Ogilvie issued for $5.00. This act of price-cutting resulted in Merriam filing a suit against Ogilvie, charging violation of the rights of the firm which had been publishing the dictionary for years. The courts, however, ruled that Ogilvie had the right to issue the dictionary.

For some reason which is not clear George Ogilvie decided to give up his Chicago firm; he moved to New York and transferred his titles to J.S. Ogilvie and Co., a firm owned by his brother. The transfer is made more peculiar because of the emnity which existed between the two brothers, but by the end of 1886 one of the more colorful figures in Chicago publishing had become a part of the New York literary scene.

The fact that most of the nineteenth-century firms did not extend into the twentieth century is frequently used to substantiate the claim that Chicago did not support publishing endeavors. For example, seldom are Chicago firms discussed by historians of the period. When they are recognized, these companies are generally dismissed as having been too small or too derivative. Yet, when *Publishers' Weekly* issued its list of U.S. publishing firms at the close of the 1880's, there were approximately fifty publishers in the city who had issued enough books to become part of this national list. (See Appendix B.) And even this was not a complete survey; hence, such firms as the Fergus Printing Co. and Henry A. Sumner do not appear. On the eve of the Exposition, before the advent of Stone and Kimball or Way and Williams, Chicago publishers had achieved recognition in the country. Frequently the strength of the firms was dependent upon a single individual whose death seriously weakened the company. But if publishing never clearly materialized in the city, the printing industry did. Certainly, when one thinks of the big houses, it is common to think only in terms of New York City or Boston; but at a particular moment in the history of publishing in the United States, the Chicago firms played a significant role.

CHAPTER 6

Chicago Literature
at the Crossroads

Of the novels published immediately after the fire perhaps not a single one captured the imaginations and the fancies of readers all over the world as much as Reverend E.P. Roe's *Barriers Burned Away* which appeared in 1872. Published in London, it became an immediate best-seller. It was a sentimental work with the sensationalism of the Chicago Fire and the moralistic preachments of its central character, Dennis Fleet. It is the story of a young man from the country who has to make his way in the sprawling, defiant city. Embodied in the novel are the myths and the realities of Chicago life. There is the all-pervasive belief in the American Dream and in Chicago as the place where this dream can be realized. Yet, underlying the apparent romantic elements of the novel are some characteristics which anticipate the realistic novels of a later period. There is the introduction of an urban sense of history and of the businessman who is totally committed to business with portraits of the young, groping, commercially-oriented society of the new city emphasizing the inevitable distinctions between the North, West, and South Sides of Chicago. There is the unspoken belief that events in Chicago are symptomatic of American civilization. Roe echoed the anti-immigrant attitude which was gaining a foothold in the city only to be rejected by the protest novelists of the twentieth century. In Dennis Fleet the reader sees the power of the individual to defy his environment without meeting that inevitable defeat so often presented. And in spite of Roe's own philosophical bent, he was aware that the city ultimately would demand a new set of values for survival in it.

In many ways Roe's novel was the hope of idealists all over the city. There were those who had a dream of a Chicago which could be. For them the Fire of 1871 had been the promise of a new beginning. But by the end of the decade it was apparent that the barriers were more firmly entrenched than ever. The new city had been created. Perhaps it was more beautiful than the old. Perhaps it had more to offer than the old. But the commercial spirit which had made the first Chicago controlled the second.

The immediate problems which attended the rebuilding of the new city had passed by 1880. There were obvious signs of the devastating fire if one looked closely, but there had emerged a glistening, magnificent city which had been created with new buildings. While all of this was taking place, there were those who insisted that a Chicago "culture" should also develop. They became increasingly concerned lest the swift transition from the frontier town to the modern industrial city be taken as a sign that Chicagoans were only interested in signs of material progress. The city's life has constantly been marked by self-consciousness and defensive pride, but these traits became more exposed as Chicagoans tried to convince themselves—and the rest of the nation—of their greatness. And it was a strange task that the image-makers had set for themselves. From the Fire of 1871 to the World's Columbian Exposition of 1893 the creators of the new city used the old techniques of business success which had produced the first Chicago, but they were concerned about developing a cultural climate similar to that of the East. In short, there was an underlying desire to be accepted by older and more traditional societies. This was intensified by the general respect of Chicagoans for what was termed "New England stock."

As Chicago developed its many elites, apparent contradictions evolved. Some of these were based primarily on regional concerns. In spite of protests to the contrary, it was a common practice in the city to look toward the East very much as Americans have traditionally looked toward Europe. As a result, New Englanders were viewed as being more socially acceptable than those from other sections of the country. Still another conflict arose between the native and foreign born as the contributions of the latter group to American culture were frequently ignored in the creation of the new community. In the days before the fire ex-New Englanders (confused in the minds of some with being the same as "native" Americans) had dominated Chicago's business and social scene even though the number of foreign immigrants who achieved commercial success is impressive and in spite of the fact that the early city prided itself upon being a class-less society. Thus, it is not surprising to see New Englanders assuming leadership in the post-fire period. There were others in Chicago who viewed place of origin as totally inconsequential in the matter of creating a city. An incipient struggle developed between those who had a great respect for the cultural heritage of New England and those who had cast their lots with the metropolis of the prairie, as they placed a greater emphasis upon *what was to be* rather than upon *what was.* This latter group was strongly committed to business and material matters much to the chagrin of those who wanted to minimize the importance of the marketplace. Yet, the businessman who stood in the vanguard, who was largely responsible for the image of Chicago as the place where materialism was THE ruler, was almost always categorized by place of origin. Although a few of them were from the South, concidentally many of the city's commercial leaders were New Englanders. Like the true frontiersmen, their spiritual predecessors, they gave no quarter for the superficialities of organized society and supported "democracy"—limited though was their interpretation of the true democratic system. It is common to read in the city's folklore of Marshall Field and George Pullman walking to their downtown offices from their elaborate Prairie Avenue homes. The fact that a coachman allegedly followed at a discreet distance has been lost in the image of two powerful financiers walking to work.

There was a strange ambiguity which expressed itself in various ways, and it was more complex than simply being a conflict between the East and the West although it tended to be discussed then—as it is now—in those simplistic regional terms. What essentially was at stake was an understanding of the true nature of the city and the method by which that city would be preserved for posterity. The issue which permeated all segments of the city's life manifested itself in various ways. Perhaps the city's architects resolved the issue before anybody else. They were the first artists to sense the tremendous opportunity to express the urban experience and to shed fidelity to the East when they rushed in to help rebuild the city. It is an interesting footnote to history to observe that the expression of a new urban experience was demonstrated through commercial structures rather than through the immediate creation of a distinctive domestic residential style. Much of this, however, was initially overlooked because the forces of gentility scored an architectural coup and victory with the World's Columbian Exposition.

The writers of the city were keenly aware of many of the problems which existed between the fragmented groups. They early noted that the regional conflict was simply one of many possible ones. Hugh Duncan in his *The Rise of Chicago as a Literary Center* . . . (Totowa, N.J., 1964) aptly noted that it was difficult for the literary artist in Chicago to define THE elite.

Whether it was E.P. Roe writing of Chicago 'society' in 1872, Chatfield-Taylor in 1891, Fuller in 1895, or the works of Read, Payne, Herrick, Potter, or Patterson in the late 90's and early years of our century, there is no doubt about the position of the New England 'puritan.' Nor is there any doubt that he was preferred to the men and women of Chicago who were in quest of an elite upon which to model themselves. The problem for Chicago writers dealing with the problem of 'society' as for the successful business family, was not so much how to get into society, but *what* 'society' was worth getting into (p. 6).

Part of the problem hinged upon the initial inability of the writers to come to terms with the urban experience as the architects had done.

While one might eschew simplistic reductions of a complicated spirit which was prevailing in the city, the problem can—for the sake of discussion—be viewed as essentially a conflict between those who supported urban imitation and those who were convinced that the new or re-created city could exist by its own ground rules. It was this struggle between the advocates of the genteel eastern tradition and the advocates of a distinctively different city which would represent the western spirit that occupied much of the latter part of the nineteenth century and which was made manifest in practically every aspect of Chicago's life.

The genteel tradition is a difficult one to define partly because it meant so many different things to so many different people and because it had such varying manifestations. Essentially, it was a product of the post-fire period, although it had some roots in the early city. Its exponents were those who felt that in re-building the city, it was necessary to eliminate the frontier qualities (many of which had made the city great in the first place) and substitute what they considered to be the "pattern" of the East. Clearly associated and intricately intertwined with the principle of gentility was the mandate for good taste. While there was much talk about it and the need either to have it or to raise its standards, nobody ever successfully defined it. Elements of their notions of good taste were just as evident in the types of essays which were written and discussed in the "literary clubs" as in the kinds of homes which the elite built and furnished for themselves. They rejected as being in poor taste crudeness in any form and that included the growing realistic movement. Because they knew little and cared less about the native cultures of the immigrants who were flooding into the city, they summarily dismissed the foreign born in the city as being simply "problems" who would not disappear. They saw no incongruity in the fact that they found the music of Beethoven and the poetry of Schiller as well as of Goethe so inspiring at the same time that the anti-German attitude was growing in intensity. In some ways the spirit of the genteel movement was predicated upon the existence and reality of a dream world; hence, when the Exposition was raised in Jackson Park on Lake Michigan, they felt they had succeeded in bringing their dream to life. Certainly that dream world was all that Chicago could hope for. Yet the White City was a fleeting creation behind which the Black City of reality stood out in bold relief.

Literary life reflected the same divisive argument which was prevailing throughout the city. There were those who contended that the redevelopment of the city should follow those patterns and concerns which they thought existed in a vague territory often described as "the East." No doubt it was to Boston which they referred most frequently, but each eastern city had its advocates as well as some of the older southern ones. On the other hand, there were others—not so influential in the financial, commercial, social, and political spheres, to be sure—who kept insisting that Chicago had to develop along its own lines, that it could not repeat the life of "the East." This argument finally settled into one of whether it was to be a genteel tradition of the romantic school which the city's writers would follow or be something unique and distinct to the region. Possibly the emerging realism which was beginning to be discussed in literary circles might settle the dilemma. Among its literary advocates, the genteel tradition resulted in an attempt to follow both the neo-classical and romantic traditions for in each tradition writers found the basis for their attempts to be part of a continuous cultural tradition. Some of this same group wanted to establish the fact that Chicago was "just like" other communities; and they spent much time trying to prove similarities rather than capitalizing upon differences. They rejected, and rightly so, the notion that material written in Chicago should somehow be less than what was expected from writers of other regions in terms of form and style. Into this tradition came another group totally convinced that the "good life" could and would come with the rejection of the many foreign immigrants who were pouring into the city, forgetting for the moment that Chicago itself was a city of immigrants.

The opponents of this tradition were perhaps not as well organized, but they did produce some notable work. The newspapers, either consciously or subconsciously, led the way in the development of realism in Chicago writing. They knew what the city was, they knew the people, they knew the broken dreams and unfulfilled hopes, and were able to see exactly what the city was doing to those who had been drawn to it. They were not so naive as to believe that a cultural tradition could be created by an elite willing it into existence. Yet, they were just as convinced that the city needed a clear definition of itself.

By the 1880's it was becoming apparent that this hard-to-define conflict between the advocates and opponents of the genteel tradition was an important element in the production of literature in particular and in the general expression of the city's quality of life. Part of this conflict was largely supported by the elite who were chafing at the condescension which often was displayed toward them by easterners. It was an attempt to put the "show-them-we-are-just-as-good" attitude into literary form. Because the advocates abhorred the use of realism (it was too mundane and ordinary for them), they were devotees of the romantic tradition.

Too frequently, however, the genteel tradition is confused with romanticism. Every romanticist in Chicago neither subscribed to nor supported this tenuous tradition. And many who did placed so much emphasis upon classical literature and art that it is frequently difficult to separate them from other neoclassicists. Eugene Field, for example, was an ardent supporter of the romantic as well as the classical literary traditions. He went so far as to attempt translations of such poets as Horace and Livy. Garland's forays into the realistic movement did not impress Field who commented in his article, "The Battle of the Realists and Romanticists" (July 27, 1893) that Garland was "an apostle of realism" which Field continued to describe as having heroes who "sweat and do not wear socks . . . heroines [who] eat cold huckleberry pie and are so unfeminine as not to call a cow 'he.'" But Field did not take kindly to those who imitated eastern ways or paid obsequies to the East. He was unimpressed that Garland was being influenced by Howells. At the same time he ridiculed those Chicagoans who lionized every eastern visitor and looked for approval from that section of the country. The question frequently arises concerning the actual power of the genteel tradition in effecting changes in the urban structure. Bernard Duffey was to claim in his *Chicago Renaissance in American Letters* (East Lansing, Mich., 1953) that this movement in "nearly twenty years of supremacy had failed to establish the kind of social or intellectual structure which could support a major literature (p. 74). The spirit of gentility—while strong within the clubs and social structure—never became as supreme as its practitioners believed, but it did make some important contributions to the physical city through visible means. The idea of a leisure class civilizing the city (and ultimately the world) was as important in nincteenth-century Chicago as the idea had been to Plato's philosopher-king. Inspiring though the notion may have been, it could not produce great works of urban art. Its practitioners had to be satisfied with their discussions of their essays on art, music, and letters in their restricted clubs.

One of the more positive aspects of the genteel tradition was its emphasis upon education, not only for the young but also for adults. Continuing education, as the twentieth century might term the movement, was an integral part of the city's life and was not limited to the elite in their complicated club structures. Throughout the city lecture series were relatively common and popular as the case of the Dime Lecture Series, designed for the workers, will attest. A cursory perusal of the newspapers of the period will reveal that many celebrities came to Chicago to lecture. And the newspapers reveal that these lectures were well-attended. Among the many notables who came into Chicago during the 1880's were some of the outstanding writers of England: Oscar Wilde, Matthew Arnold, and Charles Dickens. American writers were represented by Petroleum V. Nasby, Mark Twain, George Washington Cable, and Bret Harte. Diverse religious opinions were represented by the visits of Joseph Smith, Henry Ward Beecher, and Robert Ingersoll.

During this same period the Chicago elite of the 1880's took seriously the biblical question: "Am I my brother's keeper?" And they eagerly answered in the affirmative, and began "to do things" for the benefit of the less fortunate. Much of this activity was not, however, as altruistic as it might appear on the surface. It is ironic that they often chose those philanthropic endeavors which usually lent glory to their own names. Mrs. Bates, one of Fuller's finely drawn characters in *With the Procession,* summed up the attitude of the elite quite well. Speaking to David Marshall, she said:

. . . the man who enjoys the best position and the most consideration is not the man who is making money, but the man who is giving
it away—not the man who is benefiting himself, but the man who is
benefiting the community.

Yet, she makes clear that there is an "art" to such philanthropy.

As I have said so many times to Mr. Bates, 'Make it something that
people can *see.*' Imagine a man disposed to devote two or three hundred thousand dollars to the public, and giving it to help pay off the
municipal debt. How many people would consider themselves benefited
by the gift, or would care a cent for the name of the giver? Or fancy
his giving it to clean up the streets of the city. The whole affair would
be forgotten with the coming of the next rain-storm. 'No,' said I to
[Mr. Bates], 'it must be something solid and something permanent; it
must be a building.' . . . (p. 95).

This visible philanthropy gave to the city not only the University of Chicago but also such magnificent institutions as the Newberry Library, the Crerar Library, the Art Institute, the Chicago Symphony and dotted the landscape of the city with some of its outstanding structures. Perhaps today one might wish to argue with the paternalistic nature of such philanthropic endeavors of nineteenth-century Chicago, but no one could argue that these things did not add luster to the city. Among the women, the favorite charities usually involved homes and lunch-rooms for "working girls." And it is not surprising to note in the fiction dealing with the period, constant references made to these charities which occupied the time of the women as their husbands continued to make money in the city.

And thus it was that no facet of Chicago life remained untouched by the advocates of the genteel tradition. If, ultimately, the movement had little lasting effect upon literary production; the movement was signficant in helping Chicagoans—or at least a powerful group of them—define their roles in the city. In the final analysis the events and productions of the 1800's are as much as result of their failures as of their successes.

I

Periodical literature was the first to reflect clearly the issues which revolved around the genteel tradition. Before the golden age of Chicago's literature or the first renaissance of the latter half of the 1890's, there was considerable literary activity in the city. Much of it was centered within the world of journalism where the men and women who worked for magazines as well as for newspapers were slowly defining the city for themselves. In the pre-fire city the goals of many writers were quite similar, but the magazines generally became products of a genteel culture which many believed could exist in Chicago inasmuch as they were convinced such a life existed somewhere. Some of the tendencies which had led to the proliferation of pre-fire journals were still present in the city; as a result, the 1880's seemed an active place for the creation of new magazines and newspapers. The caution of the 1870's disappeared, and the records show an inordinate number of attempted journalistic efforts, many of which were doomed to failure—just as in the past the supply could not really exceed the demand. The motivations for these attempts varied from effort to effort, but underlying all of them was obviously a belief that they had a chance to succeed. There were still those who felt it important to continue a drive toward the creation of a western literature which would demand the respect of the literary establish-ment. In this hope they shared the optimism of the editors of the 1840's and 1850's who felt that a western literature was possible. But unlike the earlier writers who had substantially wanted to create this literature for themselves, now the attitude was to create it in order "to show" others what could be done in the com-mercial marketplace of the Midwest.

As has been noted in Chapter 3, many of the journals which developed during the 1840's and 1850's demonstrated a deliberate attempt to establish an identifiable western literature. Based upon the faith of both editors and readers, there was a belief that the region not only could become a cultural center on the prairie but also could produce a distinctive and unique literature. This belief was intricately connected to their notion that the power and the independence of the city was ultimately connected to the possibility and the probability of a regional literature. Such provincialism—if one would call it that—gave way in the late 1870's and in the 1880's to the notion that a western literature was acceptable only as long as it adhered to the same standards followed in other places. The excessive pride of the earlier period was tempered and conditioned by a desire to be found acceptable by older communi-ties. The gambling spirit of the past gave way to a more cautious approach. No longer did many Chicagoans wish to be categorized by their peculiar, frontier qualities and habits. Thus, as the rest of the nation was embarking upon the local color movement, the Chicago writers of the genteel tradition were rejecting localism. As a result, before regionalism became a dominant motif in Ameri-can letters, Chicago writers of the 1840's and 1850's had at-tempted it, and later writers in the city had found it wanting for their purposes.

Part of the story of Chicago's literature during the decade of the 1880's and in the opening years of the 1890's is demonstrated by the types of magazines which were developed during the period. Perhaps nowhere else was the desire to be like the East made more apparent and obvious than in those journals which gave tacit approval to the genteel tradition and by so doing became the organs for that tradition. While some of the existing journals made clear that there was a market—limited though it often was—for literature in the commercial marketplace of the middle border, the magazines of the period illustrated the growing complexity of Chicago's character. In the emerging cosmopolitanism of these journals there was some interest and concern with such matters as the relationship between capital and labor (and certainly this was more apparent after the Haymarket Riot of 1886), but social concerns were not as prominent as one might expect from magazines developed in Chicago during a period when the nation had turned its attention to problems of society and issues of the economy. All of the magazines in Chicago, however, shared an evolving sense of the importance of Chicago as a major metropolitan center and illustrated the increasing complexity of this particular city. For those who did not wish to be burdened with too much reading material dealing with weighty subjects, there were illustrated magazines whose pictures told the news. These frequently gained tremendous circulations. And there are examples of other magazines moving from western communities east to Chicago. By the 1880's the self-consciousness of Chicago lent itself to the establishment of a series of literary magazines. Some of them were devoted to popular fiction (both serials and short stories), poetry, and literary criticism; others were merely designed to present articles of interest written as formally as possible. Some were purely western in approach; others were more cosmopolitan seeking manuscripts from the East and from England. But all of them were committed to the idea that Chicago could be an outstanding literary center. Some of the more chauvinistic went so far as to maintain that the city's literary millenium had already arrived.

When one considers the magazines which included short stories and serializations of longer works, there are several generalizations which can be made. First of all, there were a number of works not only by established eastern writers but also by Chicagoans and westerners. Thus, the native writers had an opportunity to be heard. But much of this fiction was of the typical ephemeral type with an emphasis upon romance, nature, and adventure. Chicagoans were beginning to search for that usable past which has always figured so prominently in a community's literary development. The frontier, which was far more remote than it had been to the earlier writers, now formed a common backdrop for stories of trappers and Indians. Many of these stories were somewhat reminiscent of those first early western stories which had appeared in the 1850's. Thus, one can note, that by the end of the nineteenth century when the historical romance was increasing in popularity there had already been established an interest in the genre. Certainly it did little to define the urban nature of the city, but it did much toward defining that tradition or usable past which is so necessary for a group of people in search of the origins. There were also some "urban" stories, but these were more often than not done with a sentimental approach and resulted in didactic tales explaining the virtuous requirements of urban life. The stories about nature tended to present an idyllic view of the prairie and man as being inspired by the awesomeness as well as the splendor of his surroundings. In this setting man could absorb, so these stories suggested, the goodness of the Universe. Sometimes elements of adventure were combined in order to portray the many discoveries of the frontiersmen who were men larger than life, the heroes of the West. Occasionally, but not too often, nature is seen as vicious and superior to man. The defeat of man by nature produced a type of gloom which was left primarily to another age to develop.

Among the so-called literary magazines some achieved a distinction which might seem unusual to the modern reader. One of the early journals of this period was not begun in Chicago but moved to the city two years after its founding in Omaha. It has already been mentioned in connection with *Alliance*. *Western Magazine*, (1877-84) a monthly with Mrs. Helen Elkin Starrett as its editor, was in the forefront of the attempts to define a Chicago culture. Unfortunately, the magazine in search for more subscribers went through a period of questionable expansion. Had it not taken over the faltering *Alliance* in 1882 and had it not attempted to change its format into the *Weekly Magazine,* all indications are that it would have survived as an excellent example of what could be done with western literature. Mrs. Starrett had a sense of the various moods of her public and could appeal to them while at the same time indoctrinating them into a strong belief in the existence of a clearly-defined culture of the West. At the same time, she had some appeal for those outside of the city, and for a while the magazine was widely circulated in the East

The magazine had two important departments; one contained "select articles from our best western writers," and the "Eclectic Department" presented "the cream of European literature." Thus *The Western Magazine* appeared on the surface to offer something for the exponents of the western tradition and for those willing to transcend the confines of region. In May, 1879, the magazine made the declaration:

Give a prompt and willing support to the only periodical that illustrates our western country; and in the not far distant future we will furnish a magazine equal in size and variety of attractions to the standard monthlies of the eastern states.

This declaration does not differ significantly from the one which Rounseville had made as he embarked upon his *Western Magazine* in 1857. The promise of the journal was further enhanced by Mrs. Helen Elkin Starrett who had, by this time, achieved a degree of national fame as a journalist. She had served the famous Holland's Springfield *Republican* in Massachusetts, edited a newspaper in Kansas, and written some excellent columns for Joseph Pulitzer's St. Louis *Post-Dispatch.* In addition to the volume of poetry which she had written, Mrs. Starrett was a popular lecturer on the western circuit. Her faith in the West was as dedicated as was her belief in the possibilities of *Western Magazine.* Nor was she alone. The Chicago *Tribune,* viewing the editorial duties of Mrs. Starrett, maintained that the journal would be "the foundation of great things in the literary history of Chicago." In September of 1880 there appeared a letter entitled "A Welcome Suggestion" which was signed by a "Well-Wisher and Reader." The letter, written by Frederick Ives Carpenter when he was a high-school student, early demonstrated his concerns which he was later—as a professor of English at the University of Chicago—to re-echo. Like many of his predecessors, Carpenter was pleading for a distinctive journal which would adequately reflect the literary and intellectual interests of the city. He found in the *Western Magazine* the possibility for a literary voice for the city. He was, however, concerned about the management of the journal which was apparently too provincial for his tastes although he was aware of what it could become. He noted, for example:

. . . your magazine is the rising sun of our hopes. Will it be long before the *Western Magazine* is recognized as a worthy representative of our literary interests, before you allow it to become metropolitan?

He observed:

Rushing, trade-maddened Chicago is well-supplied with periodicals that uphold its myriad trade and labor and religious fields of activity. Yet not a sheet for its literature. Why should New York have its *Scribner's* and *Harper's,* Boston its *Atlantic,* Philadelphia its *Lippincott's* and we only our dailies and the denominational religious weeklies?

He then offered some suggestions which apparently did cause some changes in policy. He was certain that the magazine "can make a career."

Broaden your interests; admit fiction (the modern home of geniuses) and literary criticism; or at least, if we are not ready for that— literary gossip. Do this for the sake of the cosmopolitan culture that any metropolis like this possesses, and which calls for this.

Whether or not the letter from a high-school student was responsible for the subsequent changes is open to debate; however, very shortly after the publication of the letter some significant changes were made in the organization of the journal. First of all, the title was followed by a sub-title which referred to the *Western Magazine* as "A Literary Monthly." Then Mrs. Starrett began a section called "The Club" in which the essays from many of the clubs were presented to the readers of the journal. Mrs. Starrett noted in an editorial that there was "no more significant sign of social progress than the spread of literary and social clubs, whether women's clubs, art clubs, social science clubs, or study clubs." She found the club structure of the city actually cemented those interested in literature into one big fellowship, and she was willing to address the journal to this group. The fact that this group was essentially part of the genteel tradition was lost on Mrs. Starrett who herself was quite interested in socio-political problems.

When the merger with *Alliance* took place in 1882 and the journal became the *Weekly Magazine*, Mrs. Starrett assured her readership that the literary qualities would not be overlooked, and the new magazine would continue to "present to its readers each week the same choice collection of literary matter"; however, this was to be augmented by a new department "of great interest devoted to discussions by able and well-known writers on the important political, social, and economic topics" of the day. Thus in any given week, the magazine might contain a sermon by Reverend David Swing, the controversial, beleaguered, but popular clergyman of Chicago; a collection of short fiction as well as some poems; a letter from Washington on some aspect of a pressing social issue; and reviews of the political situation by William Starrett, her husband.

In spite of its commitment to freedom of expression and freedom of subject choice, it is interesting to note that the magazine was supported in part by the capitalists of the city. How much freedom was possible after the magazine had accepted the financial support of George M. Pullman, Marshall Field, and Charles B. Farwell is—even today—purely speculative, although Mrs. Starrett and her husband had little involvement with the financial arrangements of the magazine. Unfortunately, in the merger with *Alliance* Mrs. Starrett had agreed to accept the same business manager who had so mishandled the affairs of *Alliance*. It was not long before *Weekly Magazine* was also facing bankruptcy and by 1884 it was forced to cease publication.

While one may scoff at many of the "creative" efforts being proffered by Chicago's writers during this period, one must accept the dedication and commitment to literary criticism as it evolved in *The Dial*, which was founded in 1880 by A.C. McClurg and Company with Francis Fisher Browne as the editor. Originally designed as an outlet for book reviews and book notices from McClurg's as well as from some of the publishers represented by the Chicago firm, *The Dial* soon became an outstanding example of balanced critical judgment and proved that a journal devoted to literary excellence could exist in Chicago without being limited either by purely regional matters or by the business structure. Herbert Fleming noted in his work, *Magazines of a Market-Metropolis:*

> In a section where literary appreciation was much more predominant than the creative literary interest—writing and publishing—it is perhaps remarkable that such a journal as *The Dial* did not come earlier. The West was buying books. The West began to criticize books (p. 512).

What many, however, failed to perceive was to view *The Dial* as the logical culmination of many earlier critical efforts. From the beginning of journalism in Chicago, from the 1830's and 1840's, there had been some attempts made to evaluate both American and European literature as it flooded into the city. Many of the essays and lectures of the early clubs reflect this critical interest. And the articles which appeared, buried as they often were in now-obscure journals, lacked the sophistication of later works. Short-lived though these journals were, they demonstrated early efforts at literary criticism. In fact, Browne himself in his involvement with *Western Monthly* (1869-70) and subsequently with *Lakeside Monthly* (1871-74) had attempted critical journals. Both *The Owl* (1874-76) and *Literary Review* (1879-80) were immediate predecessors which were also concerned with literary criticism.

From an early age Browne was firmly convinced that an outstanding literature was neither hampered nor aided by the place or the time of its production. While he believed in the West and was an advocate for the region, he also believed that a literature produced in the region would not be more peculiar than that from any other section of the nation. He believed, in other words, that good literature transcended time and place. Unwittingly he became the spokesman for one phase of the genteel tradition. As he viewed American writers, he saw Whitman's poetic innovations as intolerable radicalism; yet, it is to the credit of *The Dial* that by the 1890's it had altered its editorial opinion of Whitman. Longfellow was viewed as the greatest poet to be produced in this country, and there was a great deal of interest in the few poems by Emily Dickinson which had emerged by this time. Yet, unlike many of his counterparts, Browne supported the realistic work of Ibsen as a step in freeing dramatic literature from some of its more archaic characteristics and saw Oscar Wilde as a genius who was being unfairly judged by his contemporaries. While he had his strong likes and dislikes, Browne tried to submerge them beneath his judicious approach to literature and thereby gave to Chicago as well as to the rest of the nation a magazine of top quality.

The journal probably reached its zenith in the 1890's after A.C. McClurg and Company had relinquished its control. This is not to suggest that the journal was actually hampered by the association because Browne got some of the best writers of the period to review books, but obviously there would be those who felt that the independence of the journal was seriously curtailed by its association with a book publisher and distributor. In announcing the new arrangement in *The Dial,* A.C. McClurg and Company announced:

The change looks wholly to the good of the paper, which, it is believed, will be better served by its publication as a separate and independent enterprise. It is perhaps natural that a critical journal like The Dial should be to some extent misunderstood through its connection with a publishing and book-selling house. To relieve the paper from this disadvantage and to make its literary independence hereafter as *obvious* as it ever has been *real,* is the prime object of the present change.

Browne assumed full ownership and management which he held until his death in 1913.

While it maintained a certain distance from some of the immediate literary concerns of Chicago, the journal did become in the 1890's involved in the issue of local and regional literature. This was especially true as Chicago prepared for the World's Columbian Exposition, and *The Dial* joined other apologists for the city in citing the cultural attributes of the city which were so frequently derided in the eastern press. At no point, however, did Browne reject the standards which he had established for himself even in the face of the anger of Hamlin Garland who refused to subscribe to *The Dial* because he thought it was too medieval and who condemned the journal for referring to the work of James Whitcomb Riley as "doggerel." Any journal which would make that judgment, according to Garland, was "not a critical journal" but "a conservative rear guard" magazine. Brown's response to Garland displays quite clearly the editor's beliefs and commitment to literary standards. At the same time it explains the role of Chicago in the midst of Garland's insistence upon regionalism:

Shall a literary fact or a critical opinion not be given because it would be 'disloyal'? Shall criticism be geographical? . . . For twenty-five years . . . I have been devoted to [western literature's] development and advancement. This devotion is not now to be impugned by eleventh hour converts who think that because I, through the Dial, will not make it my mission to exploit them and their narrow cult, am unable to see anything 'this side of England.' . . . We must show that we are willing to have it tried by the standards of world literature, rather than by the standards of the back settlements.

The Dial remained in Chicago until 1919 when it was moved to New York and ceased publication in 1929. Those of the twentieth century who were familiar with the journal probably ignored the facts of its beginning because it had become so much a part of the national literary scene. But as a product of the literary activities of the 1880's in Chicago, *The Dial* proved the possibilities of such a journal were not idle speculation. Fleming, on the other hand, maintained:

> After all is said about the *Dial* as a symbol of the growing metropolitan independence of criticism in Chicago, that which stands out as most striking concerning the developments of the eighties is [the journal's] origin in a book-distributing agency erected, like other freight distributing houses, along with the railroad systems which made the dot on the map marked "Chicago" a metropolitan center (p. 517).

Whether one ultimately decides that the *Dial* was a direct response to the commercial city is a moot point. What is important is that there was produced in Chicago a magazine of high quality which became the answer to *Harper's, Scribner's,* the *Atlantic,* or *Lippincott's,* and during its own day it was just as well-known. Unfortunately, Browne's son who took over in 1913 did not have the same commitment to literature as his father had had, and the sale of the magazine with its subsequent move to New York closed one of the most successful chapters of Chicago's literary history.

Perhaps in many respects one of the most successful literary journals of the period was *The Current* which existed from 1883 to 1888 as a weekly. Edited until 1885 by Edgar L. Wakeman, *The Current* attempted to bring to Chicagoans the best of American and European literature. Its articles and stories tended to be of a general nature with little or no reference to western regionalism.

For example, the issue for February 28, 1885 (Vol. III, 135-136) contained an article entitled "Hawthorne's Delineation of New England Puritanism." In addition to Hawthorne (who was apparently a favorite with *Current* readers judging from the number of articles on him), there are numerous references to Tennyson and Poe. Among the longer works of the journal was the appearance of E.P. Roe's *An Original Belle* as a serial beginning in Volume II (December 6, 1884) and continuing throughout Volumes III and IV. Another frequent contributor was Joaquin Miller. One of its unique features which might have some historic significance for readers today is the fact that each article, story, and poem carried the facsimile autograph of the author, undoubtedly, a costly device. Perhaps nowhere is the editorial philosophy of *The Current* more clearly defined than in the article "A Plea for Romance" by Edgar Nash which appeared on December 6, 1884. At the same time the article demonstrates the critical perceptions which had been adopted by the genteel movement in Chicago. The opening statement sets the elements of the argument to be pursued by Nash:

Whenever the question is asked, what is the most noticeable feature of American life of today? it is quickly answered with one word— 'Materialism.' The answer is frequently given at greater length, for the question is asked in many forms, but this one word summarizes the invariable reply. It is seen in business, society, religious thought, and very strikingly in our literature. Its appearance in the world of letters is sometimes called 'naturalism,' and then again it is designated as 'realism,' but in this connection these words mean nothing more nor less than materialism. It has taken so strong a hold upon the American mind and literature that Howells is right in describing it as 'the only literary movement of our time that seems to have any vitality in it.' In American fiction it is all-powerful, as a glance at any of the leading periodicals will quickly convince the inquirer. The idealist has been crowded to the wall. The romancer brings his products in vain to the market. There is no longer any demand for his wares. Yet with all this eager striving to get 'nearer to the heart of humanity,' as they express it, and to deal with men and things and conditions as they are found in the world about us, it is still pertinent to inquire whether grace, beauty and fancy have not been sacrificed to satisfy this fierce clamor for realism, and whether this latest literary movement is healthy and strong and one from which good results can come.

He then proceeds to trace the evolution of this new spirit in literature by focusing upon French literature with a very perceptive analysis of the role played by Zola in its development.

The materialism which seems to be steadily growing in favor with American novelists has attained its highest development in modern French fiction. Emile Zola has outstripped all competitors in portraying life as it is. He leaves out nothing. He lays bare the existence about him precisely as he finds it, and in doing it displays that fine literary skill which is the glory of Frenchmen. He is a great artist in word painting, yet it is safe to say that few American readers, no matter how ardent may be their love and admiration for 'art for art's sake,' read one of his novels without a feeling very much akin to disgust at the bareness and sickening aspects of his realism. The Anglo-Saxon mind naturally selects subjects different from the French, for the life about us is different, but the same methods are faithfully and oftentimes laboriously followed. Characters are portrayed with the same regard for detail, and there is clearly apparent the same regard for detail, and there is clearly apparent the same endeavor to magnify and give importance to the small and petty incidents of life. In place of the *roue,* the *demi monde,* the intrigues and orgies, we are shown the commonplace society young man, the insipid society young woman, and the stupid ball or reception. Page after page is devoted to the long drawn out analyses of the mental operations of dullards. We are wearied either with tedious moral and mental vivisection, cruel to the spectator if not to the subject. Many of our modern works of fiction are, in short, French novels without their vivacity and wickedness.

Turning his attention to the matter of romance, he notes:

In striking and delightful contrast with the productions of these writers are the works of the Norwegian Bjornsterne Bjornson, of the

German George Ebers, Wilhelmine Von Hillern and the lamented
Auerbach, of the English Blackmore and Shorthouse, whose 'John
Inglesant' has won a position upon the shelves of every library of
standard novels, and, indeed, of a score of other writers beyond the
sea who have added imagination to their skill at character-painting
and story-telling. Their beautiful tales are of rare power, breathing a
spirit so fresh, pure and delightful that they fairly charm the reader.
Yet these writers possess none of the much vaunted realism of our
American novelists. Their characters are frequently fanciful and impossible, and their plots often appear wretched when measured in the
yardstick spirit. But their productions are strong, healthy, and elevat-
ing. They afford intense pleasure and are profitable reading.

Nash maintains that in spite of the move toward the commonplace
in writing, the public has not been thoroughly convinced; and he
believes that readers actually prefer a writer such as Hawthorne to
to those who were in the process of popularizing the realistic
method.

In spite of this clearly-defined tendency toward 'naturalism' in
novels, if a careful and candid judgment of the great reading public
of this country could be obtained upon the question who is the greatest
American writer of fiction, it is hard to believe that it would be in
favor of Howells, or James, or Fawcett, or Lathrop, or any of the
realistic school. Indeed, the conviction has been steadily becoming
deeper and more widespread that the modest, shy, retiring author of
'The Scarlet Letter' is not only the most distinctively American novelist, but wrote the most finished style, displayed the finest imagination
and left upon his work an imprint more akin to genius than any writer
who went before or has yet succeeded him. But Nathaniel Hawthorne
was distinctively a romancer, and from the weird unreality of his tales,
from his creations rather than from his characterizations, arises the
charm that stamps his novels as works of genius.

Nash continues by addressing himself to the effects of the new
method of writing upon the readers of it.

If it be permissible to speak of a novel apart from the literary point of view, now that 'naturalism' has become the ideal and art is omnipotent, the effect of this materialistic tendency upon the reader may be considered. By using introspectively the analytical methods applied by the 'realists' in dissecting their characters, the conclusion becomes almost inevitable that its influence upon the reader is depressing. The impression is given, and it is all the more unfortunate if the facts justify it, that this is a wearisome, commonplace world, where hope and ambition are folly, and the very best that men can do is to endure without murmuring the dull existence which a mysterious providence has inflicted upon them. The romancer is apt to present a brighter and more optimistic view of life and duty. If reality must needs be so dreary, a longing for something a little less real is very natural.

In conclusion Nash asserts:

There has been some good work accomplished by American writers of fiction. Excellent novels have been written by Edward Eggleston, George W. Cable, Harriet Beecher Stowe, and a few others. But the influence of the more advanced realism of the Howells-James school, supported as it is by two powerful magazines, is discouraging a finer class of literary work, and cultivating a taste in which the novelist's art overbalances and almost crushes out of existence real genius. The beautiful and romantic elements of life are passed unnoticed, while the prosaic part of existence alone is portrayed and magnified.

"A Plea for Romance" is representative of the type of literary criticism which was common in *The Current*, and it also explains why the fiction in that journal seldom employed the realistic method. If realism supported urban life and values, *The Current* rejected these and substituted a romantic approach to the city which consisted of moralistic, didactic tales of rewarded virtue.

The associate editors, G.C. Matthews and John McGovern, shared Wakeman's interest in literature and believed that the new movement was not bringing out the best in American letters. Along with these three men, Professor David Swing was a "special edi-

torial contributor." Wakeman, however, could not continue to
obtain the work of the "big names" of American and European
literature and still make money. There was apparently a conflict
between Wakeman and his associate editors. When it appeared, the
issue of September 5, 1885 (Vol. IV, #90) no longer carried
Wakeman's name. Only those of Matthews and McGovern appeared. The lead editorial assured readers that *The Current* was in
good shape, that Wakeman should be praised for what he had accomplished, and asked forbearance for what he was unable to do.
By the following year (Vol. V, January-June, 1886), Matthews
and McGovern became the editors, and the period of *The Current's* attempt to go beyond its means ended. One of the first
changes to be made was the elimination of the facsimile signatures,
which necessarily reduced production costs. But the magazine was
too deeply in debt and folded as an independent publication in
1888.

Given the popularity of the magazine, the question naturally
arises: would *The Current* have survived in a different locale?
Perhaps, however, its downfall was a result of philosophical and
personality conflicts more than the place of publication. From all
reports it appears that both American and European writers were
eager to have their works published in *The Current*. In his spoof
"The Convention of Western Writers" which appeared in *Culture's
Garland,* (Boston, 1887), Eugene Field has an unnamed character
raise the question: "But have you never written anything for 'The
Current'?" And Field comments: " . . . this question would be
put with an expression of countenance that seemed to add, 'If
you *have,* you must be all right; but if you *haven't,* you can't
amount to much" (p. 77). Underlying Field's humor was the fact
that publication in *The Current* was viewed as acceptance into
THE literary establishment and was indicative of the magazine's
popularity. Wakeman, an excellent administrator who knew the
field of journalism well, had trouble with financial management.
Even though he sought manuscripts from England and was willing
to pay for them, he could not maintain his initial editorial bril-

liance. John McGovern, on the other hand, was a writer of some promise who believed so fervently in the West that he was willing for the journal to be purely a local and regional product. Perhaps the existence of *The Current* would have extended beyond its life of five years had Wakeman and McGovern been able to compromise. But during that period Chicago was treated to a magazine of high quality although it shifted from its emphasis upon world literature to become a mouthpiece for regionalism before it ceased publication and became a part of *America* in 1888.

In 1884 two journals appeared which were short-lived but which were destined to have some effect upon the Chicago literary scene. Both of them ceased publication in 1887. *The Rambler* was designed as a magazine of humor, not a frontier crude humor but a humor which was in keeping with the dictates of the genteel tradition. The sub-title of the magazine summarizes fairly well the major emphasis of the weekly magazine which called itself "a journal of men, manners, and things." Begun by Reginald DeKoven and Harry B. Smith, both of whom were writers of light operas, the journal was imitative of the New York *Life*. Later Elliott Flowers took it over and declared:

> We wanted to do for Chicago what *Life* does for New York. The manager of the Western News Company said: 'Put a New York date on it, or the West won't take it.' We did not do so. But he was right.

While clearly there were those who still preferred eastern products to those of a home-grown variety, that was not really the problem with *The Rambler* which appealed to a leisure class which Chicago did not wish to admit it had, and perhaps in reality it really did not have. The sophisticated humor was lost on many of the readers, and the magazine's downfall was a clear indication that the genteel tradition was not as yet ready to support a school of subtle humor in Chicago. It was still the frontier tradition which controlled humor, and Eugene Field—who was never accused of subtlety— was as far as the city could apparently go at this time.

Closely associated with *The Current* and *The Rambler* as a voice
of the genteel tradition was *Literary Life,* a monthly which existed
from 1884 to 1887 with Rose E. Cleveland, the sister of President
Grover Cleveland, as editor. Bernard Duffey in his *Chicago Renaissance* . . . has referred to the journal as a "genteel protest
against Philistia" (p. 57). And so it was as it attracted eastern attention with its non-localized materials. It is a good example of a
journal which was *in* Chicago without being *of* the city. There was
little aside from its dateline to identify it with Chicago. The city's
writers were conspicuously ignored as the magazine presented literary articles of general interest with much emphasis upon the personal lives of American and British writers. No less a personage
than Charles Dudley Warner found the magazine amazing, and
there were indications that it would be used to support the contention that Chicago had arrived as a thriving literary center. In fact,
Rose Cleveland viewed the journal as *"The Century* of the West."
    Herbert Fleming records that Miss Cleveland told him:

> I was interested in *Literary Life* for three months, and then dropped
> it because of a wide divergence between myself and its business
> manager as to policy in its management. During the three months in
> which I did my rather amateurish 'editing' it was quite successful,
> and would in the hands of a more discriminating manager, or a less
> fastidious editor, have been a profitable enterprise (p. 524).

While certainly the business management was a problem, there
is another issue which must be considered in the demise of the
journal. Perhaps had Miss Cleveland moved to Chicago, she could
have had better control over a journal which ostensibly was designed for the city's literati. She chose, however, to remain at her
New York home; in so doing, she gave the impression of wishing
to be removed from the Chicago scene. This did not help the struggling journal at all.
    But if *Literary Life* can be characterized and possibly doomed
by an absentee editor, *America* was signally operated by the most

active Chicagoans of them all: Hobart C. Chatfield-Taylor and Slason Thompson, whose excessive involvement in city affairs may have been their undoing. The weekly appeared from 1888 to 1891. Clearly devoted to the "upward movement" in Chicago life and letters, *America* was strongly opposed to foreign immigration. The same attitude which had been expressed decades before by Danenhower's *Native Citizen* surfaced again. This time more vociferously than Danenhower would have ever dreamed. *America,* in spite of its political essays which were so biased that they had value only for those who believed in the theory "Chicago for the native-born," made its major contribution as a journal of literary critcism. It was similar to the *Dial* in its appeals to the supporters of the genteel tradition in the city; but unlike the *Dial,* whose importance it rivalled, *America* never achieved the broad scope of the former journal nor did it last as long. While it clearly illustrated the assets and liabilities of the genteel movement, its tendency to examine literary as well as political issues within the context of a dubious nativism severely limited its national appeal. Yet, one must acknowledge that the popularity of this weekly which called itself "a journal for Americans" reveals some of the restrictive aspects of the genteel tradition. But both Chatfield-Taylor and Thompson could justify their extreme support of the anti-immigrant forces in the city as well in the country.

It must be remembered that as the 1890's opened Chicago was busily preparing to entertain the world at the World's Columbian Exposition of 1893. It appeared even to the casual observer that all of the boasting of the city as well as its phenomenal growth had been productive. For those supporters of the genteel tradition this was to be their "moment of triumph." Such weekly journals as *The Current* and *America* kept emphasizing the "good life" and made clear to their subscribers that Chicago could become a cultural center of great magnitude as well as a vortex of commercial activity. The anti-immigrant attitude of *America* was viewed by the editors as a positive quality. Hence, the magazine contained news items of interest from Chicago and the nation with especial emphasis upon the "American way of life." In a general section entitled "Americanisms" there was a weekly count of the number of immigrants who arrived not only at the New York port but also at other ports of entry. Undoubtedly the use of the numerical count was either to inspire those already settled to action against the new arrivals or to overcome themselves with fear. Much of the specific diatribe of the journal was directed against the new German immigrants. The editors of *America* constantly demonstrated much concern about the dangers to the public school system, especially from Roman Catholic parochial schools which at this time were largely populated by the children of German immigrants. The magazine also included fiction on the subject. For the October 2, 1890, issue (Vol. V #1) the Chicago writer Robert P. Peattie wrote a short story entitled "Nightmare of Teutonized America" (12-16). The short story is supposed to have been written by one Esek Sladder who on April 19, 1929, wrote a sketch "for the memory of what was once America." As the story progresses, the Germans have taken over the nation and have sent the Americans to a reservation to live. The fear which the short story evidences is multiplied time and time again in the pages of *America*. Thus Peattie's prediction that the nation would be German in less than thirty years was not really supported by the evidence of the city. But the journal viewed itself as a watchdog preserving the "native stock." In the November 6, 1890, issue (Vol. V, #6) the following poem appeared:

I Wish I Was A Foreigner

by

An American

I wish I was a foreigner, I really, really do,
A right down foreign foreigner, pure foreigner through and through;

Because I find Americans, with all of native worth,
Don't stand one-half the chances here with men of foreign birth.

It seems to be unpopular for us to hold a place,
For we are made to give it up to men of foreign race.
The question of necessity and fitness we possess
Must never be considered—who cares for our distress?

Perhaps it is not wicked to be of foreign birth,
Or to mutter a mild protest when an alien wants the earth;
But the latest importations is sure to strike a job,
And be the sooner qualified to strike and lead a mob.

A Dutchman or an Irishman, a Frenchman or a Turk,
Comes here to be a voter, and is always given work;
A native-born American is here, and here must stay;
So it matters little how he lives, he cannot get away.

The Spaniard and Bohemian, the Russian and the Pole,
Are looking toward America with longings in the soul,
Because the politicians will receive with open arms,
And the goddess of our freedom bid welcome to her charms.

But the law-abiding Chinaman from the celestial shore,
Because he has no franchise, is driven from our door;
Americans and Chinamen are not in much demand,
The one remains neglected while the other's barred the land.

So I wish I was a Dutchman, or some other foreign cuss,
I'd lord it o'er the natives—who don't dare make a fuss.
But my blushes tell the story, I am native to the soil;
So the aliens hold the places—visitors must never toil.

While the political concerns cannot be minimized in any study of *America,* the journal actually prided itself on its contributions to literature. As the city prepared for the Exposition, literary developments were used as evidence of Chicago's cultural maturity by the apologists for the city. Since much of the city's contribution to American letters might have gone unnoticed in the face of the work of writers from either Europe or the eastern establishment, the editors of *America* made certain that the Chicago writers received due notice. Maurice Thompson, who served as the literary editor

for a while, was most aware of the existence of a Chicago writing
group. In his column of November 6, 1890, entitled "Literature"
he wrote an article "A Hint to Chicago" which begins as a review
of Eugene Field's *Little Book of Western Verse*. Claiming that the
book "suggests a good deal to the conscientious critic," Thompson
continues:

> The fact that the book is a Western product—a volume of poetry
> by a man Western-born—is of itself interesting in view of certain
> other facts. The 'Wild and Woolly West' may be an area hard to mark
> out with lines; but I believe it includes Indiana and the country west
> of it to the Pacific shore. Within that area—at St. Louis—, I am
> told—Mr. Field was born about forty years ago; therefore, he is of
> the Woolly West to the manor born. According to that sort of criticism
> which has been imported from London and placed on the New York
> and Boston markets, Mr. Field ought to be a 'Child of nature,' whose
> lack of culture would make him a striking exponent of Western life.
> The curious part of it is that the 'Little Book of Western Verse,' while
> it contains some very funny dialect pieces, is notable chiefly for poems
> that show Mr. Field's refinement of thought and depth of feeling
> through an atmosphere of liberal and deep culture. He is ambidex-
> trous, painting frontier rudeness and lawlessness with one hand while
> with the other he depicts life from the point of view of the high-bred
> scholarly, altogether gentle gentleman. Mr. Field is not a cow-boy
> poet, swaggering in person through his rhymes and meters. He knows
> the West and sings its life, but he sees both sides of that life, its rude
> side and its polished side, and he does not write with a fearful eye cast
> upon Eastern critics. His independence of spirit is the best badge of
> his genius, as it is the truest mark of his Western manhood.

Clearly establishing the distinction between the writer of merit and
the writer who does peculiar things to appeal to a section of the
country which expects nothing from the Midwest, Thompson
voices one of the concerns which plagued the exponents of the
genteel tradition. They consistently rejected the notion that western literature was going to be any more distinct than that written

by anybody who has a basic idea of the tradition of the literature of English poetry. Thus, if a western literature should arise, Thompson would insist that it be judged on the basis of its authenticity as well as upon its literary quality. He continues his review by asserting:

What I like most about this little book is what I may call forthrightness of expression. Mr. Field has been a close student of English literature, from Chaucer to Andrew Lang, (and what conscientious poet is not?) and his study shows through his work; but he has thoughts and words wholly his own; he uses them with elegance and with bullet-like directness. Even in his lightest and apparently most careless pieces he shows this outright vigor, this curiously-individual way of presenting things.

Within this context Thompson is able to explain the dialect poems.

. . . I am conscious in reading them of some unmistakable signs of absolute authenticity, and this significance gives them great value. They are not 'dialect' for the mere dialect's sake, but carry in them the genuine rollick, swagger and breadth of life of plain and mine, ranch and 'booming' town.

Yet, Field's work, in his opinion, is balanced and outstanding because "over against these 'woolly west' verses are set some exquisite bits of refined and earnest art, tender lullabies, sweet sentimental melodies and touching songs of love, graceful paraphrases and translations—humorous conceits and quips, and a number of imitations, or rather experiments, in which excellent use is made of Old English forms, are also here to speak for themselves in unmistakable language." The critic notes that since *The Little Book of Western Verse* as well Field's *Little Book of Profitable Tales* have already been reviewed in the journal, he does not plan to do another review. He simply wishes to use Field and his work to illustrate some more important issues concerning literature and its production in the Midwest as well as in Chicago.

What I would say concerns more particularly the significance of the literary attitude of the West at this moment. Chicago is the second city in size in America; in importance it is scarcely as low as the second. Potentially, if not actually, it is the great American center. The Exposition will finish an impression already deepening in the world's mind that Chicago better represents American forces, aims and results than any other city in our country.

I recall that in a little crude novel written some years ago I made one of my imaginary people say that New York was soon going to snatch from Boston the right to be called America's literary center. That prophecy was much hooted at by certain critics. I could afford to wait, not having much at stake. But the waiting was not so long after all. The fact is accomplished.

If I cannot so confidently prophesy about Chicago, it may be laid to my greater experience. A man is not so audacious after he begins to find out how little he knows; but I will venture to say that Chicago, despite her overwhelming immersion in beef, pork, and wheat, is destined to share with New York the literary control of America. A few years ago New York capital was afraid of books, just as Chicago capital is now. It had a few well-to-do publishers, while Boston queened it over the literary markets. Everybody said: 'Oh, New York is given over to gross trade, she can never be a literary center.' Does anybody know what changed all this. I know. It was a trio of men— Holland, Smith, and Scribner. These three, when they founded the old *Scribner's Magazine,* turned the tide. That magazine and its successor, the *Century,* should have the credit of opening New York's doors to the literary world, and no one thing has done more for the wealth of that great city. I do not mean by this statement to disparage other magazines; but a glance back at the old volumes of *Harper's,* for instance, will show that the old *Scribner's* set the pace for the new gait, and that the old *Century* kept up the rush and the lead till *Harper's* slowly awoke and dashed up to the line. Now New York has its platoon of powerful magazines, while Boston with her *Atlantic,* solitary, but good as the best, drones along in the same old fashion. Recently Philadelphia has been taking a new growth, and it looks as if she might take again something like her ancient place. *Lippincott's Magazine* is forming itself, and after some dangerous experiment, on good lines, and under the guidance of Curtis and Bok the *Ladies' Home Journal* is assuming an aspect of power with a circulation of over half a million. Centers are shifting, or rather centers are multiplying.

The publisher of a great magazine told me recently that the subscribers for his journal—his clientele, in fact—were largely in the West, with a gradual increase in the South. The free school is multiplying the demand for literature. Where the bulk of population is, there will be, if it is not already, the bulk of readers. A few years ago there was no young man in the West—Western-born, I mean—who could write what Eugene Field has written. The light has come to us. Mr. Field is not alone or lonely. He is one, a bright particular one, of a young brood of writers distinctively Western, and yet distinctively American and notably cultivated.

Like so many others in the city Thompson saw the Exposition as a point of beginning for the city's cultural life.

The time is ripe for a first-class magazine of literature and art in Chicago. The coming of the World's Fair is the golden point. I shall expect to be laughed at for saying this; but it is true, nevertheless. This magazine should be American, not merely Western, for in fact there is no longer any West. It should not be provincial, for that would confine its influence and limit its welcome. Started on its course now and brought up to a high standard by the time the Exposition is one, and all eyes are upon Chicago, it would be an assured success, not as a Western magazine, but as a world's magazine issuing from one of the world's greatest cities and out of the heart of the world's greatest country. The time is as ripe in Chicago for such a venture as it was in New York twenty years ago, when Holland, Smith, and Scribner changed the center of literary forces from Boston to New York by the founding of their magazine.

I remarked awhile ago that nothing ever did so much for New York City as the founding of the *Century* (old *Scribner's*) magazine. It gave such an impetus to art and letters in the country, that for a time it looked as if everybody meant to be an artist or a writer. The

book business has come to be one of the large divisions of New York
trade. What an influence the magazines wield is suggested by their
advertising pages, which are growing cumbersomely numerous.

One strong, good, first-class magazine issued from Chicago would
soon make the book-trade of the city second only to that of New
York.

And so Thompson concludes his "A Hint to Chicago." The idea
expressed by him was the unspoken idea underlying so many of
the attempts to establish journals during the course of Chicago's
history. And the later history of *The Dial* would suggest that
Chicago came close to producing just such a journal.

A few months after his message to Chicago, Thompson noted
in his column of March 26, 1891, that there were many successful
authors in the city and included a list of sixty-six noting at the same
time that he was excluding those who had produced "translations,
compilations, scientific legal and medical books" although a general medical book such as Dr. N.S. Davis' very popular *Principles
and Practice of Medicine* did appear. The list is of interest today
for the great diversity of writing interests which it displayed.

It should be noted, however, that Thompson did demonstrate
some broad literary concerns. He was not always involved with
the so-called "western" writers. There are many instances of his
concern for form in literature. For example, in his column for
October 30, 1890, he wrote an article on "Editors and Short Story
Writers" which asserted that the influence of the city or "urban
attraction" was a mitigating force against the development of the
American short story. Arguing that the current trend of magazine
fiction was a deterrent to the short story form, Thompson said:

> Editors are men, when they are not women; and are subject to the
> forces of their immediate environment. What is in the air immediately
> around them has, in their understanding, a world-wide significance.
> This is unfortunate for literature, since it has come to pass that the
> magazines control the trend of literary taste and the scope of dra-

matic invention in fiction, and the magazines are controlled, in a large degree, by men who measure everything by the urban standard of taste. Now the fact is that the extra-urban influence is the preservative of the true dramatic vision, the conservator of invention of lyric purity, of forthright expression. Men of the urban centres have wondered how the plowboy Burns, the peasant Millet, the strolling actor Shakespeare, the Californian Bret Harte, and many another outsider have been able to touch and electrify the endless chord of universal sympathy. I can tell how they did it. They did it by having held that cord in their very hands, by having looked at it with their own eyes. They knew its substance and what could affect it. Moreover, if Burns—for instance—had lived in a day like ours, he would have found out right suddenly that the magazine editor held the key to the situation, and proposed to have a hand in the final touching-up and toning-down of his lyrics.

Echoing his concern about the growing emphasis upon realism, Thompson maintained that realism had run its course because "people are tired of extreme realism of the commonplace." However, he noted, that it is unfortunate that editors preferred dialect pieces especially the dialect of "New England and the Negro." Thus because the editors were people of tunnel visions they constantly refused to "accept materials of high imaginative quality." His complaint against editors as tastemakers was often voiced by those who felt much of the best work being done in the midwestern literary circle was rejected on the basis that it did not fit into the preconceived editorial notion of what midwestern literature ought to be.

By the following year, however, *America* demonstrated an awareness of the merits of the growing realistic movement. In two reviews—one of Dr. Gunsaulus' two-volumed sixteenth-century romance (*Monk and Knight: An Historical Study in Fiction*) and the other of Garland's excursion into realism (*Main-Travelled Roads: Six Mississippi Valley Stories*)—the attitude of the journal seems more objective than some of its earlier criticism. While apparently the reviewer wanted to like the Gunsaulus book, he admitted that it is a weak novel which "does not transport you into an atmosphere and surroundings of the sixteenth century." This, of course, is a problem inherent in romantic fiction. The reviewer was distressed because "the reader never loses his point of view in the nineteenth century"; however, the critic should have discerned that the value of the book lies in its awareness of a sense of history. At the same time the reviewer is proud that the city "can show such products from the studies of its authors and the presses of its printers."

The review of Garland's book is entitled "Pictures of Western Farm Life." The reviewer is distressed at the portrait drawn of the Midwest but acknowledges its validity. The analysis of the book of short stories provides a vehicle for the discussion of realism and demonstrates a growing acceptance of it as a technique while abhorring its content.

If we are to believe the writers of fiction of today the existence led on Western farms is a grim epic of hard work and discontent. The Southern plantation or the New England farm may give opportunities for a life which is at least not insupportable, but the Western farmer, according to the talented apostles of realism, is a drudge who has a mortgage to pay and has no chance of ever paying it. He works from daylight to dark in weather that is either terribly hot or perilously cold when it is not frightfully muddy and wet. He never goes anywhere and always finds himself worse off at the end of a harvest than he was before. As for the farmer's wife, she always has dishes to wash and a crowd of hungry men to cook for. Besides she is a prey to chronic weariness. It is clear that she would be infinitely better off if she were dead. The farmer's boy eats with his knife and looks like a fright, while his sister gets tanned and consequently is very miserable. All are hopeless and penniless and weary beyond expression. They are also unfashionable and their views are narrow.

It is not our wish to criticise the accuracy of the pictures drawn of the Western farmer, particularly those drawn by Mr. Garland, which are singularly vivid and very true, but we do desire to express our regret that the seamy side of the Western farmer's life is the only one revealed. There can be no question that there is squalor on many Western farms; but it is just as certain that thousands of farmers at the West have homes of comfort and even elegance, that their families are reared with the greatest of care, that the work is so arranged that slavish toil is unknown, and that neither the farmer nor the farmer's son could be tempted to leave their fertile acres. The wife and the daughter have no reasonable desire which is not gratified; bountiful hospitality is the rule, whole neighborhoods living in such harmony and simple friendship that they compose one great and peaceful family. That is the side of Western farm life that the gentle purveyors of realistic fiction habitually overlook. Yet there is nothing else so beautiful anywhere. It has kindness and the grace of the old Southern plantation life without the taint of despotism and servility. The farmer of this class does not tramp around in the mud, cursing his luck and dodging the interest on a chattel mortgage. He knows a better way than that. He prefers to drain his land so that there will be no mud worth mentioning, to carry on his farm work like an intelligent American and not like a dunce, to make money and not to lose it. He leaves the misery and the penury to those farmers who manage everything badly and who are assisted in their mismanagement by a high tariff, a woful ignorance of everything from cookery to the rotation of crops and an insatiable desire for politics, plug tobacco, yellow dogs, and circus parades. Even the Farmers' Alliance, which is going to bring on the millennium not later than week after-next, will not be able to teach such farmers thrift.

Mr. Garland's stories, though very powerful, are inexpressibly sad. They deal with the horror of hard work. His characters toil and droop and languish on the treadmill of fate. In "A Branch Road," a young farmer runs away from his betrothed in a gust of foolish rage, and, returning seven years later, finds that she is married to his rival and is working herself to death in the farmhouse kitchen. He makes fierce love to her and elopes with her, taking her baby along. In "Up the Coule," a young man who has achieved success in the city returns to the farm where his mother and brother live, finds them very poor and working like serfs. The farmer brother is ferocious through pride and disappointment at his lot. Nothing can be done, however, fate being inexorable. "Among the Corn Rows" is less gloomy. A young settler on the frontier goes back to his old home in Wisconsin to get married to some one of the girls whom he knew there. He finds the buxom daughter of a barbarous old Norwegian plowing corn under the eye of her father, courts her and carries her away, while the savage foreigner roars out his rage. The home-coming of a sick soldier is the subject of "The Return of a Private." Its pictures of the lonely wife's longing for her husband, and of the husband's joy at getting back to his poor possessions, are at once pathetic and beautiful. "Under the Lion's Paw" has to do with the injustice of a land-owner to his hard-working and deserving tenant. In "Mrs. Ripley's Trip," a poor, work-worn housewife goes away to see her 'folks,' after twenty-three years of preparation for the visit, and then a few days later hurries back through the snow eager to resume her drudgery.

Mr. Garland's portraits of his farm people are distressingly vivid. Here is Agnes, formerly a beautiful girl, as she appears to her old lover who sees her the wife of his rival:

> She was worn and wasted incredibly. The blue of her eyes seemed dimmed and faded by weeping, and the old-time scarlet of her lips had been washed away. The sinews of her neck showed painfully when she turned her head, and her trembling hands were worn, discolored and lumpy at the joints.

Here we have the portraits of the man from the city and his unfortunate brother who lives on a farm:

> The two men stood there, face to face, hands clasped, the one fair-skinned, full-lipped, handsome in his neat suit; the other tragic, sombre in his softened mood, his large, long, rugged Scotch face bronzed with sun and scarred with wrinkles that had histories, like sabre-cuts on a veteran, the record of his battles.

Here is a young girl at the plow:

> The heat grew terrible. The corn came to her shoulders, and not a breath seemed to reach her, while the sun, nearing the noon mark, lay pitilessly upon her shoulders, protected only by a calico dress. The dust rose under her feet, and as she was wet with perspiration it soiled her till, with a woman's instinctive cleanliness, she shuddered. Her head throbbed dangerously, The corn must be plowed, and so she toiled on, the tears dropping from the shadow of the ugly sun-bonnet she wore. Her shoes,

coarse and square-toed, chafed her feet: her hands, large and strong were browned, or more properly burnt-on the backs by the sun.

Even nature is coarse at times in these stories. The jay is given to yelling and flying wild geese "sprawl sidewise." Yet, for power, truth and pathos it would be difficult to find six stories by another American author which would bear comparison with these.

Less than a month after the appearance of these two reviews, *America* issued an article "The Growth of Realism" which supported the method of William Dean Howells.

Mr. Howells, the chief of the American guild of novel writers, has long been engaged in the self-appointed task of solving social problems by telling stories in which such problems are kept prominently in view. While thus engaged he has achieved distinct success as a novelist. But has he helped on any reforms? And do his writings have a permanent value? The future must answer these questions, for the present has not made up its mind in regard to them. It is worthy of note that his books show systematic painstaking preparation. He is a conscientious workman, a good mechanic. Before taking up his pen, or oiling his type-writer, as the case may be, he provides himself with something to say. His descriptions are as accurate as are reproductions by a camera. His conversations are natural, and in his later works are seldom commonplace; on the contrary, they are usually so brilliant as to be almost unique in fiction. Of movement, however, there is not much.

The province of fiction is to amuse. If the novelists all become reformers, what will be left for the preachers? Must they take up the work neglected by the story-writers? In this day of balance-sheets and inter-state commerce laws the people are in danger of taking themselves too seriously. When in their moments of relaxation they provide themselves with one of Mr. Howells' masterpieces, and read a story dealing with the evils of plutocracy or with the problems of heredity, they do not get very far away from the serious side of life with which they have been engrossed so steadily during their working hours. Even when Mr. Howells is most amusing, black Care is in the audien--

wearing a sorry grin. This wise novelist is very much in earnest, even when his wit is most keen. His genius paces slowly, with its hands behind it, and muses as it goes. But while its glance is penetrating, the burden on its mind recalls continually the squalor of existence. It will not let us boast and swagger in its company. Tinsel-decked uniforms worn by men of heroic size, who are expert swordsmen and skilled in pistol practice, are frowned on by it. We who tread in his contemplative footsteps see that our coats are rather shabby, that there are some dangers before which we quail and that altogether we see rather ordinary people leading colorless lives.

There are still writers who cry out against this sort of thing. They say that people who read books desire to get away from themselves, to have their blood stirred by battles and pageants and picturesque villainies. Mr. Howells serenely and steadily refuses to accept their standard of art as his own. It is sad that the writers themselves do not succeed very well in demonstrating the superiority of their school of fiction over that of Mr. Howells when they try their skill at telling stories. Either they are not such good workmen as he is or else there is something the matter with their stock of genius. That their theory is sound has been shown conclusively by the man who wrote "Guy Mannering" and the man who wrote the "Three Musketeers," to mention no others.

These romantic writers who scoff at Mr. Howell's theory of art would do well to copy that gentleman's thorough methods. There ought to be as much care shown on the one hand in describing a battle or an earthquake as there is on the other in describing a tea party or a conversation in a horse-car. So long as the retailer of heroics persists in peddling damaged goods he will not succeed in vindicating his calling, particularly when the head of the opposition persists in being wise and witty, accurate and up to date. Mr. Stevenson, who is the pride and hope of the romantic school, is different from his brethren because he is painstaking and has soul above mere claptrap. With him the aim of novel writing is entertainment for the novel reader. If it be true that his best plots come to him in dreams, it is clear that they cannot be over-burdened with social questions and problems of existence. Does Mr. Stevenson in "The

Master of Ballantrae" or Mr. Howells in "A Hazard of New Fortunes" give the more rational example of the art of novel-writing?

It must have become apparent to the reading public that most of the critics who a few years ago disapproved of Mr. Howells with great emphasis are now silent, or nearly so, or are quite willing to admit that Mr. Howells has mastered them. The thoughtful reader, they find, must have his novelist as well as the mental swashbuckler. Though Mr. Howells refuses to wade in blood on land, or to sail on pirate ships at sea, he has managed to interest a large and growing audience with the performances of prim Bostonians and other people equally averse to melodrama. It remains to be seen whether these sober-minded readers would cling to their favorite if some broad-shouldered author should start in with a halloo and go to weaving romances full of mystery and blood-letting. If this sanguinary person should delay his coming much longer it is not impossible that when he does finally appear the reading public will gaze at him sternly over its eye-glasses—will say coldly, 'Please go away, you are too noisy,' and then will return calmly to Howells.

As an independent voice, the significance of *America* cannot be underestimated in the opening years of the 1890's. Whatever problems it may have had at its inception were smoothed out, and it became a first-rate journal of cultural thought and a spokesman for the genteel tradition in most things. Its political leanings, of course, were less than in keeping with the democratic spirit but at least they were forthright and unfortunately had a number of supporters among Chicago's cultural elite. Hence, because of its success, its subscribers were shocked to learn on September 24, 1891:

With this number AMERICA completes its sixth volume, and ends its independent existence. Next week it will be merged in the *Graphic,* whose publishers have purchased its business, good-will, subscription list, advertising contracts and those incorporeal hereditaments which are the realty of a periodical's existence.

It will never be known the extent to which its anti-immigrant attitude eventually lost support and led to its demise; however, in the last editorial entitled "The Transfer of 'America,'" the editor noted:

> With this transfer goes all that AMERICA'S editor and proprietor can deliver, except his personal association and opinions. These latter were not included in the bargain for two good reasons—they were not for sale and the publisher of the *Graphic* was already supplied with a full line of assorted opinions of his own. What was therefore distinctively personal about the political faith of AMERICA dies with it. What lines of thought in politics and literature it held in common with the *Graphic* will live in the survivor.

Then, in a review of its aims, goals, and accomplishments, the editor explained the reasons for the sale of *America*:

> This consolidation will certainly prove of value to weekly journalism in Chicago, and indirectly in the country at large. In the three years and a half of its existence AMERICA has built up what the Chicago Tribune has been generous enough to call an enviable reputation for itself. In respect to several subjects, too much slighted in the columns of the daily press, it has been as a voice crying in the wilderness. The preservation of American manhood by the restriction of foreign immigration, the purification of our voting system, the enactment of uniform laws regarding citizenship in the different states, the adoption of an educational qualification for voters, the compulsory diffusion of primary school education on the American plan in American schools, a firm but moderate opposition to the political and educational policy of the Roman Catholic Church in the United States, an abiding faith in the potency as well as the alembic in which all races, classes and creeds can alone be fused into the best material for American citizenship—these and cognate themes which will occur to the reader, were the especial campaign of education in which AMERICA engaged.

> With a subscription list extending into every state and territory in the Union, and an exchange list that became a burden through its

size, the diffusion of AMERICA'S peculiar views has been remarkably wide. If some of its seed has fallen on stony ground, some has found congenial soil and borne fruit. The columns of its contemporaries have been broadened by frequent approved quotations from it.

In such reflections the editor of AMERICA has found his chief compensation for the labor and money involved in getting out what was virtually a magazine for the price of a weekly. With increasing responsibilities in another line of business the oversight and labor of editing it became too onerous to be long continued. Rather than see what was built up with such expense and industry decline through enforced neglect, the sale to the publisher of the *Graphic* was made.

The Graphic, which had been established in 1888 as an illustrated weekly, was not at this time as well known as *America*; however, in this final editorial *The Graphic* was explained as being to the *Mid*-West "what the *Illustrated London News* is to England, what *Harper's Weekly* is to New York and the East. . . ." Defensively, the editorial continued by asserting "it is admirably printed and many of its illustrations give the lie to the recent sneer of the New York Critic, that there were no wood-engravers in Chicago. Its pages prove not only that we have first-class engravers in the West, but that we can furnish interesting subjects for their skill." Finally, as a journal to record the World's Columbian Expositon the editorial noted "during the next two years the *Graphic* will be in a position to do valuable service for Chicago" and explained the merits of *The Graphic:*

It has facilities to illustrate the World's Fair beyond those possessed by any ephemeral publication which must depend upon the drippings from 'headquarters' to make both ink and paper ends meet. The absorption of AMERICA will enable the publisher of the *Graphic* to strengthen its letter press and place it beyond the range of possible competition in this field.

Yet in spite of the promised strength of the merger, the editorial was willing to honor unexpired subscriptions "should any of the subscribers to AMERICA feel dissatisfied with the transfer to the *Graphic*" because "this is but a just recognition of the principle that when a man orders and pays for a cottage piano his vendor does not fulfill his obligation by tendering him a concert grand." "The Transfer of 'America' " ended with the following paragraph: "And so, fond reader of AMERICA, farewell. Next week the postman will bring you another weekly in its stead in which the writer trusts you will find much to exalt, refine, and entertain your soul." When this magazine ceased publication, one chapter of Chicago's literary history came to a close. Somehow the *Graphic* —while relatively successful as a picture weekly—never became as popular as *America* nor did its readers take it seriously.

In retrospect one is obligated to view *America* not only in terms of what it actually accomplished but also in view of Hobart Chatfield Chatfield-Taylor and Slason Thompson. Both men supported the concepts of gentility in literature and the romantic philosophy. They were initially firmly convinced that the evolving spirit of realism in American literature was the result of foreign influences and was not in the best interest of the nation. The fact that these two men became a team perhaps shows their commitment to their principles because in many ways they were an unlikely pair. Thompson, a Canadian, had been trained as a lawyer and had moved to California where he passed the bar; however, he became a journalist first in San Francisco then in New York city. Like many others convinced of the opportunities in the Midwest, he moved to Chicago where he worked with several different publications. His strong attachment to the literary scene in the city is perhaps dominated by his devotion to Eugene Field whose biographer he became. Yet, throughout his career, questions of political and sociological concerns most interested him. Chatfield-Taylor, on the other hand, was a native Chicagoan who had—in a sense—been to the manor born. As a child, he had lived in the West Division when it was the bastion of some of the old New England and southern families. He had gone East to attend Cornell University and upon graduation was eager "to do" something of a literary nature in his native city. He actually believed that it was possible to change the city and produce a "culture" reminiscent of that of older societies. As an active participant in the genteel movement, he was convinced that Chicago not only needed to be changed but also that such a change was possible. He was not as strongly committed to current issues of a political nature nor did he write the biting satires which so frequently came from Thompson; yet, both men shared an aversion to the foreign immigrants who were flooding into the city.

To combine the political with the literary was an interesting experiment even at that time. And Chatfield-Taylor's independent income undoubtedly helped *America* to interest some notable English and American writers. Reportedly Bret Harte, for example, was paid $500.00 for "Jim." The early contributors to the magazine were some of the popular writers of the period. Andrew Lang, Swinburne, James Russell Lowell, Frank Stockton, Charles Dudley Warner, Oliver Wendell Holmes, Ella Wheeler Wilcox, James Whitcomb Riley, Hamlin Garland, and Eugene Field are examples of writers whose work appeared in an early issue. In spite of the limiting view of literature which the editors held, they were willing to open the magazine to recognized writers; hence, it is not surprising that Hamlin Garland, whose *Main-Travelled Roads* became so successful, was asked to contribute to the magazine. Julian Hawthorne, whose name carried a lot of weight with people who remembered his father's tales fondly, was the first literary editor who was subsequently followed by Maurice Thompson.

It was not feasible to continue to pay for manuscripts for a journal which never achieved an extensive subscription list. Rather than face bankruptcy, the magazine's policy shifted; and Chatfield-Taylor, Reginald DeKoven, and Harry Smith—using various pseudonyms—began to produce the bulk of the "literary and cultural" articles. This phase of the magazine, however, soon was eclipsed as Chatfield-Taylor left the publication in less than a year.

When Thompson was left as the sole editor, there was an editorial which stated that there would be "no deviation from the high literary entertainment" although Thompson, who was now completely in charge of the editorial and business phases of the magazine, insisted that the journal would "continue to urge the restriction of all immigration by consular inspection and a per capita tax, the making of citizenship essential to the privilege of suffrage, and the limitation of the right to vote to citizens who can read and write" and would support any effort designed to maintain "America's free schools, American morality, and American nationality." All of this *America* did with a vengeance, employing any means to get its message across from the direct cartoons of Thomas Nast to the more subtle innuendoes which can sometimes be more deadly. Throughout its existence the magazine demonstrated clearly the relationship between the genteel tradition and the principles of an aristocracy based upon not only wealth but also an assumed elitism which was a result of a combination of culture and taste. The *Graphic* was able to absorb the physical *America* and admittedly was popular during the period of the World's Columbian Exposition, but the illustrated weekly never took the place of *America*.

The role of *America* as a major literary journal was partially assumed in the 1890's by *The Dial* which had been founded in the previous decade. But unlike *America*, *The Dial* had been reluctant to assume that the realistic method had validity, but as the voice for the genteel tradition in the city, it was without rival. Yet as the approaching Exposition neared, *The Dial* became more and more defensive of the city and its cultural life. Such articles as "The Literary West" (October 1, 1893), "Western Indifference to Western Authors—A Reviewer's View" (October 16, 1893), "A Western Style in Literature" (November 1, 1893), "The West, Once More" (October 16, 1893), and "Chicago's Higher Evolution" (October 1, 1892) appeared; however, *The Dial* prided itself for being committed to literary standards rather than to regional literature.

In addition to *America* and *The Dial* there were other journals which dealt with some of the same issues and ideas. With few exceptions they gave voice to those who believed that Chicago's cultural life was soon to rival that of the East, most especially Boston. One publishing company had an interesting approach to magazine publishing and to the matter of the elevation of taste in Chicago. *Belford's Magazine* unwittingly addressed itself to that phase of the genteel tradition which attempted to relate to the cultural life of Europe and attempted to treat serious subjects in a manner which would make them have general appeal. During its second year (1889) the magazine moved to New York: however, in June of that year there was an editorial attempt to explain the magazine as an interpreter of American life. It observed:

When the best blood of Europe sought these shores as laborers or pirates, they sought to conquer a continent. The victory achieved between the first landing and now is simply a marvel of industry, endurance, energy, and enterprise. In this struggle of man versus matter we have become materialists.

The editorial comment then addressed itself to reading and literature.

Out of sixty odd millions of population, about 3,000,000 read books, and these mainly novels. To attempt the publication of a monthly devoted to the discussion of grave subjects, to be to the thoughtful reformers of this country what the *Westminster* of London has been to the Liberals of England, would be commercial insanity. Successful American magazines are devoted to pictorial exhibits, which, although they are artistically done, yet make only picture-books, to be looked at, not read.

Three years later the magazine returned to Chicago, but the optimism of its early years had gone; and the editors admitted that the true "literature" of the West could not be contained in a periodical because "it has been acted, it has been *done*." And so the failure of the magazine in 1893 was not surprising.

Throughout the 1880's and into the 1890's Chicago's writers were busy, publishing companies were issuing reprints of European books as well as first editions of Chicago books with frequency, literary clubs were busy and people were reading. The fledgling Chicago Public Library was doing well under the guidance of William F. Poole. With the death of Walter Newberry's widow in 1885, the provisions for a library as set forth in his last will and testament of 1868 were executed by the end of the 1880's. All of these activities and events indicated that there was a great interest in books and writing. While the newspapers—and there were many of them—steered clear of the elitist approach to the city's cultural life, the people who were the tastemakers were convinced that the day of gentility had arrived for Chicago.

This was further reinforced by the general interest in self-improvement which was made evident by the several types of journals which gained prominence during the period. In former years the tasks of the "upward movement" and personal improvement were fulfilled by the multitude of cultural clubs which prevailed in the city. Now there were journals which performed the same function but which were able to reach a wider audience. Such publications as *Correspondence University Journal* (1884-86), *The University* (1885-86), *Home Library Magazine* (1887), and *National Magazine* (1889-94) did not have long runs; but they were designed to provide educational materials to the general public. There were also those journals which reflected the specific interests of trade and religious groups which performed a similar function. All of these magazines are further evidence of the diversity of the growing population in the great midland metropolis. While a few of these journals attained spectacular circulations, they along with the many successful publishing companies contributed to the sense of the importance of the printed word in the city.

While much activity was related to the genteel tradition in some way, there was a journal which demonstrated conclusively the possible popularity of humor and local color. It disturbed the delicate sensibilities of some but found favor with a large audience. *The Arkansaw Traveler,* which had been founded in 1882 by Opie Read, was moved to Chicago in 1887 from Little Rock when Read decided that Chicago—as a railroad center—would be far better for his weekly journal of humor which was designed to entertain those on trains and at railroad stations. Herbert Fleming in his *Magazines of the Market-Metropolis* recalls his interview with Opie Read who explained the move to Chicago.

> Chicago had become the great railway center. Our paper was sold chiefly on railway trains. We moved to Chicago so as to be in position for reaching the largest number of railway passengers most easily. The mailing facilities of Chicago as the central point in a spider's web of railways, also led us here. In those days, schoolboys were not used extensively for the sale of weekly papers. Besides making sales on the trains through the news companies, we had a subscription list. For years Chicago had been a great point for the sale of subscription books. For our weekly of general circulation the business manager, P.D. Benham, my brother-in-law, found that it was not possible to get advertising in the same proportion to the number of subscribers as with a local newspaper. The advertising patronage came from the general agencies, and in those days magazine advertising was not done so generally as it is today. We counted on sales and subscriptions.

The magazine consisted of humorous sketches, stories, and poems written in a southern dialect and presenting an array of southern characters. As an exercise in local color *The Arkansaw Traveler* was highly successful. Read, however, left it in 1892. It is difficult to know whether his departure was based upon his displeasure with the group which had seized financial control of the journal or because he really felt he was wasting his talents on the sketches which train readers enjoyed but soon discarded. At any rate, he remained a vital and vigorous part of the city's literary scene and produced a number of books. The magazine continued until 1916, but it was during the period of Read's editorship that it had its greatest appeal and spawned an entire literature designed for "railroad travelers."

II

At the time that the so-called literary and serious magazines were often reinforcing the romantic by giving support to the historical romance or to the imagined interests of the East, Chicago newspapers were unwittingly becoming the vehicles for the development of realism in Chicago writing. They stressed the human interest story whereby the readers were exposed to vignettes of the successes and tragedies in the city not only of the famous but also of the "man on the streets." Here was in reality the drama of urban existence, and the newspapers made the most of it. Stories about the jails, the poverty-stricken, the treatment of immigrants, and the young working girls in the city were all subjects for discussion. The city was described as the force which shaped and was shaping the lives and the destinies of so many. Many of these journalistic efforts were by struggling reporters who frequently demonstrated great insights into the basic meanings of the city.

Newspapers during this period underwent some drastic changes in policy which ultimately influenced what they produced and proved an ample training ground for many of the writers who were to gain fame and recognition in succeeding years. After the Fire it became more and more apparent that if a newspaper intended to compete in the marketplace of public opinion, it would have to go beyond having *clear* writers, it would have to have *good* writers who could aid in the molding of public opinion. And there would have to be a broadening of the operational base in order for the papers to appeal not only to all of the many groups in the city but also to every member of the family. Thus, by the 1880's Chicago newspapers had embarked on their period of great influence which was to last for several decades.

The strictly utilitarian news and business sheets of the past gave way to the deliberate appeal to family reading. Emerging out of all of this was a new emphasis upon signed articles by columnists whose names often did become household words. The anonymity of the feature writers passed into oblivion. Because many readers were neither book readers nor magazine subscribers, the newspaper came to exert great influence based upon the assumption that everybody is exposed at some time to a newspaper. And the assumption was not too wrong. By the 1890's there were practically thirty daily newspapers in the city, some of which—undoubtedly —were designed to catch the coming expected crowd who would attend the Exposition. Generally these papers seemed less cosmopolitan than New York papers because there was a peculiar blend of the urban habit of mind with rural values and concepts. This may not have been helpful to a large city newspaper; however, it had the benefit of being quite agreeable to the small town editors in surrounding communities who used the news from the Chicago papers and simply added specific items of appeal for their locales. It can honestly be said "as Chicago read, so read the countryside" as the city papers provided the pattern, the news, the format, and often the writers for the papers of surrounding communities. "I saw it in a Chicago paper" undoubtedly lent authenticity to many late nineteenth-century conversations. Making much of telegraphic news services and special correspondents, Chicago newspapers were not as provincial as they appeared on the surface. During this period, the newspaper world was enhanced by the formation of a series of associations and clubs. In the area of the dissemination of the news the recently-established press associations made possible greater news coverage; however, they also created a general sameness among the papers. Organizations such as the City Press Association and Western Associated Press bought and sold dispatches to which most Chicago papers subscribed.

The Press Club of Chicago, while not the first such organization, was established in 1880, and Wilkie maintained in his *Personal Reminiscences of Thirty-Five Years of Journalism* (Chicago, 1891) that he and Melville Stone had the idea of such a group after the disaster of trying to entertain Mark Twain in December of 1879 with no suitable place for the press. The Press Club, whose first president was Wilkie, was organized exclusively for members of the literary departments of the several papers. "Before the present club . . . there had been no less than six efforts to establish press clubs," according to Wilkie who asserted that these previous attempts had failed because when funds were low outsiders such as "lawyers, actors, and other professional men" were admitted to membership. He continued by basing the success of the new organization upon excellent management and a homogeneous grouping. To be eligible for membership "a man must have supported himself by his pen . . . for a year prior to application." He further felt that the Press Club had helped to eliminate the Bohemian quality which many people had associated with the press (pp. 306-307).

Perhaps one of the most effective associations for the press had nothing to do with the business of gathering news; rather it was an organization which emphasized the possible cameraderie of the members of the press corps in Chicago. The Whitechapel Club was organized in 1889 for the sole purpose of providing a means for newspaper people to get together. Among the first members were such well-known journalists as Opie Read, George Ade, John T. McCutcheon, and Finley Peter Dunne. Although it was committed to an examination of some of the important socio-economic and political issues of the day, the Whitechapel Club became associated with a rowdiness and an abandonment which belied its serious intent. Located in a section of Calhoun Place which was called "Newspaper Alley," the club made available to its members, some of whom were not journalists, a place of total relaxation. Such men as Franc B. Wilkie in his *Personal Reminiscences of Thirty-Five Years of Journalism* (Chicago, 1891), Opie Read in *I Remember* (New York, 1930), Charles H. Dennis in "Whitechapel Nights," (*Chicago Daily News* of July 29, 1936), and Elmer Ellis in *Mr. Dooley's America* (New York, 1941) have recorded the days of the Whitechapel Club.

With this new emphasis upon cameraderie among the city's journalists, the major newspapers—with one exception—continued to grow. The *Tribune,* for example, assured its continued growth not only by absorbing smaller and less successful papers but also by making a deliberate appeal to the rights of capital. It opposed any relief for the working class including the adoption of the eight-hour day. Strikes it viewed as a subversive tool, and it continued to support in principle the Republican Party. In spite of its clearly-defined political goals—which were supervised by Joseph Medill from 1874 when he gained control of the paper until his death in 1899—the *Tribune* managed to have some innovative columns as well as features. Elias Colbert, the commercial editor, and George P. Upton, the music critic, were two outstanding journalists whose affiliations with the *Tribune* continued over a long period of time. Upton eventually spent fifty-seven years with the paper. But there were other journalists who submerged themselves in a variety of pseudonyms for the pleasure of the *Tribune* readers. There was, for example, "Rural, Jr.," who wrote of farm and garden matters and "Veterinarian," who handled the column "Field and Stables." And while the *Times* was always associated with spectacular journalism, the columnists for the *Tribune* were also sent on often-daring missions in order to have some spectacular news for the readers.

The *Inter-Ocean,* a post-fire paper, also continued to grow under the leadership of J. Young Scammon and those who had earlier been disenchanted with the *Tribune.* Its motto "Republican in everything, Independent in nothing" made clear the political philosophy; however, when William Penn Nixon became editor, some of the community projects which had been ignored by the *Tribune,* were supported; and in the 1890's the paper entered into its most influential period.

After the death in 1884 of its mercurial editor, Wilbur Storey, the *Times* floundered, was absorbed by Carter Harrison who purchased it in 1891, and combined it in 1895 with the *Herald.* But for all practical purposes the *Times* was dependent upon its well-known editor. When he boastfully announced during his productive period "I don't wish to perpetuate my newspaper. I am the paper! I wish it to die with me so that the world may know that I was the *Times,*" he was far more correct than perhaps he knew. As the Democratic paper, it was more than a match for the *Tribune* and the *Inter-Ocean.* In fact, there were a number of similarities between the *Tribune* and the *Times* in terms of dictatorial editors, columnists who were significant, innovative features, and general public appeal. Medill, of course, never became quite as vindictive as did Storey who really pioneered in the use of telegraphic communiqués and in the use of foreign correspondents. There were many outstanding writers who were connected with the *Times,* who—after the apparent decline of Storey—tried to maintain the paper. Among them were Franc B. Wilkie, Horatio W. Seymour, and Finley Peter Dunne.

Of all of the newspapers, this was the period of greatness for the *Daily News.* Its growth was based upon Melville Stone's ability to predict trends and to give the reading public what it most wanted without in any way compromising his own high standards for what a newspaper ought to be. With Stone's assumption of the control of the editorial policy of the *News* he made it clear that the reader was of primary importance; therefore, any advertising or political ties must be loose enough to permit absolute freedom. Not only must the news be lively as in Wilbur Storey's *Times* but it had to be absolutely reliable (as was not always the case in the *Times*). To read it in the *Daily News* had to be tantamount to declaring the event a matter of gospel. Stone was convinced that a favorable public opinion would ultimately be developed through public respect. In the final analysis the reader should be entertained, and this meant employing a staff of first-rate writers.

There was a conscious and deliberate attempt to recruit the best writers of the period. So the journalistic roster of the *Daily News* read like a who's who of important men and women not only of letters but also of scholarship. From the Chicago *Herald,* which had gone out of existence, Stone took John Ballantyne to become his managing editor and Slason Thompson to become the chief editorial writer. Both Robert and Elia Peattie also became associated with the paper. Stone also instituted a procedure which he apparently took from the London *Times*. He maintained, on call, outstanding scholars who could write—whenever necessary—articles within their special disciplines. These scholarly editorial assistants gave to the paper added dignity and appeal. There was Frank Reilly, the first medical correspondent for a paper; Professor W.S.B. Mathews in music; Colonel Gilbert A. Pierce in politics; William Morton Payne, literary criticism; Professor James Langlin in economics who must have joined the staff in the 1890's since he was affiliated with the University of Chicago; and there was Professor Richard T. Ely in sociology from the University of Wisconsin. Stone was also willing to go outside of Chicago for necessary talent. Hence, from Indiana he recruited John T. McCutcheon the cartoonist and George Ade who was first a reporter and then a columnist. From Denver, Colorado, came Eugene Field. Eventually Finley Peter Dunne, from Chicago's westside, was to write sports news for the paper. Prior to his time, sports news had been primarily a record of who played, who won, and who lost. Dunne created a lively language which we now associate with sports writers, and he went on to develop his stories of the streets of Chicago and his Mr. Dooley tales.

The use of the feature writer was not, of course, a new phenomenon. It had been a characteristic of journalism although some editors—notably Wilbur Storey of the *Times*—did not really approve of this even though he eventually permitted Franc B. Wilkie to use a pen name. But Stone in the 1880's decided that the emphasis upon a feature writer was one way to increase circulation and appeal. Thus it was that the newspapers, especially the *Daily News,* provided a training ground for many of the writers who were to gain recognition in succeeding years. In fact the roster of so-called Chicago writers is in reality a list of those who served an apprenticeship as reporters for Chicago papers.

With the arrival of Eugene Field as a columnist in 1883, the *Daily News* could not be surpassed. Field was destined to play a major role among the journalists in the conflict between the romantic and realistic traditions of literature. He used humor to support Chicago's budding institutions; at the same time, he used it as a weapon against the strivers of the city's society. While he did not long for the East (Chicago was probably as far East as he wanted to go) and was in favor of the establishment of a western literature, he did not—and could not—accept the brand of realism which was sweeping the country through the patterns established by Howells and which he also saw in Garland. Yet, ironically, he was a model for so many of the writers who were later to be associated with the realistic movement.

When Field arrived in Chicago, those who supported the contentions of the genteel tradition were demanding frequently, and producing romances in the style of the older communities. They were the men and women of the literary clubs who spent a great deal of time researching, discussing, and debating such issues as "Was Homer Really Blind?" They were concerned about classical and European literature and made a great effort to invite and entertain eastern writers in Chicago. There were the others in the city who had little tolerance for this type of endeavor. They felt it inconsistent with the rising commercial city to spend time dealing with such long ago and far-away issues. And so in their newspapers and journals they tried to define and defend "western man." Ambiguities which existed between these two groups strangely enough existed in Field's work. There was the Field of the *Daily News* who was hard-hitting in his support of westernism without supporting the phoniness of the genteel tradition. This was perhaps illustrated by Field's addiction to the Saints' and Sinners' Corner as well as to the eventual publication of *Culture's Garland* which was based upon selections from his column "Sharps and Flats" and which used as its imprimatur a garland of link sausages. Then there was the Field of the remembered poems of childhood as well as of the barroom stories which were not repeated in polite society.

A cursory comparison of his earlier work with that of his Chicago period indicates that he certainly lessened his tendency toward violence and grim humor after coming to Chicago. From the *Complete Tribune Primer* which appeared in Boston (1901), six years after his death, there is this short piece which gives an example of his earlier approach to humor:

> This is a gun. Is the gun loaded? Really, I do not know. Let us find out. Put the gun on the Table, and you, Susie, Blow down one barrell, while you, Charlie, blow down the other. Bang! Yes, it was loaded. Run, quick, Jenny, and pick up Susie's head and Charlie's lower jaw before the nasty blood gets over the new carpet.

Another example which is perhaps less biting but certainly which is not attuned to a "family paper" also appeared in *Complete Tribune Primer*:

> Mama is beating poppa with the mop handle. The children are fighting over a piece of pie in the kitchen. Over the piano there is a beautiful motto in a gilt frame. The beautiful motto says: 'there is no place like home' (p. 67).

Once in Chicago Eugene Field was forced by circumstances to alter his work. The bitterness disappeared because the *Daily News* was billed as a "family paper" and as such had to appeal to all members of the family. Although a great deal is made of his satire and his freedom as a journalist, the truth of the matter is he was heavily edited. If this censorship really disturbed him, there is not a great deal of evidence of it. So in spite of the hard-hitting nature of the newspapers, it seems fairly clear that they too were concerned about the advertisers and the people who were "footing the bill." Furthermore, with all of its avowal of an emphasis upon independence and journalistic freedom, the *Daily News* did not wish to alienate deliberately the Establishment. As has been reported, one of the major duties of John Ballantyne—the managing editor—was to read Field's columns before they appeared in order to make certain that the "slings and arrows" did not penetrate too deeply into those supporters of the genteel tradition in Chicago. When Field got carried away, Ballantyne (on order from Victor Lawson) simply deleted the offending·and offensive passage. Field was permitted to poke fun at Chicago's *nouveaux riches* without attacking them. It was a tight rope which he had to walk. And that he could do it was perhaps a credit to his own fortitude. Of course, the question remains "what would his career have been if he had been permitted to write without this tacit censorship?" Perhaps, another man with such an acid pen might have gone down to defeat in Chicago, but Field succeeded because he had that approach to humor which in its final form did not alienate.

It was clear that he appreciated America and the West in general and Chicago in particular. Field had great love for and pride in his adopted city; but he hated the sham and pretensions of the elite. Whenever he could he poked fun at them—not in anger—but in an attempt to make them aware of their foolishness which occurred whenever they tried to imitate some of the older, more established communities. He wanted only the best for his nation and for his adopted city. He firmly believed that Chicagoans could exist on their own terms, without any reference to the East or to Europe. Imitation, he believed, resulted in all of the weakest manifestations of a culture being copied. Ultimately, he believed the world was governed by a series of moral laws; and if one used common sense, one could discover these eternal verities and be happy. His satires, then, are directed toward those whose pretensions outweigh their sense of reality, who try to be something which they are not. It was the false, the pretentious, or the sham which annoyed Field, and he poked fun at the *Current, Literary Life,* and *America* with their sometimes officious attempt to be the arbiter of taste. For example, while laughing at Chicago's culture in *Culture's Garland* Field defined what is meant when a Chicagoan refers to a "hand well known in literature." According to Field it "is a horny, warty but honest hand which, after years of patient toil at skinning cattle, or at boiling lard, or at cleaning pork, has amassed sufficient to admit of its master's reception into the crême de la crême of Chicago culture" (p. 168).

Field believed that man should be true to his nature, and ultimately he believed that there were certain eternal truths which persisted—truths of life and death—which no doubt led to some of his best children's poems. It is important to note that Field was not a reformer; hence, his attacks on the elite were not politically motivated. In his poetry he voiced the kind of sentimentality which many nineteenth-century families found inspiring and reassuring as he reinforced his own belief in the immortality of man's soul.

Eugene Field became a success. His columns and poems were read, he was quoted, he was lionized; but his career illustrates rather clearly both the assets and liabilities of a journalistic career for a man who wants to be taken seriously as a literary artist. The exigencies of the daily columns somehow sapped his creative energy, and part of his life was unfulfilled. Judgment is still divided on Field. Perhaps had he lived beyond his forty-fifth year, one might have a clearer view of his destiny. Perhaps had he lived longer, he would have become more aware of his own direction. That he wanted to write seriously is clear from the wistful letters which he wrote to his friends. And toward the end of his life there was growing evidence that the eccentric side of him with its emphasis upon fun-loving practical jokes was being submerged as he devoted himself to presenting the great literature of the classical world to his Chicago audiences in understandable terms. This accounts for his interest in re-doing the works of Horace, who was a Roman satirist very similar to Field. There have been a series of studies of Field, and they all—more or less—try to find the answer for his thwarted career. But perhaps, after all, he did on the *Daily News* what he could do best, and perhaps he never would have risen from the Denver *Tribune* cynic if he had not gone to Chicago. When one tries to total his life in terms of contributions, he aided greatly the realistic movement in literature by his insistence upon reporting life as he saw it around him. At the same time the realism of Field did not admit the ugly or the mundane. It was left for later writers to put that realism into more overt terms.

Thus it was that the newspapers provided—perhaps unwittingly —the motivation for the development of realism in Chicago writing. While Eugene Field was certainly not the city's first journalist to achieve a degree of fame, he was probably the first to become a nationally-recognized personality. In the present-day cult of the celebrity, such acclaim may be taken as a matter of course; in the nineteenth century, it was rare indeed. While the work of the advocates of the genteel tradition cannot be minimized, it was ultimately the work of the Chicago newspapers and journals which would provide the impetus for the golden age of Chicago's literature. It was from the ranks of the journalists—with few exceptions—that modern Chicago literature received its writers.

III

The fiction which appeared in the magazines during this period was singularly characterized by its avoidance of those realistic subjects which were being presented in the newspapers. Short stories were marked by their adherence to the romantic tradition and were often full of tales of love and nature. The rural aspects of these stories avoided the grimness of the regional story as popularized by Hamlin Garland; instead, the reader was presented with lovely landscapes, happy people, and the American Dream translated into agrarian terms. There were, of course, still stories of Indians, advance scouts, trappers, and settlers. The Indians were either portrayed as the "noble savage" or as a barbarian but never as a human being. The scouts, trappers, and settlers were portrayed as frontiersmen who were the essence of bravery and who managed—in spite of the frequent perils of nature—to establish homesites in the wilderness. When the city appeared in fiction, it became a place to test the virtue of the country lads and lasses who decided to try for their fortunes. The good are rewarded, and the immoral are punished. So simplistically are these few urban tales presented that the city became for the authors a means by which to re-tell age-old romantic tales of virtue rewarded and sin committed to everlasting damnation. If the fiction of this period had any distinction, it was in its almost total rejection of the social, economic, and psychological problems which were plaguing the residents of major cities like Chicago.

In addition to the fiction which appeared in the journals, there was growing evidence that a Chicago novel was beginning to emerge by the opening of the Exposition in 1893. (See Appendix C: The Chicago Novel, 1850-1893). While many of the novels produced in the city had appeared to be romantic such as the two "travel" novels by Henry Blake Fuller, *The Chevalier of Pensieri-Vani* (1890) and *The Chatelaine of La Trinité* (1892) or the historical romance, *Monk and Knight,* by Reverend Gunsaulus, there was a growing interest in the type of realism which had been used by Reverend E.P. Roe in his *Barriers Burned Away* of 1872. Slowly there developed a novel of the city, but paramount to the early urban novels was the attempt to include the best of both the romantic and the realistic traditions. This resulted in a novel of manners not unlike those which had been produced by Jane Austen.

Hobart Chatfield Chatfield-Taylor turned to fiction when he left *America.* His early novels looked at the social scene of which he was an integral part and sometimes satirized the growing seriousness with which the elite now viewed themselves. At the same time he was convinced that it was the life of the upper classes which should form the subject for Chicago fiction. Thus he portrayed the society woman and the "gentleman" of business, but these portraits were rough sketches because even he was not so certain what a "lady" or a "gentleman" should do in the commercial market-place of the Midwest. Should a lady devote herself to entertaining after the fashion of the great houses of England, or should she seek fulfillment by trying to establish some social settlement for working girls in the city? Should a gentleman devote himself solely to his business, or should he be shown in his downtown club as a man of leisure whose business miraculously could run itself? These initial questions as well as the inevitable comparison between Chicago society and that of the older and more established communities of the East as well as of Europe concerned Chatfield-Taylor in his early novels. But it became clear that the society novel—at least as he envisioned it—could not exist in a vacuum in Chicago, and it was not long before this novel had to merge with the more effective "business" novel or with the "dynasty" novels as represented initially by Fuller's *On the Stairs* (1918) but subsequently refined and expanded by a later group of women novelists. The novel of manners, then, could exist only as a part of the story which recounted the development of a family fortune where the central figure remained the businessman. The sections of these novels which deal with society and the manners of the people tend to be well-done; however, it was clear that these sections could not be divorced from the larger issues of the novels. Yet, in his *An American Peeress* (1891) and *With Edge Tools* (1891) Chatfield-Taylor explored Chicago society and attempted to deal with this emerging phenomenon. By the publication of *Two Women and a Fool* (1895) he was able to view the Chicago scene far more realistically as did his character, Dorothy Temple who declared: "Life here is nothing but a scramble, you must grow used to it" (p. 143); but this "lady" of society also recognized that "there is an enthusiasm about Chicago life which is resistless" (p. 144). Hence, she was able to devote her time to the establishment of a social center on the West Side which was worlds apart from her Prairie Avenue residence. It did, however, remain the task of the later novelists of the twentieth century to chronicle more faithfully this life of "scramble" which did prove "resistless" to many.

While the work of Chatfield-Taylor was in keeping with the genteel spirit which was so pervasive in the period before the Exposition—indeed, he was a guiding figure in the movement—the

1880's saw the development of an urban novel which the advocates of the genteel tradition would have preferred to have had unwritten. Duncan refers to these as "urban thrillers," but they are essentially crime stories which use Chicago as a locale—a type which through the years has remained a popular form of fiction. Although it leaves much to be desired as a novel, *Mysteries of Chicago* (1881), which had appeared in 1879 as *Suppressed Sensations*, is designed as an exposé of the type of crime for which the city was famous. The anonymous author, later revealed as James Maitland, declared:

> Other cities can boast of desperate thieves, thugs, and murderers . . .
> But it is not in the lower and brutal grades of crime that Chicago
> stands pre-eminent.

The writer goes on to declare that Chicago is known for "a certain looseness of morals . . . which has no parallel in any other city in the world" and for what he calls "ingenious rascality and blood-curdling scoundrelism [for which] the outlaws of the Garden City carry off the palm" (pp. 5-6). While the city as a place of evil is a rather traditional notion, especially within the romantic framework, these "urban thrillers"—which were sensational—did include significant elements of realism.

A series of novels—to use the term loosely—were produced by one Shang Andrews who did not condemn the city. Set in Chicago, the novels demonstrate that the author apparently knew the city well enough to give—even to later readers—a sense of place. Streets, buildings, and neighborhoods are drawn realistically; but the action is not totally dependent upon the locale. These stories, representative of a specific genre, combine the techniques of the urban thriller with an exposé of the sexual exploits of the main characters. They appeared in the late 1880's and early 1890's, printed on cheap paper, with unnumbered double-column pages. *Cranky Ann: The Street Walker* (1886), which Andrews referred to as "this great Chicago story," is the tale of a woman, seduced in early childhood, who is forced into a life of prostitution. The author promises that the story is a "startling exposition of midnight doings in the great metropolis of the West." The action, which takes place in 1876 and is designed "to paint a startling picture of Chicago by day and by night," recounts how the very respectable Mr. Baldwin, who lives in a "palatial residence on Wabash Avenue," is introduced to the seamier side of his city. The promotional "blurb" tells the reader:

The Underground Hellholes are unearthed with faithful and fearful accuracy. *Sin in Silk* is pictured with vivid truthfulness. *The Dark Dens of the City* are described so plainly that the reader will tremble as he reads. *The Horrible Crimes of Assignation Hags* are portrayed to the very Life. The Devilish Designs of those Female Fiends are exposed in words that Burn and lines that Lacerate. In fact, the WHOLE BOOK . . . is one continuous Sensation, from the first page to the last.

The reader is then promised:

Whoever takes it up to read will never lay it down until the last word is reached, and then he or she will only wish that there were more. 'It is THE BEST STORY I HAVE EVER READ' is the unanimous verdict of all who peruse it. If it were purely fiction, it would be a Grand Romance. But as it is actually A TALE OF TRUTH, it cannot but command more earnestly the attention of the public.

As is common in this type of story, the conclusion presents a moral regeneration which is as unbelievable as it is speedy. But interestingly enough, the element of suffering which one tends to expect in the sensational fiction of the nineteenth century is absent. Instead, the conclusion represents a "free will" choice made by the central character who is tolerated—not rejected—by the urban environment.

Nellie O'Brien, the central figure of *Wicked Nell: A Gay Girl of the Town* (1892), is twelve years old in 1869 when the novel opens. Already she has gained the reputation as one of the "best" prostitutes in the "Red Light District," then located in the vicinity of Wells and Jackson Streets. She is coarse, brash, sullen, and proud of her profession. In a scene undoubtedly designed to pull nineteenth-century heartstrings, her mother is led to the bar from which Nellie conducts her "business." But she refuses to go home in "memory of her dear, departed father" and says: "Mother . . . I will *NOT* go home! I will *NOT* be good! I will *NOT* reform! I will always be 'Wicked Nell, a gay girl of the town.' " But this declaration is made before Mr. Brown falls in love with her. After a series of adventures, Nellie—the reader is startled to learn—is attending "a female seminary not two hundred miles from Chicago" under the auspices of Mr. Brown. In contrast to the city, the seminary is equated with the beauty and peacefulness of nature. After three years, Nellie has become a lovely young lady and is ready to marry Mr. Brown.

Andrews describes Nellie as a "wild child of the street" and promises that the story will be "thrilling in the extreme." He continues:

While under the spell of a terrible enchantment the wayward creature seems really devil-possessed, and exhibits a hardness of heart that a demon in hell could not excel. She laughs with horrid glee at a mother's awful curse, defies the officers of the law, damns everything good, and in every possible way endeavors to be the wickedest girl in Chicago. She drinks, swears, fights, lies, steals, and takes pride in being abominably bad.

Yet he claims "underneath all there is something noble in this wicked girl. She is not so bad as she tries to make herself." And he tells the reader that this "is a well-told tale—one that will be carefully preserved long after trashy yarns are dead and forgotten —and is destined to take front rank among the great realistic romances of this fast age."

While they have little to recommend them, the novels of Shang Andrews do attempt to use the "Red Light District" as a major locale for fiction. Years later Alston J. Smith declared in his *Chi-cago's Left Bank* (Chicago, 1953) that the significance of this section of the city should not be overlooked.

No other tenderloins in the world, save possible those of New Orleans and Paris, have intrigued authors as have the succession of red-light areas . . . that decorated the Chicago scene. These pur-lieus, for better or for worse, were of the essence of the city from its earliest days, part and parcel of a brash, brawling, bawdy city that was chronologically and geographically close to the frontier and glad of it. They were an integral part of Chicago's self-conscious bigness; no other city in the world could boast of so much vice, such elaborate bagnios, such colorful madames, such a phalanx of demi-mondes. Successful vice was as much a part of the Chicago story as successful meat-packing or successful railroading . . . It was this open, un-blushing bawdiness, so different from the furtive, back-alley whoring of the East, that captured the imaginations of a whole series of writers . . .

Smith continues by suggesting "the Chicago house of ill fame, *circa* 1900, is the classic prototype of the bagnio in American art, letters, and drama." In an attempt to establish a relationship be-tween "the artist, the writer, the musician, the actor, and the prostitute," Smith contends that they "share a common rootless-ness" and finally concludes:

There are some world cities that are culturally incomprehensible unless one understands the netherworlds . . . Paris is such a city. So is Shanghai . . . So is New Orleans. And so, more than any of these, is Chicago. In these places (unlike Dublin or Madrid or Boston or Denver) the writer or artist must know the underworld before he can understand the upper-world. Take Monmartre out of Paris or the Vieux Carre out of New Orleans and you throw away the key that unlocks the city's heart. Similarly, if you know nothing of 'The Sands,' 'Little Cheyenne,' North Clark Street, or the 22nd Street tenderloin of recent memory, you cannot know Chicago. In giving flavor to Chicago, the Armours, Swifts, and Ryersons must take a back seat to the Kennas, Colosimos, Capones, and Everleighs. This is nothing to be proud of, but it is a fact that must be taken into account (pp. 136-37).

Without the sophistication of later writers such as Nelson Algren or Willard Motley, Shang Andrews did attempt to give literary voice to a section of the city which was frequently ignored in the nineteenth century. His tales are sensational and melodramatic, but he was a forerunner of that rather typical tale of the Chicago-after-dark variety. Had he done as well with character and plot development as he did with setting, it is conceivable that he might have made a significant contribution.

The 1880's also saw the publication of *Zury: The Meanest Man in Spring County* (1887) and *The McVeys* (1888) by Joseph Kirkland. It is, of course, perfectly true that these novels are not about Chicago, but they were part of the midwestern literary scene so influenced by the thriving urban metropolis which controlled the cultural life around it. Joseph Kirkland's association with the midwestern scene included his history of the city, *The Story of Chicago* (1892), which is a somewhat romanticized account of the city which met the genteel standards for recounting the past. His novels, on the other hand, are grim reminders that life close to nature is not as beautiful as many had said. Before writers were able to deal with the city honestly, they had to face what the countryside actually meant. Once this occurred, it was possible to apply the techniques which they had used to the city. When this was done, the rise of urban literature as it is currently known was possible. And these techniques were consistently applied to Chicago after the World's Columbian Exposition. Zury, of course, is a product of the times, and his declaration "money was life; the absence of money was death" could have been the motto of any Chicago entrepreneur who stopped at nothing in order to succeed. Zury, however, soon learned—unlike the Chicago businessman, that hard work alone would not necessarily produce success. Out of this grim realization there arose a body of realistic literature which dealt quite faithfully with the indifference of nature as represented through man's inability often to eke out a living even though he had put in the hours of hard work. Interestingly enough, many of these early writers of the grimness of the country were centered around Chicago.

Dorothy Dondore in her *The Prairie and the Making of Middle America* (1926) cogently observed:

. . . in the realistic movement that stormed the critical outposts in the eighties and that down to the present day has produced some of the least ephemeral of our literature, it is unquestionably true that Middle Westerners have been the leaders. The explanation of this phenomenon is not, however, so simple. In part it was due to a world-wide reaction from romance; this would not explain, however, its centralization in one locality. Perhaps the absence of a stately past such as dignified the genteel decay of New England and the South pivoted attention on the raw realities of the present. The clear air and broad horizons of the prairie may have tended to sharpen the vision. More probably the absence of hampering tradition, the spur of the adventurous pioneer blood that won the frontier, continued to incite in literature as in politics to revolt—revolt as much against the blatant self-satisfaction of the western promoter as against the academic strictures of the Atlantic conservatives. Certainly no more sriking manifestation of the insufficiency of mere material prosperity could be found than this pitiless blazoning forth of its deficiencies by this most prosperous section of the world's most prosperous nation (pp. 326-327).

What is of probable interest to the modern reader is the absence of social and protest novels during this period. When one remembers the speed with which Chicago was rebuilt and the recouping of the fortunes by so many, one also must remember that the lot of the working man was far from ideal. Plagued by long hours, almost inhuman working conditions, housing of the most inferior kind, little or no concern for sanitation, the lower classes of Chicago might have been inspired by the manifestation of wealth around them; however, as they waited for their "American Dream" to be fulfilled, they were forced into the direst poverty. The conditions which led to the Haymarket Affair were not isolated; they were rampant in the city. Immigrants had been arriving in Chicago with a degree of regularity only to be met by hostility and indifference. Each national group was packed into its own ethnic ghetto and from this viewpoint, there was little attractive about Chicago. Even the cultural institutions—which by now were open to all—could mean little to people who worked twelve to fifteen hours a day in order to make it possible for the elite to continue to buy "pictures" for the city. Yet, no literary champion arose to plead their cause. Instead, some utopian novels appeared in the early 1890's which presented a Chicago which could arise. Both *A Tramp in Society* (1891) by Robert Cowdrey and *The People's Program* (1892) by Henry L. Everett believed that the ideal city would arise when the principles of socialism governed the lives of the urban dwellers. While not specifically rejecting what Chicago had come to represent, they were convinced that things would be even better once the ownership of everything was in the hands of everybody. In essence their protests were masked beneath their alternate plans. *The Beginning: Romance of Chicago As it Might Be* (1893) was apparently a group effort of "a small debating club of workingmen" and proposed moral regeneration as the means by which the city would be changed. Such an ideal state could exist if everyone returned to the basic principles of religion, and the anonymous authors thought this could occur by 1922. One of the problems faced by the writers of the utopian novel in Chicago was predicated upon the fact that they were forced to admit that the city had grown fantastically successful in such a short period. They were aware of the method of its growth and were aware that their plans would not have produced a comparable example of material success. Even though these works appeared after considerable labor problems in the city, their protests—if they might be called such—were mild in comparison to the actuality of the events.

There are certain characteristics which one tends to associate with Chicago fiction. Using such authors from Fuller to Dreiser and ultimately from Colter to Bellow one tends to view Chicago literature—especially its fiction—as being essentially naturalistic with environmental and/or economic determinism pervading the work. One tends to emphasize the fact that a sense of rejection of the dominant commercial spirit exists along with the recognition that there is an extreme emphasis upon the present with little or no regard for the past either as a fact or as a necessary historic symbol. This view of Chicago fiction is undoubtedly a product of the times. The promise of the American Dream somehow never materialized for thousands of Americans and as great economic fortunes were being made in Chicago, they were made at the expense of thousands more who worked in the factories and the other hell-holes of the city. And eventually Chicago literature did react—as did American literature—to these prevailing conditions. When this occurred, the great social literature of the twentieth century developed, Yet, one must acknowledge that the seeds for this literature were sown in the nineteenth century, often in obscure places by obscure writers.

Given the role of the Chicago novel in the closing years of the nineteenth century and into the twentieth century there is little about its production prior to Fuller's *The Cliff-Dwellers* (1893) which would suggest the major role which it would assume in the future evolution of the American novel. At the same time, these early novels do have some interest because one can see the tentative treatments of what eventually were to become major themes. If the Chicago novelist did not rise to the occasion in the 1880's and opening years of the 1890's this was partially due not only to the genteel spirit but also to what they were able to observe. Their nearness to the subject prevented the type of perspective which later novelists were able to assume. Furthermore, the urban novel as a distinct form was still being hampered by an unrealistic view of the city.

When the novel of social protest finally evolved, it developed out of a sense of urban frustration and attacked—as had some of the earlier novels—the growing emphasis upon business as well as upon material success. The city had promised so much but had delivered so little to the immigrants and to those who had come into the city trying to realize their dreams of American success. There was a call—often unheeded—of a return to a more simple way of life. Hence, into the twentieth century many of the protest novels returned to the precepts of that "small debating club of workingmen" who felt that "the ideal state will be when we have arrived at that stage of moral perfection where we can dispense with all government control" (pp. 3-4).

IV

During the nineteenth century western versifiers were many, and western poets were few. Much of the verse of the period appeared in magazines and journals; and much of it has deservedly been forgotten and ignored. In 1859 William T. Coggeshall, the state librarian of Ohio, issued a call for western literature as had many sectional loyalists before him. However, his call appeared in a discourse entitled "The Protective Policy in Literature." He argued that a regional literature would best serve the interests of the West and would make the West understandable to other sections of the nation. The following year he produced *The Poets and Poetry of the West: with Biographical and Critical Notices.* This work of 1860 contains the poetry of 152 writers from Kentucky, Ohio, Indiana, Missouri, Michigan, Illinois, Wisconsin, Iowa, Minnesota, and Kansas. In his introduction Coggeshall noted:

Not more than ten of the writers herein represented can be classed as literary men and women in that sense which conveys the idea of the pursuit of literature as a profession. The poets of the West are, or have been, lawyers, doctors, teachers, preachers, mechanics, farmers, editors, printers, and housekeepers. They have written at intervals of leisure, snatched from engrossing acres and exacting duties. Their literary labors, consequently desultory, have rarely been given to elaborate performances, but rather to the emotion, the impulse, or the passion of the hour; and yet it may be justly claimed that this volume presents a collection of poems, remarkable for variety of topics and versatility of treatment, exhibiting in a greater degree the feeling than the art of poetry, but preserving some specimens of descriptive and some lyric verse, which are likely to keep the memories of their authors green for many generations yet to come (p. vi).

He excuses the exclusion of humorous poems by ascertaining the lack of an extensive body of that literature. The fact that western humor figured so prominently in the development of American literature is lost as he observed:

In poetry breathing an earnest spirit of moral and political reform; expressing just appreciation of material beauty; revealing domestic affections; representing noble aspirations for intrinsic worth and force, the West is rich; but in humorous poems (except by way of parody) and in the more pretending styles, which are wrought by elaborate culture, it is far from opulent.

He explains these absences, however, by noting:

The reasons are obvious. The earliest poem of the West was written in 1789. The regular chronological order of this volume comprises a period of only forty years—a period significant for perilous wars, for hard work, for amazing enterprise; all of which furnish materials for literature; but, until the mellowing influences of time have long hung over their history, repel poetry (p. vi).

Later he noted that "soldiers, hunters, and boatmen had among them many songs, descriptive of adventures incident to backwoods life, some of which were not destitute of poetic merit; but they were known only around camp fires, or 'broad horns,' and tradition has preserved none which demands place in these pages" (p. 14).

Thus covering a period from 1820 to 1860 the anthology represents a group of men and women who—in their day—were the accepted poets of the region. Very much as Ralph L. Rusk was to do sixty-five years later in his *The Literature of the Middle Western Frontier*, Coggeshall focuses his attention on the "culture" of such centers as Lexington, Kentucky, and Cincinnati, Ohio; as he reports that before 1820 "there was . . . decided rivalry between Cincinnati and Lexington for literary pre-eminence" (p. 14). In most western communities, before the settlement of Chicago, there was a genuine interest in a sectional literature. This may have been due in part to the truth of Coggeshall's statement that "the men who began the settlements of the North-West, on the Ohio River . . . in 1788, were men of culture; and, while cheerfully undertaking the perils and deprivations incident to a wilderness traversed by Indians, they provided that the refinements of art and literature should not altogether be denied them" (p. 13). There were others who agreed with Bishop who in *An Introductory to a Course of Lectures in History* (1823) noted that the time would come "when the mouth of the Columbia, or the head waters of the Missouri, shall be the seat of Empire and the abodes of the arts and refinement, and London and Paris may be as Ninevah and Babylon are" (p. 4).

A different approach to the West—though equally as romantic —came from James Hall who in his *Letters from the West* (1828) noted:

I shall never forget the intense interest which I felt, while a boy, in gazing at the brawny limbs and sun-burnt features of a Kentuckian, as he passed through the streets of Philadelphia. The rough, hardy air of the stranger, the jaded paces, of his nag, the blanket, bear-skin, and saddle-bags—nay, the very oil-cloth on his hat, and the dirk that peeped from among his vestments, are still in my eye; they bespoke him to be of distant regions, to have been reared among dangers, and to be familiar with fatigues. He strode among us with the step of an Achilles (p. 5).

The faith in western production is not echoed by Rusk who chronicled the literary history of the region up to 1840 with primary focus upon Cincinnati, Lexington, Louisville, St. Louis, and Detroit.

The reflection in literature of the vast phenomenon of the pioneer West is to be seen properly only in the great bulk of mediocre pamphleteering and journalism—and, to a much lesser extent, bookmaking—of men who wrote only incidentally to their participation in the economic, political, and religious turmoil which engaged almost their whole attention. The few self-conscious writers of the frontier, striving ineffectively for a certain artistic achievement, had their eyes fixed on an ideal rather than a reality. They yielded to the spell of a legend or looked beyond their own time to a future in which they firmly believed . . . this same romantic haze obscured the vision of almost every Western writer who attempted to add to his actual experience of life the element of imagination. The few who acquired a style of any charm were usually those who were thus incapable of picturing the real West (pp. 77-78).

In spite of the justified pessimism of critics such as Rusk, the result is that before Chicago was founded there did exist a western poetic tradition which—although it had serious limitations—had produced a great deal of activity. If one views this activity in terms of the cyclical theory of the evolution of literature, then it becomes clear that the bulk of writing which exists before the production of something "distinctively unique" does serve a purpose in the development of the culture of a people. Thus Rusk's ultimate conclusion unwittingly serves as an explanation for the cyclical theory as one might translate it into midwestern terms.

When an Easterner wrote, he was conscious of the fact that he was an American; but when a Westerner attempted authorship, he was troubled by the consciousness of the fact that he was not only an American but a Westerner. Unfortunately, though the Western writer could speak his frontier convictions courageously so long as he had to do with what seemed to him matters of fact, once upon the border-land between fact and imagination, he too often sought either to idealize the life with which he was actually acquainted or else disguise his identity as a frontiersman by copying conventional themes in no way connected with the West. Lacking unusual power of artistic achievement, he thus often failed to put into his tales and novels the one thing which might have made them of great value—a faithful delineation of pioneer life (pp. 272-273).

As one views the development of literature and the various responses of writers to the multi-faceted incidents in Chicago, one might be struck by the fact that the poets did not—as a rule —respond to the conditions of the city as readily as did the prose writers. Yet, to view the evolution of a poetic tradition is to view a set of problems which excluded those writers who were concerned with the more mundane matters of building a socio-economic or a socio-political theory in a new land. Thus there remained a belief in a type of pastoral poetry which would in some way reflect the concerns of the times. There was—in addition— the expected array of didactic poetry, designed to present the universal concerns of RIGHT and WRONG to the readers. So while Coggeshall and others were calling for and identifying a western literature, what they really were accepting was a literature—as closely patterned after the subjects which they accepted as "poetic material"—by western writers. Like the first poets of the nation, the early western poets dealt with matters of nature; and like the early poets, the western poets tried to make their work "regional" by describing the prairie. Consequently, there are many poems which deal with the prairie. There are also more patriotic poems than one might imagine, but this might be explained when one considers that many of the settlers viewed their hardships as contributing to the growth of the nation.

Some of the earliest poets of Chicago have already been dis-

cussed in terms of the romantic offerings of such writers as Horatio
Cooke and William Asbury Kenyon, both of whom are literary
curiosities but certainly not poetic giants. And it is interesting
to note the continuation of the belief that Kenyon's work was the
first published collection in Chicago in spite of the availability of
Cooke's volume which appeared a year earlier. It is also interesting to note—although it is not unduly surprising—that the long
prose tradition is unmatched by an equally successful poetic tradition.

Before the golden age of Chicago's literature or the first renaissance of the 1890's, there was considerable literary activity in the
city. Much of it revolved—as already noted—around the journalists and the magazines or newspapers for which they worked.
Some of the tendencies which had led to the proliferation of pre-
fire journals were still present in the city; as a result, it was an
active place for the creation of new magazines and newspapers in
the 1880's. The motivation for these creations frequently changed;
but underlying all of them was obviously a belief that they had a
chance to succeed. After the fire, then, as the new city was being
created, there were those who felt it important to continue the call
for a western literature which had figured so prominently in the
early literature of the 1840's, 1850's, and 1860's.

One of the leaders of the post-fire literary movement (if one is
willing to consider it organized enough to have a "leader") was
Benjamin Franklin Taylor. In 1886 S.C. Griggs and Co., issued
his *Complete Poetical Works,* and with this work he assumed a
national stature unmatched by any poet up to his time. Actually, a
great deal of his work spanned nineteenth-century Chicago, and
early in the city's history one can find his name figuring prominently on the mastheads of local newspapers and journals.

Benjamin Franklin Taylor, a New Yorker by birth, was the son
of a college president and early was introduced to books. In 1838
he graduated from Madison University where his father had
served, and his literary career began with the publication of an
erudite analysis of language somewhat reminiscent of Noah Web-

ster's *Dissertations upon the English Language* of 1789. Taylor's work was entitled *Attractions of Language; or a Popular View of Natural Language, in all its varied Displays in the Animate and Inanimate World; and as Corresponding in Instinct, Intelligence, and Reason* and was published in 1843. Two years later, convinced that the tales of success in the West were not exaggerated, Taylor decided to move to Chicago. He began his long and distinguished career in journalism when he became the literary editor of the Chicago *Evening Journal*, a paper which had begun publication in 1844 with the same optimism which had guided the establishment of so many newspapers, magazines, and journals during the 1840's. There was an inherent belief that in the raw, embryonic city there were literary possibilities. The paper appeared Monday through Saturday. The Saturday edition which was larger and might be compared to the modern Sunday paper editions contained a long column entitled "Saturday Literary Notices" which consisted of book notices and reviews of new works. Many of these were written by Taylor. Since the use of the by-line did not come into vogue until some years later, Taylor's work was rarely identified, but in keeping with the usual procedures, his work appeared throughout the paper—sometimes as lead articles, sometimes as fillers.

Using a pseudonymn he produced *Short Ravelings from a Long Yarn, or: Camp and Marsh Sketches of the Sante Fe Trail* which was ostensibly taken from the notes of Richard L. Wilson and which appeared in 1847. There is little indication that this was more than a limited edition literary curiosity. The important thing is that by 1847—just ten years after the city's incorporation—there was a man committed to writing. By 1848 Taylor with the Reverend Mr. J.S. Hurlbut—following the lead of the popular magazines of New York and Philadelphia which were designed for women—began the *Lady's Western Magazine*. Taylor was designated editor-in-chief. Like many other early journals, this one was not able to survive in the marketplace of the Midwest and was forced to close in 1849, less than a year after its establishment.

But once again its very existence attested to the desires of some to create a literary life in the new city.

It is apparent that Taylor was in the forefront of the movement to create a Chicago literature and/or literary tradition. How much interest was actually engendered by his activities is a moot point, but it is a safe assumption that these were all parts of the attempt to "civilize" the midwestern outpost and to give a semblance of culture to the city. Taylor was also active in the Young Men's Association, one of the many clubs devoted to the "uplift" movement during the early days of the city. Not only did he try to persuade people to attend the lectures of the Association but he also gave space to the activities of the Association in the *Journal.* He gave some of the lectures; for example, on February 26, 1852, he delivered "The Battle of the World" which was subsequently published in that same year by A.H. and C. Burley of Chicago.

In 1854 he published *January and June: Being Outdoor Thinking and Fireside Musings* which appeared simultaneously in Chicago and New York. The book, a collection of prose and poetry, became extremely popular and was reprinted several times. By 1860 its third edition was published by one of the leading houses in the city, D.B. Cooke and Company. According to Andreas ". . . his writings attract attention, and [have] a vigor of style hitherto almost unknown in the literature of the West." He was included among Coggeshall's western poets and was represented by the long "Rhyme of the River," which apparently elevates the Chicago River beyond recognition. The first stanza celebrates the river in idealistic terms:

> Oh, River far-flowing,
> How broad thou art growing,
> And the sentinel Headlands wait grimly for thee;
> And Euroclydon urges
> The bold-riding surges,
> That in white-crested lines gallop in from the sea.

He does note a few stanzas later:

> In the great stony heart
> Of the feverish mart,
> Is the throb of thy pulses pellucid today;
> By gray mossy ledges,
> By green velvet edges,
> Where the corn waves its saber, thou glidest away;

The poem extends for nineteen more stanzas. His use of the six-line aabccb stanza and varying metric patterns is an interesting variation from so much of western verse. But the harsh realities of the city and its river are shaded beneath the pastoral tradition. Two romantic poems "June Dews" and "Shall I Know Her Again" describe the delights of the early days of summer as well as unrequited love.

The patriotic "God Bless Our Stars" is indicative of the epic sweep of much of Taylor's work as he managed to compress it into a series of eight-line stanzas.

> "God Bless our Stars for ever!"
> Thus the Angels sang sublime,
> When round God's forges fluttered fast,
> The sparks of starry Time!
> When they fanned them with their pinions,
> Till they kindled into day,
> And revealed Creation's bosom,
> When the infant Eden lay.
>
> "God bless our Stars for ever!"
> Thus they sang—the seers of old,
> When they beckoned to the Morning,
> Through the Future's misty fold,
> When they waved the wand of wonder—
> When they breathed the magic word,

And the pulses' golden glimmer,
   Showed the waking granite heard.

"God bless our stars for ever!"
   'Tis the burden of the song,
Where the sail through hollow midnight
   Is flickering along;
When a ribbon of blue Heaven
   Is a-gleaming through the clouds,
With a star or two upon it,
   For the sailor in the shrouds!

"God bless our stars for ever!"
   It is Liberty's refrain,
From the snows of wild Nevada
   To the sounding woods of Maine;
Where the green Multnomah wanders,
   Where the Alabama rests,
Where the thunder shakes his turban
   Over Alleghany's crests;

Where the mountains of New England
   Mock Atlantic's stormy main,
Where God's palm imprints the Prairie
   With the type of Heaven again—
Where the mirrored morn is dawning,
   Link to link, our Lakes along,
And Sacramento's Golden Gate
   Swinging open to the song—

There and there! "Our stars for ever!"
   How it echoes! How it thrills!
Blot that banner? Why, they bore it
   When no sunset bathed the hills.
Now over Bunker see it billow,
   Now at Bennington it waves,
Ticonderoga swells beneath,
   And Saratoga's graves!

Oh! long ago at Lexington,
   And above those minute-men,

The "Old Thirteen" were blazing bright—
　There were only thirteen then!
God's own stars are gleaming through it—
　Stars not woven in its thread;
Unfurl it, and that flag will glitter
　With the Heaven overhead.

Oh! it waved above the Pilgrims,
　On the pinions of the prayer;
Oh! it billowed o'er the battle,
　On the surges of the air;
Oh! the stars have risen in it,
　Till the Eagle waits the Sun,
And Freedom from her mountain watch
　Has counted "thirty-one."

When the weary Years are halting,
　In the mighty march of Time,
And no New ones throng the threshold
　Of its corridors sublime;
When the clarion call, "Close up!"
　Rings along the line no more,
Then adieu, thou blessed Banner,
　Then adieu, and not before!

His representation in the Coggeshall anthology ends with the brief
"The World's Embodied Thought," which uses one of Taylor's
favorite verse patterns.

Lo! there, the breathing thought,
　The poets sang of old,
And there the burning word,
　No tongue has fully told,
Until the magic hand,
　The bold conception wrought,
In iron and in fire it stands—
　The world's embodied Thought.

Lo! in the panting thunders,
　Hear the echo of the Age!

Lo! in the globe's broad breast, behold
The poet's noblest page!
For in the brace of iron bars,
That weld two worlds in one,
The couplet of a nobler lay
Than bards have e'er begun!

That Coggeshall included five of Taylor's poems is to be noted
in a work which contains so few of the so-called Chicago poets. In
his critical note Coggeshall observed: "Mr. Taylor has written
some of the most beautiful literary sketches, and some of the sweet-
est gems of poetry, that have been penned in the Western country.
His originality of thought, scope of imagination, and power of
language are remarkable. His resources appear inexhaustible, notwithstanding the fact that he has been a writer for the public press
for over a dozen years, and suffers the wear and tear of daily
journalism" (p. 416).

With the advent of the Civil War Benjamin Franklin Taylor
became a war correspondent for the *Journal* and his "letters" were
published as articles and communiques from the front. These
published letters became the basis for his next popular book which
was once again published simultaneously in Chicago and New
York. Appearing in 1872 as *Mission Ridge and Lookout Mountain, with pictures of Life in Camp and Field*, it was published in
Chicago by S.C. Griggs and Company and in New York by D.
Appleton and Company. The initial essay gives an indication of
Taylor's sympathy. As he wanders through Chicago's Rosehill
Cemetery, he thinks of the soldiers whom he has known and who
have been killed. He recalls his life as a war correspondent and
his travels through the war-torn country. He describes the land,
the people, and the battles. Juxtaposing the local color tradition
with the reality of war produced a work which went through several editions. His description of the battles of Mission Ridge
and Lookout Mountain helped to make his national reputation as
a war correspondent. The second and third editions were pub-

lished in Chicago, 1875 and 1888, by S.C. Griggs and Co. with the title *Pictures of Life in Camp and Field*. Subsequently, his later life as a free lance writer saw his work appearing in such national publications as *Atlantic, Harper's* and *Scribner's*. At the end of the Civil War and with his decision to free lance, Benjamin Franklin Taylor decided to travel throughout the country. This led to another book, published in 1874 by S.C. Griggs and Co., entitled *The World on Wheels and Other Sketches*. These sketches which had appeared a year earlier in the New York *Examiner* and *The Chronicle* were based upon his thoughts about the United States as he traveled by train along with his descriptions of the Midwest. In a rather perceptive, though humorous sketch, Taylor notes that cities are made by trains. Some of his light sketches are used for didactic purposes; for example, he notes:

The more you travel, the less you carry. The novice begins with two trunks, a valise, a hatbox, and an umbrella. He jingles with checks. He haunts the baggage-car like a 'perturbed spirit.' He ends with a knapsack, an overcoat, and a linen duster. Bosom, collar, wristbands, he does himself up in paper like a curl. He is as clean around the edges as the margins of a new book (p. 62).

This is followed by the observation:

We throw away a great deal of baggage on the life journey that we cannot well spare; a young heart, bright recollections of childhood, friends of the years that are gone. And so we 'fly light,' but we do not fly well (p. 62).

Without being dubbed a local colorist, Taylor was fulfilling one of the dictates of the movement: he was intent upon explaining one region to another region.

In a subsequent edition in 1875 of *Pictures of Camp and Field* reviews from the Chicago *Tribune* appeared for *The World on Wheels*. Said the *Tribune*:

The pen-pictures of B.F. Taylor are among the most brilliant of the day. They are like the music of GOTTSCHALK played by GOTT-SCHALK himself; or like skyrockets that burst in the zenith, and fall in showers of fiery rain. They are word-wonders, reminding us of necromancy, with the dazzle and bewilderment of their rapid succession.

Another over-statement appeared in the St. Louis *Dispatch* which was equally laudatory and which appeared as an advertisement in the 1875 edition of *Pictures of Life in Camp and Field*. Said the *Dispatch* reviewer:

Another of Benj. F. Taylor's wonderful word-painting books . . . In purity of style and originality of conception, Taylor has no superiors in this country. The book before us is a gem in every way. It is quaint, poetical, melodious, unique, rare as rare flowers are rare. He has an exquisite faculty of illustration that is unsurpassed in the whole range of American literature.

In addition to these works, Benjamin F. Taylor had issued a book of poetry entitled *Old Time Pictures and Sheaves of Rhyme*. Both the third and fourth editions had been published by S.C. Griggs and Co. in 1874 and 1875 respectively. In the same advertisement John Greenleaf Whittier commented:

It gives me pleasure to see the poems of B.F. Taylor issued by your house [S.C. Griggs and Co.] in a form worthy of their merit. Such pieces as the 'Old Village Choir,' 'The Skylark,' 'The Vane on the Spire,' and 'June' deserve their good setting. . . . I do not know of anyone who so well reproduces the home scenes of long ago. There is a quiet humor that pleases me.

The advertisement goes on to record the views of *The Albany Morning Express* which compared Taylor to Whittier.

Unless it be Whittier, we know of no American poet so sweet, tender and gentle in his lyrics as B.F. Taylor. No writer of today sings the praises of rural life and scenery so eloquently, and we do not wonder that many of his poems have become classics. The holiday volume of his happy verses, *Old Time Pictures and Sheaves of Rhyme* is a very eloquent and daintily bound volume . . . Taking up this handsomely printed book, we have to linger on the delightful imagery and graceful diction of its pages, glowing as they are with pure and tender thoughts, and the indescribable music of sunny fields and rural joys. No one can read it but will be the better for so doing.

Old Time Pictures and Sheaves of Rhyme, in spite of the advertisements for it, illustrates both the strengths and weaknesses of Taylor as a poet. Certainly it is as delightful as the critical comments would suggest. It is totally romantic with its emphasis upon home, the beauty of nature, and the joys which come from living. The subjects cover a wide range of interests but tend toward romanticism in a philosophical way. Nature, man, life, death are among his major concerns; however, there are also some indications of regional interests. In "The Isle of Long Ago" there is the use of an extended metaphor, one of the typical Taylor devices. The island is presented as being man's mind in which are stored all of the pleasant remembrances of things past. In the first of seven stanzas Taylor establishes not only the metaphoric nature of the poem but also banishes any sense of obscurity which might have resulted from the title. The reader is told that the island is in "the middle of the River Time, in the ocean of years, and in the realm of Tears." The next two stanzas note that the island is subject to the influences of the years, the seasons, as well as night and day. But these do not have adverse effects. Rather the island is blessed by a "sweet spring, cloudless sky, and tropical climate." It is, in other words, a place of perfection. Thus the island provides a place of refuge for the harassment of everyday life. One can go to his "island" and regain its "treasures."

> There are brows of beauty and bosoms of sorrow—
> They are heaps of dust, but we love them so!
> There are trinkets and tresses of hair.

There are fragments of songs that nobody sings,
and other bits and pieces of long ago things,
left only to the memory.
There are hands that are waved when the fairy shore,
by the mirage is lifted in air.
And we sometimes hear through the turbulent roar,
Sweet voices we heard in days gone before,
When the wind down the River is fair.

As the poem ends, Taylor notes the importance of his "island" because it is a place to which one journeys even while asleep. These precious memories and thoughts which are so exclusively subjective have their counterparts in the fact that although certain memories belong to only a single person, everybody has a set of pleasant memories. Hence, Taylor spoke to all as he recounted the happiness of his own memories.

The universal quality of life and death is the subject of "Going Home." The "carriage for one," so aptly described in the first stanza, is the hearse which carries the "lone rider." Death as the great equalizer is portrayed graphically as the reader realizes that no matter what one's station in life may have been, he must ride in the carriage belonging to some one else on his journey to the cemetery. He notes, for example, in the third stanza:

He rode in state, but his carriage fare,
was left unpaid to his only heir.
Hardly a man from hovel to throne
takes to this route in coach of his own,
But borrows at last and travels alone.

In "a note to the reader" the genesis of the poem is explained:

A poor disheartened emigrant returning to his home in the East from the Far West, met in the streets of LaPorte, Indiana, a hearse on its way to the City of the Silent. He turned aside, halted, and with his wife and two children, watched the sad procession. The poor fellow told his story to someone never suspected of a spark of poetry, who, as he watched the meeting [of the hearse and the farm wagon both of which were carrying its occupants home] from the sidewalk, said, 'Well, one is going East and the other going West, but they're both bound the same way after all—both going home.

"Dearborn Observatory, Chicago" illustrates how Taylor could use a local scene in order to present a poem dealing with a theme which transcended regional concerns.

> From my chamber last night I looked out on the sky
> No mortal can reach without waiting to die,
> And I saw a few ships of Infinity's fleet,
> And the light at their bows lit the dew in the street
> That dying men crush with irreverent feet.
> Broadside to this port ridged and roughened with graves,
> Not a boat from the shore, not a gun from the waves,
> There they lay off and on in the Blue of the Blest
> Like the thoughts of the Lord in His Sabbath-day rest!
> Are we chained here for life? Are we bound to the clod
> When the lark with a song springs directly from the sod
> To the breakers of day and the glory of God?
> Have you heard of the man who was calling the roll
> Of the stars till the Seraphim called for his soul?
> Who began the Lord's census and prayed for clear night
> While he counted for life the squadrons of light?
> Do you know how the Pleiads made sail at the word
> And Arcturus bore down, till he fancied he heard
> The wash of the sky as it rocked off a shore
> It never had touched at a signal before?
> Port of Entry for stars! Where great admirals come
> And flotillas report to a Herschel at home—
> In that wonderful tower whose window commands
> Not a thing in the universe fashioned with hands,
> There's an eye at the window that never can sleep,
> That no ages can dim and that never can weep—
> Always gazing at life, never seeing the graves,

Though the land with its tombs mocks the sea with its waves—
That beckons a world and it dawns into sight,
Gives a glance at the blue and it sparkles with light,
Sweeps a field that the Lord had forgotten to sow,
When He scattered the worlds like His treasures of snow,
And a sun blossoms out from the infinite space
Like the first flowers of spring in God's garden of grace.

Certainly the questions and observations raised by "Dearborn Observatory, Chicago" could have been raised anywhere, and the localized title does nothing more than provide the vehicle for the poetic persona.

"Fort Dearborn, Chicago" is one of his longest and most ambitious historical poems whose introduction tells of the first fort and of the massacre of 1812 which occurred a few miles from the fort. The poem, however, is designed to recount the city's history before and after the Fire of 1871. As the poem begins, there is an idyllic description of the prairie just before the 1803 construction of the fort. This idyllic view is disturbed by the Fort. During a time of human terror the fort is destroyed, but the prairie remained the same although it is changed by the ruins of the fort. But man—like nature—cannot be conquered, and soon there are other settlers on the prairie, working the land and believing firmly in their own manifest destiny. The grandeur of the land and the magnificence of the place are conveyed in the opening lines of the poem.

Born of the prairie and the wave—the blue sea and the green,
A city of the Occident, Chicago lay between;
Dim trails upon the meadow, faint wakes upon the main,
On either sea a schooner and a canvas-covered wain.

I saw a dot upon the map, and a house-fly's filmy wing—
They said 'twas Dearborn's picket-flag when Wilderness was king;
I heard the reed-bird's morning song—the Indian's awkward flail—
The rice tattoo in his rude canoe like a dash of April hail—
The beaded grasses' rustling bend—the swash of the lazy tide,
Where ships shake out the salted sails and navies grandly ride!

I heard the Block-house gates unbar, the column's solemn tread,
I saw the Tree of a single leaf its splendid foliage shed
To wave awhile that August morn above the column's head;
I heard the moan of muffled drum, the woman's wail of fife,
The Dead March played for Dearbon's men just marching out of life,
The swooping of the savage cloud that burst upon the rank
And struck it with its thunderbolt in forehead and in flank,
The spatter of the musket-shot, the rifle's whistling rain—
The sand-hills drift round hope forlorn that never marched again!

I see in tasselled rank and file the regiments of corn,
Their bending sabres, millions strong, salute the summer morn;
The harvest-fields, as round and red as full-grown harvest moon;
That fill the broad horizons up with mimic gold of noon;
I count a thousand villages like flocks in pastures grand,
I hear the roar of caravans through all the blessed land—
Chicago grasps the ripened year and holds it in her hand!
"Give us this day our daily bread!" the planet's Christian prayer;
Chicago will her open palm, makes answer everywhere!

Using a theme which is frequently repeated in Chicago's history and literature, Taylor focuses upon the fact that Chicago defied nature as it was constructed in an unlikely place and in an unlikely way. This defiance has led many Chicagoans—both natives and emigrants alike—to use the fact as evidence of the city's greatness. And Taylor is no exception as he notes:

I hear the march of multitudes who said the map was wrong—
They draw the net of Longitude and brought it right along,
And swung a great Meridian Line across the Foundling's breast,
And the city of the Occident was neither East nor West!
Her charter is no dainty thing of parchment and of pen,
But written on the prairie's page by full a million men;
They use the plowshare and the spade, and endless furrows run,
Line after line the record grows, and yet is just begun;
They rive the pines of Michigan and give them to the breeze—
The keel-drawn Charter's draft inscribes the necklace of the seas,

'Tis rudely sketched in anthracite, engraved on copper plate,
And traced across the Continent to Ophir's Golden Gate!
The Lord's Recording Angel holds the Charter in his hand—
He seals it on the sea, and he signs it on the land!
Unroll the royal Charter now! It "marches" with the West,
Embossed along its far frontier, Sierra's silver crest;
Along its hither border shines a scared crystal chain:
God cursed of old the weedy ground, but never cursed the main,
As free to-day from earthly sin as Eden's early rain!

The growth of Chicago is compared to the growth of ancient
Rome, a growth which ultimately must foreshadow doom.

"I found a Rome of common clay," Imperial Caesar cried;
"I left a Rome of marble!" No other Rome beside!
The ages wrote their autographs along the sculptured stone—
The golden eagles flew abroad—Augustan splendors shone—
They made a Roman of the world! They trailed the classic robe,
And flung the Latin toga around the naked globe!

Chicago, however mighty it became, was no city of marble. Rather
it was a city built hastily of wood. And so Taylor notes that the
successful and prosperous territory on the prairie once again faces
disaster. This time it is the Fire of 1871.

"I found Chicago wood and clay," a mightier Kaiser said,
Then flung upon the sleeping mart his royal robes of red,
And temple, dome, and colonnade, and monument and spire,
Put on the crimson livery of dreadful Kaiser Fire!
The stately piles of polished stone were shattered into sand,
And madly drove the dread simoom, and snowed them on the land!
And rained them till the sea was red, and scorched the wings of
            prayer!
Like thistle-down ten thousand homes went drifting through the air,
And dumb Dismay walked hand in hand with frozen-eyed Despair!
Chicago vanished in a cloud—the towers were storms of sleet,
Lo! ruins of a thousand years along the spectral street!

The night burned out between the days! The ashen hoar-frost fell,
As if some demon set ajar the bolted gates of hell,
And let the molten billows break the adamantine bars,
And roll the smoke of torment up to smother out the stars!
The low, dull growl of powder-blasts just dotted off the din,
As if they tolled for perished clocks the time that *might* have been!
The thunder of the fiery surf roared human accents dumb;
The trumpet's clangor died away a wild bee's drowsy hum,
And breakers beat the empty world that rumbled like a drum.

The terror of the fire is enough to disturb the dead. Yet, in spite
of the loss of life and the destruction of property, men and women
rose to the occasion as they fought bravely. The world responded,
and the prairie was ready to receive a new city.

O cities of the Silent Land! O Graceland and Rosehill!
No tombs without their tenantry? The pale host sleeping still?
Your marble thresholds dawning red with holocaustal glare,
As if the Waking Angel's foot were set upon the stair!
But ah, the human multitudes that marched before the flame,
As 'mid the Red Sea's wavy walls the ancient people came!
Behind, the rattling chariots! the Pharaoh of Fire!
The rallying volley of the whips—the jarring of the tire!
Looked round, and saw the homeless world as dismal as a pyre—
Looked up, and saw God's blessed Blue a firmament so dire!
As in the days of burning Troy, when Virgil's hero fled,
So gray and trembling pilgrims found some younger feet instead,
That bore them through the wilderness with bold elastic stride,
And Ruth and Rachel, pale and brave, in silence walked beside;
Those Bible girls of Judah's day did make *that* day sublime—
Leave life but *them*, no other loss can ever bankrupt Time!
Men stood and saw their all caught up in chariots of flame—
No mantle falling from the sky they ever thought to claim,
And empty-handed as the dead, they turned away and smiled,
And bore a stranger's household gods and saved a stranger's child!
What valor brightened into shape, like statues in a hall
When on their dusky panoply the blazing torches fall,

Stood bravely out and saw the world spread wings of fiery flight,
And not a trinket of a star to crown disaster's night.
"Who runs these lines of telegraph?" A clock-tick made reply:
" 'The greatest of the three' has brought this message from the sky,
The Lord will send an Angel down to work these lines to-day!"
Charge all the batteries good and strong! Give God the right of way!
And so the swift evangels ran by telegraphic time,
And brought the cheer of Christendom from every earthly clime;
Celestial fire flashed round the globe, from Norway to Japan,
Proclaimed the manhood of the race, the brotherhood of man!
Then flashed a hundred engines' arms—then flew the lighting trains;
They had that day the right of way—gave every steed the reins—
The minutes came, the minutes went—the miles fled just the same—
And flung along October night their starry flags of flame!
They all were angels in disguise, from hamlet, field, and mart,
Chicago's fire had warmed the World that had her woe by heart.
"Who is my neighbor?" One and all: "We see her signal light,
And She our *only* neighbor now, this wild October night!"

And so a new and grander city arose, but it was a city which owed
its new life as much to the world as to its own citizens who kept
faith with the destroyed city.

"I found Chicago wood and clay," the royal Kaiser cried,
And flung upon the sleeping mart the mantle of his pride;
It lay awhile—he lifted it, and there beneath the robe
A city done in lithograph, the wonder of the globe;
Where granite grain and marble heart, in strength and beauty wed,—
"I leave a mart of palaces," the haughty Kaiser said.

Thus as the poet views the city on the second anniversary of the
great fire (October 8, 1873) he sees the rebuilding of the great
city. And he concludes that Chicago, the Prairie Flower, will
withstand all disasters not only because the people of the city are
committed to its growth but also because God is the city's De-
fender.

Now, thanks to God, this blessed day, to whom all thanks belong—
The clash of silver cymbals, the rhyme of the little song—
Whose Hand did hive the golden bees that swarm the azure dome,
Whence honey-dews forever fall around this earthly home—
Did constellate the prairie sod and light it up with flowers—
That hand defend from fire and flood this Prairie Flower of ours!
This volume of the royal West we bring in grateful gage,
We open at the frontispiece and give it to the Age,
Who wrote the word "Chicago" twice upon the title-page!

Old Time Pictures and Sheaves of Rhyme was followed by another travel book, a form which gained a great deal of popularity in nineteenth-century America. *Between the Gates* appeared in 1878 and dealt primarily with California with emphasis upon San Francisco. It was also published in Chicago by S.C. Griggs and Co. and was later reprinted in 1883, another testimony to his popularity. Then, in 1886—a year before his death—his Chicago publisher issued the *Complete Poetical Works of Benjamin Franklin Taylor,* a book which sold widely and was used as an indication of the literary activity which could take place in the Midwest.

Many of the poems in the 1886 collection had appeared elsewhere and marked Taylor as a poet who usually transcended time and place and who dealt with universal themes and subjects. His use of the city in his "Chicago" is certainly quite different from Sandburg's "Chicago" or that of Turbyfill, but the motivation of it was the same sense of pride that has marked the "Chicago booster."

A wide-winged bird, a schooner brown,
    Swam shoreward in a lazy way,
And shook her lifted plumage down,
    Where in the wild-rice cradle lay,
    As tender as a water-cress,
    The Moses of the Wilderness!
An empty Egypt lay in sight,
    No Sphinx to stare the ages out,

No Pharaoh nor Israelite,
  A painted savage lounged about,
  A paddle in his gray dug-out,
And watched the child beside the lake;
  Fort Dearborn's guns were marble mute,
The world walked in by trail and wake,
  As silent as a naked foot.
Ah, picket line beyond the law,
  Where cloudless nights were such a boon,
For half the year the sentry saw
  His nearest neighbor in the moon!

This Moses rent his swaddling bands,
  He sprang upon his youthful feet,
And beckoning to the drowsy lands
  Made half the world Chicago Street,
That found at last, where'er it went,
The gate-way of the continent.
Some Samson gave a mighty lift
And sent the ponderous gates adrift:
By dust and wave, by wheel and sail,
And glitterring wake and ringing rail,
  In cloud and calm, and day and night,
In lumbering wain, and lightning train
  That flies as if its load were light,
The engines with their hot simoom
Throb redly through the midnight gloom,
The genii pant, the giants row,
The hosts are going West to grow!
The world is coming up the road!
The highway clear, the gate-way broad!

A monotone from farthest West!
  Was it a growl of heavy breath
  Through White Nevada's snowy teeth?
Or murmur from a Thunder's nest?
  Or echoes of the coming world
  From Rocky Ranges backward hurled?
Like trumpet's mouth the opening roar,

It widens, deepens more and more,
  Until, behold in lengthened line,
  With fragrant leaves and silken shine,
The train from China at the door!
And all the while the nerves of wire
Are thrilled with quick electric fire,
And East and West talk back and forth
Round the great circles of the earth
With instant words that never wait,
Like lovers at a garden gate
When roses blow and moon is late!

In 1887, the year of Taylor's death, *Theophilus Trent; Old Times in the Oak Openings* appeared. Although S.C. Griggs and Co. published the would-be novel a year after *Complete Poetical Works,* this last book published during his lifetime does not really do justice to Taylor's literary career. His death in Cleveland, Ohio, was followed by his burial in the University Cemetery of Hamilton, New York. Thus it was that Taylor was returned to the land of his birth.

Assessing the role of Benjamin Franklin Taylor in the creation of a literary climate in Chicago is difficult. Was he a prime mover, or was he merely a followerer? From the outset, while still a young man in Hamilton, New York, he had decided to cast his lot as a man of letters. Certainly Chicago provided a congenial atmosphere for his literary hopes, and he took advantage of the many newspapers and magazines to do the work which he most enjoyed. While he frequently described unique midwestern scenes, he did pay some especial attention to Chicago. His city, however, was not the bustling, urban community with its emphasis upon the commercial life—although he did allude to this aspect of it. Rather the city was generally presented as a placid beautiful community which grew out of the prairie. His prose and his poetry illustrate his interest in approaching his subjects philosophically, and many of his subjects—love, nature, life, death, the ultimate goodness of man—were general enough to be appealing to readers everywhere. While he demonstrated that he could deal with subjects realistically as he did in his Civil War studies as well as in his descriptions of people and places, Taylor was essentially a romantic writer who never subscribed to the dictates of the move toward realism which followed the Civil War. Consequently, to search for a realistic view of the city is to search in vain. He was committed to the idea of a *western* literature, but he was enough of an easterner to attempt to use the established and traditional poetic forms as his tools. Thus the type of experimentation which many of his peers associated with the search for a literary tradition, Taylor rejected. Relying instead upon neo-classical forms, images, and allusions while utilizing a romantic approach to life, Taylor became a poet *in* Chicago rather than a Chicago poet. Yet, he manifested his faith in the possibility that the city could become a literary center by having all of his major works published in the city at a time when many Chicago writers sought eastern publishers. Furthermore, from his first days as a columnist on the Chicago *Evening Journal* he insisted that literary activity could take place in the city without being limited by an urban vision. Early he made clear that culture—as evidenced by poetry—was not regional. He made—perhaps unwittingly—a lasting contribution with his capture of the prairie in poetry.

As Taylor was ending his career in Chicago, Eugene Field was amusing people with his columns in the Chicago *Daily News*. The importance of Field as a journalist cannot be minimized since he became one of the first newspapermen to become a national celebrity in the 1880's. He is perhaps remembered by many today as the poet of childhood. Although there has been some question raised concerning whether he composed "Little Boy Blue" ultimately it matters little whether he simply reworked somebody's idea or created his own, generations of children and adults alike have found a degree of comfort in the eternal values of life as represented in "Little Boy Blue" and "Wynken, Blynken, and Nod." For example, few children and adults can forget the sadness of "the little toy dog . . . covered with dust" nor "the little toy soldier . . . red with rust" which were once new and put into place by "our Little Boy Blue." As the years pass, the little boy does not return; but "the little toy friends are true," and the poem ends:

> . . . faithful to Little Boy Blue they stand,
>   Each in the same old place—
> Awaiting the touch of a little hand,
>   The smile of a little face;
> And they wonder, as waiting the long years through
>   In the dust of that little chair,
> What has become of our Little Boy Blue,
>   Since he kised them and put them there.

During the same period when he was writing sentimental children's poetry, Eugene Field had also turned his attention to classical poetry. It was not, however, the classicism which was favored by supporters of the genteel tradition; rather it was the humor of Horace that captured much of his attention. He spent much time paraphrasing a great deal of the work of the older poet because he wanted to give Horace to his readers "in the garb and vernacular of the present. . . . Horace belongs to us, to this age, to this century, to this decade, to this year—yes, to this very day! And he belongs to every people that appreciates the geniality, the poetry, the charity, and the gracious, saving frailty of human nature." Thus spoke Field in his preface to *Echoes from the Sabine Farm* which was published in 1894.

A perusal of Field's verse reveals a wide range of subjects and attitudes. That many of his poems are humorous should not be surprising. He was fond of paraphrasing not only Horatian odes but also his contemporaries. *Hoosier Lyrics*, which appeared posthumously in 1905 and which contains much work which had been previously published, opens with a parody of James Whitcomb Riley, who by this time was considered to be the poet laureate of the Midwest by many of his enthusiasts.

We've come from Indiany, five hundred miles or more,
Supposin' we wuz goin' to get the nominashin, shore;
For Col. New assured us (in that noospaper o' his)
That we cud hev the airth, if we'd only tend to biz.
But here we've been a-slavin' more like hosses than like men
To diskiver that the people do not hanker arter Ben;
It *is* fur Jeems G. Blaine an' *not* for Harrison they shout—
And the gobble-uns 'el git us
                    Ef we
                    Don't
                    Watch
                    Out!

The poem continues by utilizing stanza patterns of several of
Riley's best-known poems. Entitled "Hoosier Lyrics Paraphrased"
it also spoofs the current political situation as Field saw it.

In "The Red, Red West" there is the expression of Eugene Field
as a western man committed to the growth and the uniqueness of
his region.

I've travelled in heaps of countries, and studied all kinds of art,
Till there isn't a critic or connoisseur who's properly deemed so smart;
And I'm free to say that the grand results of my explorations show
That somehow paint gets redder the farther out West I go.

I've sipped the voluptuous sherbert that the Orientals serve,
And I've felt the glow of red Bordeaux tingling each separate nerve;
I've sampled your classic Massic under an arbor green,
And I've reeked with song a whole night long over a brown poteen.

The stalwart brew of the land o' cakes, the schnapps of the frugal
    Dutch,
The much-praised wine of the distant Rhine, and the beer praised
    overmuch,
The ale of dear old London, and the port of Southern climes,—
All, *ad. infin.*, have I taken in a hundred thousand times.

Yet, as I afore-mentioned, these other charms are naught
Compared with the paramount gorgeousness with which the West is
    fraught;
For Art and Nature are just the same in the land where the porker
    grows,
And the paint keeps getting redder the farther out West one goes.

Our savants have never discovered the reason why this is so,
And ninety per cent of the laymen care less than the savants know;
It answers every purpose that this is manifest:
The paint keeps getting redder the farther you go out West.

Give me no home 'neath the pale pink dome of European skies,
No cot for me by the salmon sea that far to the southward lies;
But away out West I would build my nest on top of a carmine hill,
Where I can paint, without restraint, creation redder still!

One of his poetic contributions can be seen in his ability to turn
a phrase in such a manner that an ordinary idea receives a different—if not new—dimension. That the bulk of his poetry is unknown today, including that designed for "male audiences," is perhaps unfortunate for those who wish to understand the variety of
midwestern literature; yet, so much of his poetry was in direct
response to people and to situations of his day that it frequently
becomes obscure to those who have no knowledge of the events or
people who occasioned his poetic outbrusts. Thus this ephemeral
verse—little of it revised for posterity—frequently appeared in his
columns and later some of it can be seen in the various collected
editions of his works. Whether he longed to be a better poet is a
moot point. In "A Lamentation" he said:

> Oh, if I were a poet
> The world would surely know it—
> Ye gods! how I would go it
>   From morning until night!
> I'd write no rhymes jackassic,

> But carmina as classic
> And as redolent of Massic
> As old Horace used to write!

Perhaps this is so; however, he remained—even in his own day—primarily the conscience of a striving society as he ridiculed those segments of Chicago life which were filled with sham and pretensions. And to later generations he remains the poet of childhood who somehow transcended his time and his place.

If Benjamin Franklin Taylor's work represents the poetry of urban rejection during the nineteenth century and Eugene Field's the poetry of childhood, Harriet Monroe's early work represents the poetry of the genteel movement. She is usually thought of in terms of the twentieth century because of her establishment in 1912 of *Poetry: A Magazine of Verse* and for her connection with that journal as well as some of the innovative patterns in American poetry until her death in 1936. Certainly these represent her greatest contributions. But no consideration of the 1880's can be complete without a consideration of her work and her life as an integral part of the genteel tradition.

By the time of the dedication of the Auditorium in 1889, she had become a force in Chicago's literary circles. Unlike Taylor and Field, she was a Chicagoan. She was born in 1860 in the city which she later described in her autobiography, *A Poet's Life* (New York, 1938) as "the little rapidly growing city . . . even then conscious of its destiny" (p. 1). Her early literary efforts were re-inforced by her two-year study in a Georgetown convent where the writing of poetry was an integral part of the study of Rhetoric. But in 1888 she received her first real support by the acceptance of her poem, "With Shelley's Poems," by Richard Watson Gilder, the powerful editor of the influential *Century*. This became her first published poem. There is little about the sonnet to foreshadow her later work.

> Now do I send you to the heights of song,
> My brother! Let your eyes awake as clear

As morning dew, within whose crystal sphere
Is mirrored half the world; and listen long,
Till in your ears, famished to keenness, throng
The bugles of the soul—till far and near
Silence grows populous, and wind and mere
Are phantom-choked with voices. Then be strong—
Then halt not till you see the beacons flare
Souls mad for truth have lit from peak to peak;
Haste on to breathe the intoxicating air—
Wine to the brave and poison to the weak—
Far in the blue where angels' feet have trod,
Where earth is one with heaven, and man with God.

During the time of her first published poem she was at work on *Valeria*, a tragedy, and on the ode "Niagara's Song." The ode was refused by *The Century*, and speaking in retrospect in *A Poet's Life* Monroe noted:

The ode, as I now read it after so many years of hard-boiled experience with the 'new movement,' seems singularly old-fashioned, of a school which I soon withdrew from—in the tradition of Shelley's 'Cloud' and certain rhythmically rolling poems of Swinburne, and full of *thou* and *thee*, *dost* and *doth*, and other duly accredited 'poetic' words (p. 88).

While she had decided upon a literary career, she had unconsciously decided that the role of the poet or at least poetry should have public appeal. Thus it was that she penned the words for the "Cantata," sung at the momentous occasion of the opening of the Auditorium, a landmark not only in Chicago's history but also in the architectural history of the world. She celebrated her city with the lines:

Hail to thee, fair Chicago! On thy brow
America, thy mother, lays a crown.
Bravest among her daughters brave art thou,
Most strong of all her heirs of high renown.

The poem continues by noting several phases of Chicago's history. The days of the frontier are described. Then the territory's first settlers are introduced when the Indians arrive for a pow-wow on the shores of Lake Michigan. Monroe used the romantic concept of the noble savage; when the white settlers arrived, there was a period of grasping for the land without concern for the earlier settlers, but Monroe, however, does not completely condemn these later settlers because she realizes that the city has gone through a period of great growth. Although she recognized the selfish motives which led to the founding of Chicago, she praised the ultimate result which the great city demonstrated.

> . . . weary nations heard
>   As they dreamed on the breast of time,
> Till the yearning world was stirred
>   With the thrill of a birth sublime.

The city was subjected not only to urban growing pains but also was forced to face financial panics, war, fire, and other disasters. But with each problem there were those in the city who were prepared to fight for the existence of the city. Thus, the spirit of triumph over all foes—physical, material, and spiritual—could also be celebrated.

> New thoughts are thine: new visions rise
>   Before thy clear prophetic eyes.
> On to the future, where the light
>   Streams over fields of glory,
> Thy soul doth take its morning flight
>   From slumberous ages hoary.
> Out of the dark an eagle to the sun
>   Speeds on. Awake! 'Tis day! The night is done.

Perhaps one of the best statements of her views of literature during this period is her sonnet "On Reading a Modern Romance," which—like the historical romances of Catherwood—returned to those periods when men were heroes of action and seemed to be larger than life. The genteel movement's attempt to recapture those days was destined to failure. The price had to be paid for the great material success of the nineteenth century. Spiritual sterility was the outcome; but as she looked back in that sonnet, she could note:

Across a shadow of these morbid years,
Whose growth luxuriant, tangled, loads the air
With perfume and decay; whose soil does bear
Rich rottenness, while rooted beauty rears
Heaven-seeking boughs through a hot mist of tears—
Oh, through this breathless region let the blast
From happier centuries sweep pure and fast
And strong upon our fevers and our fears!
Hark! The clear voice of man's imperial youth
Cries warning to his weary middle age—
Sings of the days when newly found was truth
Nor blasted yet by doubting Time's bleak rage;
When men bowed low to nature, holiest shrine
Of God, and, rising, knew they were divine.

Yet even then Harriet Monroe was realistic enough to recognize—in spite of her participation in the activities of the genteel movement—that late nineteenth-century America in general and Chicago in particular may not be as grand as the romantic urge might suggest. She had seen duplicity in operation, and the decline of her father's fortunes and legal practice had taught her a great deal about the power of money in the city. Culture alone would never be a measure of success in a commercial market-place; and the city of her birth—a city which she loved—was such a market-place. Others of the movement, such as Hobart C. Chatfield-Taylor, tried to close their eyes to the realities of the city. Or when they voiced them, as did Henry Fuller, they tried to dismiss the physical city and its monstrous structures. But unlike her other associates among the so-called "old Chicagoans," she could view the passing of the "old" Chicago as a necessary event—unpleasant though it might be—in the growth of the city. Perhaps this phase of her career came to a conclusion with the writing of "Columbian Ode." It was delivered on the 21st of October, 1892, at the dedicatory service for the buildings which would be opened the following year for the World's Columbian Exposition. *Triumphant, proud, grand* describe the poem from the Chicagoan who convinced a group of businessmen that there was the need for a poem to celebrate the grandeur of the occasion. The poem begins with a salute to the nation:

> Columbia, on thy brow are dewy flowers
> Plucked from wide prairies and from mighty hills,
> To this proud day have led the steadfast hours;
> Now to thy hope the world its beaker fills.

The following lines chronicle other nations, "elder-born of Time," who will be represented at the Exposition, and the section concludes:

> Now unto these the ever-living Past
> Ushers a mighty pageant, bids arise
> Dead centuries, freighted with visions vast,
> Blowing pale mists into the Future's eyes.

She then tells the story of the discovery of America and the significance of the nation's history. In one of the few personal passages she pays tribute to her brother-in-law John Root who died before the Fair opened:

> Back with the old glad smile comes one we know—
> We bade him rear our house of joy today;
> But Beauty opened wide her starry way,
> And he passed on. . . .

And the poem ends with a celebration of Democracy who "dares wake and rise/ From the sweet sloth of youth." And she notes:

> By storms made strong, by many dreams made wise,
> He clasps the hand of Truth.

And Democracy will ultimately conquer the world, and eventually "the long march of time/ . . . Shall lead man up through happy realms of light/Unto his goal sublime." Later in her edition of *Chosen Poems* (1935) she was to note accurately:

> Except for an early blank-verse tragedy of medieval Italy, . . . a Shelley sonnet in the *Century* . . . , and a few easily forgotten other poems, my 'literary career' . . began with the *Columbian Ode*. It will perhaps strain too severely the credulity of present-day readers if I assure them that this psalm of joy, this paean of triumph, this prophecy of world-wide peace and lasting international amity, was an accurate expression of the feeling of the time, of the impassioned exultation which opened to the world the classic gates of the beautiful Columbian Exposition (p. vii).

Chosen Poems: A Selection from My Books of Verse does bring together those works which she considered her best efforts. In her introduction she recalls her life as a poet:

> Putting this book together has been a very emotional exercise. It has reminded me of the epochs I have lived through—the incredible and revolutionary changes in political systems, social creeds and attitudes, scientific theories and inventions, religious assumptions and practices—in every department of human living and thinking as well as in the arts. This book is by no means an adequate mirroring of these volcanic upheavals, but to a certain degree it offers evidence of what has been going on in the world and in human minds during the last more-than-forty years (p. vii).

She then evaluates her work during the period of the genteel movement and dismisses much of it. That she continued to write poetry and became more attuned to the modern world can be seen in her varied selections. That she became a supporter of the new and innovative in poetic technique can be demonstrated not only by her poetic efforts but also by her commitment to her journal, the first such magazine devoted exclusively to poetry. But in the 1880's and opening years of the 1890's she became if not the strongest at least the best-known advocate of the genteel tradition in poetry. And her work has survived in part because she was perceptive enough to realize that change was necessary, that Chicago was to be a distinct community and not a carbon-copy of some by-gone village of a by-gone age. But in her "Cantata" of 1889 and in "Columbian Ode" of 1892 she celebrated the Chicago of the dreamers.

That there were other poets of the period is a matter of record. The newspapers and magazines were filled with the efforts of budding and accomplished poets in the city. Both Elwyn A. Barron and Rev. Frank Gunsaulus published long works in blank verse. During the time there were predictions that Barron's *The Vikings* (1888) and Gunsaulus' *Phidias and Other Poems* (1891) would propel their authors into national prominence. Such was not the case. Neither did the publication of Louis J. Block's mystical *Dramatic Sketches and Poems* in 1891 do much to alter the fact that Taylor, Field, and Monroe were the best that the Chicago of the 1880's had to give to the literary world. Their work was indicative of the various phases of the genteel spirit in the city in those days before the World's Columbian Exposition, but it was not until Sandburg's magnificent celebration to the "hog butcher of the world" that the city entered the poetic consciousness of world literature. But the poetic efforts which preceded Sandburg are still an integral part of the city's literary history.

V

As the decade of the 1880's came to a close, it was apparent to the perceptive Chicagoan that his city's "culture" was at the crossroads. Would the genteel tradition be the true voice of the

West? Or would the realistic method be adopted in literature? The genteel tradition certainly controlled the magazines as well as some major aspects of the printing and publishing industries. While the newspapers—both dailies and weeklies—were recording the news and presenting it to an ever-growing population, there were various attempts throughout the period to create "literary" and serious magazines. Traditional types of literary criticism and interests filled the pages of those journals devoted to proving Chicago was just like the more established communities. Thus, mixed with a self-conscious pride was a self-conscious defensiveness. Of course, after the Fire of 1871 the popular story weeklies—which in some ways formed a bridge between the daily newspapers and the more "literary" journals—achieved wide circulations as they had appeal not only for Chicagoans but also for others throughout the country.

Newspapermen such as Eugene Field were intent upon displaying the city as it actually was. The sham and pretensions of the genteel tradition were constantly ridiculed; yet some of them were not prepared for the starkness of the realistic method as it was being practiced by the followers of Howells. Generally, however, in the 1880's and into the 1890's the city continued to be an exciting place for all types of journalistic endeavors. Although the number of newspapers being established in no way matched the number of magazines, the newspapers became increasingly clear about their urban mission. It was their portrayal of urban characters and conditions as well as their use of an urban language which set forth a new set of urban symbols. This ultimately paved the way for the novelists of the 1890's and the subsequent social protest fiction.

Much of the poetry being created in the city continued to reject Chicago as a central subject, although there was some occasional poetry which dealt with the region. Novelists, on the other hand, were beginning to discover ways to use the city in fiction. There was an increased sense of place which became more and more dominant. The railroad strike of 1877 and the Haymarket Affair of 1886 had raised some serious questions, but the literary artists were not equipped nor ready to answer them. The spokesmen for the oppressed had not as yet raised their voices in protest. The vocal minority in the genteel tradition—with a firm commitment to what it considered the "standards" of the East and with a determination to gain acceptability—could assert that Chicago was indeed as "cultured" as Boston and could cite supporting evidence. But Boston did not have the Union Stockyards. Boston was an old society which in the nineteenth century would take comfort in its seventeenth-century origins. In Chicago there was a rejection of the French culture of the seventeenth century as well as the defeat of the Fort Dearborn Massacre. For Chicago, only the present existed. Harriet Monroe could rhapsodize and sing of the greatness of Chicago, but there were enough indications by the 1880's that the city was not going to be a cultural imitation of the other great cities of the world. Its commercial architecture, for example, had already made that plain. Thus, as the 1880's came to a close, there were two ideologies vying for the control of the city. Which would prevail and set the pattern for Chicago's literary culture?

ILLUSTRATION 18.—Joseph Medill (1823–1899) bought an interest in the Chicago *Tribune* in the early 1850's. In 1874, after serving a disastrous term as mayor of the city, he became the editor of the newspaper. Under Medill the *Tribune* became one of the most powerful newspapers and Republican voices in the Northwest. He literally "ran" the *Tribune* until his death.

ILLUSTRATION 19.—Eugene Field (1850–1895), whose move to the Chicago *Daily News* in 1883 from the Denver *Post* corresponded with the great days of the *Daily News,* was opposed to the genteel tradition as it was being practiced in the Chicago of the 1880's. He did a great deal to satirize those Chicagoans who pretended to have "culture," and he unwittingly supported the development of the realistic movement in Chicago writing.

ILLUSTRATION 20.—"Nearly everybody who reads the English Language in, around, and about Chicago reads the Chicago Daily News" so said the *Post Office Review.* The advertising broadside, "A daily paper for one cent a day . . . ," was issued in 1881 by Shober and Carqueville Lithographing Company.

ILLUSTRATION 21.—Hobart C. Chatfield-Taylor (1865–1945), scion of a wealthy Chicago family, was an active participant in the literary life of the nineteenth-century city. Urbane and well-traveled, he was a staunch supporter of the genteel tradition and an avid believer in the "manifest destiny" of Chicago. He produced some of the early society novels using the city and its suburbs as the locale.

ILLUSTRATION 22.—The Reverend Frank W. Gunsaulus (1856–1921), popular Congregational minister and author of a number of works including *Monk and Knight: An Historical Study in Fiction* (1891), was a member of the literati who spent much time in the Saints' and Sinners' Corner of McClurg's Bookstore.

ILLUSTRATION 23.—Opie Read (1852–1939) founded the *Arkansaw Traveler* in 1882 and subsequently moved it to Chicago from Little Rock, Arkansas, in order to be closer to a central point for rail distribution. Once in Chicago, he produced several novels and became a well-known figure in the city's literary life.

Epilogue:

An End and Another Beginning

BY 1893 THERE were still many frontier characteristics apparent in the thriving midwestern city, but there was no doubt that Chicago had become a major urban center. The city had rebuilt itself. The financiers of the city were men whose influence was becoming more national. The historical accounts of the period reveal that the "men of Chicago" were spoken of in reverential voices. All of the country recognized their power and prestige. The cultural development of the city was beginning to bear fruit. The establishment of the numerous self-improvement clubs before the Fire and of the major social clubs, some of which were modeled after the clubs of Boston, were augmented by those established immediately after the Fire. In these clubs there was an interest shown in literature, art, music, theater, and—of course—Chicago.

On the surface, then, it appears that Chicago had accepted the challenge of rebuilding itself and had met the task with dispatch and with success. It was generally agreed that the city had been given a unique opportunity to rebuild itself. It could eliminate its old mistakes and could create an ideal city in the Mississippi Valley. The accomplishments of the decade were many. The 1870's saw the production of a new material city as well as the formation of some outstanding literary and cultural clubs for the elite. But there was disturbing evidence that all was not well in the garden city. The ideal city had not been realized by the end of the decade, but there had been established—almost as if by mutual consent— an agreement to the principles of the genteel tradition to which many of the writers subscribed led by an elite who stressed the fact that in the re-making of the city there could be created a place

357

which would rival the culture and the beauty of older eastern communities. The decision-makers and the leaders of Chicago shared this belief. It is perfectly true that there was nothing genteel about their operations in their factories and banks, but commercial enterprises (even successful ones in Boston) were not known for their gentility.

As the genteel tradition or upward movement developed, the people involved took it and themselves very seriously. It was a hard-to-define movement, only a part of which was concerned with literature. The major goal was to elevate "taste." Without ever defining the term, they talked about "taste" by appealing to it, by believing in it. Taste became the sword by which they cut through anything which did not please them. It never really became a moral movement in the ethical sense, but they defined good and bad in terms of "taste." Thus, while the men and women of society re-created their elaborate club structures, dedicated themselves to what has been called "a general spirit of uplift," and talked about "taste" as well as the need to have it, the men and women of letters were still devoted to their newspapers and periodicals. Only those writers who were acceptable to the eastern establishment were considered "worthy" by the elites who formed the genteel tradition because they were very much concerned about the "image" of their city. Although there was a general interest in things "literary," the newspapers and magazines were convinced that they must show some monetary gain. Hence, there developed magazines which made a deliberate effort to capture the market. And many of them were highly successful.

In fact, the genteel tradition reached its zenith in the 1880's as it gave support to "the conspicuous consumption of the arts" by people who had acquired a great deal of wealth in the marketplace of the city. Although the business and social elites were frequently satirized, their "conspicuous consumption" of the arts contributed to the metropolitan character, metropolitan attitudes, and to the development of some of the outstanding cultural institutions of the city. For example, by 1882 the Art Institute had a substantial brick building which was followed in 1887 by a four-story, brownstone Romanesque structure, located at the southwest corner of Van Buren Street and Michigan Avenue. Designed to house the school and museum, it has been aptly described by Fleming in his *Magazines of a Market-Metropolis* (1906): "there in the heart of the market city, on a boulevard which was fast becoming the fine-arts avenue of Chicago, was a material temple fixing in the public mind the idea of art" (p. 519).

The interest in the graphic arts was matched by an interest in music. Theodore Thomas, the acknowledged outstanding musician of the country, and his orchestra filled winter engagements in the city. They gave concerts during the summer months in the famous Exposition Building (designed by W.W. Boyington of the Water Tower fame) which stood on the site of the present Art Institute until 1887. And it was this orchestra which formed the basis for the Chicago Symphony, which is known today throughout the world as one of the most outstanding symphonic organizations. As they toured the country each year introducing Americans to some of the finest works of Europe, foreign opera companies made Chicago one of their major stops. Even the theater was alive and well as road companies composed of outstanding American and English actors performed for Chicagoans who hungrily patronized the theater. That there was little or no native drama did not disturb those who felt that "culture" should be imported rather than home-grown.

The supporters of the genteel tradition—often carefully barricaded in their town villas and country homes—successfully closed their eyes to the gigantic commercial structure which was winning world admiration. They knew they were part of a thriving city, but their refusal to see the city as it actually existed was symptomatic of some of their larger problems. For example, in order to rebuild the city as hurriedly as possible and in order to circumvent the labor unrest within the city, widespread immigration from Europe was encouraged. Workers—both native and foreign—had flocked into Chicago. They had helped to rebuild the city while sharing the general discontent of the worker in America. The panic of 1873 did little to alleviate the conditions which existed. And so while the beautiful Chicago arose once again on Lake Michigan, there was widespread unhappiness in the factory areas and among the poor. Sooner or later the city would have to deal with the problem, but the elite said in effect: "Not now." Hence, the tragedy of the Haymarket Affair of 1886 might have been averted if people had understood the significance of the railroad strike of 1877.

The World's Columbian Exposition of 1893 has captured the interest of so many historians. From its opening, the elusiveness of the White City has been overlooked as the eloquence about it sometimes soared to unprecedented heights. Perhaps there might be more unanimity about its beauty than upon its effect. But like other modern Camelots, the Exposition provided material for a number of dream sequences. On the more practical level, however, the story of Chicago's preparation for the World's Fair has generally placed a great deal of emphasis upon the city's role and has highlighted the attitudes of other cities. It appeared, even to the casual observer, that all of the boasting of the city along with its phenomenal growth had been productive. For those supporters of the genteel tradition this was truly to be their "shining hour." The magnificent classical structures which had been raised in Jackson Park, on the shores of Lake Michigan, were to house what has frequently been called a "turning point" in American civilization. Little did they realize that this "triumph" was to be their "swan song" as a viable force in Chicago's culture.

By 1893 the city was all aglow with the potentialities of the Exposition. In spite of the multitude of problems which led to the Fair both in the city and in the nation, it opened on May 1, 1893, accompanied by a burst of civic pride. Created on the shores of Lake Michigan in Jackson Park was the classical dream, directed by Daniel H. Burnham and supported by the leading architectural firms of the nation. Truly a dream city which offered much to spectators had been built in Chicago.

There was fun at the Exposition. Certainly the Midway provided a variety of activities including George Ferris' newly-invented Wheel. But no side show rivalled the appeal and the popularity of the exotic dancer, Little Egypt.

There was certainly beauty at the Exposition. Not only had the planners demonstrated the efficacy of a plan which led to a movement toward urban planning in this country but also with the new electric lights bathing the fair grounds and the white buildings with thousands of bulbs each night, the result—according to viewers—was awe-inspiring.

There was education at the Fair. The World's Congress Auxiliary—an attempt to broaden the appeal of an international fair—emphasized its motto: "Not Things but Men." There were enough seminars and forums for the most dedicated. These were, according to the Auxiliary's statement of purpose, "organized to provide for and facilitate the holding of a series of congresses of thinkers, or to supplement the exposition that will be made of the material progress of the world by a portrayal of the achievement in science, literature, education, government, jurisprudence, morals, charity, art, religion, and other branches of mental activity." The educational activity took many forms. The Board of Lady Managers, chaired by Mrs. Potter Palmer, made certain that women were represented; and Sophia Hayden's Women's Building became the setting for lectures and classes of interest to women. Through the Parliament of Religions, held from September 11-27, there was an increased sense of human unity, and this meeting became the first modern ecumenical conference. Henry Adams, the lonely visitor to Chicago, was right when he said that the Fair provided "lessons" to be learned.

There were heartbreaks at the Exposition. One such heartbreak eventually ended in triumph. The 25th of August had been billed as "Colored Americans Day." The newspapers had expected a clown show and had indicated as much. The venerable Frederick Douglass and others associated with him feared lest the day provoke unnecessary racial incidents. The hecklers arrived, but so did some of the outstanding people of Negro America. Before the conclusion of the day's activities, the vendors who had arrayed themselves in front of the auditorium with watermelons had to leave with their unsold wares. The scoffers were silenced. Among the participants, Frederick Douglass thrilled the crowd with his oration, "The Race Problem in America"; and the young, unknown Paul Laurence Dunbar captivated the audience with his poetry. The following day the Chicago newspapers praised Dunbar, "the colored poet," and gave him the first major press recognition which he received. But one tragedy was not averted. On the final day of the Exposition—Chicago Day—Carter Harrison, the mayor of the city, still thrilled with the triumphs of the day answered his doorbell only to be struck by an assassin's bullet. On that note of sadness the World's Fair of 1893 came to a close.

The Exposition which had meant all things to all people was undoubtedly a fairyland. But it could not last forever. The contrasts between it and the real city were too great and reinforced the ambiguities of American life. The preceding international fairs had taken place in finished cities, but this one had occurred in a city which itself was still in the process of becoming. Yet, as the dream city rose and fell in Chicago, one could conclude from all contemporary reports that truly for one brief shining moment there was a Camelot in Chicago.

The Exposition furnished Chicago's writers with their first collective relationship with writers from this nation as well as from foreign countries. The locus for much of this activity was the Literature Congress which brought together some of the outstanding writers of the world. The Chicago writers acquitted themselves well, and many visitors left the city believing that there was a viable school of literature existing in the metropolis of the Midwest where the forces of the romantic tradition came face-to-face with those who supported realism in literature. Brought into the open, the conflict was discussed in varying ways. Charles Dudley Warner feared the superficial and the inability to understand the importance of artistic standards. George Washington Cable addressed himself specifically to the problems of fiction and rejected the tendency to equate the methods of science with those of fiction. The confrontation between Mary Hartwell Catherwood and Hamlin Garland has been reported. Each brought to the discussion a belief in the direction of American literature. While Catherwood was concerned about "form," Garland was a supporter of local color. Many of the questions raised during this meeting have subsequently become academic. Sir Walter Besant's declarations that a literary work should have a "message," that it should have "a thing to say, a story to tell, a living man or woman to present, a lesson to deliver—clear, strong, and unmistakable" were used by both the romanticists and the realists to support their respective contentions.

Besant was more aware than many of the questions being raised about literature in the conference. His letter, addressed to Charles C. Bonney who was the president of the World's Congress Auxiliary, appeared in the *Dial* (August, 1893):

. . . At the moment of leaving Chicago and the Literary Conference, I beg permission . . . to convey to you . . . our most sincere congratulations on the success of the Congress . . .

Permit me, sir, if I may do so as a simple visitor, without the appearance of impertinence, to congratulate your splendid city on the place which this Exposition has enabled it to take among the great mother cities of the world. Among all your business activities, and in the eager pressing forward of your people, rejoicing in vigorous youth, confident in a splendid future, reckless of what they spend because of the strength and resources within them, I rejoice to find springing up a new literature.

Speaking further of this "new literature," he observed:

Whatever may be the future of this literature, which rises on the frontier line of East and West, it will at least be free from old traditions. I wish for your authors that independence which we in the old

country are struggling to conquer; at least it will be their fault if they
do not achieve it at the outset . . .

And he concluded:

> I leave your city with memories of the greatest kindness and hos-
> pitality. . . I carry away a delightful memory, not so much of a
> Chicago rich, daring, young, confident, as of a Chicago which has
> conceived and carried into execution the most beautiful and poetic
> dream—a place surpassing the imagination of a man, as man is
> commonly found—and a Chicago loving the old literature, discerning
> and proving that which is new, and laying the foundations for that
> which is to come, a Chicago which is destined to become the centre
> of American literature in the future (p. 74).

Like most of the foreign visitors, Besant was impressed with
the types of contrasts which he saw in the city. And by 1893 Chicago certainly was a place of contrasts. It was a self-made society
composed of self-made people who had achieved success by following the laws of the frontier, who were determined to show their
"culture" to the world. There were outstanding art collections in
the city, a magnificent opera house, an orchestra, libraries with
exceptional holdings, and residences which rivalled anything to be
seen in New York, London, Paris, or Venice. There were those
who said it was a wicked place and pointed to the many vice dis-
tricts. Others said it was a city of churches and cited the fact that
some of the most significant church structures had been built and
some of the nation's best known clergymen occupied pulpits in
Chicago. The contrasts were made even more startling by the
White City of Jackson Park with its gleaming, white, classical
structures in the midst of a city whose soot-dirtied commercial
buildings of skeleton frame construction were accepted as a fact of
life. As a footnote to history, Maitland's *Dictionary of American
Slang* (1891) defined a skyscraper as a "tall building such as those
rising in Chicago." Everywhere there were the ambiguities of urban
living, but somehow 1893 provided for many a dream of what they
thought could be.

Hence, it was a surprise to most critics and Chicagoans when Henry Blake Fuller, one of the leading practitioners as well as exponents of the genteel tradition, published *The Cliff-Dwellers* in 1893. In spite of its melodramatic plot (which was overlooked by most readers) the novel ushered in a new way of using the city in fiction. The business world was the underlying force in the drama of urban living, and the portrait of the businessman—while less than flattering—was singularly impressive because it was so credible. In the final analysis, however, critical attention was directed to Fuller's comments and observations about the city. The novel, which Fuller called his "little essay in realism," recognized what Chicago was and what it could never be. With neither bitterness nor undue emotion Fuller noted:

. . . the name of the town, in its formal, ceremonial use, has a power that no other word in the language quite possesses. It is a shibboleth, as regards its pronunciation; it is a trumpet-call, as regards its effect. It has all the electrifying and unifying power of a college yell.

'Chicago is Chicago . . . it is the belief of all of us. It is inevitable; nothing can stop us now' (p. 243).

In retrospect, one can see that the period represented the "coming of age" of Chicago fiction and to some extent the city's poetry. Fuller's landmark novel had been preceded by *The Chevalier of Pensieri-Vani* (1890) and *The Chatelaine of La Trinité* (1892) both of which found favor with unperceptive readers who viewed them as delightful, romantic tales rather than as Fuller's initial use of his comparative statement about the Old World and the New. In her review of *The Cliff-Dwellers* Lucy Monroe, the sister of Harriet, noted in *The Critic* (March 18, 1893) that the first two novels by Fuller "have led us to expect from this graceful writer a certain elegance of diction, a polished and perfumed style, satire so delicate that it masquerades as the most gallant courtesy, and a felicitous humor which falls on the just and unjust alike with an exquisite fanciful caprice" (p. 168).

Given the events and the promises of 1893, the city was not prepared for *The Cliff-Dwellers* nor for the novels which followed in rapid succession and which repeated the themes as well as the techniques of Fuller's novel. Truly the pioneers of the business novel were alive and well in Chicago. The city furnished the only laboratory which they needed. Before the decade ended Opie Read's *The Colossus* (1894), Fuller's *With the Procession* (1895) Will Payne's *Jerry, the Dreamer* (1896) and *The Money Captain* (1898) as well as Robert Herrick's *The Gospel of Freedom* (1898) had been published. These novels were similar; they issued strong statements about the nature of the city and used as a central figure the Chicago businessman who, in less than sixty years, had created a major American city. The portraits were not pleasant; certainly they were not in keeping with that life of leisure which the genteel tradition had advocated nor did they use the philosophy of a dying romanticism. By 1905 and the publication of his *Memoirs of an American Citizen,* Robert Herrick—in a series of novels—had analyzed the city. Ultimately this genre reached its zenith with the publication of Theodore Dreiser's *The Titan* in 1914.

In twenty-one years, from the tentative explorations of Fuller in *The Cliff-Dwellers* to the fully-developed analysis of the intricate relationship between the businessman and the city in *The Titan,* a type of urban novel which has been accepted as typical of American civilization came into being. After the period beginning in 1893 and ending in 1914 American fiction would never be the same. Writers might select any subject, but the Chicago writers had made clear that hovering in the background there would always be this specter of business which made urban life possible. Some turned to rural scenes or to the past to avoid facing these more realistic issues, but these seemed pallid in the face of the vibrant Chicago novels.

Both Upton Sinclair in *The Jungle* (1906) and Frank Harris in *The Bomb* (1909) protested against the importance of a business culture. Their novels became interesting literary curiosities in the annals of Chicago history, but the protest novel as such was a much later development. The novels of social protest developed out of a sense of urban frustration. Initially they were directed against the emphasis upon business. The city from its inception had promised much but delivered little to the immigrants from foreign lands and to those who could not fit into the mold of "Success." In time there were many types of protest, but much of it was directed against the materialism of the city. For example, Robert Herrick concerned himself with the relationship between big business and the university (ostensibly committed to the precept "Know the Truth, and it shall make you free") in his 1929 novel, *Chimes,* a thinly-disguised story of the early days of the University of Chicago. Subsequently, the neighborhood novels of James T. Farrell, Richard Wright, Willard Motley, Nelson Algren, and William Brashler were to contain protests against an establishment which cared little for those people destined for the various twentieth-century ghettoes. But William T. Stead, the English clergymen who visited Chicago to see the Exposition and stayed long enough to write *If Christ Came to Chicago* (1894) understood as did the city's novelists the underlying principle of the prairie metropolis. Said Stead:

It is impossible to describe Chicago as a whole. It is a congeries of different nationalities, a compost of men and women of all manner of languages. It is a city of millionaires and of paupers; a great camp of soldiers of industry, rallying round the standard of the merchant princes in the campaign against poverty. This vast and heterogeneous community, which has been collected together from all quarters of the known world, knows only one common bond. Its members came here to make money. They are staying here to make money. The quest of the almighty dollar is their Holy Grail (p. 123).

It must not be imagined that realism had no advocates in the Midwest before Fuller and his followers. Joseph Kirkland, in the tradition of Edgar W. Howe's *The Story of a Country Town* (1883), produced in *Zury: The Meanest Man in Spring County*

(1887) an excellent study of the region as did Hamlin Garland in *Main-Travelled Roads* (1890). These works faithfully recorded what the authors had seen, but these were not urban works. By the turn of the century Howells was able to praise the nineteenth-century novelists of Chicago. In his "Certain of the Chicago School of Fiction," which appeared in the *North American Review* (May, 1903), he was firmly convinced that Fuller had led the way to a "new" novel.

The peculiar Chicago note . . . is not less perceptible in the writer who came to Chicago full Boston-grown than in those to the manor born. The republic of letters is everywhere sufficiently republican; but in the metropolis of the Middle-West, it is so without thinking; it is so almost without feeling; and the atmospheric democracy, the ambient equality, is something that seems like the prime effect in literature of what America has been doing and saying in life ever since she first formulated herself in the Declaration (p. 739).

Howells was undoubedly unaware of the long writing tradition which had produced the writers who are cited in his article. From the first newspapers and tentative literary journals in Chicago there had been attempts to find a "western voice." Perhaps no other community had tried as long nor as hard to create a literature. Within this context the failures become almost as important as the successes. Consequently, by the turn of the century Chicago's place in fiction was fairly well assured. Although the idea evoked strong antagonisms and equally strong defenses, the fact remained that the city unwittingly was providing the raw material for a clear statement on American civilization. Howells found in the Chicago writers the essence of "democratic kindness" which tended to strip from their writing all pretenses and imitative qualities. "The democracy which was the faith of New England became the life of the West, and now it is the Western voice in our literary art" (p. 738).

The democratic qualities which Howells praised in the Chicago school of fiction were present in Fuller's Chicago novels, but they were also evident in John Calhoun's *Democrat* of 1833. Even during the period of the anti-immigrant journals, the city's literature displayed what has vaguely been referred to as "the spirit of America." Howells noted that Fuller "had to reason to his democracy through the misgiving inspired by the Beautiful in the lands of tradition and convention, and it is the chief wonder of his very extraordinary work that after being a chevalier of vain thoughts, he should have become a fellow-citizen of such solid realities" (p. 738). While Howell's comment about Fuller is quite correct, there were others whose lives in Chicago forced them into "solid realities." And upon them ultimately rests the foundation of the city's literature.

While the business novel was coming of age in Chicago, poetic activity was strangely resisting the inroads of realism. This was in part due to the interests and concerns of Harriet Monroe, but more important it was a result of the generally-accepted notion that there were certain subjects which were not the fit province of poetry. William Vaughn Moody, Robert Herrick's colleague at the University of Chicago, did much toward displaying an interest in psychological realism. But his most revealing attitude toward realism was displayed in a letter which was postmarked July 2, 1903, in which he said, after reading the ghost stories of Howells: ". . . It is very striking to see . . . how Howells seems to be drifting back toward the poetic envisagement of life with which he began years ago." He allowed that Howells approached "his subject nominally under the aegis of Science," but continued:

How impressive it is to see how almost all earnest minds, and exactly by reason of their earnestness, have sooner or later to abandon the realistic formula, or at least to so modify it that it ceases to have any meaning *qua* realism.

The years immediately following the Exposition gave rise to a flurry of literary activity. Hamlin Garland remained in the city and tried to organize the writers under the "realistic banner." Among those with increased interest in the written word were a number of publishing companies, heirs to those who pioneered in the city shortly after the fire. The companies of the 1890's were convinced that the day of Chicago had arrived. Unlike many of their predecessors, these new companies were determined to become more than regional curiosities. Among these firms perhaps no one of them had greater impact than Stone and Kimball which did not survive for a long period but which—as Hamlin Garland noted later—built up "the book-making art in Chicago."

The genteel tradition hung on with reminiscences of its triumph, but 1893 made clear—if not before—that Chicago would never be the dream White City of the Exposition. It was a unique, distinct place. And so it was that the 1890's saw the end of one Chicago and the beginning of a literary history which was to contain the giants of urban literature. The days of Theodore Dreiser, Carl Sandburg, Floyd Dell with the men and women of the Chicago Renaissance, James T. Farrell, Richard Wright, Nelson Algren, and Gwendolyn Brooks were not too far in the future. But such a pantheon of writers could not appear until there was an acceptance of the city as it was and not as someone had dreamed it could be. The old days were soon forgotten, if indeed they were ever remembered, and the early voices from the prairie had been silenced; but in many ways the work of the later writers was the fulfillment of that call for a "western" literature which had been made years before. At the end of the nineteenth century Chicago's literature was providing a pattern for urban fiction. It was a writing which bore the earmarks of its past, but it was essentially writing of the present for the future. The end of one epoch was simply a step toward another beginning.

from *The Artistic Guide to Chicago and the World's Columbian Exposition* (1892)

ILLUSTRATION 24.—By the time of the World's Columbian Exposition the city considered itself to be a cultural center. In one block stood the Auditorium, the Studebaker Building, and the Art Institute.

ILLUSTRATION 25.—Newberry Library on Chicago's North Side was another showplace used during the days of the World's Columbian Exposition to substantiate the claim that Chicago was a "cultural center."

from *Pictorial Chicago and Illustrated
World's Columbian Exposition* (1893)

ILLUSTRATION 26.—One of the showplaces of Chicago at the time
of the World's Columbian Exposition was the Rand-McNally building
at 160–174 Adams Street.

from *Pictorial Chicago and Illustrated World's Columbian Exposition* (1893)

ILLUSTRATION 27.—When the World's Columbian Exposition opened, the University of Chicago—located on the Midway—had been in existence for a year. Later the University's "Alma Mater" was to recognize the fair: The City White hath fled the earth,
But where the azure waters lie,
A nobler city hath its birth,
The City Gray that ne'er shall die.
For decades and for centuries,
Its battlemented tow'rs shall rise,
Beneath the hope filled western skies . . .

APPENDIX A

NINETEENTH-CENTURY JOURNALISM: SELECTED NEWSPAPERS AND MAGAZINES 1833-1893

Contrary to popular belief, from the inception of the city there was a great deal of writing; and it spawned all genres as well as subjects. While it is true that the magazines and newspapers tended to emphasize their "western" qualities, they proceeded— for the most part—to reproduce the kind of work known in the East. With the extensive development of the newspaper in Chicago during the 1850's, 1860's, and 1870's, it appeared that if anything unique developed in Chicago writing, it would be through this medium. In retrospect one might conclude that the Chicago papers did not live up to their potential, but it must be remembered that during the nineteenth century it was the world of journalism that freed writing from many of its out-dated and out-moded notions.

Even a cursory study of the city will suggest that Chicago was an urban area beset by many problems. One of the most significant was the city's attempt to define its image. As a result, there were many conflicting forces in operation. The strange ambiguities of the city could be seen in many areas during the time. Perhaps in architecture these paradoxes can be graphically illustrated. During the decade of the 1870's the men and women of Chicago were actively engaged in rebuilding the city. Within a three-year period most of the major structures had been rebuilt. Needless to say, the pre-fire iron-fronts which had been so popular were found to be defective. The twisted and melted iron of the days immediately after the fire were silent reminders that untreated and unprotected iron was not a deterrent to fire. The buildings which rose in the 1870's were frequently undistinguished imitations of Italian Renaissance and modern Gothic structures, but the erection of them made clear that Chicago was indeed "open for business."

The architects who had adopted the Italian Renaissance and modern Gothic styles immediately after the fire began to respond to the needs of the city and its commercial nature. An office building, they decided, did not need to resemble an Italian villa. It should be honestly rendered in terms of what it was. In a series of buildings which proved to the world that skeleton frame construction was nothing more than what could be seen, Chicago's architects showed that these buildings could be aesthetically pleasing. Unfortunately, Jenney's Home Insurance Building of 1883 has been destroyed, but it led the way to the development of the now-famous Chicago School of Architecture which reached a high point in the 1890's. From the firm of Burnham and Root came in 1886 the famous Rookery, perhaps still one of the most distinguished and vibrant buildings on LaSalle Street. In that same year there was the construction of the only existing Richardson building in the city, the home of John J. Glessner on Prairie Avenue—a house which gave the neighbors some concern because of its unusual appearance. Before the Exposition, the Gold Coast of Chicago was on the South Side; and Prairie Avenue was the center of it where lived Pullman, Marshall Field, Philip Armour, and the Keith Brothers. There was the culmination of the work of Adler and Sullivan in the construction of the Auditorium in 1889, a building which illustrated one of the clearest statements of the union between commerce and art. Yet, outstanding and innovative as were such structures as the Rookery or the residence of Glessner or the Auditorium, it was the starkness of the buildings which utilized skeleton frame construction which captured the imaginations of the world's architects and propelled Chicago into prominence as an architectural center even before the Exposition. But the supporters of the genteel tradition—often carefully barricaded in their town villas and country homes—successfully closed their eyes to the gigantic commercial structures in the downtown area which were winning world admiration.

This refusal to accept an integral part of the city was symptomatic of some larger problems.

Before they were influenced by those who wished to portray the city as it could be rather than as it was, the city's writers were very much concerned with all facets of urban living. And perhaps nowhere was this better displayed than in the world of journalism which early demonstrated an optimism concerning the city's importance. In many ways, these first writers were men and women who preceded the architects in displaying the reality of the city. It was not long, however, before some of them were committed to a vision of the city which bore little resemblance to the real world. But throughout there was maintained an interest in THE WEST and in Chicago as the "center" of the Northwest Territory.

Because of the tendency to restrict one's consideration of journalism to the more "literary" publications, there is frequently a disregard for the importance of other types of newspapers and magazines. It is easy to forget that among the annals of trade and religious journals can be found the names of men and women who eventually became outstanding in literary circles. No one interested in late nineteenth-century American literature can forget that Edward Eggleston edited religious journals in the Chicago area. Neither can one overlook the years spent by Sherwood Anderson in the early twentieth century as he wrote articles for such Chicago-based trade magazines as *Agricultural Advertising.* If for no other reason, a study of the city's journalism will reveal that trade and specialized publications often served as a training arena for men and women who were to assume significant places in the city's and nation's literature.

At the same time, such a study will also suggest the initiation of patterns which were to become popular. For example, from 1857 to 1862 James Grant Wilson edited the *Chicago Record,* an interdisciplinary monthly, which was the first in the region to present through its articles and focus the relationship between literature, fine arts, and religion. While the fame of *St. Nicholas* is accepted as one of the foremost periodicals for young people, its immediate forerunner was a Chicago journal, *The Scholar* (1873-76) which itself had developed in the wake of the popularity of such works as *The Little Corporal.* Failing in the city, it was sold and became an integral part of *St. Nicholas* in 1876 when that well-known eastern magazine was established. For those who have relied heavily upon the biennial editions of *Who's Who in America* it comes as a shock that this indispensable reference tool began in 1890 as a series of biographical supplements which were circulated to subscribers of the major newspapers in Chicago. Eventually A.N. Marquis was convinced that he had something valuable in his sheets which appeared periodically. He expanded his work, and *Who's Who in America* gives no indication that it was once part of Chicago journalism. Among the more unusual works at the time was the establishment in 1891 of the monthly *Park and Cemetery,* which began as *Modern Cemetery* and which was apparently the first journal to address itself exclusively to the need for planning and beautifying cemeteries.

During the nineteenth century there were some important "firsts" in the city's journalism. Many of these are now taken for granted without realizing that the pioneers were part of that budding group of literati on the Middle Border. This is, perhaps, most apparent when one studies the development of the foreign language press. *Gazeta Polska w Chicago* (est. 1873), the oldest Polish newspaper in the nation, and *Svornost* (est. 1875), the oldest Bohemian daily, were founded in Chicago. Both *Svenska Tribunen-Nyheter* (est. 1869) and *Svenska Kuriren* of 1884 became two of the most important Swedish newspapers in the United States. It is perhaps of some interest that Victor Lawson who was to achieve fame for his role in the development of the Chicago *Daily News* should have received valuable newspaper experience when he purchased an interest in the Norwegian *Skandinaven* in 1873, a daily and bi-weekly paper which had been established in 1866. One of the most influential Italian publications in the country, *L'Italia,* was begun in 1886; and three years later the

German-American press was augmented by *Abendpost* (est. 1889), not the first such publication but certainly one which achieved great respect. Throughout the nineteenth century the foreign language press remained powerful and active.

The move toward greater freedom for women became a national phenomenon after the Civil War as many abolitionists turned their attention to such reform issues as women's suffrage and temperance. One of the early journals in the country devoted exclusively to the issues and problems of rights for women was the *Balance,* which was issued shortly after the Fire of 1871 and continued for approximately five years. Women assumed active roles and some of them became well-known and popular editors. Although Mrs. M.L. Rayne and Mrs. M. Cora Bland were in charge of magazines which made their major appeals to female audiences, others—such as Mrs. Myra Bradwell (founder and editor of Chicago *Legal News,* the oldest publication of its type in Chicago), Mrs. Helen E. Starrett, Frances Willard, and Mary B. Willard—made their contributions in male-dominated circles.

It is not surprising that a commercial city should have supported a business-oriented journalism. It is also interesting to note that unlike other cities where political affiliations have always been of paramount importance in newspaper history, Chicago's commitment to the world of business is demonstrated in the first official paper of the city which was one devoted to mercantile enterprises. While there were newspapers which preceded it, the *Democratic Advocate and Commercial Advertiser* (1844-46) set the tone for the city's daily newspapers.

Given the nature of the city, it is not strange that there was a proliferation of trade newspapers and magazines. Few trades were without their publications, and some of them even went on to achieve either national or international distinction. From such diverse works as the *Reporter,* established in 1868 to deal with the growing granite and marble industry, the *American Poultry Journal* (est. 1874), *National Laundry Journal* (est. 1878), *National Harness Review* (est. 1879), *Western Druggist* (est. 1879), and *American Artisan and Hardware Record* which began in 1881 as an outlet for discussions of several related industries such as stove-building, tin-work, hardware, heating, and ventilation, the city's name became associated with its industrial life. These same journals represent not only the oldest of their types in the country but also extremely influential ones in their trades. Generally speaking, many of the trade journals, with their emphasis upon a lay understanding of the mechanical and the technical, might be considered as forerunners of the multitude of "do-it-yourself" magazines which still continue to flood the market. Thus it is not surprising that such a publication as *Popular Mechanics* (1903) would eventually begin in Chicago.

Just as the trade magazines reflected the city's mercantile interests so also did those magazines relating to printing illustrate one attempt—albeit feeble—to relate the industrial with the humanistic. Frequently they combined their dedication to printing techniques with "literary" articles. *Rounds' Printers Cabinet* (est. 1856) was the second journal of its type in the country, but eventually it became one of the most important publications devoted to matters of typography. Almost equally significant was *The Inland Printer* (est. 1883).

The long and successful history of the *Prairie Farmer* (est. 1843) and the host of journals which followed it are testimonies to the agricultural interests of the region; at the same time they reflected significant changes in the metropolis of the Middle Border. Fifty years later *Sports Afield* (est. 1889) moved from Denver to Chicago in order to be more centrally located for purposes of distribution. Once in Chicago, the oldest magazine for sportsmen in the country included some excellent long articles on many aspects of life in the West and Midwest. Whether publications dealt with agriculture or with sports, they shared a common interest in extolling the virtues of the region as they pioneered in their respective areas.

Balancing the temporal nature of commercial, trade, and laudatory journalism were the many religious and medical serials. From

Northwestern Baptist (1842-44), the first religious periodical in the city, and the *Illinois Medical and Surgical Journal* (1844-49), the first medical magazine, journalism in Chicago seemed at times to be dominated by those works devoted to man's spiritual and physical well-being. Examples of the innovations and pioneer efforts of the editors and publishers along with the journalists in the city could continue; suffice it to say, Chicago journalism offered variety and a corpus worthy of further study.

An attempt to survey nineteenth-century journalism in Chicago, a task which is virtually impossible, is made more difficult due to several factors. There was the destructive force of the Fire of 1871 which eliminated so many pertinent records. Often a newspaper or magazine disappeared completely, and the only notice of its existence was to come through some mention of it in contemporary accounts of the period. Many journals, operating on an initial shoe-string, could not recoup their losses and ceased publication. Then there was the fire of 1874 which is seldom mentioned but which was equally destructive. Still another problem exists in the repeated use of certain names. For example, there was a *Commercial Advertiser* which existed during 1836-37 as an abolitionists paper edited by the fervent Hooper Warren, heir apparent to the work of those men and women who early saw the inhumanity of slavery. From 1844 to 1846 Ellis and Fergus issued the *Democratic Advocate and Commercial Advertiser* which used outstanding community leaders as "visiting" editors. *A Commercial Advertiser* appeared again in Chicago life from 1847 to 1858. This was substantially different from the other two. It was edited by Alfred Dutch and was committed to the philosophy that the city as well as the country should be run by businessmen. During 1864 the W. S. Spencer Co. issued for a short time the *Union Banner and Commercial Advertiser*. It was followed the next year by one John R. Robinson's *Commercial Advertiser and Counting Room Manual*. Beginning in 1873 and extending to 1880 the *Chicago Commercial Advertiser* appeared weekly. Although it had a number of editors, Charles S. Burch was the guiding spirit until the newspaper became, in 1880, the *Industrial World and Commercial Advertiser,* a name which lasted for two years. After 1882 it went through a number of name changes and eventually merged with *Iron Trade Review* at the close of the century. Furthermore, more common names such as *Tribune* and *Daily News* also occurred with a degree of frequency during this period.

It is also difficult to assign categories to many of the newspapers and magazines. I have done so merely to give some idea of the range of interests displayed in the world of Chicago journalism; however, one must bear in mind that the general newspaper frequently had a particular political orientation as in the case of the *Tribune* which began as a paper which editorially supported those principles which were to become the platform of the Republican party just as the *Times* supported the principles of the Democratic party. All cases, however, were not this clear-cut. For example, the *Daily Democratic Press* was begun in 1852 by John L. Scripps and William Bross as a politically independent newspaper. It was one of the first so-called general newspapers to place a great deal of emphasis upon its "Commercial" department; and the "Financial Page" became an integral part of its daily offerings, a section which was soon included in other journals. Soon after its establishment, it began to subscribe to the tenets of the Democratic party and became quite vocal in its support until the Kansas-Nebraska Act of 1854. Both Scripps and Bross could not reconcile their own points of view to that proposed by Douglas in his act, and the two editors took their paper into the Republican camp; and in 1858 the *Daily Democratic Press* merged with the Chicago *Tribune.* There were other newspapers which switched party affiliations through their histories although perhaps not as dramatically as did Scripps and Bross.

In addition to political shifts, there were the inevitable changes in editors and ownerships through the course of a single journal, especially those which had particularly long runs. As might be expected, these shifts brought about changes in editorial policies. Furthermore, the frequency of appearance often deviated from its original issue. A journal might begin as a weekly, later become a daily, and—in some rare instances—become a weekly again. In other cases, there were different editions which had separate editorial boards. The Appendix does not record all of these changes. Hence, when a journal is noted as being a "monthly," this refers to the frequency of its appearance in the year of its establishment. The following listing does not indicate the many mergers which took place. The combining of resources was so common that ultimately the history of journalism in Chicago is a history of the various combinations which took place.

Perhaps nowhere is the theory "for every action there is a reaction" more discernible than in Chicago's world of journalism. From 1833 it was apparent that every successful journal would be met by another which hoped to capitalize upon the former's success. John Calhoun's *Democrat* of 1833 was faced with the competitive *American* which began in 1835 with William Stuart as the editor and which presented the opposing political views. The earliest "literary" journals were soon priced out of the market by other "literary" magazines. The first weekly Sunday paper, the *Vacuna* (1856) was forced to compete with the *Sunday Leader* (1857) which appeared with the same purpose and appealed to the same audience. Alfred Sewall's successful *Little Corporal* (1865-75) had to struggle for survival in the wake of the many imitations which followed its establishment. These examples may be firm illustrations of the free enterprise system and the benefits of competition; but the city often could not support all of these journals, and many were forced to cease publication because the limited market could no longer sustain them.

Most of the following newspapers and magazines began and terminated in the nineteenth century; but a surprising number of them extended beyond 1893, and their decline was a twentieth-century phenomenon. As can be noted, often the journals lasted for less than a year. They may not be important as documents, but they indicate something about the nature of productivity in a city which was not known for the extent of its literary activities in those days. That so many journals were attempted tells us something about the nature of that faith which these writers and editors had in the possible success of their ventures as well as their belief that they could succeed in Chicago. There were apparently some men and women in the city who were professional editors, and one can find their names recurring repeatedly with diverse journals.

Ultimately, the complete story of journalism in Chicago has yet to be written. Such pioneer works as *The History of Chicago* (3 vols.) by Alfred Andreas which ends with 1885, Herbert E. Flemings, *Magazines of a Market-Metropolis* . . . (1906), and Franklin W. Scott's, *Newspapers and Periodicals of Illinois: 1814-1879* (1910) give excellent—albeit—partial portraits; yet the intricacies of the world of journalism in early Chicago remains untapped. The various newspaper directories are invaluable although even they do not give a complete survey of the newspapers and magazines which were established during the nineteenth century.

The following lists give some indication of the scope of the world of journalism, but they do not pretend to include all of the journals; neither do they indicate the peculiar histories of so many of them. Ordinarily such lists might be considered of dubious value; however, they do—when taken together—show the interest in as well as the productions of the city's journalistic world. Many notable historians of American journalism, such as Frank Luther Mott, have suggested that little was produced in Chicago. Perhaps the city did not issue newspapers and magazines which were readily accepted by other communities, but those produced in the city—at least the successful ones—had enough subscribers to sustain the publication. Maybe a person in Boston or Charleston would not read *The Prairie Farmer* nor *The Watchman of the Prairies,* but thousands of people in Chicago and in the surrounding region did. In the final analysis the history of a city's writing must be based upon what was produced in that location. Its existence cannot be denied merely because it does not follow the patterns of other locales nor have appeal for those outside of the city.

KEY TO APPENDIX A

The journals which appear in Appendix A have been divided into nineteen categories: Agriculture, Art, Commercial World, Education, Family, Foreign Languages, Juvenile and Youth, Literary, Medical, Music and Drama, Negroes, Newspapers—General, Newspapers—Neighborhood, Recreation (Games and Sports) and Travel, Reform, Religious, Scientific, Secret Societies, and Women. The fact that a newspaper or magazine appears under one heading does not preclude it having columns which conceivably could fit in another category. These designations were made on the basis of what appeared to be the dominant appeal of the journal. Those works which might be termed "Miscellaneous" (and admittedly there are many of them) have been eliminated.

For most of the categories the following information is given:
Est. . . . the year in which the periodical was founded
Name . . . the first title used for the newspaper or magazine
Termination, if before 1893 . . . the date represents as closely as possible either the date the journal ceased publication or—in some few cases—the date when the periodical moved to another city. If the symbol + appears, it means that the work continued after 1893. A question mark after the date indicates that the journal probably was discontinued during that year.
Freq. . . . refers to how often the journal appeared. Since the frequency of appearance changed for many of these works, the denotation—unless otherwise stated—refers to its frequency at the time of its establishment. The following abbreviations are used in this column:

d.	daily	bm.	bi-monthly
w.	weekly	m.	monthly
sm.	semi-monthly	q.	quarterly
tw.	tri-weekly	bw.	bi-weekly
f.	fortnightly	o.	occasional publication for a specific event but which had a large circulation

Ed. or Pub. Since many of these journals underwent numerous editorial changes as well as shifts in ownership, it was impossible to record all of the names. The name given in the charts is either the first editor or the one who did the most toward developing the periodical. In some instances where the publishing firm was more significant in establishing the editorial policy, the name of the company is substituted for that of an editor. A question mark indicates that it was impossible to determine the person or firm who had chief editorial responsibility for the publication. ———— indicates that the name of the publisher is the same as that of the journal.

1. Agriculture

John Wright's role as the first editor of the long-lived *Prairie-Farmer* belies his ultimate importance as a Chicago "booster." Throughout his career he emphasized the possible significance of the city as one destined to be "GREAT." Called a "visionary," even by his contemporaries, he used an agricultural magazine to voice his hopes for the city. The scarcity of strictly agricultural journals also belies the importance of agriculture to the city. As it became the center for bidding and trading agricultural futures, the city became the focal point for the farmers of the Middle Border.

Est.	Name	Termina-tion, if before 1893	Freq.	Ed. or pub.
1841	*The Union Agriculturist and Western Prairie Farmer*	1843	w.	John S. Wright
1843	*The Prairie Farmer*	+	w.	John S. Wright
1848	*Western Farmer*	1869	w.	W. B. Davis
1855	*Western Farm Journal* [moved to Chicago in 1875]	1877	w.	Dr. G. Sprague
1856	*Western Enterprise*	1857	w.	E. Porter Little
1858	*Emery's Journal of Agriculture*	1859	w.	Henry D. Emery
	Northwestern Prairie Farmer	1860?	w.	James C. Medill and Charles Betts
1861	*American Bee Journal*	+	m.	Mrs. E. S. Tupper and George W. York
1862	*Farmer's Voice and Rural Outlook*	+	m.	H. A. Bereman
1863	*Western Rural*	1883	w.	H. N. F. Lewis
1866	*Northwestern Farmer*	1869	m.	Northwestern Farmer Co.
1867	*Journal of the Farm*	+	m.	Baugh and Sons
1868	*Bonham's Rural Messenger*	1872?	m.	Jeremiah Bonham
	Western Agriculturist and Livestock Journal	+	m.	T. Butterworth
1870	*National Live Stock Journal*	1888	m.	John P. Reynolds
1873	*American Miller*	+	m.	Arthur J. and Harley B. Mitchell, S. S. Chisholm
	Scientific Farmer	1875?	m.	Dr. T. A. Bland
	Bee Keepers' Magazine	1874	m.	H. A. King
1875	*National Farmer*	1879	m.	M. E. Cole
	Milling	+	m.	J. F. Mueller
1876	*American Poultry Journal*	+	m.	C. J. Ward
1877	*Farm and Garden*	1881	bm.	?
	Farmers' Review	+	w.	A. Moore and
			m.	Hannibal H. Chandler Co.
	Better Farming	+	m.	———
1878	*Farm, Field, and Fireside*	+	m.	R. L. V. Powis

Est.	Name	Termination, if before 1893	Freq.	Ed. or pub.
1879	Agriculture and Family Gazette	1879	m.?	Ray Lespinasse
	Illustrated Champion	1879	m.	Warder, Mitchell and Co.
1881	Breeders' Gazette	+	w.	Alvin H. Sanders
1882	American Elevator and Grain Trade	+	m.	Arthur J. and Harley B. Mitchell
	Farm Implement News	+	w.	E. J. Baker
	Western Plowman	+	sm.	C. J. Ward et al.
1883	American Sheep Breeder	+	m.	W. W. Burch
1884	Dairy World	+	m.	Thompson Pub. Co.
1885	American Florist	+	w.	J. C. Vaughan
	American Swineherd	+	m.	James Baynes and Sons
	Markets	+	w.	W. O. Hoffman
1886	Orange Judd Farmer [western ed. of American Agriculturist]	+	w.	Orange Judd Co.
1887	Farmer's Voice	+	w.	———
1891	Chicago Dairy Produce	+	w.	George Caven and S. B. Shilling
	Wool Markets and Sheep	+	w.	———
	Irrigation Age	+	m.	J. E. Forrest
1892	Gardening	+	sm.	Michael Barker
1893	Corn Belt	+	m.	C. B. and Q. Railroad Co.
	Hay Journal	+	w.	———

2. Art

The Art magazine was a product of the 1860's, and these first ones were short-lived. Earlier magazines did—on occasions—address themselves to the subject, but for the most part they were satisfied with the inclusion of illustrations which were substitutes for "art." For a serious discussion of the subject many Chicagoans relied upon eastern magazines. By the end of the century, however, there had been developed a considerable interest in Art.

The Central Art Association, publishers of *Arts for America,* was committed to the distribution of study courses to the various clubs and was convinced that "art is no longer devoted to the painting of pictures." There was a great interest in the history of art, and many general magazines as well as newspapers contained articles on the subject. The genteel tradition and its supporters tended to emphasize the importance of knowing about the various European artistic traditions. And it is not surprising that the founders of the Art Institute specialized in European rather than American art.

Est.	Name	Termination, if before 1893	Freq.	Ed. or pub.
1867	Art Journal: An American Review of the Fine Arts	1871	m.	Martin O'Brien
1868	American Builder and Journal of Art	1872	m.	Stanley Waterloo and Charles D. Lahey
1870	Arts	1874	m.	Joseph H. Hiursch and Co.
	Art Review	1872	m.	E. H. Trafton
1877	Eye	1888?	m.	Hutchins and Cotmer
1878	Artist	+	m.	G. F. Thomas
	Indicator	+	w.	O. L. Fox
1880	Picture and Art Trade	+	m.	J. Sawtelle Ford
1885	Home Art	+	m.	————
1892	American Illustrated	+	m.	Peninsula Pub. Co.
	Arts for America	+	m.	H. A. Pierce and Central Art Ass'n.
	Brush and Pencil	1892	m.	Art Institute

3. Commercial World

It was in the world of business that newspapers and magazines displayed their greatest growth. Magazines devoted to banking, railroading, insurance, legal matters, and real estate interests were widespread as were specific trade journals, exclusive of general agriculture. Some of these journals have been discussed in earlier chapters; however, the following list gives an indication of a group of popular titles in the nineteenth century. The single common pattern used by these publications was perhaps expressed by the first one which was established in 1844. The *Democratic Advocate and Commercial Advertiser* issued by William Ellis and Robert Fergus, the printers, emphasized the importance of business to the city. By the time it had folded, Alfred Dutch began his weekly Chicago *Commercial Advertiser* which made clear that whatever was good for business was good for Chicago. All of the journals, however, were not that overtly chauvinistic about their city; but all of them appeared to accept tacitly the theory of the importance of Chicago as a commercial center, and they existed as long as there was a specific need for them or as long as the editor and/or proprietors could support them. They were almost always devoted to limited business interests of Chicago and the surrounding regions.

For several years after the Fire of 1871 these magazines and newspapers continued. By the late 1870's, however, they were becoming so specialized that they ceased to have much interest for the general reader. Out of this shift of focus, the trade paper— one directed to a special audience whose interest rested in a given profession or trade—became increasingly popular. Thus by the 1880's many of the papers had become organs of particular firms and industries, and the city was no longer of primary interest to the editors although there remained a sense of that nebulous "Chicago spirit" in these publications.

Although the following list by no means represents a complete list of all such publications edited or produced in the city, the list does give some idea of the scope of this type of journalism as well as its diversity. With few exceptions, the publications listed are those which had unusually large circulations and had some appeal although they seldom replaced the general newspaper.

Est.	Name	Termination, if before 1893	Freq.	Ed. or pub.
1844	*Chicago Democratic Advocate and Commercial Advertiser*	1846	w.	William Ellis and Robert Fergus
1847	*Commercial Advertiser*	1858	w.	Alfred Dutch
1850	*Commercial Register*	1850	w.	J. F. Ballantyne
1852	*Chicago Daily Express and Commercial Register*	1852	d.	W. J. Patterson
1853	*The Christian Banker*	1853	m.	Seth Paine
	The Christian Shoemaker	1853	m.	F. V. Pitney
1855	*The Chicago Bank-Note List*	1864	sm.	Granger Adams
1856	*Commercial Letter*	1868	d.	P. L. Wells and Thomas Wignall
	Rounds' Printers Cabinet	1881	m.	S. P. Rounds
1857	*Daily Union*	1858	d.	Louis Schade
	Northwestern Bank Note and Counterfeit Reporter	1860	sm.	Isaac A. Pool
	Real Estate Newsletter and Insurance Monitor	1858	m.	Gallaher and Gilbert
	Real Estate Register of the Northwest	1858	m.	G. W. Yerby
	Wells' Commercial Express and Western Produce Reporter	1871	w.	Joel Henry Wells
	Western Railroad Gazette	+	m.	A. N. Kellogg
1859	*Phillips' Northwestern Money Reporter and Insurance Journal*	1871	w., m., sm.	B. W. Phillips
	Report of Suits, Judgments, Chattel Mortgages	?	d.	Edward Bean
1860	*Market Review and Price Current*	+	w.	P. L. and J. H. Wells
1861	*Daily Record and Hotel Register*	1870	d.	John J. W. O'Donoghue
	Insurance and Railway Register	+	m.	J. A. Nichols
	Legal Adviser	+	w., m.	E. M. Haines
	Lumberman's Advertiser and Weekly Price Current	+	w.	Nathaniel A. Haven
	Merchants' Monthly Circular and Illustrated News	1866	w., m.	———

Est.	Name	Termination, if before 1893	Freq.	Ed. or pub.
1862	American Spirit and Wine Review	+	sm.	J. T. Pratt
	Iron and Steel	+	w.	Hemby-Hutchinson Pub. Co.
	McElroy's Bank Note and Reporter	1863	m., sm.	Thomas McElroy
1863	Journal of Commerce	+	m.	J. E. C. Heyer
	Railroad Gazette	1882	w.	Stanley G. Fowler
1864	American Law Manual	1867	q.	E. M. Haines
	Builder and Woodworker	+	m.	F. J. Hodgson
	Templar's Offering	1871	m.	Rolla A. Law
	Union Banner and Commercial Advertiser	?	m.	W. S. Spencer and Co.
	United States Review [insurance]	1876	sm.	R. R. Deardon
1865	Commercial Advertiser and Counting Room Manual	?	m.	John R. Robinson
1866	Banking and Insurance Chronicle	1868	w.	?
	Chronicle [insurance and real estate]	1872	w.	J. W. O'Donaghue
	Daily Commercial Report and Market Review	1878	d.	D. D. Michaels
	Price Current and Manufacturers' Record	+	w.	John C. W. Bailey
	Real Estate and Building Journal	+	w.	R. C. Smyers
1867	Western Merchants Courier	1875	m.	H. B. Bryant
	Inside Track	1869?	m.	A. N. Kellogg
	Northwestern Review [insurance]	1874	w. m.	R. R. Deardon
	Specimen	1881	q.	Marder, Luce, and Co.
	Union	1868	m.	Chicago Typographical Union
	Union Stock Yards Exchange	+	d.	H. L. Goodall

Est.	Name	Termination, if before 1893	Freq.	Ed. or pub.
1868	Chicago Merchants' and Manufacturers' Record	?	d.	J. C. W. Bailey
	Chicago Railway Review	+	w.	Willard A. Smith and Stanley G. Fowler
	Daily Law Record	1871	d.	R. R. Stevens
	Market Reporter	1869	d.	B. Frank Howard
	Real Estate and Building Journal	+	w.	S. A. Chappell
	Reporter [marble and granite trade journal]	+	m.	Francis N. Nichols
	Western Postal Record	1881	m.	J. S. Elwell
1869	Bureau	+	m.	C. W. Jenks
	Daily Commercial Bulletin	+	d., w.	B. Frank Howard
	Land Owner	+	m.	J. M. Wing
	Legal News	+	w.	Myra Bradwell
	Spectator	1880	m.?	J. H. and C. M. Goodsell
1870	American Cabinet Maker, Upholsterer, and Carpet Reporter	1881	m.?	J. Henry Symonds
	Argus	+	sm.	Rollins Pub. Co.
	Bench and Bar	1874	m.	James A. L. Whittier
	Commercial Reporter	1871	w.	T. G. Wilcox
	Dry Goods Price List	1880	w.	August Schooley
	Herald [insurance]	1877	m.	Powell and Steele
	National Live Stock Journal	+	m.	John P. Reynolds
	Observer	?	m.	J. Clement
	Publishers' Auxiliary	1873	w.	A. N. Kellogg
	Smax Money Maker's Journal	1870	w.	R. W. Chappell
1871·	Advertiser's Assistant	1872	m.	Cook, Coburn, and Co.
	Chicago National	1874	m.	John H. Holmes, W. C. Cockson, and the National Life Insurance Co.
	Commercial Enterprise	1875	w.	———
	Dry Goods Reporter	+	w.	C. W. Spofford
	Financier	1873	w.	W. H. Boardman
	National Car Builder	1881	m.	James Gillett

Est.	*Name*	Termina- tion, if before *1893*	*Freq.*	*Ed. or pub.*
	National Hotel Keeper	+	d.	F. W. Rice
	Newspaper Union	1878	w.	Samuel H. Williams
	Rand-McNally Railway			American Railway
	Guide and Hand Book	+	m.	Guide Co.
	Tailors' Intelligencer	1874	m.	Salisbury Brothers and Co.
1872	Grocery and Drug			
	Price List	+	w.	A. C. Schooley
	National Hotel Reporter	+	d.	Frank Glossop
	Railroad Monthly	1873?	m.	Story and Camp
	Watchmakers' Magazine	1873	m.	E. R. P. Shurley and the Horological Association
1873	Advocate	1887	m.	Martin Ryan and the Protection Life Insurance Co.
	Agents' Guide	1880	m.	James P. Scott
	Chicago Commercial			
	Advertiser	+	w.	Charles S. Burch
	Electrotype Journal	1881	q.	A. Zeese and Co. and H. H. Newhall
	Electrotyper	1881	q.	Schniedewend and Lee Co.
	Grocer's Criterion	+	w.	R. J. Bennett and Eugene Hall
	Industrial Age	1879	w.	J. A. Noonan *et al.*
	Investigator [insurance]	+	w.	J. S. Bloomingston
	Journal of the American			
	Bureau of Mines	1875?	m.	W. C. McCarty
	Master Mechanic	1874?	m.	Evans, Comstock, and Co.
	Northwestern Lumberman	+	w.	William B. Jackson and Judson, Dicey Co.,
	Wilson's Reflector	1880?	m.	Mrs. M. H. Fuller and the Wilson's Sewing Machine Co.
	Workers' Lamp	1887	m.	C. G. Smith
1874	American Furniture Gazette	+	m.	Marshall D. Talcott
	Babcock Fire Record	1874	m.	George Mathews
	Commercial Price Current	+	w.	R. H. Wheeler

Est.	Name	Termination, if before 1893	Freq.	Ed. or pub.
	Engineering News	+	m.	George H. Frost
	Furniture Trade	1880	m.	Charles E. Brackett
	Grocer	1879	w.	George P. Engelhard
	Insurance Critic	1879	sm.	George W. Reed
	Liquor Trade Review	1884?	m.	Thomas Marshall
	Sewing Machine World	+	m.	A. M. Leslie and Co.
	Watchmaker and Metal Worker	1881	m.	John H. Mather
	Western Manufacturer	1882	m.	Fox Co.
	Western Photographic News	1876	m.	C. W. Stevens
1875	Grain and Provision Review	1888	w.	Cole and Co.
	Great South-West	1876	m.	George Rice
	Hotel World	+	w.	Frank Glossop and H. J. Bohn
	American Trade Journal	1881	q.	———
	Confectioner and Baker	+	m.	J. Thompson Gill
	Insurance Press	?	w.?	George Cohen
	Mercantile Price Current	1886	d., w.	Chicago Mercantile Pub. Co.
	Paper Trade	+	f.	J. Fred Waggoner
	Printing Press	1876	q.	Henry R. Boss
	Western Trade Journal	+	w.	Henry Clay Brace
1876	American Horse-Shoer and Hardware Journal	1881	m.	———
	Fancy Grocer	1879?	w.	Ferdinand Fish
	Railway Age	+	w.	Elisha H. Talbot
	Railroad Conductor's Brotherhood Magazine	1880	m.	J. Ward Boyles
	Shoe and Leather Review	+	w.	Clinton Collier Co.
	Western Brewer and Journal of the Barley, Hop, and Malt Trades	+	m.	J. M. Wing and H. S. Rich
1877	Amateur Mechanic	+	m.	Samuel Harris
	Board of Trade	1877	m.	M. T. Lane and Co.
	Epicure Confectioner, Baker, and American Caterer	+	m.	Thompson Pub. Co.
	Fair Play [liquor interests]	+	w.	Frank Brooks
	Hardware and Implement Trade	1877	w.	Tucker and Smith
	Hardware and Iron List	1879?	m.	A. C. Schooley

Est.	Name	Termination, if before 1893	Freq.	Ed. or pub.
	Insurance Herald	1885	w.	George I. Yeager
	Law Journal	+	w.	Judge John Gibbons
	Leaf	1881	w.	J. Irving Crabbe
	Monthly Casket	1880	m.	Edward U. Jones
	National Board of Trade	1879	w.	E. A. Saxby
	Railway Master Mechanic	+	m.	Railway Purchasing Agent Co.
	Western Shoe and Leather Review	1881	w.	C. E. Rollins
1878	*American Furniture Gazette*	1881	m.	————
	Champion of Fair Play	+	w.	Robert J. Halle
	Chicago Mining Review	+	m.	————
	Exposition Daily Press	1878	d.	Creswell, Wanner, and Co.
	Grocer	+	w.	O. L. Deming
	National Laundry Journal	+	sm.	Charles Dowst
	North-Western Commercial Traveler	1881	m.	Hatch and C. D. Chase
	Railroader and Railway Enterprise	1879	m.	Day K. Smith
	Railway Master Mechanic	+	m.	O. H. Reyolds
	Railway Purchasing Agent	1886	w.	Willard D. Smith
	Railway Times	+	w.	Walter D. Crosman?
	Real Estate Journal and Weekly Bulletin	1878	w.	Bulletin Pub. Co.
1879	*American Contractor*	+	w., m., q.	B. Edwards and Co.
	American Stockman	+	d., sw., w.	E. W.. Perry
	Bookseller and Stationer	1881	m.	J. Fred Waggoner
	Chicago Illustrated News	1879	sm.	Interstate Industrial Exposition
	Commercial Graphic	1880	w.	W. F. Fawcett
	Druggist and Paint and Oil Review	+	m.	G. H. Engelhard
	Jewelers' Journal	+	m.	S. R. Stephenson
	Lakeside Watch	+	m.	W. C. Vosburgh
	Merchants' Bulletin	+	w.?	Jerome Chapman
	National Harness Review	+	m.	Jefferson Jackson

Est.	Name	Termina-tion, if before 1893	Freq.	Ed. or pub.
	Railway Advertising Bulletin	+	d.	C. H. Shaver
	Sewing Machine Advance	+	m.	A. M. Leslie and Walter Scates
	Western Clothing, Furnishing, and Hat Reporter	1881	m.	Charles H. Moore
	Western Confectioner and Baker	+	m.	J. Thompson Gill
	Western Druggist	+	m.	G. P. Engelhard
	Western Stationer	+	m.	J. Fred Waggoner
	Western Undertaker	+	m.	Herbert S. Fassett and F. H. Hill Co.
1880	*American Artisan Hardware Record*	+	w.	American Artisan Press
	American Builders' Association News	+	w.	American Builders Co.
	Commercial Union	+	w.	Publishers' Commercial Union
	Railway Mail	+	w.	A. E. Winrott
	Stationer and Printer	+	sm.	J. Sawtelle Ford
	Western Broker	+	m.	————
	Western Firemen and Journal of Public Works	+	w.	T. E. Smith
1881	*American Artisan and Hardware Record*	+	m.	Daniel Stern
1882	*American Jeweler*	+	m.	George K. Hazlitt Co.
1883	*Inland Architect and News Record*	+	m.	Inland Pub. Co.
	Inland Printer	+	m.	J. W. Langston and F. H. Hill
	Paint, Oil, and Drug Review	+	w.	D. Van Ness Person
1884	*Mida's Criterion*	+	sm.	William Mida
	Rand McNally's Bankers Monthly	+	m.	Rand McNally Co.
1885	*Butcher and Grocery Clerks' Journal*	+	m.	————
	The Detective	+	m.	International Association of Chiefs of Police
	National Builder	+	m.	F. T. Hodgson and C. A. Miller

Est.	Name	Termination, if before 1893	Freq.	Ed. or pub.
1886	Commercial Collector	+	q.	Credit Co. Pub. Co.
	Roadmaster and Foreman	+	m.	————
	Timberman	+	w.	J. E. Defebaugh
	Western Bottler	+	m.	H. Gathmann
1887	Bakers' Helper	+	m.	H. R. Clissold
	Registered Pharmacist	+	m.	————
	Western Electrician	+	w.	————
1888	Economist	+	w.	————
	Financial Review	+	m.	Credit Co. Pub. Co.
	General Manager [railroading]	+	m.	Lanward Pub. Co.
	Mixed Stocks	+	m.	————
	Monumental News [marble and granite]	+	m.	R. J. Haight
	Office Men's Record for Accountants	+	q.	Record Pub. Co.
	Stone [marble and granite]	+	m.	D. H. Ranck Pub. Co.
1889	Furniture Herald	+	m.	————
	Independent	+	m.	————
	Monumental News	+	m.	R. G. Haight and John Weston
	Photo-Beacon	+	m.	————
1890	American Pressman	+	m.	Robert Sawyer
	Black and White [insurance]	+	m.	Kellogg and Son
	Hide and Leather	+	m.	R. C. Jacobson
	National Corporation Reporter	+	w.	U.S. Corporation Bureau
	Street Railway Review	+	m.	Windsor and Kenfield
1891	Chicago Stockman	+	w.	Will F. Baum
	Embalmer's Monthly	+	m.	Trade Periodical Co.
	International Confectioner	+	m.	T. F. Harvey
	Park and Cemetery	+	m.	R. J. Haight
1892	Clay Record	+	sm.	————
	Commercial Stamp Trade Journal	+	m.	————
	Electrical Engineering	+	m.	————
	Insurance Post	+	sm.	Charles A. Hewitt
	Shears	+	m.	George E. Jenks
	Starchman	+	m.	————
	Western Painter	+	m.	Charles H. Webb

Est.	Name	before 1893 Termination, if	Freq.	Ed. or pub.
1893	*Harman's Journal of Window Dressing*	+	m.	Harry Harman
	Hotel Monthly	+	m.	John Welly
	Illustrated Glass and Pottery World	+	m.	———

4. Education

The first two "educational" journals made clear that they were also "literary" magazines. Just before the *Northwestern Educator and Magazine of Literature and Science* ceased publication, James L. Enos—editor—complained about the reception which the magazine had received, but he was also aware of the journal's accomplishments. Said he in the February (1849) issue:

[The magazine] was commenced under the most unfavorable circumstances, in a country where no like publication had ever circulated, where the people were comparatively little imbued with a love for education—or at least, that inculcated by professional teachers—and with the privations incident to a new country pressing heavily upon them; yet notwithstanding these difficulties, the influence of the Educator has steadily increased, and within the last three months the circulation has nearly doubled.

Needless to say, the "literary" aspects of the *Northwestern Educator . . .* and *The Eclectic Journal . . .* were submerged beneath materials which dealt with the many theories of professional education.

Prior to 1893 there existed a series of magazines devoted almost exclusively to pedagogical matters. Few of them, however, extended beyond 1893 and most of them folded before. With the establishment of the Normal School in 1869 there was a great deal of interest in teaching methods and in the training of teachers, but it was not until John Dewey's work at the University of Chicago that the Chicago writers on educational matters became part of the national scene. After 1893, and extending into the twentieth century, educational journals tended to be more interested in the welfare of teachers and the political questions of the profession. Discussions of methodology were relegated to highly specialized journals which had little or no interest for the general public. In this connection the following theses might be of interest:

Beck, John M. "Chicago Newspapers and the Public Schools, 1890-1920." Ph.D. Dissertation, University of Chicago, 1958.
Duffie, Burton. "Educational Policies of Two Leading Newspapers," Master's Thesis, University of Chicago, 1939.
Farley, Mancy Lee. "Educational Publicity in the Newspapers of Chicago. A Study of Six Dailies." Master's Thesis, University of Chicago, 1927.
Johns, Elizabeth. "Chicago Newspapers and the News." Ph.D. Dissertation, University of Chicago, 1942.

Est.	Name	Termination, if before 1893	Freq.	Ed. or pub.
1847	The Northwestern Educator and Magazine of Literature and Science	1849	m.	James L. Enos
1850	The Eclectic Journal of Education and Literary Review	1851	m.	O. F. Bartlett
1859	Northwestern Home and School	1863?	m.?	J. T. Eberhart
1868	American Journal of Education	1879	m.	Rev. E. N. Andrews and Grace Hurwood
1869	Teachers' Golden Hour	1871	m.	Tomlinson Brothers
1870	Schoolmaster	1871	m.	John Hull and Albert Stetson of Illinois Normal University and William E. Phelps

Est.	Name	Termina-tion, if before 1893	Freq.	Ed. or pub.
1872	Chicago Teacher	+	m.	Jeremiah Mahony
1873	Western Journal of Education	1876	m.	John W. Brown
1875	School World	1876	m.	William H. Gardner
1876	Drew's College Journal	1881?	m.	Drew's Business College
	Educational Weekly	1890?	w.	William E. Phelps
	Gaskell's Magazine	1887	m.	A. J. Scarborough and G. A. Gaskell Co.
1877	Practical Teacher	1888	sm.	Klein and Kimball
	Social Science Journal	1881	m.	Miss S. A. Richards for the Illinois Social Science Association
1879	Western College Magazine	+	m.	American Educational Co.
	Western Educational Journal	1881	m.	J. Fred Waggoner
1887	Free Kindergarten	+	q.	Free Kindergarten Ass'n.
1888	Kindergarten Magazine	+	m.	Kindergarten Literature Co.
1893	School Review [except July and August]	+	m.	University of Chicago

5. Family

One of the highly-touted characteristics of a certain type of periodical literature was its appeal "to all members of the family." This inevitably was used by newspapers which wanted consistent subscribers and which recognized the importance of women as consumers. The so-called "family" magazine in the nineteenth century was closely related to the journal of general miscellany and was designed with all members of the family in mind. They frequently contained some short fiction "suitable for women and children," poetry, fashions for men and women as well as for the home, and puzzles and games. The non-fiction included commentary (generally simply written) on public affairs and issues.

In Chicago this type of magazine did not appear until after the Civil War and never became as popular in the city as in the East. It is not to be confused with the "family story" magazine which was extremely popular and which has been included with the "literary" magazines.

Est.	Name	Termina-tion, if before 1893	Freq.	Ed. or pub.
1868	*Home Eclectic*	1871	m.	Sumner Ellis
1870	*Family Circle*	1871	sm.	C .H. Cushing
1873	*American Home Magazine*	1873	m.	Charles T. Taylor and Co.
1874	*American Homes Magazine*	1874	m.	F. W. McClure
1877	*American Home*	1881	bm.	Mrs. Theodore C. Campbell
1878	*Call*	1884	w.	T. J. Morrow
	Family Journal	1885	m.	Miss C. T. Stalph
1886	*Household Realm*	+	m.	Webster Pub. Co.
1891	*Household Guest*	+	m.	———
1892	*Banner of Gold*	+	m.	———

6. Foreign Languages

The nineteenth-century foreign languages press in Chicago cannot be underestimated. While there have been some notable studies on the contributions of the various ethnic groups to the cultural life of the city, much still needs to be done on the literary contributions made not only to Chicago but also to the rest of the nation by those immigrants who continued to write in their native languages. It is perhaps too easy to assume that foreign immigrants entered the city in the nineteenth century and remained hidden in their various ethnic enclaves. It is of interest to note, for example, the advertisement used by the German *Freie Presse* in E. P. Remington's *Newspaper Directory* of 1898:

Do you know there are over 400,000 Germans in Chicago who are a thrifty, well-to-do class of people, and have money to spend for worthy articles? If you want to catch their trade advertise in the columns of their favorite papers, *Freie Presse* published daily and weekly and *Daheim,* the great German Sunday paper . . . (p. 385).

The following journals represent those which were apparently most popular. There were others, however, which were so specialized that they never became a part of the dominant culture of the city. Those which are listed, while written in foreign languages, were decidedly urban papers. They spent a great deal of time telling their respective publics how to survive in the city, giving local and national news, and especially giving guidance on how to react to the local political structure. In addition, there were columns which included news from "back home" as well as some fiction and poetry. In short, the foreign language press had appeal for those who either had not learned English or who wished to maintain their ethnic ties. Notably absent from this group are the numerous instances of newspapers and magazines which were far more isolationist in intent. This was especially true of many of the Yiddish papers which—though well read in the Jewish communities of the city—dealt infrequently with the urban scene of Chicago.

The number and lengths of existence of these journals seemed highly dependent upon the extent of the political influence of the group. Thus, it is not surprising that the largest numbers of periodicals should have come from the Germans and the Scandinavians who exerted considerable pressure in the city. The German press, however, gained a great deal of notoriety during the 1880's as the fomentor of dissent in the city. Needless to say, this attitude was reinforced by the editorial activities of August Spies, Michael Schwab, and Albert Parsons as well as the suspicious attitude which prevailed against "foreigners" before and after the Haymarket Affair of 1886.

It is of further interest to note that the German newspapers were essentially politically motivated with extremely strong ties to the Democratic party, although there were one or two powerful Republican papers. The German journals generally took part in all sides of the pertinent issues of the day. On the other hand, the Scandinavian press was strongly religious. Many of these newspapers were founded elsewhere in Illinois as religious organs and were moved to Chicago after they had been in existence for a few years. It is also of interest to realize that in spite of their religious origins, the Scandinavian newspapers frequently supported strongly the principles and doctrines of the Republican party.

Perhaps one of the typical Scandinavian newspapers was *Det Gamla Och Det Nye Hemlandet,* a Swedish Lutheran journal. It began in 1854 as *Hemlandet* in Galesburg, Illinois, where there was a powerful Swedish settlement. At the time it was the only Swedish newspaper in the country. Edited by the Reverend T. N. Hasselquist, the newspaper also sponsored a companion monthly, *Det Rätta Hemlandet* (1856-73), which was concerned with devotional and ecclesiastical matters. The two journals moved to Chicago in 1858 where Reverend Hasselquist was joined by a series of editors, most of whom were clergymen. The magazine, which had the same editorial staff, merged with the newspaper in 1873; but by the early 1870's the religious nature of the newspaper was being minimized, and it clearly became a Republican journal which just happened also to be Lutheran.

The periodicals listed here are representative of the popular journals of the day, and many of them continued into the twentieth century; however, their scopes frequently became more circumscribed as succeeding generations became less attached to the home land and more integrated into urban society.

Est.	Name	Termination, if before 1893	Freq.	Ed. or pub.

BOHEMIAN

Est.	Name	Termination, if before 1893	Freq.	Ed. or pub.
1868	*Narodni Noving*	1870	w.	Joseph Sladek
	Nova Doba	1871	w.	Joseph Pastor
1869	*Pokrok*	?	m.	?
1873	*Chicagsky Vestnik*	+	w., m.	Josef Langmayer
1875	*Amerikan*	+	w., bw.	August Geringer
	Svornost	+	d., w.	August Geringer
1876	*Raresek*	1886?	w.	Reischel Gutes
1877	*Duch Casa*	+	w.	August Geringer
1879	*Sokol Americky*	+	m.	G. Reisl for the United Bohemian Gymnastic Association
1890	*Krestansky Posel*	+	w.	Hrejsa and Vanek Bohemian Methodist Church
	Pritelditek	+	w.	Bohemian Benedictine Press
1891	*Denni Hlasatel*	+	d.	Bohemian Typographical Union
1892	*Tydenni Hlasatel* [Sunday edition of *Denni Hlastatel*]	+	w.	Bohemian Typographical Union
1893	*Katolik*	+	bw.	Bohemian Benedictine Press

DUTCH

Est.	Name	Termination, if before 1893	Freq.	Ed. or pub.
1882	*Nederlander*	+	w.	J. G. Y. Esnorff

FRENCH

Est.	Name	Termination, if before 1893	Freq.	Ed. or pub.
1855	*De Journal de L'Illinois*	1858	w.	A. Grandpre and Claude Petit
1861	*L'Observateur de Chicago*	+	w.	S. E. Pinta
1870	*L'Amerique*	1871	sw.	S. E. Pinta
1892	*Courrier de Chicago*	+	w.	M. Hadida

Est.	*Name*	Termina- tion, if before *1893*	*Freq.*	*Ed. or pub.*
		GERMAN		
1845	*The Chicago Volksfreund*	1848	w.	Robert B. Hoeffgen
1848	*Illinois Staats-Zeitung*	+	w.	Robert B. Hoeffgen
1854	*Deutsche Amerikaner*	1854	m.	George Schlaeger
1855	*Boebachter van Michigan*	1856	w.	J. E. Committi and Frederick Becker
	Union	+	d., w.	Frederick Becker and George Schlaeger
	Der National Demokrat	1862	d.	Dr. Ignatius Koch
1856	*Demokrat*	1880	d.	W. Kuhl
	Abend Zeitung	1858	d.	J. E. Committe and Frederick Becker
1857	*Zeitgeist*	1858	w.?	Ernest Georders and Charles Hess
1860	*Home Land*	1860?	w.	W. Kuhl?
	Katholisches Wochenblatt	+	w.	Franz Xavier Brandecker
1862	*Telegraph*	+	d., w.	Dr. Ernest Schmidt
1863	*Blätter*	+	w.	Henry Hoiser
	Hausfreund	1871	w.	Joseph Hartman and United Evangelical Church
1864	*Deutsch-Amerikanische Monatshefte*	+	m.	Caspar Butz, Carl Schurz
	German-American	1872	m., w.	Caspar Butz
	Herald of Truth	1867	m.	Mennonites
1866	*Belletristiche Zeitung* [Sunday ed. of the *Chicago Union*]	1876	w.	Hermann Lieb
	Reform	1867	d.	B. F. Bross
	Westlische Unterbaltungs Blätter	1880	w.	Herman Lieb and Frederick Becker
1867	*Anzeiger*	1867	m.?	George F. Cross
	Juxbruder	1871	w.	Dr. A. C. Lebell and H. von Sangen

Est.	Name	Termination, if before 1893	Freq.	Ed. or pub.
1868	*American Messenger*	1871	m.	American Tract Society
1869	*Lutherische Kirchenfreund*	1881	sm., m.	Rev. J. D. Severinghaus
1870	*Deutsche Arbeiter*	1870	w.	German Central Union of Workingmen
	Freie Presse	+	w., d.	Richard Michaelis
	Illinois Volks-Zeitung	1872?	d., w.	German Printing Co.
	Landwirth und Hausfreund	1871	w.	Carl Kron
	Westliche Odd Fellow	1871	m.	J. B. Wing and Co.
1871	*Americanischer Farmer*	1874	w.	Julius Silversmith
	Daheim [Sunday ed. of *Freie Presse*]	+	w.	Richard Michaelis
1872	*Kneip Zange*	1873	w.	Miller and Wagner
1873	*Eulenspiegel*	1883?	w.	Moritz Langeloth
1874	*Arbeiterfreund*	+	w.	Rudolph Ruhbaum
	Volks-Zeitung	1876	w.	Social Democratic Printing Ass'n.
	Vorbote	+	tw.	Conrad Conzett, August Spies, Michael Schwab, *et al.*
	Westen	+	w.	Herman Raster
1875	*Chicagoer Neue Freie Presse*	+	d., w.	German-American Pub. Co.
	Chicagoer Handels-Zeitung	1880	w.	Hermann Lieb
	Chicagoer Wespen	+	w.	Dr. A. C. Lebell
	Guardian	1881	m.	H. F. Holcomb
1876	*Arbeiter Zeitung*	+	tw., w., d.	Social Labor Party and Conrad Conzett with August Spies and Michael Schwab
	Chicagoer Socialist	1879	d.	Socialist Printing Ass'n.
	Erholungs-Stunden	+	w.	George Brumder
	National Demokrat	1877	d.	George Braham
1877	*Beobachter*	+	w.	A. Paessler and Paul Geleff

Est.	Name	Termination, if before 1893	Freq.	Ed. or pub.
	Bunder-Posaune	1879	m.	Publishing Committee of the German National Y.M.C.A. and Rev. J. D. Severinghaus
	Chicagoer Volks-Zeitung	+	d.	Chicago Press Society
	Deutsche Americanische Mueller	1881	m.	E. A. Sittig
	Deutsche Warte	+	w.	Dr. H. Duemling
	Katholischer Jungend-Freund	1881	bw., w.	Rev. A. J. Thiele and August Brenz
	Neue Zeit	+	w.	Chicago Press Society
1878	Champion of Fair Play	+	w.	R. J. Halle
	Conditor, Koch, und Baecker Zeitung	1879	bw.	F. Lisiewski and Co.
	Jewish Advance	1881	w.	Rev. Henry Gersoni
	Plattdeutsche Nachrichten	+	w.	———
	Plattdeutsche Zeitung	1881	w.	Edward Cook
	Volksfreund	1880	d. w.	Edward Rummell
	Westliche Schutze und Jagd Zeitung	+	m.	John J. Pinzel
1879	Bundes Banner	1881	m.	Rev. J. D. Severinghaus
	Fackel [Sunday ed. of Arbeiter-Zeitung]	+	w.	Social Democratic Party
1880	Rundschau	+	w.	———
1882	Brewer and Malster	+	m.	Eugene A. Sittig and Co.
	Calumet Anzeiger	+	w.	———
1886	Auswander	+	m.	Emigrant Pub. Co.
	Deutsche Industrie	+	m.	Eugene A. Sittig and Co.
1887	American Brewers' Review	+	m.	———
1888	Gegenwart	+	m.	Theodore G. Steinke
1889	Abenpost	+	d.	Frederick Glogauer
1890	Concordia	+	bw.	———
	Schuh und Leder	+	sm.	Press Pub. Co.
1891	Abendblatt	+	w.	Staats-Zeitung Co.
	Katholisches Sonntagsblatt	+	w.	William Kuhlmann
1892	Republikaner	+	d.	———
	Vereins-Zeitung	+	w.	Forst and Schaedlich

Est.	Name	Termina-tion, if before 1893	Freq.	Ed. or pub.
		ITALIAN		
1867	*L'Unione Italiano*	1869	w.	Italo-American Printing Co.
1868	*Il Messaggiere Italiano dell' Ouest*	1885?	w.	Italo-American Printing Co.
1886	*Italia*	+	w.	O. Durante
		LITHUANIAN		
1892	*Lietuva*	+	w.	Stanislaus Rokosh
		POLISH		
1873	*Gazeta Polska w Chicago*	+	w.	Wladyslaw Dyniewicz
1874	*Gazeta Polska w Katoliscka*	+	w.	John Barzynski and the Polish Literary Society
1882	*Dzienswiety*	+	w.	W. Smulski
	Zgoda	+	w.	Polish National Alliance
1890	*Dziennik Chicagoski*	+	d.	Polish Pub. Co.
	Dziennik Polski	+	d.	Gazeta Chicagoska Pub. Co.
	Nowe Zycie	+	w.	J. R. Niemczewski
1893	*Kuryer Swiateczny*	+	w.	N. K. Zlotnicki
		SCANDINAVIAN		
1852	*Frihed's Banneret*	1853	w.	Mouritzon and Kjoss
1854	*Det Gamla Och Det Nye Hemlandet*	+	w.	Rev. T. N. Hasselquist and other Swedish Lutherans
1855	*The Svenska Republikanaren*	+	m.	S. Cronsioe
1858	*Det Rätta Hemlandet*	1873	m.	Rev. T. N. Hasselquist *et al.*
1864	*Sändebudet*	+	f.	Victor Wittig and Swedish Methodists

Est.	Name	Termination, if before 1893	Freq.	Ed. or pub.
1865	*Skandinaven*	+	d., bw.	Norwegian-Danish social action group— John Anderson and Victor Lawson
	Svenska Amerikanaren	1873	m.	Hans Mattson
1868	*Fremad*	1871	w.	S. Beder
1869	*Christelige Talsmand*	+	w.	Norwegian-Danish Methodists, C. Hansen
1869	*Svenska Tribunen-Nyheter*	+	w.	Frank Anderson
1870	*Agerdyrkning and Oeconomie*	1871	?	Barthene and Rene
	Dagslyset	1874	m.	Marc Thrane of the Freethinkers' Society
	Missionaren	1873	m.	Swedish, E. Norelius and Rev. J. P. Nyquist
	Missionären	1877	m.	Norwegian-Danish Methodists, Rev. J. H. Johnson *et al.*
	Nya Velden	1876	w.	P. A. Sundelius
	Justitia	1871	m.	Isidor Kjellberg
	Ungdoms Vännen	1881	sm.	*Hemlandet*
1873	*Augustana Och Missionären*	+	w.	Rev. Hasselquist
	Nya Svenska Amerikanaren	1876	m.	Magnus Elmblad and Gottfried Cronwell
	Vart Nya Hem	1878?	m.	A. Chaiser and Co.
	Zions Vakt	1873	w.	Swedish Baptist Church, Dr. J. A. Edgren
1874	*Fra Moderlandene*	1876	w.	Albert Fougner
	Handels und Industrie	1876	w.	Hejmdal Pub. Co.
	Hejmdal	1877	w.	Reichel and Salmonsen
	Hyrdestemmen	+	w.	Norwegian-Danish Methodists, Rev. Christian Treider
	Missions-Vännen	+	m., w.	Mission Synod, A. W. Hedenschoug
	När Och Fjeuan	+	m.	*Hemlandet*
	Norden	1881	w.	Hallwarde Hande
	Den Nye Tid	1881	w.	Scandinavian sect of the Socialist Labor Party

Est.	Name	Termination, if before 1893	Freq.	Ed. or pub.
1875	*Budbarren*	1878	w.	Lars C. Svendson
1876	*Folkets Rost*	1879?	w.	Joe Ellerson
	Svenska Tribunen	+	w.	Hans Mattson and Carl Gustaf Linderborg
1877	*Bladet*	+	f., w.	John Martenson, Swedish Lutherans
	Evangelisk Tidskrift	1885	m., sm.	Dr. J. A. Edgren, Swedish Baptists
	Kristelige Talsmand	+	w.	Norwegian-Daniel Methodist Episcopal Church, Rev. Christian Treider
	Nad Och Sannung	1880	m.	Charles Lindell and Rev. Carl A. Ewald
	Norsk-Amerikanske Independent	+	w.	O. M. Peterson
	Svenska Amerikanaren	+	w.	Herman Roos and Nels Anderson
	Svenska Posten	1877	sm.	Peter Roos
1878	*Barn-Vannen*	1889?	m.	Rev. A. Hull and Charles Lindell
	Faederneslandet	1880?	w.	Olson and Co.
	Tilskueren	1880	m.	Louis Pio
	Verdens Gang	+	w.	Nels Sampson and Co.
1879	*Famalje Altaret*	1880?	m.	Rev. A. Hull
	Folke-Vennen	+	w.	Norwegian Lutherans, W. Mortenson and Crook, Rev. J. Z. Torgerson
1881	*Posten*	+	w.	C. Rasmussen Pub. Co.
1884	*Fosterlandet*	+	w.	Swedish Pub. Co.
	Svenska Kuriren	+	w.	Alex J. Johnson
	Svenska Tribunen	+	w.	Swedish Pub. Co.
1885	*Nya Wecko Posten*	+	w.	Swedish Baptists, Rev. E. Wingren
1890	*Evangelisten*	+	tm.	R. A. Jernberg
	Humoristen	+	w.	Gus Broberg

Est.	Name	Termina-tion, if before 1893	Freq.	Ed. or pub.
	SPANISH			
1889	*Illustracion Norte-Americana*	+	m.	Hickox and Read Pub. Co.
	YIDDISH			
1885	*Chicago Weekly*	+	w.	Jewish Courier Co.
1888	*Jewish Courier*	+	d.	———

7. Juvenile and Youth

In the wake of the success of Alfred Sewall's *Little Corporal* (1865-1875), a monthly magazine for children, there appeared a number of imitations. With few exceptions they were highly didactic monthlies. After the Fire of 1871, many ceased publication, others merged and continued for a few more months. By the late 1870's the popularity of the juvenile magazine had waned, and those which remained tended to be supported by various church groups as supplementary Sunday School material. They frequently combined the work of a few professional writers with a great deal of amateur talent. Unless otherwise noted, all of the following appeared monthly.

Est.	Name	Termina-tion, if before 1893	Ed. or pub.
1843	*The Youth's Gazette* [weekly]	1883	Kiler K. Jones
1853	*The Youth's Western Banner*	1853	Isaac C. Smith and Co.
1862	*Index Universitates*	1871?	John S. Mabie, Thomas W. Goodspeed, *et al.*

Est.	Name	Termination, if before 1893	Ed. or pub.
1865	The Little Corporal	1875	Alfred Sewall
	Young Catholic's Friend	1880?	J. J. Kearney
1866	Brown School Holiday Budget	1866	S. P. Rounds, Jr. and Tad Lincoln
1869	College Times	1871	University of Chicago students
	Little Folks	1877	Adams, Blackmer, and Lyon Pub. Co.
1870	Leedle Vanderer	1876	C. F. Harris
	Little Corporal's School Festival [quarterly]	1873?	Alfred L. Sewall
	Little Watchman [semi-monthly]	1872	L. H. Dowling
	Young Folks' Monthly	1883	H. N. F. Lewis, Mrs. Annie R. White, et al.
	Young Folks' Rural	1883	H. N. F. Lewis, J. D. Tallmadge, et al.
	Young Pilot	1871	Franklin H. Tinker
1871	Amateur Monthly	1872	Charles C. Hoyt and Will E. Gard
	Child's Paper	1871	?
	Child's World	1871	?
	Little Men	1872	Charles C. Diehl and Frank F. Morrill
	Our Boys	1873	Charles C. Hoyt
	Young Hero	1872	Will E. Gard
	Young Messenger	1872	Walter T. Dwight
	Youth's Cabinet	1872	John L. Whelan
1872	Child's Friend	1873?	C. G. G. Paine
	Literary Youth	1872	Edward Everett Woodbury
	Our Flag	+	Elwell and Gowell
	Our Youth	+	Charles C. Hoyt and Will E. Gard
	Volante	1881	University of Chicago students
	Young America	1872	Dicker and McLacklan
	Young Chicago	1873?	Dicker and McLacklan
	Young Industry	?	H. E. Greenbaum
	Youth's Reporter	1872?	E. E. Russell

		Termina-tion, if before 1893	Ed. or pub.
Est.	*Name*		
1873	*Little Bouquet*	1877?	S. S. Jones
	Our Boys' and Girls' Own	1875	J. A. Densmore
	Student	1874?	M. Wendell
1874	*Children's Voice*	?	W. Billings
	Every Child's Paper	1878	Miss E. C. Pruden
	Every Youth's Paper	1878	Miss E. C. Pruden
1877	*Young Folks Weekly*	?	H. N. F. Lewis
1878	*Newsboys' Appeal*	1880	J. J. Tobias
	Our Little Folks' Magazine	+	P. W. Raidabaugh
	Our Picture Gallery	+	Chicago Engraving Co.
	Our Youth's Friend	+	Pub. Ass'n. of Friends
	Picture Gallery for Young Folks	1881	Mrs. D. N. Bash
1879	*Youth's Evangelist and Little Preacher*	?	Rev. A. T. McDill
1891	*Historia*	1893	Fred B. Cozzens
1892	*Child-Garden*	+	Kindergarten Literary Co.

8. Literary

To single out one group of journals as being "literary" is undoubtedly misleading because so many of the newspapers and magazines published during this time had "literary" pretensions. For example, some of the religious journals such as *Advance* were composed of original offerings and featured some of the outstanding clergymen of the nation such as Henry Ward Beecher who were considered "good writers." Other journals prided themselves on the inclusion of "literary" pieces in each issue along with literary criticism. However, this category is used for those journals which not only emphasized the possibilities of the West as a literary center with Chicago as the capital but also those whose primary aim in each issue was to feature the poet, the essayist, the writer of fiction, or criticism. Included here are some of the oc-

casional magazines which were developed in response to the
World's Columbian Exposition. Ordinarily such publications might
justifiably be omitted; however, among these clearly temporary
journals were some of literary intent and design. Although many
of them were "illustrated" to meet popular demands for "fair
pictures," they also included some of the best contemporary
accounts of daily activities at the Fair and had a wide circulation.

These literary journals designed either for entertainment or for
cultural edification were usually free from any organizational
and/or political ties although some of the major publishers of the
city did sponsor critical journals. Ultimately the history of Chicago's literature might well be told—in part—through the following magazines and newspapers.

Est.	Name	Termina-tion, if before 1893	Freq.	Ed. or pub.
1844	*Gem of the Prairie*	1852	w.	K. K. Jones and James Beach
1845	*Garland of the West* (single issue)	1845	m.	Robert N. Garrett and Nelson W. Fuller
	Western Magazine	1846	m.	William Rounseville
1848	*Ladies' Western Magazine*	1849	m.	Benjamin F. Taylor
1852	*Chicago Literary Budget*	1855	m.	W. W. Danenhower
1853	*Sloan's Garden Magazine*	1854	w.	Walter B. Sloan
1855	*Western Garland*	1855	m.	Mrs. Harriet C. Lindsey
1856	*Pen and Pencil*	1856	w.	T. R. Dawley
	Prairie Leaf	1856	m.	D. B. Cooke and Co.
	The Flower Queen	1857	m.	Higgins Brothers
1857	*Chicago Magazine: The West As It Is*	1857	m.	Zebina Eastman
	Chicago Record	1862	m.	James Grant Wilson
1862	*National Banner*	1862	m.	Mrs. Delphine P. Baker
1865	*Literary Messenger*	1871	m.	Mrs. M. L. Rayne
	The Monthly	1871?	m.	University of St. Mary's of the Lake
1866	*Concordia*	1869	q.	H. R. Palmer and W. S. B. Mathews

Est.	Name	Termina-tion, if before 1893	Freq.	Ed. or pub.
	Frank Leslie's Chimney Corner	1871		Frank Leslie
1867	Gem of the West and Soldier's Friend	1876	m., w.	Mr. and Mrs. C. Augustus Haviland
1868	Chicago Western Home	1875	m.	Robert Collyer *et al.*
	The Chicagoan	1869	w.	H. N. F. Lewis
	Illustrated Chicago News	?	w.	Farnum and Church
	Western Book Seller	1888	m.	Western News Co.
1869	Bright Side	1872	w., sm., m.	John B. Alden
	Evening Lamp	+	w.	A. N. Kellogg
	Western Monthly	1870	m.	H. V. Reed and Francis Fisher Browne
	Western Sunday Review	1870	w.	George R. Norton
1870	Chicago Magazine of Fashion, Music, and Home Reading	1876	m.	Mrs. M. L. Rayne
	Home Journal	1871	m.	J. H. Bascom
	Our Folks at Home	?	m.	Fred D. Carson
	World Magazine	1893	m.	World Society
1871	Happy Hour	1874	m.	M. A. Fuller
	Lakeside Monthly	1874	m.	Francis Fisher Browne
1872	Bright Side and Family Circle	1873	m.	John B. Alden and C. G. G. Paine
	Carl Pretzel's Magazine Pook	1874	w.	Charles H. Harris
	Chicago Ledger	+	w.	Samuel Williams and W. D. Boyce Co.
	Chicago Librarian	1873	m.	Chicago Public Library
	Our Fireside Friend	1875	w.	Waters, Evert, and Co.
	Outlook	1873	m.	Selden Gilbert
1873	Alliance	1882	w.	Reverends David Swing, Robert Collyer, *et al.*
	Cottage Monthly	+	m.	Readle, Brewster, and Co.

Est.	Name	Termination, if before 1893	Freq.	Ed. or pub.
	Excelsior Magazine	1875	m.	M. Garland Walker
	Exposition Pictorial Advertiser	Fall, 1873	o.	Pictorial Printing Co.
	Freeman	1874	m.	W. S. Burke
	Literary Varieties	1874?	m.	Edward N. Fuller
	Turner's Minaret	1875	sm.	E. M. Turner and Co.
1874	*Carl Pretzel's National Weekly*	1893	w.	Charles II. Harris
	Northwestern Magazine	+	m.	W. S. Burke
	Novelist	1881	m.	George E. Blakely
	The Owl	1876	m.	William Frederick Poole
	Saturday Evening Herald	+	w.	Lyman B. Glover
	Western Home	1875	m.?	A. Chisholm
1875	*Index*	1891	w.	C. E. Tues
	In Door and Out	1879	m.	George E. Blakely
	Printing Press	1876	q.	Henry R. Ross
1876	*Editor's Eye*	1883?	w.?	Clarence P. Dresser
	Old Oaken Bucket	1876	m.	E. M. Turner
	Sunset Chimes	1887	m.	————
	Wild Edgerton's Weekly Evergreen	1877	w.	Brock L. McVicker
1877	*Publishers' Monthly*	1878	m.	Luther Conant
	Western Magazine	1884	m.	Mrs. Helen Elkin Starrett
1878	*Over Land and Sea*	1879	m.	————
	Western Enterprise	+	m.	John J. Sullivan
1879	*Bookseller and Stationer*	1881	m.	J. Fred Waggoner
	Hours of Recreation	1881	m.	T. S. Denison
	Library Record	1884	sm.	Union Catholic Library Ass'n.
	Literary Review	+	m.	C. E. Walker
1880	*The Dial*	+	m.	Francis Fisher Browne
1882	*The Arkansaw Traveler*	+	w.	Opie Read
1883	*The Current*	1888	w.	Edgar L. Wakeman and John McGovern
1884	*American Journal of Semitic Languages and Literature*	+	q.	University of Chicago
	Literary Life	1887	m.	Rose Elizabeth Cleveland

Est.	Name	Termina-tion, if before 1893	Freq.	Ed. or pub.
	National Printer-Journalist	+	m.	———
	The Rambler	1887	w.	Reginald deKoven, Harry B. Smith, and Elliot Flower
1885	Vanity Fair	1886	w.	———
1887	Appleton's In the Swim	1891	w.	Charles Appleton?
	Saturday Blade	+	w.	W. D. Boyce
1888	America	1891	w.	Slason Thompson and Hobart C. Chatfield-Taylor
	Belford's Magazine	1893	m.	Belford-Clarke Pub. Co.
	Commonwealth	1892	m.	———
	Graphic	+	w.	G. P. Englehard and J. A. Spencer-Dickerson
	Our Day	+	m.	Frederick L. Chapman
	Society	1888	m.	———
	Twentieth-Century Monthly	+	m.	F. W. Clements and Co.
	Wildwood's Magazine	1888	m.	"Wild Wildwood" (Fred E. Pond)
1890	Figaro	1893	w.	New York ed. of Life
1891	Halligan's Illustrated World's Fair	1893	m.	Jewell Halligan and John McGovern
	World's Columbian Exposition Illustrated	+	m.	James B. Campbell
1892	American Illustrated	+	m.	?
1893	Echo	+	sm.	———
	New Occasions	+	m.	B. F. Underwood and Frederick Upham Adams
	Queen Isabella Journal	1893	q.	Queen Isabella Ass'n.
	World Fair's Puck	1893	w.	New York ed. of Puck

9. Medical

With the establishment of Rush Medical College in 1837, Mercy Hospital in 1853, and the Hahnemann College of Homeopathy in 1855, it is not surprising that Chicago early became a medical center not only in terms of experimentation but also in the number of publications which issued from the various medical groups. While an argument raged about the relative merits of homeopathy which resulted in a "war of words" as represented by many of the magazines, those who supported the cause were highly successful in convincing many that theirs was a just cause. Of these early journals perhaps none was as significant as *The Northwestern Journal of Homeopathia* (1848-52), edited by the well-known Dr. George E. Shipman. The journal was clearly defensive, and its "object was to set forth the principles of homeopathy and to defend and confirm the views of such physicians as had undertaken its practice." Homeopathy had the further support of being advocated by some of the most respectable physicians of the city who frequently made their journals deliberately "popular" in order to sway a large portion of the reading public.

Most of the following journals were accessible to the general public although many of the titles might suggest that they were too technical for the average layman.

Est.	Name	Termination, if before 1893	Freq.	Ed. or pub.
1844	*Illinois Medical and Surgical Journal*	1849	m.	Rush Medical College Faculty and Dr. James Van Zant Blaney
1848	*The Northwestern Journal of Homeopathia*	1852	m.	Dr. George E. Shipman
	Northwestern Medical and Surgical Journal	1857	m.	W. B. Herrick and John Evans
1854	*The Chicago Homeopath*	1856	bm.	Dr. D. S. Smith
1858	*Chicago Medical Journal*	1875	m.?	Daniel Brainard

Est.	Name	Termina-tion, if before 1893	Freq.	Ed. or pub.
1860	*Chicago Medical Examiner*	1875	m.	Dr. N. S. Davis
	Medical Investigator	1875	bm.	Dr. T. C. Duncan
1861	*American Journal of Materia Medica*	1862	m.	Dr. George E. Shipman
1863	*Peoples' Dental Journal*	1871	q.	Dr. W. W. Allport *et al.*
1864	*Peoples' Journal of Health*	1871	m.	Dr. Juston Hayes
1865	*United States Medical and Surgical Journal*	1874	m.	Dr. George E. Shipman *et al.*
1868	*Medical Times*	+	m.	Dr. R. A. Gunn, Dr. Finley Ellinwood, *et al.*
	Pharmacist	1885	q., m.	E. H. Sargent and Albert E. Ebert
1869	*Druggists' Price Current*	1872	m.	Dr. H. D. Garrison
1873	*Hahnemannian Advocate*	+	m.	Hahnemann Pub. Co.
1874	*Chicago Journal of Nervous and Mental Diseases*	1875	q.	J. S. Jewell
1875	*Chicago Medical Journal and Examiner*	1884	m.	Dr. W. H. Byford *et al.*
	United States Medical Investigator	1893	m.	Dr. T. C. Duncan
1877	*Druggist*	1888	m.	Dr. H. D. Garrison?
1878	*Homeopathic Record*	1880	m.	W. F. Morrison
1879	*Western Druggist*	+	m.	G. P. Engelhard and Co.
1880	*Clinique*	+	m.	Gurnee Fellows
1883	*Journal of the American Medical Association*	+	w.	A.M.A.
	Medical Era	+	m.	———
1884	*Medical Visitor*	+	m.	Halsey Brothers Co.
1885	*Peoples' Health Journal*	+	m.	———
1886	*Dental Review*	+	m.	H. D. Justi
1887	*Medical Standard*	+	m.	G. P. Engelhard and Co.
1888	*North American Practitioner*	+	m.	Dr. John H. Holister
1889	*Practitioner*	+	m.	J. H. White Co.
1890	*Chicago Medical Recorder*	+	m.	Dr. A. R. Reynolds
1891	*Corpuscle*	+	m.	Rush Medical College
	Journal of the American Health Society	+	q.	George Dutton

Est.	Name	Termination, if before 1893	Freq.	Ed. or pub.
	Ophthalmic Record	+	m.	Charles C. Clute
1892	*American Climates and Resorts*	+	m.	A. F. McKay
	Hahnemann Pulse	+	m.	Hahnemann College
1893	*Medical Century*	+	m.	————

10. Music and Drama

It is difficult to separate the magazines devoted to the arts into specific areas. It was not unusual for a so-called "art" journal to include sections devoted to literature or to music. This is made especially clear in the semi-monthly *Western Journal of Music* (1856-57) whose stated purpose noted that the journal was to be "devoted to literature and art" as well as "to the advancement of musical knowledge and interest" with especial emphasis upon "the western states."

Est.	Name	Termination, if before 1893	Freq.	Ed. or pub.
1856	*Western Journal of Music*	1857	sm.	William H. Currie
1857	*Chicago Musical Review*	1858	m.	C. M. Cady
1863	*Song Messenger*	1875	m.	George F. Root and C. M. Cady
1864	*Academy of Music Gazette*	1867	w.	W. J. Jefferson and G. S. Utter
1866	*Musical Review*	1867	m.	H. M. Higgins
	Seven Sounds	1869	m.	H. T. Merrill
1867	*Higgins Musical Review*	+	m.	H. M. Higgins
	Opera House Programme	1870	d.	G. S. Utter and Co.
1868	*Musical Independent*	1873	m.	W. S. B. Mathews and the Lyon and Healy Co.
1871	*Lorgnette*	1871	w.	Crosby Opera House

Est.	Name	Termination, if before 1893	Freq.	Ed. or pub.
1873	*Goldbeck's Journal of Music*	1876	m.	Robert Goldbeck
	Vox Humana	1879	m.	Charles Barnard
1877	*Musical Review*	+	m.	George B. Armstrong
1878	*Amusement World*	+	w.	Frank I. Jervis
1879	*Conductor's Magazine and Repository*	1879	w.?	J. Ward Boyles
1880	*Indicator*	+	w.	O. L. Fox
	Stage and Field	+	w.	B. H. Bockholt
1881	*Musical Times*	+	w.	————
1884	*Presto*	+	w.	E. D. Abbott
1891	*Dramatic Times*	+	w.	Dramatic Magazine Press
	Music	+	m.	————
1893	*National Home and Music*	+	m.	Chicago Book and News Co.

11. Negroes

Thirteen years after the Civil War the first Negro newspaper appeared in Chicago. Before the War there had been a viable—albeit small—Negro community in the city. By 1840 and the first census report for Chicago, there were fifty-three Negroes listed in the total population of 4,470. Hence, when John Jones—who was to gain fame as an early entrepreneur, financier, and community leader—arrived in the city during 1845, he found a community of his people working and living together in Chicago. While the Negro population in the city increased rapidly so also did the total population of the city. According to the available statistics, the Negro population remained at less than 2 per cent of the city's total until the First World War.

While there have been many excellent studies on the Negro in Chicago during the twentieth century, there has been little done which relates exclusively to the period prior to 1900. As a result, little is known about the Negro community. In 1850 the historic

Olivet Baptist was founded, and in 1864 John Jones' attack upon the Black Laws of Illinois was published by the *Tribune* as a pamphlet. Such people as Ferdinand Barnett (who in 1878 established the first Negro newspaper in the city) and Daniel Hale Williams (the noted surgeon who founded Provident Hospital in 1891) were among the Negro leaders. But they were not alone. By 1893 Paul Laurence Dunbar found in Chicago an elite group which was extremely active in the life of the city. There were many clubs devoted to cultural uplift; probably the most prestigious was the Prudence Crandall Club, an exclusive reading and literary society after the manner of those which had been established earlier in the nineteenth century in Boston and Philadelphia.

Then—as now—that vital Negro community was committed to first-class citizenship although it was divided on the best methods which ought to be used. One of the leaders of militant protest was John G. Jones, better known as "Indignation" Jones, who became a law partner of Barnett in the 1880's. On the other hand, Daniel Hale Williams was joined by Charles Smiley and Julius Avendorph in the belief that the best way to "beat a system" was to become successful within that system.

While they do not concentrate on the nineteenth century, the following works have made a significant contribution to the study of the Negro in Chicago. Much still needs to be done on the period up to 1893.

Chicago Commission on Race Relations. *The Negro in Chicago* (Chicago, 1922).

Drake, St. Clair. *Churches and Voluntary Associations in the Chicago Negro Community* (Chicago, 1940).

———— and Horace Cayton. *Black Metropolis: A Study of Negro Life in a Northern City* (New York, 1945).

Duncan, Otis and Beverly. *The Negro Population of Chicago: A Study of Residential Succession* (Chicago, 1957).

Frazier, E. Franklin. *The Negro Family in Chicago* (Chicago, 1932).

Gosnell, Harold F. *Negro Politicians: The Rise of Negro Politics in Chicago* (Chicago, 1935).

Spear, Allan. *Black Chicago: The Making of a Negro Ghetto* (Chicago, 1967).

The two newspapers which were founded before 1893 presented essentially the voice of militant protest, but they also provided an outlet for the hopes and aspirations of a people for whom other sources of community news were closed. Thus, very much as some of the foreign language newspapers, these two served to relate means and methods for coping with the urban environment. At the same time they recorded the cultural achievement of the city's Negro population. Local poets and short story writers discovered that these publications were receptive to their works.

Est.	Name	Termination, if before 1893	Freq.	Ed. or pub.
1878	*Conservator*	+	w.	Ferdinand L. Barnett and James E. Henderson
1885	*Appeal*	+	w.	C. F. Adams

12. Newspapers—General

While many of the general newspapers had identifiable political leanings, the following represents those newspapers intended for the general public and which accepted advertising on that basis. Hence, to identify them as a specific type is merely to indicate the political persuasion of the paper editorially. Furthermore, these political leanings frequently changed with either a shift of editors or new owners. After the city's first two papers, the daily paper became a common type although there remained some weeklies which had a large reading public. The Chicago *Democrat,* the first newspaper in the city, started out as a weekly as did the Chicago *American,* the second paper. However, the *American* in 1839 became a daily and the *Democrat* became a daily paper in

1840. From that time on the type became commonplace. Although there were many weekly papers, most of them were designed for special interest groups; however, they gave summaries of political and regional events.

Needless to say, a list of this type is as abbreviated as possible. I make no attempt to record all of the changes which took place within a single newspaper, and the political affiliation noted for each entry is the initial one. Most frequently, these changed over the years. For a fuller presentation of the newspapers of Chicago, one of the newspaper directories, such as Rowell's or Chamberlain's, will give a fuller description of the internal changes which occurred with a degree of frequency. Unless other indicated, however, the following were daily papers.

Est.	*Name*	Termina-tion, if before *1893*	*Type*	*Ed. or pub.*
1833	Chicago *Democrat*	1861	Dem.	John Calhoun (1833-36) and John Wentworth (1836-1861)
1835	Chicago *American*	1842	Whig	William Stuart and T. O. Davis
1840	*The Weekly Tribune*	1841		E. G. Ryan
1842	*Quid Nunc*	1842	Ind.	David S. Griswold and Ellis and Fergus Co.
	Chicago *Express*	1844	Whig	W. W. Brackett
1844	*Daily Journal*	+	Whig	Richard and Charles Wilson
	Evening Journal	+	Ind.	Evening Press Co.
1845	*Daily News*	1846	Liberty	Zebina Eastman
1846	*Daily Cavalier*	1847	Ind.	Robert Wilson and Rev. William Rounseville
	Morning Mail	1847	Ind.	Rev. William Rounseville
1847	*Tribune*	+	Rep.	William Bross, Joseph Medill (1853-99), *et al.*
1850	*Democratic Argus*	1852?	Dem.	B. F. Seaton and W. W. Peck

Est.	Name	Termination, if before 1893	Type	Ed. or pub.
1852	Daily Democratic Press	1858	Dem., Rep.	John L. Scripps and William Bross
	Weekly Express	1853		J. F. Ballantyne
1854	Times	+	Dem.	Wilbur Storey (1861-84)
	Young America	1854	Dem.	J. W. Patterson
1855	The Native American	1856	Native Am. Party	W. W. Danenhower and Washington Wright
1856	Daily News	1856	Ind.	Walter B. Sloan
	Democratic Bugle	1856	Dem.	Charles Lieb
	Herald	1857	Ind.	T. R. Dawley
	Sunday Vacuna	1856	Ind.	T. R. Dawley
1857	Daily Ledger	1857		Seth Paine
	Daily Union	1858	Ind.	Louis Schade
	Sunday Leader	1859?		S. P. Rounds and W. H. Bushnell
1858	Herald	+	Dem.	Isaac Cook and Charles Pine
1860	Morning Post	1865	Dem.	James W. Sheahan
	Saturday Evening Review	1860	Ind.	William Pigott
1862	Telegraph	1864		G. Feuchtinger and Dr. Ernest Schmidt
1864	Workingman's Advocate	1879	Labor Party	Blake and Hayde Co.
1865	Bee	+	Ind.	William Pigott
	City Evening News	+	Ind.	J. M. Climie
	Post	1878	Rep.	William Pigott
	Republican	1872	Rep.	Charles A. Dana
1866	Record	+	Ind.	Victor F. Lawson
1869	Banner (weekly)	+	Ind.	Frank E. Stanley
1870	Sunday Democrat	1870	Dem.	George W. Ruet
1872	Daily News	1873	Dem.	H. R. Whipple
	Inter-Ocean	+	Rep.	J. Young Scammon
1873	Daily Herald	1873	Ind.	?
	Express	1880	Greenback	O. J. Smith
	Industrial Age (weekly)	1879	Labor	J. A. Noonan
1874	Daily Courier	1877	Ind.	George I. Yeager
	Post and Mail	1878	Ind.	Oliver Willard
1875	Daily News	+	Ind.	Melville E. Stone and Victor Lawson

Est.	Name	Termination, if before 1893	Type	Ed. or pub.
1876	*Irish Tribune* (weekly)	1885	Ind.	M. Ryan
	Pomeroy's Democrat (weekly)	1880	Green-back	Mark Pomeroy
1877	*Northwest*	?	Ind.	Carl Grandpré
	States (weekly)	1877?	Green-back	O. J. Smith ?
1878	*Daily Telegraph*	1881	Green-back-Labor Party	Seymour F. Norton
	Graphic (weekly)	+	Rep.	Hoffman and Lederer
	Sentinel (weekly)	1888?	Green-back	Seymour F. Norton
1879	*Morning Herald*	1879	Ind.	William Burgess
1880	*Chronicle* (weekly)	+	Rep.	D. L. Davis
1881	*Herald*	+	Ind.	John R. Walsh
	Morning Record	+	Ind.	Victor Lawson
1882	*Citizen* (weekly)	+	Ind.	———
1884	*Commercial Journal* (weekly)	+	Rep.	Evening Press Co.
1888	*Telegram* (weekly)	+	Ind.	J. P. Caulfield
1889	*Democrat* (weekly)	+	Dem.	———
	Eagle (weekly)	+	Ind.	Henry F. Donovan
1890	*Broadside* (weekly)	+	Free Trade	Norman Rapalee
	Evening Post	+	Ind.	John Walsh, Finley Peter Dunne, *et al.*
1892	*Dispatch*	+	Ind.	Joseph R. Dunlop and the Dispatch Co.
	The Public	+	Ind.	Louis Post

13. Newspapers—Neighborhood

The importance of the neighborhood in a large city cannot be underestimated. The "divisions" or "sides" in Chicago never attained the same political independence as New York's boroughs, but in some ways sectionalism was more apparent in Chicago. The city's novelists frequently used the distinctions between the West, South, and North Divisions as a means of establishing certain character types.

The neighborhood newspaper did not originate in Chicago; however, because of the nature of the city, the local paper had a great popularity among those residents who were so loyal to their sections. These papers were also highly supported by the local businessmen who often used them as a major means of advertising.

All of the following newspapers began as weeklies except the *Sun* (1869-   ) and the *Calumet* (1882-   ) which began as dailies and became weeklies.

Est.	Name	Termination, if before 1893	Ed. or pub.
1869	*Sun* [series of papers published under this name such as:	+	H. L. Goodall and the Drovers' Journal Pub. Co.
	Hyde Park Daily Sun		
	Lake Sun		
	Lake Daily Sun		
	Lake View Sun		
	Union Stockyards Daily Sun		
	Dollar Weekly Sun		
	Dollar Sun		
	Cook County Sun		
	South Side Sun		
	Cicero Sun		
	Marine Sun		
	Thornton Sun		
	Calumet Sun		
	Jefferson Sun]		
	West Chicago Banner	1881	Frank E. Stanley
1870	*Union Park Advocate*	1877	Charles E. Crandall
	Union Park Banner	1880	E. M. Turner and Co.
	West Chicago	1875	————
	West End Advocate	1881	Charles E. Crandall
1871	*Phenix*	+	M. A. Fuller
1873	*South Side News*	+	Vansant and Co.

Est.	Name	Termina-tion, if before 1893	Ed. or pub.
1875	*Enterprise and Times* [became *The Enterprise* in 1876]	+	William Caffrey and H. L. Goodall and Co.
	South Side Record	+	Vansant and Co.
	South Lawn Tribune	1888?	John K. Rowley
1878	*Englewood Eye*	+	———
	North Side Reporter	+	F. W. Brenckle
	Southwest Advertiser	+	Oliver Colhapp and Co.
1880	*West Side Chronicle*	+	Frank E. Stanley ?
1882	*Calumet*	+	———
1884	*North Chicago and Lake View Independent*	+	C. A. Blair
1886	*Englewood Times*	+	G. E. Sullivan
	Mirror of South Englewood	+	G. E. Sullivan
	Opinion	+	West Chicago Pub. Co.
	Chicago Lawn Post	+	George K. Storey
	Pullman Journal	+	———
	South Side Advocate	+	Omer L. Douney

14. Recreation (Games and Sports) and Travel

Rather late in the nineteenth century there developed a specific market for journals dealing with leisure-time activities, recreation, games and sports; most of them extended into the twentieth century. From the 1850's, however, there was evidence of an interest in the travel magazine. Though short-lived they took the opportunity to "boost" Chicago and to present the advantages of railroad travel. They are the forerunners of the present-day paperback as monthly guides to the city which are quite popular.

Est.	Name	Termination, if before 1893	Freq.	Ed. or pub.
1853	*The Traveler*	1856?	m.	James M. Chatfield *et. als.*
	Horner's Chicago and Western Guide	1853	m.	W. B. Horner
1855	*The Illinois Gazeteer and Immigrants' Western Guide* [only the August issue appeared]	1855	m.	?
1864	*Museum and Hotel Register*	1873	d.	R. V. Kennedy
1873	*Western Sporting Times*	+	m.	T. Z. Cowles
1874	*American Field*	+	w.	Dr. N. Rowe
1876	*Chicago Field*	1881	w.	C. W. Marsh *et al.*
	Dunton's Spirit of the Turf	1881	m.	F. H. Dunton and C. E. Jones
	Western Traveler	1883?	m.	D. A. Cashman
1878	*American Chess Journal*	1881	m.	Denvir Brothers
1879	*New Overland Tourist*	+	m.	Overland Pub. Co.
1881	*Horseman*	+	w.	Chicago Horseman Newspaper Co.
1884	*A Pointer* (travel)	+	m.	Reaux Campbell
1887	*Sports Afield*	+	m.	Claude King
1888	*American Checker Review*	+	m.	Denvir Brothers
	Referee (Cycling)	+	w.	———
1889	*American Traveler*	+	m.	C. E. Hunt
	Horse Review	+	w.	John C. Bauer
1890	*Sportsmen's Review and Bicycle News*	+	sm.	———
	Bearings (Cycling)	+	w.	———
1893	*Cycling Life*	+	w.	———

15. Reform

To label a newspaper or magazine as being a "reform" journal is perhaps misleading because even the daily general newspapers, those designated for the "general public," often had "reform" motives when they ardently supported one political party over another. However, in this category will be found those papers whose purposes were simply to change or influence patterns of belief or behavior as they related to a single issue. Included in this category are the short-term campaign newspapers which were issued in the city. On the other hand, such a utopian journal as *The Christian Banker* almost defies classification. In some respects it might be considered as a religious journal or as a commercial one, although it clearly had reform in its purpose as did many of the other religious publications. Included with the editor's name (when such is known) is the specific cause which the journal advocated.

That many of these periodicals were short-lived is to be expected. Reform papers then—as is true today—had a brief duration either because the cause was a passing one or because the journal lacked a broad-based support of the community.

Est.	Name	Termina-tion, if before 1893	Freq.	Ed. or pub.
1836	Chicago *Commercial Advertiser*	1837	w.	Hooper Warren and the Abolition Movement
1838	*Voice of the People*	1838	w.	Whig Young Men's Ass'n., campaign paper
1840	*Hard Cider Press*	1840	w.	William Stuart, campaign paper
1842	*Chicago Republican*	1844	w.	A. R. Niblo and F. W. Cleveland, re-election of President Tyler
	Western Citizen	1855	w.	Zebina Eastman, Anti-Slavery
1845	*The Spirit of Temperance Reform*	1845	w.?	J. E. Ware
1846	*Daily News*	1846	w.?	Zebina Eastman *et al.*, "liberty paper"

Est.	Name	Termination, if before 1893	Freq.	Ed. or pub.
	The Western Herald	1847	w.	J. B. Walker and B. F. Worrall, Anti-Slavery, Anti-Masonic, Temperance, Society of Friends
	The Liberty Tree	1848	m.	Zebina Eastman, Anti-Slavery
1848	The Field-Piece	1848	d.	*Journal,* campaign paper
	Free Soil Banner	1848	d.	Free Soil Party, campaign paper issued by *The Western Herald*
1849	The Chicago Temperance Battle-Axe	1849	w.?	Charles J. Sellon
1852	The Daily Times and Citizen	1853	d., tw.	Zebina Eastman, Anti-Slavery and Free Soil
1854	The Maine-Law Alliance	1854	w.	Dr. Charles Jewett et al.
	The Saturday Evening Mail	1854	w.	George R. Graham, Temperance
	The Free West	1856	w.	Hooper Warren and Zebina Eastman— Freedom Party
1855	Western Crusader	1856	w.	Thomas Williams and Orlo Strong, Temperance
1856	Daily Patriot	1856	d.	campaign paper
1860	Rail Splitter	1860	d.	Charles Lieb, Lincoln campaign paper
1863	New World	1873	w.	C. P. Russell, Temperance
1864	Workingman's Advocate	1879	w.?	John Blake, James Hayde, pro-labor union forces
1865	Home Circle and Temperance Oracle	1871	m.	S. M. Kennedy
	Western Temperance Advocate	1868	w.	Rev. J. C. Stoughton and Sons of Temperance

Est.	Name	Termination, if before 1893	Freq.	Ed. or pub.
1866	*National Prohibitionist*	1871	?	Prohibitionist Party
1867	*Irish Republic*	1871	m.?	Michael Scanlan
	Lyceum Banner	1873?	bw.	Mrs. H. F. M. Brown and Mrs. Lou H. Kimball, women's rights
1868	*Sorosis*	1869	w.	Mrs. M. L. Walker, women's rights
1869	*Advocate of Peace*	1874	m.	American Peace Party
	Agitator	?	m.	women's rights
1872	*Balance*	1877	m.	Maria Hawley and Mary Tomlin, women's rights
	Humane Journal	+	m.	A. W. Landon for "humane propaganda"
1873	*American Working People*	1873	m.	R. C. Machesny
	Express	1880	w.?	O. G. Smith, Greenbacks
	People's Paper	1873	w.	Edward N. Fuller, Grange paper
1874	*Crusader*	1881	m.	Mrs. M. E. DeGeer and Mrs. C. V. Waite, Temperance
	Union Signal	+	w.	Women's Temperance Pub. Co.
1875	*Temperance Monthly*	1876	m.	Mrs. C. Augustus Haviland
	Temperance Record	+	m.?	John Meagher
1876	*Washingtonian*	1893	m.	Daniel Wilkins and the Washingtonian Home Ass'n., Temperance
1878	*Alarm*	1884	w.	A. R. Parsons, Workingman's Party and socialist reform
	Citizen's League	1879	w.	Frederick Dalton, Temperance and Prohibition
	Chicago Review	1880?	w.	W. C. Crum, Temperance
	Lever	+	w.	Lamont and Walkup, Prohibition

Est.	Name	Termination, if before 1893	Freq.	Ed. or pub.
	Socialist	1878	w.	Frank Hirth and A. R. Parsons
1879	*Illustrated Temperance Tales*	1880	m.	Fleming H. Revell
	Signal	1881	w.	Mrs. Mary B. Willard, Temperance
1887	*Young Crusader*	+	m.	Women's Temperance Pub. Co.
1888	*Young Women*	+	m.	Women's Temperance Pub. Co.
1892	*Eight-Hour Herald*	+	w.	Labor reform

16. Religious

Given the nature and the image of the city, it is often surprising to discover that there was a strong religious press in Chicago. Beginning with the *Northwestern Baptist* (1842-44), these periodicals did much toward the development of "literature." With rare exceptions, the men and women who wrote for the religious press were highly trained and were interested in making religion as well as church activities an integral part of urban life. Consequently, most of the journals were designed for the general public and were not technical theological tracts.

While it is true that the sermon provided staple fare for many of these publications, there was also an emphasis upon political commentary, social issues, general essays, fiction, and poetry. The nineteenth-century religious press in the city was dominated by the Protestant denominations. This was reinforced by the popularity of such clergymen as R. W. Patterson, S. S. Jones, David Swing, Robert Collyer, and Frank Gunsaulus who were also part of the city's literati. Edward Eggleston, perhaps best known for his novel, *The Hoosier Schoolmaster* (1871), edited several journals in Chicago.

In the 1870's and 1880's the Protestant press was also dominated by those who were opposed to foreign immigration. As a result, the anti-Roman Catholic spirit in the city was supported by those who feared that the Protestant tradition was in jeopardy. During the period there were some Roman Catholic journals written in English, but most of them were written in other languages until the twentieth century.

Only those religious journals in English are listed in this section; the others appear in Section # 6: Foreign Languages.

Est.	Name	Termination, if before 1893	Freq.	Ed. or pub.
1842	*Northwestern Baptist*	1884	sw.	Thomas Powell
1843	*Better Covenant*	1847	w.	Rev. Seth Barnes and Rev. William Rounseville
1847	*Watchman of the Prairies*	+	w.	Rev. Luther Stone, Baptists
1848	*Herald of the Prairies*	1849	w.	Rev. J. B. Walker and B. F. Worrall
	New Covenant	1886	m.	Rev. W. E. Mauley, Universalists
1849	*Prairie Herald*	1853	w.?	G. S. F. Savage and Rev. A. L. Chapin, New School of Presbyterians and the Congregationalists
1852	*The Christian Era*	1852	w.	Rev. Epaphras Goodman
	Northwestern Christian Advocate	+	w.	General Conference of the Methodist Episcopal Church
1853	*The Chicago Evangelist*	1855	m.	Rev. R. W. Patterson and the "New School" Presbyterians
	The Christian Banker	1853	m.	Seth Paine
	The Christian Shoemaker	1853	m.	F. V. Pitney
	Christian Times	1865	w.	Rev. Leroy Church
	Congregational Herald	1861	w.	Rev. John C. Holbrook

Est.	Name	Termination, if before 1893	Freq.	Ed. or pub.
	New Church Independent and Review	1880	m.	Swedenborgians
	Standard	+	w.	Leroy Church, Edward Goodman, Baptists
	Northwestern Christian Advocate	+	w.	James V. Watson and Rev. Thomas Eddy
1854	The Chicago Protestant	1854	m.	Hays and Thompson
	The Israelite	+	w.	Leo Wise
1856	Manford's Monthly	1881	m.	Rev. Erasmus Manford, Universalists
1857	Northwestern Presbyterian	1871?	w.	Rev. E. E. Erskine
	Presbyterian Expositor	1860	m.	"Old School" Presbyterians
1859	Christian Instructor and Western United Presbyterian	1880	m.	Morrison and McCoy, pubs.
1860	Baptist Monthly	1861	m.	W. Stuart Goodno
	Bible Students	+	m.	Society of Friends
	Congregational Review	1871	bm.	G. S. G. Savage
	Home Visitor	+	m.	Mrs. Mary G. Clark *et al.* for the Chicago Home for the Friendless
	Life Boat	1871	m.	Edward Eggleston and John W. Dean
	Northwestern Pulpit	+	m.	Illinois Baptist General Ass'n.
1861	Presbyterian Recorder	1862	w.	Lake, Quinlan, and Raymond
1862	American Churchman	1871	m.?	Hugh M. Thompson, Episcopalians
	Northwestern Church	1865	w.	Rev. Thomas Smith, Episcopalians
1864	Advent Christian Times	1877	w.	Second Adventists, W. L. Hines, and William Sheldon
1865	Christian Times and Witness	1867	w.	J. A. Smith and Leroy Church, Baptists
	Evangelist	1881	w.	B. W. Johnson, B. J. Radford, and Evangelical Church

Est.	Name	Termina-tion, if before 1893	Freq.	Ed. or pub.
	Northwestern Sunday School	1866	q.	Rev. J. H. Vincent et al.
	Religio-Philosophical Journal	+	w.	S. S. Jones, Spiritualists
1866	Sunday School Teacher	1869	q.	Edward Eggleston
	Western Pulpit	1871?	m.	Rev. R. F. Shinn
1867	Advance	+	w.	W. W. Patton, J. B. T. Marsh, Congregationalists
	Christian Freeman	1871	m.	Free Will Baptists and Christian Freeman Ass'n.
	Columbian Ed Western Catholic	+	m.	J. J. Thompson
	Herald of the Coming Kingdom and Christian Instructor	1871	sm.	Thomas Wilson and George Moyers
	Heralds of Peace	1870	sm.	W. E. Hathaway, Society of Friends
	Liberal	1870	w.	James Walker, Free Thought Movement
	New Republic	1870	m.	Rev. W. B. Christopher
	Western Catholic News	+	w.	Catholic News Pub. Co.
1868	American Messenger	1871	m.	American Tract Society
	Christian Cynosure	+	w., bw., m.	Rev. J. Blanchard, National Christian Ass'n
	Gospel Pulpit	1869	q.	Rev. W. J. Chaplin, Universalists
	Present Age	1872	w.	Spiritualists
	Sunday School Messenger	+	w.	Rev. Andrew L. O'Neill et al.
	Sunday School Scholar	1873	m.	Rev. Andrew L. O'Neill et al.
	Western Catholic	1881	w.	David Barry and Co.
1869	Baptist Quarterly	1870	q.	American Baptist Pub. Society
	Everybody's Paper	1879	m., sm.	Fleming H. Revell, Evangelical Movement

Est.	Name	Termina-tion, if before 1893	Freq.	Ed. or pub.
	Macedonian and Record	1871	m.	American Baptist Missionary Union and Home Mission Society
	Missionary Advocate	1880?	sm.	Home Mission Society
	National Baptist	1871	m.	American Baptist Pub. Society
	National Sunday School Teacher	1881	w.	Edward Eggleston
	Universe	1871	m.	H. N. F. Lewis
	Young Reaper	1870	sm.	American Baptist Pub. Society
1870	Examiner	1871	m.	Rev. Edward C. Towne, Evangelical Movement
	Interior	+	w.	W. A. Gray, Rev. Arthur Swazey, Cyrus McCormick, Presbyterians
	Methodist Quarterly Review	+	q.	D. D. Whedon
	The Ray	1872	m.	Union Park Baptist Church
	Sunday School Helper	1872	m.	S. A. Briggs, Universalists
	Sunday School World	+	m.	American Sunday School Union
1871	Baptist Union	1875	w.	Rev. G. H. Ball
	Foundlings' Record	1876	m.	George E. Shipman
	Heavenly Tidings	1872	m.?	Y.M.C.A.
	Restitution	1874	m.	Thomas Wilson, Servants of Jesus Christ
1872	Bell	1875	m.	Young People's Ass'n. of the Western Avenue Baptist Church
	Chicago Pulpit	1873	w.	Carpenter and Sheldon
	Diocese	1874	m.	Roman Catholics
	Religio Politico Party	1873?	m.	Mrs. A. Buffam
1873	Catholic Vindicator	1877	w.	Dr. D. W. Nolan
	Christian Voice	1879	m.	Fleming H. Revell,
	Occident	+	w.	Julius Silversmith, Radical Reformed Judiasm

Est.	Name	Termina-tion, if before 1893	Freq.	Ed. or pub.
1874	*Catholic Pilot*	1881	w.	M. J. Cahill
	The Cross and the Sword	1874	w.	Nowlan and Cunningham
	Illustrated Bible Studies	1879	m.	non-sectarian Sunday School journal
	Men	+	w.	Fleming H. Revell Y.M.C.A.
	Our Rest	1880	sm.	H. V. Reed and the Second Advent Movement
	Truth	+	m.	Fleming H. Revell
1875	*Christian Register*	+	w.	Rev. T. J. Mumford, Unitarians
	Morning Star	1879	w.	George T. Day, I. D. Stewart, Baptists
	Sunday School Gem	1879?	w.	David C. Cook
	Watchman	1886	sm.	W. W. Van Arsdale, Y.M.C.A.
1876	*Appeal*	1880	bw.	Bishop Samuel Fallows and Reformed Episcopal Church
	Christian Sunday School Teacher	1881	m.	non-denominational
	Highway Papers	+	m.	Isaiah Reid, Evangelical Movement
	International Lesson	1880	m.	Fleming H. Revell
	Sunday School Advocate	+	w., sm.	Rev. J. H. Vincent
	Teachers' Quarterly	+	m.	Evangelical Movement
	Words of Life	1880	m.	Fleming H. Revell
1877	*Church and School*	+	m.	David C. Cook
1878	*Living Church*	+	w.	Rev. Samuel S. Harris and Episcopalians
	New Unity	+	w.	Alfred C. Clark
	Pamphlet Mission [became *Unity* before the end 1878]	+	m, sm., w.	Rev. Robert Collyer, Rev. Jenkins Lloyd Jones, *et al.*
	Witness	1881	w.	Rev. Thomas J. Lamont, Evangelical Movement

Est.	Name	Termina-tion, if before 1893	Freq.	Ed. or pub.
1879	*Bible Class Scholar*	+	q.	Evangelical Movement
	Carnival Herald	1879	d.	Mrs. Elizabeth Boyton Harbert
	Day Spring	+	m.	Fleming H. Revell
	Spiritual Record	+	m.	First Society of Spiritualists of Chicago
1880	*Biblical World*	+	m.	Evangelical Baptists
	Free Methodist	+	w.	D. P. Parke and B. T. Roberts
1882	*Free Thought*	+	m.	H. L. Green
	Lutheran Witness	+	sm.	Lutheran Pub. Board
1883	*Friends' Bible School*	+	q.	Society of Friends
	Mission Studies	+	m.	Women's Board of Missions
	Sunday School Lesson Illustrator	+	m.	Fleming H. Revell
1884	*Christian Oracle*	+	w.	non-denominational
	Midland	+	w.	United Presbyterians
1885	*Daily Jewish Courier*	+	d., w.	H. S. Wolf
1886	*Faith and Record*	+	m.	George E. Shipman
1887	*Congregational News*	+	m.	
1888	*Open Court*	+	m.	Frederick L. Chapman
	Our Youth's Friend	+	m.	Society of Friends
	Universal Truth	+	m.	F. M. Harley and Co.
1889	*Children's Home Finder*	+	m.	Children's Home Society
	Evangelical Episcopalian	+	m.	F. J. Walton
	Progressive Thinker	+	w.	John R. Francis, Spiritualism
1890	*Baptist Union*	+	w.	Baptist Young People's Union of America
	Ram's Horn	+	w.	Frederick J. Chapman
1891	*Christognosis*	+	m.	M. B. Van Eps, Christian Scientists
	Reform Advocate	+	w.	Block and Newman

Est.	Name	Termina-tion, if before 1893	Freq.	Ed. or pub.
1892	*New World*	+	w.	Dr. Thomas O'Hagan, Roman Catholic
1893	*Progressive Thinker*	+	w.	J. R. Francis, Spiritualists

17. Scientific

Around the hospitals, medical schools, and colleges as well as around the Chicago Academy of Sciences (1859) there developed a group of men and women who were committed to the idea that SCIENCE as a discipline ought to be understandable to the general public. Up to the Civil War periodical literature of a scientific nature was dominated by the medical journals; however, in 1862 Chicago obtained duplicates of the collection of Robert Kennicott's most recent exploratory trip with the originals going to the Smithsonian Institution. From 1862 to 1865 Kennicott worked diligently for the purposes and goals of the Academy of Sciences. During those years he was extremely active in a movement to increase public awareness in scientific issues. This included bringing to the city such men as Louis Agassiz to lecture. All of this was support for part of the plan of cultural uplift sponsored by many of the older societies and clubs in the city.

Not only was there a popularizing of scientific subjects but also there was an emphasis upon science as an integral part of life. The work of such men as Dr. James Coulter and Dr. Asa Gray in Botany, for example, is illustrative of the small coterie of scholars who created a public for their work. For the non-specialist who had an interest in the various fields, the magazines and newspapers were adequate. While few of them reached spectacular circulation figures in twentieth-century terms, these journalistic efforts did have a respectable number of subscribers.

The extremely technical journals as well as medical periodicals have not been included in the following list. Popular medical journals can be found in Section # 9: Medical.

Est.	Name	Termination, if before 1893	Freq.	Ed. or pub.
1872	*Lens*	1873	q.	Microscopical Society of Illinois, J. A. Briggs, ed.
1874	*Scientific Manufacturer*	1878?	sm.	Thomas S. Sprague
1875	*Botanical Bulletin*	1876	m.	Dr. James M. Coulter
1876	*Botanical Gazette*	+	m.	Dr. James M. Coulter and Dr. Asa Gray
1877	*American Antiquarian*	+	bm.	Stephen D. Peet
1878	*Mining Review and Metallurgist*	+	m.	Edward A. Taft
1885	*Black Diamond* [dealt with coal and gas]	+	w.	H. A. Beschoff
1889	*Domestic Engineering*	+	m.	J. S. Palmer
1890	*Monist* ["scientific philosophy"]	+	q.	Open Court Pub. Co.
1891	*Ice and Refrigeration*	+	m.	H. S. Rich and Co.
1893	*Journal of Geology* [8 issues per year]	+		University of Chicago

18. Secret Societies

While there was a strong feeling against secret societies and various aspects of Masonry in some quarters of the city, there was some support for these groups either on the basis of genuine fellowship which the organizations brought or because they provided a means to control certain aspects of urban life. It is indeed significant that the first journal of a secret society should have been edited by a clergyman who is so closely associated with the early literary development of the city. *The American Odd Fellow and Magazine of Literature and Art,* a monthly edited by

William Rounseville, appeared in 1848. It was followed by a number of short-lived journals.

Est.	Name	Termination, if before 1893	Freq.	Ed. or pub.
1855	*Ashlar*	1861	m.	Allyn Weston
1857	*The Trestle Board*	1857	m.	J. J. Clarkson
1863	*Voice of Masonry*	1883	m.	Robert Morris and J. C. W. Bailey
1864	*Mystic Star*	1874	m.	Rev. James Billings *et al.*
1867	*Olive Wreath*	1869	m.	W. D. Chaplin for the Odd Fellows
1869	*Western Odd Fellow*	1871	w.	J. B. Wing and J. Ward Ellis
1873	*Masonic Record*	1878	m.	C. H. Carson
1885	*Independent Forester*	+	m.	T. W. Saunders
1888	*Pythian Record*	+	m.	————

19. Women

The following journals were designed specifically for female readers and were designed to cover articles of a general nature as well as fashions. Reform magazines or those which addressed such matters as women's liberation are not included in the following list.

Est.	Name	Termination, if before 1893	Freq.	Ed. or pub.
1863	*Volunteer*	1863	d.	"ladies of the Northwestern Fair"
1866	*Ladies Repository*	1871	m.	J. W. Wiley
1869	*Ladies' Own Magazine*	1874	m.	Mrs. Cora Bland
	Matrimonial Bazar [sic)]	1879	m.	B. H. Burtin and Co.
	Matrimonial News and Special Advertiser	1883	bw.	C. G. Harton
1871	*Mother's Journal*	1871	m.	Mrs. Mary G. Clarke

Est.	Name	Termination, if before 1893	Freq.	Ed. or pub.
1872	*Bridal Bells*	1877	sm.	Eugene T. Gilbert
	Ladies' Friend and Shopping Guide	1875	w., m.	J. A. Densmore
1873	*Bridal Veil*	1879	sm.	H. M. Habel
1877	*Clothing Gazette*	+	m.	John McGreen
	Cosmopolitan	1880	m.	C. A. Vosburg
	Mirror of Fashions	1880	w.	J. D. Goodrich
1880	*Home Literature*	+	w.	M. J. Cahill
1881	*Elite*	+	w.	———
1883	*Helping Hand*	+	m.	———
1887	*Climax*	+	m.	———
1889	*American Messenger*	+	m.	Frederic Drake
	Apparel Gazette	+	sm.	Waldo Fairchild Co.
1893	*Four Hundred*	+	m.	Persinger and Sullivan
	Woman's Rural Journal	+	m.	Graham-Keer Co.

In addition to the journals which can be assigned to specific categories, there were numerous periodicals which appeared before 1893 which defy classification. The extent and number of such *miscellaneous* journals can be determined through a study of such works as Scott's *Newspapers and Periodicals of Illinois* (pp. 52-149) or the numerous newspaper directories for the nineteenth century. Suffice it to say, there was every indication that Chicagoans viewed their town as a cosmopolitan city and produced more than enough periodical literature for themselves as well as for surrounding communities. Ultimately, the number of journals which were begun is not as important as the fact that a substantial number of them were in existence by 1893 and continued into the twentieth century.

There is still much work to be done in this area in spite of the fact that a study of the work prior to October, 1871, is severely hampered by the destruction in the fire of 1871 of so much vital material.

APPENDIX B

THE CHICAGO NOVEL: 1833-1893

Until 1850 there was no Chicago "novel" as such; and even those which appeared immediately after Edward Bonney's *The Banditti of the Prairies* . . . can be called "novels" only by a loose definition of the genre. Short fiction, however, did appear in various newspapers and magazines before 1850. Given the mercantile nature of the city, early fiction followed a strange course. As it developed, it tended to consist of romantic froniter tales which recorded the adventures of the newly-arrived settlers. The inevitable sameness of the prairie was duly noted by writers who were also struck by the beauty of the place. There were, of course, the expected conflicts with the Indians who by this time were presented as being essentially hostile. Many of these were written in the style of Cooper and appeared in the magazines of the city as well as in the journals of the Midwest. Singularly significant by their absence were the tales which chronicled the evils of the city. One need merely to compare the type of fiction which was flooding Philadelphia and other large urban centers to note that Chicago writers for a long time rejected the notion that they were in a metropolitan area. Thus while the East read those stories which reinforcecd urban problems, Chicagoans were reading adventure stories set on the prairie.

Two works which illustrate the popular frontier story are Solon Robinson's *Me-Won-I-Toc: A Tale of Frontier Life and Indian Character* (1867) and *The Heart of the West: An American Story* by an Illinoian (1871). Strictly speaking, of course, these are not Chicago novels; but they are typical of the concerns of Chicago fiction from the 1850's through the 1860's. Many of these might be termed "local color" efforts in their deliberate use of those characteristics deemed peculiar to the region; however, there was

441

also a strong historical element in these works as a large number of writers used the facts of the frontier and their interpretation of Indian life to present the midwestern territory. This genre culminated with the work of Catherwood who returned to the days of the French occupation.

The long fictional works which appeared before 1872, with the possible exception of the products of Major John Richardson— the Canadian soldier, tangentially might be called "Chicago novels"; however, with the publication of Rev. E. P. Roe's *Barriers Burned Away* (1872) there was a "Chicago novel" which was destined to continue to the present day. If one assumes that a distinctive national, ethnic, regional, or urban literature arises when a group recognizes how it differs from other established groups, it may be well to note Juliette Kinzie's *Wau-Bun* of 1856, erroneously categorized as a novel by many critics. Although it is a personal narrative, her work has implications for fiction because she sounded a note of prophecy when she made it clear that the hero of the new territory would be a man of finance rather than a man of military honor. She thus articulated a truth which was apparent in other locales but which was generally subverted in order to illustrate the more traditional concepts of the importance of honor, fidelity, religious commitment, morality, *ad infinitum*.

Although the emphasis upon the commercial aspects of life permeated much of the non-fiction produced in the city, it was not until E. P. Roe's novel of 1872 that the newer patterns became discernible in fiction. Roe suggested that it was possible for a young man to come into Chicago and survive the vicissitudes of urban living. He claimed, as had Juliette Kinzie, that existence in the city called not necessarily for unnatural strength but rather for a new way of looking at the urban environment. The old norms of *good* and *evil* were not always workable when dealing with the culture of the city. Hence, unlike the eastern writers, the Chicago novelists were willing to accept either the evil of the city or its amorality as facts with which heroes could deal without succumbing to moralistic diatribes.

By 1893 the terms "Chicago novel" and "Chicago novelist" conveyed restricted meanings even though there was not complete agreement on all aspects of them. Generally, however, "Chicago novel" came to relate specifically to long fiction in which the city played some integral part in the development of the characters as well as of the action. And as the confusion of meaning became increasingly minimized, the "Chicago novel" tended to refer to a work which accepted the businessman as the cultural hero of the city. "Chicago novelist" tended to refer to those writers who viewed the city in terms of its metaphoric relationship to human existence. They used the city in such a way that it was more than just a locale or setting for the action. It assumed the role of becoming a conditioning force. While many of these novelists not only lived and worked in Chicago but also were part of the city's nebulous literary establishment, many were outsiders who simply managed to capture the dominant significance of the urban experience as represented by Chicago.

Nineteenth-century critics such as Thomas Morton Payne and Maurice Thompson were not as concerned that a writer capture "the spirit" of Chicago; hence, they included any writer as a "Chicago novelist" who lived in the city no matter what subjects such a writer selected. Frank Gunsaulus, the clergyman—for example—was considered to be a "Chicago novelist" although his two-volumed *Monk and Knight* (1891) is a medieval romance. Because of the shift of meanings for the requirements of the Chicago novelist and/or novel, it is difficult to compile a bibliography of the "Chicago novel." One of the earliest novelists in the city was William Bushnell who was certainly an important force in the development of the city's literature as he edited some of the early journals of the town. Yet his novels *Prairie Fire: A Tale of Illinois* (1855), *The Pearl of Panama; or, The Spaniard's Vengeance* (1867), and *Ah-Meek, The Beaver; or, The Copper-*

Hunters of Lake Superior (1867) are certainly not remotely "urban." Some time later the first two novels by Henry Blake Fuller also raise serious questions. While clearly he can be identified with Chicago as the author of *The Cliff-Dwellers* (1893) and *With the Procession* (1895) as well as much of his later work (which includes his participation in the various literary organizations of the city), Fuller began his career with *The Chevalier of Pensieri-Vani* (1890) and *The Chatelaine of La Trinité* (1892). Both have European settings, but it was clearly Fuller's life in Chicago which formed the basis for his comparative statements on the differences between the Old World and the New.

As one examines the fiction of the period which tentatively explored the city, it is important to be cognizant of the substantial number of "dime" novels which appeared from the close of the Civil War to the World's Columbian Exposition. Many of these used the locale and the mystique of Chicago. These sentimental-gothic novellas did little to advance the cause of literature but were fascinating tales that displayed the extent to which a city's surface details could become incorporated into its literature. Many of these "dime" novels were "detective" stories whose authors showed adeptness at the use of local color elements.

The following list of novels excludes most of the Chicago-based "dime" novels and juvenile tales because the city seldom has any significant role. There are, however, some notable exceptions. Consequently "dime" novels which illustrate the urban locale as an important controlling element in the narrative are included. Furthermore, this list gives some indication of the extent of fiction as the Chicago novel was growing to maturity. It was an evolutionary process which occurred from the earliest renderings of the place to the city of Opie Read's *The Colossus* (1893) or Theodore Dreiser's *The Titan* (1914). The inclusion of a novel in the following list does not mean to suggest that all of the works are of equal literary merit.

1850   Edward Bonney, *The Banditti of the Prairies; or, The Murder-
       er's Doom! A Tale of the Mississippi Valley*
       Henry A. Clarke, *The War Scout of Eighteen Hundred and
       Twelve*
       Major John Richardson, *Hardscrabble; A Tale of Chicago*
1852   ———, *Wau-Nan-Gee; or, The Massacre at Fort Dearborn,
       a Romance of the American Revolution*
1867   *Luke Darrell; the Chicago Newsboy*
1869   Juliette Kinzie, *Mark Logan, the Bourgeois*
1871   ———, *Walter Ogilby: A Novel*
1872   E[dward] P[ayson] Roe, *Barriers Burned Away*
1873   Mary Healy Bigot, *Lakeville*
       Martha J. Lamb, *Spicy: A Novel*
1876   Martha Louise Rayne, *Against Fate: A True Story*
       Shang Andrews, *Chicago After Dark*
1879   Anne E. C. Bailey, *My God! Whose Wife Am I? or, The Lost
       Heir*
       Emma van Deventer, *Shadowed By Three*
       [James Maitland], *Suppressed Sensations* by a "Reporter"
1880   Bessie Albert, *How Bob and I Kept House: A Story of Chi-
       cago Hard Times*
1883   [Blanche Machetta], *Marked "In Haste": A Story of Today*
1884   Robert Cartwright Givens, *Land Poor: A Chicago Parable* by
       Snivig C. Trebor [pseud.]
       Blanche Machetta, *Stage-Struck; or, She Would Be an Opera
       Singer*
1885   Robert Cowdrey, *Foiled by a Lawyer: A Story of Chicago*
       Symmes Jelley, *Shadowed to Europe: A Chicago Detective on
       Two Continents*
       Mrs. A. A. Wellington, *By a Way That They Knew Not*
1886   Shang Andrews, *Cranky Ann, the Street Walker. A Story of
       Chicago in Chunks*
       Helen Dawes Brown, *Two College Girls*
       Martin Foran, *The Other Side*
       Martha Louise Rayne, *Her Desperate Victory*
1887   Lillian Sommers, *For Her Daily Bread*

1888   [John Smith Draper], *Shams; or, Uncle Ben's Experience with Hypocrites*. By Benjamin Morgan.
       Franc B. Wilkie, *The Gambler*
1889   Sarah Davieson, *The Seldens in Chicago: A Domestic Tale*
       John McGovern, *Daniel Trentworthy: A Tale of the Great Fire of Chicago*
1890   Edgar Rice Beach, *Stranded: A Story of the Garden City*
       Joseph Kirkland, *The Captain of Company K*
       Lillian Sommers, *Jerome Leaster of Leaster and Co.*
1891   Allan Arnold, *Belle Boyd, the Girl Detective: A Story of Chicago and the West*
       Hobart C. Chatfield-Taylor, *An American Peeress*
       ————, *With Edge Tools*
       Robert Cowdrey, *A Tramp in Society*
       Katherine Donelson, *Rodger Latimer's Mistake*
       Carter Harrison, *A Summer Outing and the Old Man's Story*
1892   Henry L. Everett, *The People's Program: The Twentieth Century Is Theirs: A Romance of the Expectations of the Present Generation*
       Austin Granville, *The Fallen Race*
1893   Shang Andrews, *Irish Mollie; or, a Gambler's Fate. The True Story of a Famous Chicago Tragedy*
       The Beginning: A Romance of Chicago As It Might Be
       Blanche Fearing, *Asleep and Awake* by Raymond Russell [pseud.]
       Henry B. Fuller, *The Cliff-Dwellers*
       Marietta Holley, *Samantha at the World's Fair*
       Hyland C. Kirk, *The Revolt of the Brutes: A Fantasy of the Chicago Fair*
       Charles B. McClellan, *Uncle Jeremiah and the Family at the Great Fair*
       Donn Piatt, *The Reverend Melancthon Poundex: A Novel*
       Opie Read, *The Colossus*
       Eloise O. R. Richberg, *Bunker Hill to Chicago: A Story*
       Cora M. Thurston, *Polly and I*

APPENDIX C

NINETEENTH-CENTURY PUBLISHERS OF FICTION IN CHICAGO

When Chicagoans counted the writers in the city, there was the inclusion of the large body of scholarly work in science, linguistics, religion, history, and philosophy. Such works as John W. Foster's *Prehistoric Races of the United States of America* (1873), William Frederick Poole's *Anti-Slavery Opinion Before the Year 1800* (1873), William Mathews' *Oratory and Orators* (1879), George P. Upton's *Women in Music* (1881), and Edson S. Bastin's *Elements of Botany* (1887) gained unusual popularity as products of Chicago's scholars. Among the clergymen the work of David Swing, Robert Collyer, Frank Gunsaulus, and James Vila Blake was well-received. Among the historians Alfred T. Andreas, Joseph Kirkland, and William Bross did much to make Chicagoans aware not only of their heritage but also of the greatness of the United States. Shortly after his death, Abraham Lincoln achieved a reputation of legendary proportions ably assisted by such biographers as Isaac Arnold and Francis Fisher Browne. Even George Howland, superintendent of schools, and Kate Newell Doggett, the founder of the elitist Fortnightly Club, produced scholarly transactions of infrequently-read foreign works. All of this was used to prove that there were people in the city interested in academic pursuits. During the early 1890's literary developments were used to show evidence of Chicago's cultural maturity by apologists for the city.

By 1893 there had developed an active printing and publishing industry in the city which issued not only the work of Chicago writers but also that from other sections of the country. This industry never reached the point where it was willing to support a native literature to the exclusion of all else. But such firms as

Ellis and Fergus, S. C. Griggs, and finally Stone and Kimball as well as Way and Williams did a great deal toward promoting Chicago writers as well as Chicago subjects. But for many of the firms there was nothing particularly unique about them to separate them from others in the country. In the days before effective copyright laws, they did their share of pirating both American and European works. The surprise for many people is not what they published but the fact that they were publishing at all in the lakeside metropolis.

Much of the city's early printing was done by the Daily Democratic Press. In fact, in the 1850's S. C. Griggs used the Democratic Press to do a great deal of his printing. In the 1860's more printers appeared on the scene. The story of publishing in Chicago is complicated by the fact that until the 1880's it was frequently difficult to distinguish between a printer, publisher, and bookseller. In fact, all three functions were generally provided by a single firm. One has merely to survey the imprints of the pre-fire period to note the consistency of this observation. Such firms as Geer and Wilson, W. W. Barlow, T. M. Halpin, John C. W. Bailey, and W. S. Spencer were printers, publishers, and booksellers. In this period the act of publishing often simply meant the act of printing. The elaborate editorial offices which today are associated with the industry were generally absent. There was also the procedure whereby a newspaper on occasion would issue a pamphlet or book and then supervise its distribution. By, however, the end of the 1870's and into the 1880's there was a clearer understanding of the distinct aspects of publishing and a separation of functions. In 1888 *Publishers' Weekly* was able to include more than fifty Chicago firms in its national listing of book publishers in the United States.

Excluding the subscription firms and specialized publishers as well as the multitude of printers, the following list represents the city's leading publishers up to 1893. Only one of the listed firms —Sherwood—was devoted almost exclusively to textbooks. And Callaghan was the only law publisher. The others on the list—in

spite of some names which would indicate the contrary—were in
the business of general book publishing. (Those marked by an
asterisk * were included in the 1888 survey noted by *Publishers'
Weekly*.) The two firms for which Chicago ultimately became
noted, Stone and Kimball and Way and Williams, were later developments whose work in the 1890's did not always match the
earlier companies in terms of dollar sales but which because of
their inventories and authors have become extremely important
in the consideration of the city as a literary center, especially after
1893.

    American Publishing Co.
* John Anderson and Co.
    A. H. Andrews and Co.
    J. C. W. Bailey
* Belford, Clarke and Co.
    Brentano Brothers
* J. C. Buckbee and Co.
* Callaghan and Co.
* W. J. Chase
* W. A. Chatteron and Co.
* Chicago Book Publishing Co.
    Coburn and Newman Publishing Co.
    W. B. Conkey Co.
* C. A. Cook and Co.
* David C. Cook Publishing Co.
* Ezra Cook
    Cook County Review Co.
* Adam Craig Co.
    A. E. Davis Co.
    Dearborn Publishing Co.
* T. S. Denison
    Dibble Publishing Co.
    Dixon and Shepard
* R. R. Donnelley and Sons
* Donahue and Henneberry
* Dramatic Publishing Co.

* E. O. Excell
* Fairbanks and Palmer Publishing Co.
* A Flanagan Co.
* T. H. Flood and Co.
* G. A. Gaskell Co.
  Milton George Publishing House
  Goodman and Dickerson
* S. C. Griggs and Co.
* George C. Hall Co.
  F. M. Harley Publishing Co.
* W. H. Harrison, Jr., Co.
  George K. Hazlitt and Co.
  Homewood Publishing Co.
  Horton and Leonard Co.
* Interstate Publishing Co.
  Jameson and Morse
* Jeffrey Printing Co.
  W. B. Keen, Cooke, and Co.
* W. T. Kenner Co.
* Charles H. Kerr and Co.
  Knight and Leonard Co.
* Laird and Lee Co.
  Lewis Publishing Co.
* A. C. McClurg Co.
* Charles MacDonald and Co.
* McDonnell Brothers
* J. B. Martindale Co.
* A. N. Marquis and Co.
* S. A. Maxwell and Co.
  Morrill, Higgins and Co.
* L. P. Miller and Co.
* E. B. Myers and Co.
* F. T. Neely Co.
  New Era Publishing Co.
  George W. Ogilvie and Co.
  Open Court Publishing Co.
  Augustus J. Palmer and Co.
* R. S. Peale and Co.

* Purdy Publishing Co.
* Railway Age Publishing Co.
* Rand, McNally and Co.
* Fleming H. Revell Co.
* Rhodes and McClure Publishing Co.
  S. P. Rounds Co.
* Sanitary Publishing Co.
* M. Schick Co.
  F. J. Schulte Co.
* Frank Shepard Co.
* George Sherwood and Co.
  N. C. Smith Publishing Co.
* A. G. Spaulding and Brothers
  Stone and Kimball
* S. W. Straub and Co.
  Henry A. Sumner and Co.
  Union Book Concern
* C. V. Waite and Co.
* Jessup Whitehead
* S. R. Winchell and Co.
* Woman's Temperance Publishing Association

During the latter part of the nineteenth century, Chicago publishers began to understand the importance of fiction as a trade item. Of the eighty-five active firms, most of them were engaged in the publication of fiction. The following lists are representative rather than comprehensive. They indicate the extent of activity of some of Chicago's publishing houses in a period when one tends to think of publishing centers being located in the East. At the same time, it must be remembered that few of these firms really specialized in fiction. Rather these titles represent an attempt to "cash in" on a popular market. Furthermore, it is apparent that many of the authors who were published by these firms were considered—with few exceptions—to have an already-established audience. While many of these firms pioneered in varying aspects of publishing and the book trade, few of them were willing to take too many chances with unknown novelists. This may explain —in part—a reluctance to publish Chicago writers.

When one considers the following lists, there are several observations which can be made. In addition to the general lack of Chicago talent, the lists indicate a strong interest in the popular romance which became the mainstay of the subscription book trade and the lack of a representative number of so-called "classics" of American literature.

Belford, Clark and Co.

The firm had a semi-weekly subscription series which accounts for the extensive number of romances dealing with love, marriage, and divorce. These were staples of the subscription trade. In addition, the firm gambled on popular Chicago writers such as Martha Louise Rayne and Symmes M. Jelley. Among the firm's popular writers the publication of the work of Julian Hawthorne proved to be a real coup. Both Edgar Fawcett and Edgar E. Saltus had wide reading publics, and the company was responsible for creating reading publics for the work of Edgar W. Nye and George Wilbur Peck.

The following works represent some of the fiction produced by the firm of Belford, Clarke and Co. during the 1880's and into the 1890's.

Bellamy, Elizabeth Whitfield Croom. *Old Man Gilbert,* 1888
Benjamin, Lewis. *Why Was It? A Novel,* 1888
Buel, James William. *Life and Marvelous Adventures of Wild Bill, The Scout,* 1880
Clark, Mrs. Mary J. *The Record of a Ministering Angel,* 1885
Cooper, Samuel Williams. *The Confessions of a Society Man,* 1887
Dahlgren, Madeleine Vinton. *Divorced: A Novel,* 1887
Daintrey, Laura. *Eros,* 1888
Dallas, Mary Kyle. *The Devil's Anvil,* 1889
Fawcett, Edgar. *A Daughter of Silence: A Novel,* 1890

———. *Divided Lives: A Novel,* 1888

———. *The Evil That Men Do: A Novel,* 1889

———. *How A Husband Forgave: A Novel,* 1890

———. *Mirian Balestier: A Novel,* 1888

Flagg, William Joseph. *Wall Street and the Woods; or, Woman the Stronger,* 1885

Fletcher, Robert Horne. *A Blind Bargain: A Novel,* 1889

Florence, William Jermyn. *Florence Fables,* 1888

Gally, James Wellesley. *Sand, and Big Jack Small,* 1880

Gibson, Eva Katherine. *A Lucky Mishap: A Novel,* 1883

Green, Warren. *A Blue-Grass Thoroughbred: A Novel,* 1889

Hawthorne, Julian. *A Dream and a Forgetting,* 1888

———. *The Professor's Sister: A Romance,* 1888

Hinman, Walter N. *Under the Maples: A Story of Village Life,* 1888

House, Edward Howard. *Yone Santo, a Child of Japan,* 1888

Jelley, Symmes M. *Shadowed to Europe: A Chicago Detective on Two Continents,* 1885

Jessop, George Henry. *Judge Lynch: A Romance of the California Vineyards,* 1888

Kerr, Alvah Milton. *Trean; or, The Mormon's Daughter,* 1889

Lambourne, Alfred. *Jo: A Christmas Tale of the Wasatch,* 1891

Lin, Frank. *What Dreams May Come,* 1888

McCarthy, Mrs. Emma W. *Assemblyman John; or His Wife's Ambition,* 1889

Mathews, Frances Aymer. *His Way and Her Will: A Novel,* 1888

———. *A Married Man: A Novel,* 1889

———. *The Princess Daphne: A Novel,* 1888

Mott, Edward Harold. *The Old Settler and His Tales of Sugar Swamp,* 1889

Nye, Edgar W. *Baled Hay: A Drier Book Than Walt Whitman's "Leaves O' Grass,"* 1884

———. *Bill Nye and Bommerang; or, The Tale of the Meek-eyed Mule,* 1881

———. *Bill Nye's Chestnuts Old and New,* 1888

———. *Forty Liars and Other Lies,* 1882

Peck, George Wilbur. *The Grocery Man and Peck's Bad Boy: Being a Continuation of Peck's Bad Boy and His Pa,* 1883

————. *How George W. Peck Put Down the Rebellion; or The Funny Experience of a Raw Recruit,* 1887

————. *Mirth for the Million: Peck's Compendium of Fun, Comprising the Immortal Deeds of Peck's Bad Boy and His Pa, and All the Choice Gems of Wit,* 1883

————. *Peck's Bad Boy and His Pa,* 1883

————. *Peck's Boss Book,* 1884

————. *Peck's Irish Friend, Phelan Geoheagan,* 1888

————. *Peck's Sunshine: Being a Collection of Articles Written for Peck's Sun, Milwaukee, Wis.,* 1882

————. *Peck's Uncle Ike and the Red-Headed Boy,* 1889

Piatt, Donn. *The Lone Grave of the Shenandoah and Other Tales,* 1888

————. *The Reverend Melancthon Poundex: A Novel,* 1893

Pierson, Ernest De Lancey. *The Black Ball: A Fantastic Romance,* 1889

————. *A Slave of Circumstances: A Story of New York,* 1888

————. *A Vagabond's Honor: A Romance,* 1889

Postgate, John W. *Two Women in Black: The Marvelous Career of a Noted Forger,* 1886

Rayne, Martha Louise. *Her Desperate Victory,* 1886

Saltus, Edgar Everston. *Eden: An Episode,* 1888

————. *Mary Magdalen: A Chronicle,* 1891

————. *The Pace That Kills: A Chronicle,* 1889

————. *A Transaction in Hearts: A Episode,* 1889

————. *A Transient Guest, and Other Episodes,* 1889

————. *The Truth about Tristrem Varisk: A Novel,* 1888

Shaw, Edward Richard. *The Pot of Gold: A Story of Fire Island Beach,* 1888

Spencer, William Loring. *A Friend to the Widow,* 1888

Stapleton, Patience. *Babe Murphy,* 1890

————. *Kady,* 1888

Wallace, William DeWitt. *Love's Ladder: A Novel,* 1886

Walworth, Jeannette Ritchie. *That Girl From Texas: A Novel,* 1888

Donohue and Henneberry Co.

For Donohue and Henneberry book publishing was essentially secondary; the firm specialized in printing and did all of the initial printing for Stone and Kimball. When it issued fiction, the firm promoted sensational adventure stories and became known for one of its subscription series during the latter part of the 1880's. In the 1890's Donohue and Henneberry republished the work of William Gilmore Simms and aided in the creation of another market for the American writer. Other significant works published by this house before 1893 were:

Allen, Luman. *Dane Walraven: A Tale of Old Boston,* 1892
———. *Lucia Lascar: A Romance of Passion,* 1890
[Brown, Walter.] *Mitylene: A Tale of New England and the Tropics.*
    By "Mi Esposa e Yo," Being a Narrative of the Personal Experi-
    ence of a father, his two daughters, and Their Physician, Ship-
    wrecked upon an Uninhabited Island of the Pacific, 1879.
Marean, Beatrice. *The Tragedies of Oak Hurst: A Florida Romance,*
    1891
———. *Won at Last: A Novel,* 1892
Roe, Edward Reynolds. *Balteshazzar: A Romance of Babylon,* 1890
Thayer, Emma. *The English-American,* 1890

S. C. Griggs and Co.

In the 1850's S. C. Griggs made available to Chicago readers some books which perhaps might otherwise have been lost to the city's market. Using a well-known technique, Griggs issued in the city books which were published—often simultaneously—in other cities by other firms. For example, in 1857 the New York firm of Sheldon and Blakeman published Mrs. Mary Denison's *Gracie Amber* and Mrs. Maria Richard's *Life in Israel; or Protraitures of Hebrew Character.* Both books were also printed by Griggs whose imprint also appeared on the title pages of the first editions.

As Griggs, however, moved into publishing without the attendant bookselling aspect, it became increasingly common to see the Griggs' imprint standing alone.

Carew, Richard. *Tangled: A Novel*, 1877
Casseday, Davis B. *The Hortons; or American Life at Home*, 1857
Ford, Mrs. Sallie. *Grace Truman; or, Love and Principle*, 1857
Freeman, Mrs. A. M. *Somebody's Ned*, 1879
[Higgins, Alvin S.] *The Mishaps of Mr. Ezekiel Pelter*, 1875
Livermore, Mrs. Mary Ashton. *Pen Pictures; or Sketches from Domestic Life*, 1862
Spenser, Lillian. *After All: A Novel*, 1885

Jansen, McClurg and Co.
A. C. McClurg and Co.

A. C. McClurg and Co. had been preceded by Jansen, McClurg and Co., a much more conservative firm. With the retirement of Jansen, McClurg was able to take more chances with his offerings. Those works issued after 1886 carried the A. C. McClurg imprint. Like some of the other Chicago firms, Jansen, McClurg had an arrangement with Atwood and Culver of Madison, Wisconsin whereby the two firms issued works simultaneously. Throughout the evolutionary history of the firm there was a strong interest in local color stories coupled with the usually popular sentimental romances. A. C. McClurg also became known as a firm which published much adventure as well as historical fiction. McClurg, who had an excellent "book sense," managed to publish the works of such popular writers as Joaquin Miller, John Hafferton, and Mary H. Catherwood. The firm did a great deal to "sponsor" Chicago writers and the literature of the Midwest.

Abbott, Mary Perkins. *Alexia*, 1889
———. *The Beverleys: A Story of Calcutta*, 1890
Ackerman, A. W. *The Price of Peace: A Story of the Times of Ahab, King of Israel*, 1893

Balch, Frederick Homer. *The Bridge of the Gods: A Romance of Indian Oregon,* 1890

Carpenter, Frank De Yeaux. *Round About Rio,* 1884

Catherwood, Mary H. *The Story of Tonty,* 1890

Chatfield-Taylor, Hobart C. *With Edge Tools,* 1891

Clark, Charlotte, *How She Came Into Her Kingdom: A Romance,* 1878

Coulter, John. *Mr. Desmond, U.S.A.,* 1886

Crane, James Lyons. *The Two Circuits: A Story of Illinois Life,* 1877

DuBois, Constance Goddard. *Columbus and Beatriz: A Novel,* 1892

———. *Martha Corey: A Tale of the Salem Witchcraft,* 1890

[Gatchell, Charles.] *Haschisch: A Novel,* 1886

Gunsaulus, Frank W. *Monk and Knight: An Historical Study in Fiction,* 1891

Hafferton, John. *The Jericho Road: A Story of Western Life,* 1877

[Holden, E. Goodman.] *A Famous Victory,* 1880

Marsh, Charles Leonard. *Opening the Oyster: A Story of Adventure,* 1889

Mason, Mary Murdoch. *Mae Madden,* 1876

Miller, Joaquin. *First Families of the Sierras,* 1876

———. *Shadows of Shasta,* 1881

[Munday, John William.] *The Lost Canyon of the Toltecs: An Account of Strange Adventures in Central America,* 1893

———. *The Spanish Galleon: Being an Account of a Search for Sunken Treasure in the Carribean Sea,* 1891

[Perrin, Raymond St. James.] *The Student's Dream,* 1881

[Perley, Mrs. T. E.] *From Timber to Town: Down in Egypt,* 1891

Phelps, Charles Edward D. *The Baliff of Tewkesbury,* 1893

Roberts, Charles Humphrey. *"Down the O-hi-O,"* 1891

[Robinson, Stephen T.] *The Shadow of the War: A Story of the South in Reconstruction Times,* 1884

Ruddy, Mrs. Ella Augusta. *Bachelor Ben,* 1875

———. *Maiden Rachel,* 1879

———. *Out from the Shadows: or Trial and Triumph,* 1876

[Scudder, Moses Leavis.] *Brief Honors: A Romance of the Great Dividable,* 1877

Steele, James William. *Frontier Army Sketches,* 1883

———. *West of the Missouri,* 1885

Taylor, Winnie Louise. *His Broken Sword,* 1888
Wolf, Emma. *Other Things Being Equal,* 1892
[Worthington, Elizabeth Strong.] *The Biddy Club and How Its Members, Wise and Otherwise, Some Toughened and Some Tender-Footed in the Rugged Ways of Housekeeping, Grappled with the Troublous Servant Question,* 1888

Charles H. Kerr and Co.

As a small firm willing to take greater chances than more established company, Charles H. Kerr enjoyed a measure of success as a "Chicago publisher." Among its most popular offerings were science fiction, utopian tales, and socialistic novels. Most of the firm's best-sellers were issued after 1893; however, it had produced a substantial list by that time.

Bickford, Luther H. *A Hopeless Case: The Remarkable Experience of an Unromantic Individual with a Romantic Name,* 1889
Cole, Cyrus. *The Auroraphane: A Romance,* 1890
[Fearing, Lillian Blanche.] *Asleep and Awake,* 1893
[Galloway, James M.] *A Pure-Souled Liar,* 1888
Hancock, Anson Uriel. *The Genius of Galilee: An Historical Novel,* 1891
————. *John Auburntop, Novelist: His Development in the Atmosphere of a Fresh-Water College,* 1891
————. *Silhouettes from Life on the Prairie, in the Backwoods,* 1893
[Roe, William James.] *The Last Tenet Imposed upon the Khan of Tomathoz,* 1892
Smith, Benjamin George. *From Over the Border; or Light On the Normal Life of Man,* 1890

Laird and Lee

In spite of the brief of existence of Laird and Lee, the company managed to publish some of the popular writers of nineteenth-century America. While it had its great period in the closing years of the 1890's, the firm issued significant work before 1893.

Altgeld, Emma Ford. *Sarah's Choice; or The Norton Family,* 1887
Fawcett, Edgar. *Women Must Weep,* 1891
Gardner, Fulton. *Checkered Lights: A Novel,* 1887
Gibson, Eva Katherine. *A Dark Secret,* 1889
Givens, Robert Cartwright. *The Rich Man's Fool,* 1890
Hatch, Mary R. *The Upland Mystery: A Tragedy of New England,* 1887
Holmes, Mrs. M. E. *Her Fatal Sin,* 1886
———. *The Tragedy of Redmount,* 1888
Kent, Winnifred. *Sell Not Thyself: A Novel,* 1893
Kirby, Louis Paul. *Agnes: A Story of the Streets: A Realistic Novel,* 1890
Merrill, James Milford. *Forced Apart; or Exiled by Fate,* 1886
———. *Tracked to Death; or Eagle Gray, the Western Detective,* 1886
Pinkerton, A. Frank. *Dyke Darrel, The Railroad Detective; or the Crime of the Midnight Express,* 1886
———. *Jim Cummings; or the Great Adams Express Robbery,* 1887
Read, Opie. *A Tennessee Judge,* 1893
Roe, Edward Reynolds. *Dr. Caldwell: or, the Trail of the Serpent,* 1889
Stevens, Charles McClellan. *The Adventures of Uncle Jeremiah and Family at the Great Fair,* 1893

F. Tennyson Neely Company

Whether Neely was more unscrupulous than other publishers of the period is a moot point; however, because of the suit filed by the prolific novelist Richard H. Savage against him, the firm of F. Tennyson Neely became associated with shoddy practices in the publishing world. The bulk of the firm's fiction was published after 1893 and before 1900. Such well known writers as Charles King and Opie Read wrote under the Neely imprint. For a while, Neely was successful in issuing popular fiction.

Fawcett, Edgar. *The Adopted Daughter,* 1892
Greene, Nanci Lewis. *Nance: A Story of Kentucky Feuds,* 1893

Nye, Edgar W. *Nye and Riley's Railroad Guide,* 1889
Powell, Talluah Matteson. *An English Girl in America,* 1892
Savage, Richard Henry. *For Her Life and Love,* 1893
————. *The Passing Shore,* 1893

George W. Ogilvie and Co.

Before it moved to New York in 1886, the firm of George W. Ogilvie was a popular publisher of sentimental fiction and detective stories.

Elwood, B. R. and Helen. *The Female Detective; or a Celebrated Forger's Fate,* 1885
Kutch, Archie. *Young Sleuth's Victory; or, A Detective's Adventure,* 1885
Strong, Edmund C. *Manacle and Bracelet; or, The Dead Man's Secret: A Thrilling Detective Story,* 1886
Urner, Nathan Dane. *Link by Link; or, The Chain of Evidence. A Great Detective Story,* 1886
Wallis, John Calvin. *A Frolicsome Girl,* 1886
Young, Ernest A. *File No. 114: A Sequel to File 113,* 1886
————. *Fred Danforth, the Skilled Detective, or the Watertown Mystery,* 1885
————. *Neil Nelson, the Veteran Detective; or Tracking Mail Robbers,* 1885
————. *A Wife's Honor: A Novel,* 1885

Rand, McNally and Co.

Up to the turn of the century Rand, McNally was a popular publisher of fiction in Chicago. Concentrating on the later developments in the local color movement, the firm issued a number of ante-bellum and Civil War books. During this period it also issued a great deal of the work of Richard Henry Savage whose work had been publishd by F. Tennyson Neely before the author and publisher broke over the matter of contractual relationships. The work of the company prior to the World's Columbian Exposition was typically an emphasis upon the sentimental romance.

Collins, Paul Valorous. *A Baton for a Heart: A Romance of Student Life in Paris*, 1888

Daly, James. *The Little Blind God on Rails: A Romaunt of the Gold Northwest*, 1888

Fawcett, Edgar. *Fabian Dimitry: A Novel*, 1890

Fish, Williston. *Won at West Point: A Romance of the Hudson*, 1883

Hall, Arthur Dudley. *Anselma; or In Spite of all*, 1886

————. *La Tosca: A Novel*, 1888

McGovern, John. *Daniel Trentworthy: A Tale of the Great Fire of Chicago*, 1889

Maitland, James. *Suppressed Sensations: or Leaves from the Note Book of a Chicago Reporter*, 1879

Postgate, John W. *A Woman's Devotion; or The Mixed Marriage. A Story of Rival Detectives. An American Novel Founded on Facts*, 1886

Read, Opie. *Mrs. Annie Green: A Romance*, 1889

————. *Up Terrapin River*, 1889

Reynolds, D. A. X. *Wolverton; or the Modern Arena*, 1891

Roe, Edward Reynolds. *The Gray and the Blue: A Story Founded on Incidents Connected with the War for the Union*, 1884

Ryan, Marah Ellis. *In Love's Domain: A Trilogy*, 1889

————. *Merze: The Story of an Actress*, 1889

————. *A Pagan of the Alleghenies*, 1891

————. *Squaw Elouise*, 1892

————. *Told in the Hills: A Novel*, 1891

Watson, Lewis H. *A Strange Infatuation*, 1890

Wellington, Mrs. A. A. *By a Way That They Knew Not*, 1885

White, Ten Eyck. *The Lakeside Musings*, 1884

Wiggs, Anna Oldfield. *Hayne Home*, 1890

Fleming H. Revell Co.

Fleming H. Revell was one of the few Chicago publishers who had actually been born in the city. Before Washington Street became one of the early social centers of the West Side which was made famous by the residences of such celebrated southerners as Carter Harrison and A. A. Honore (the father of Mrs. Potter Palmer), Revell was born on that street in 1849, just twelve years after the incorporation of the city. He began his business in 1869 and capitalized—as did many others—on the highly moralistic interests which followed the Civil War. As the publishers of *Everybody's Paper* and other journals of the period, he did extremely well. The period of evangelism and revivalism found a sympathetic supporter in Revell whose religious publications defined denominational lines. By the time that his sister had become the wife of the noted evangelist Dwight Moody, Revell's publishing patterns had become established.

According to George Doran, who had been hired by Revell in 1892, the Chicago publishers was extremely shrewd. In his memoirs *The Chronicles of Barabbas* (New York, 1952), Doran described Revell.

F. H. R. was a real Barabbas—one to be respected, for this must be said of him: In his business dealings there was no sign of pious palaver; he was direct and to the point. He could take a poor preacher's hard-earned $500 or a $1000 for the publication at the preacher's own expense of a volume of sermons or Bible studies without the slightest compunction, even though he realized that the same poor parson could not hope for any return—or at most for a very slight return—of his outlay. The operation was a painless one but many a poor patient suffered agonies afterward (p. 25).

While Revell is certainly to be remembered for his successes, the publisher is also known for his errors. For example, he refused to accept for publication *In His Steps: What Would Jesus Do?* by Charles Sheldon. The book went on to become one of the all-time American best-sellers after it was issued by an obscure Chicago firm, the Advance Publishing Co. He also refused the first work of Harold Bell Wright. Yet, as he turned—especially after 1893—to more general printing and to more fiction, he listed among his authors Roswell Field, the brother of Eugene.

F. J. Schulte Co.

Although it represented a small firm, F. J. Schulte Co. did a great deal for the advancement of Chicago literature primarily because the founder was willing to take chances with Chicago writers as well as with unpopular subjects. He decided, for example, to issue the work of Ignatius Loyola Donnelly whose socialistic novels were "ahead of the times." It is of some significance that Hamlin Garland placed two of his works with Schulte during this period as also did Stanley Waterloo. Both men had been quite vocal concerning the possibilities of Chicago becoming the literary capital of the United States.

Bierce, Ambrose. *The Monk and the Hangman's Daughter,* 1892
Donnelly, Ignatius Loyola. *Caesar's Column: A Story of the Twentieth Century,* 1890
———. *Doctor Huguet: A Novel,* 1891
Fawcett, Edgar. *American Push,* 1892
———. *An Heir to Millions,* 1892
Field, Roswell Martin. *In Sunflower Land: Stories of God's Own Country,* 1892
Garland, Hamlin. *A Member of the Third House: A Dramatic Story,* 1892
———. *Prairie Folks,* 1893
Holbrook, Elizabeth. *Old 'Kaskia Days: A Novel,* 1893
Read, Opie. *Emmett Bonlore,* 1891
———. *A Kentucky Colonel,* 1890
———. *Selected Stories,* 1891
Waterloo, Stanley, *A Man and a Woman,* 1892

Henry A. Sumner and Co.

During the 1880's some of the popular fiction issued from the city bore the imprint of Henry A. Sumner and Co., a firm about which little is known. Much of it was within the local color tradition; however, with the publication of John McElroy's *The Red Acorn* (1883) Henry Sumner proved that he was not afraid to tackle social subjects. Essentially, however, the novel—as a plea against war—was somewhat out of place with the usual romantic tales which carried the Sumner imprint.

Balch, William Stevens. *A Peculiar People; or, Reality in Romance,* 1881
Barnard, Edna A. *Maple Range: A Frontier Romance,* 1882
Bassett, Mary E. *A Fair Plebian,* 1883
Burnham, Clara Louise. *Dearly Bought: A Novel,* 1884
———. *No Gentlemen,* 1881
———. *A Sane Lunatic,* 1882
———. *We, Von Arldens,* 1881
Fox, Mrs. Emily. *Off the Rocks: A Novel,* 1882
Gibson, Eva Katherine. *Her Bright Future,* 1880
Hill, Mrs. Agnes. *Heights and Depths . . . ,* 1881
McElroy, John. *The Red Acorn: A Novel,* 1883
Paynter, Mary Moncure. *Caleb, the Irrepressible,* 1883
Porch, Hester Edwards. *An Ideal Fanatic,* 1883

In addition to the publishers already cited, there were others in the city. Many of them did not specialize in fiction; however, in the years before 1893, they issued at least one work of fiction which enjoyed a degree of success. That these firms were frequently short-lived should not be surprising, but taken together they give further evidence of the nature and scope of the publishing industry in Chicago between the Civil War and the World's Columbian Exposition. Generally speaking, these firms capitalized on the public interest in sentimental romances and fictionalized adventure stories; hence, they seldom published fiction which might have been considered controversial. Today some few of these firms exist merely on the title pages of obscure nineteenth-century novels.

AMERICAN PUBLISHING COMPANY
Leach, Bailey Kay. *Soulless Saints: A Strange Revelation,* 1892
A. H. ANDREWS AND COMPANY
Gibson, Eva Katherine. *A Woman's Triumph: A True Story of Western Life,* 1885
J. C. W. BAILEY
[Hill, Mrs. Agnes.] *Myrtle Blossoms* by Molly Myrtle, 1863
McAfee, Mrs. Nelly Nichol. *Gleanings from Fireside Fancies,* 1866
BRENTANO BROTHERS
[Sherman, Miss Frankie B.] *For Him; or A Promise Given and a Promise Kept* by Gipsy, 1887
CLARKE AND COMPANY
Corbin, Mrs. Caroline Elizabeth (Fairfield). *Rebecca; or a Woman's Secret,* 1867
COBURN AND NEWMAN PUBLISHING COMPANY
Humphrey, Mary A. *The Squatter Sovereign; or Kansas in the 50's. A Life Picture of the Early Settlement of the Debatable Ground. A Story Founded Upon Memorable and Historical Events,* 1883
W. B. CONKEY AND COMPANY
Logan, Belle V. *Her Shattered Idol,* 1893
Strong, Mrs. Mary F. *Margie's Mistake and Other Stories,* 1891
D. B. COOKE AND COMPANY
Smith, William L. G. *Life at the South; or Uncle Tom's Cabin As It Is. Being Narratives, Scenes, and Incidents in the Real "Life of the Lowly,"* 1852
COOK COUNTY REVIEW
[Givens, Robert Cartwright.] *The Millionaire Tramp* by Snivig C. Trebor, 1886
A. E. DAVIS
Nye, Edgar W. *Remarks by Bill Nye,* 1887
Wiggs, Anna Oldfield. *Apple Blossoms: A Novel,* 1886
DEARBORN PUBLISHING COMPANY
Nye, Edgar W. *Bill Nye Thinks,* 1888
————. *Nye and Riley's Railway Guide,* 1888
T. S. DENISON
McNutt, Cyrus F. *Broken Lives,* 1888

DIBBLE PUBLISHING COMPANY
Bloomfield, Will J. *Fay Banning,* 1893

DIXON AND SHEPARD
Paddock, Mrs. Cornelia. *In the Toils; or, Martyrs of the Latter Days,* 1879

J. E. DOWNEY AND COMPANY
Post, Charles C. *Driven from Sea to Sea: or Just A Campin',* 1884

MILTON GEORGE PUBLISHING COMPANY
Rogers, John Rankin. *The Graftons; or Looking Forward: A Story of Pioneer Life,* 1893

J. S. GOODMAN
Arthur, Timothy Shay. *Woman to the Rescue: A Story of the New Crusade,* 1874

GOODMAN AND DICKERSON
Diekenga, Inje Eildert. *Jasper Groales and His Wonderful Journeys on Christmas Eve,* 1888

F. M. HARLEY PUBLISHING COMPANY
Griswold, Sarah Elizabeth. *Out of Law into Gospel; or, God in Man,* 1893

GEORGE K. HAZLITT AND COMPANY
Matson, Nehemiah. *Raconter: Four Romantic Stories Relating to Pioneer Life, Scenes in Foreign Countries, Religious Fanaticism, Love, Murder,* 1882

HERMETIC PUBLISHING COMPANY
Phelon, William P. *Three Sevens: A Story of Ancient Initiations,* 1889
————. *A Witch of the Nineteenth Century,* 1893

HOMEWOOD PUBLISHING COMPANY
Postgate, John W. *The Strange Case of Henry Topless and Cap't. Shiers,* 1893

HORTON AND LEONARD
[Oliver Outwest.] *Adventures of Lena Ronden, a Southern Letter Carrier, or Rebel Spy: A Story of the Late War,* 1872
Smith, Stephe R. *Romance and Humor of the Road: A Book for Railway Men and Travellers,* 1871

JAMESON AND MORSE

Goodhue, James M. *Struck a Lead: An Historical Tale of the Upper Lead Region,* 1883

W. B. KEEN, COOKE, AND COMPANY

Nash, Willard Glover. *A Century of Gossip; or The Real and the Seeming,* 1876

Pinkerton, Allan. *Claude Melnotte as a Detective and Other Stories,* 1875

———. *The Detective and the Somnabulist. The Murderer and the Fortune Teller,* 1875

———. *The Expressman and the Detective,* 1874

Rayne, Mrs. Martha Louise. *Against Fate: A True Story,* 1876

Shuman, Andrew. *The Loves of a Lawyer, His Quandary and How It Came Out,* 1875

Swisher, Bella. *Struggling Up to the Light: The Story of a Woman's Life,* 1876

KEEN AND LEE

Arthur, Timothy Shay, ed. *The Mother's Rule; or the Right Way and the Wrong Way,* 1856

———. *Our Homes; Their Cares and Duties, Joys and Sorrows,* 1856

———. *The True Path and How to Walk Therein,* 1856

———. *The Wedding Guest: A Friend of the Bride and Bridegroom,* 1856

———. *Words of Cheer for the Tempted, the Toiling and the Sorrowing,* 1856

KNIGHT AND LEONARD COMPANY

Bross, William. *Legend of the Delaware: An Historical Sketch of Tom Quick. To Which Is Added the Winfield Family,* 1887

Yandell, Enid. *Three Girls in a Flat,* 1892

LEGAL NEWS COMPANY

[Fox, Mrs. Emily.] *Rose O'Connor: A Story of the Day* by Toler King, 1880

LEWIS PUBLISHING COMPANY

[Draper, John Smith.] *Shams; or, Uncle Ben's Experience with Hypocrites* by Benjamin Morgan, 1887

R. R. MC CABE AND COMPANY

[Sharon, Thomas.] *Viola; or Life in the Northwest* by a Western Man, 1874

MORRILL, HIGGINS AND COMPANY

Freeley, Mary Belle. *Fair to Look Upon,* 1892

Saltus, Edgar E. *Imperial Purple,* 1892

NEW ERA PUBLISHING COMPANY

Gordon, Helen Van-Anderson. *It is Possible: A Story of Life,* 1891

OPEN COURT PUBLISHING COMPANY

Carus, Paul. *Truth in Fiction: Twelve Tales with a Moral,* 1893

AUGUSTUS J. PALMER AND COMPANY

McKay, Ada Jean. *Silopaen: A Novel,* 1888

[Worthington, Elizabeth Strong.] *When Peggy Smiled: A Love Story* by Griffith A. Nicholas, 1888

RHODES AND MC CLURE

Givens, Robert Cartwright. *The Unwritten Will: A Romance,* 1886

Manly, Mrs. Angie Stewart. *Secrets of a Dark Plot in New York Society,* 1893

Nye, Edgar W. *Bill Nye's Cordwood,* 1887

Post, Charles C. *From the Wabash to the Rio Grande and Oklahoma: A Novel, with Characters True to Life,* 1886

Shore, Carrie L. *Connubial Bliss: Passages in the Lives of Alice and Arthur,* 1882

———. *Wedded and Saved! Spreading the Toils. Currently Wronged. The Sport of Fortune. Her Mistake. A Secret Engagement,* 1882

S. P. ROUNDS

[Baker, Mrs. Dephine Paris.] *Solon; or The Rebellion of '61. A Domestic and Political Tragedy by Delphine,* 1862

Kingsley, Adelaide Delia. *Heart or Purse: A Story of Today,* 1887

CHARLES H. SERGEL AND COMPANY

Post, Charles C. *Congressman Swanson,* 1891

N. C. SMITH PUBLISHING COMPANY

[Cohen, Alfred J.] *Conscience on Ice: A Story of the Stage* by Allan Dale, 1892

UNION BOOK CONCERN

Miller, Emily Clark. *The Parish of Fair Heaven,* 1876

JOHN R. WALSH AND COMPANY
[Chamberlain, J. E.] *Cotton Stealing: A Novel,* 1866
WESTERN NEWS COMPANY
Ford, E. L. *Madelaine Darth,* 1867
Upton, George P. *Letters of Peregrine Pickle,* 1869

Some nineteenth-century writers were perceptive enough to realize the advantages of local firms, and their works appeared simultaneously from several companies. For example, when Mark Twain's *Roughing It* appeared in 1872, the book was published in Hartford, Conn. but was also issued in a number of other places —including Chicago by the firm of F. G. Gilman. A few years later John Esten Cooke's *Justin Harley: A Romance of Old Virginia* appeared as one of the 1874 books of the Today Printing and Publishing Co.

The notations "privately printed," "printed for the author," or "published for the author" were relatively common in nineteenth-century Chicago. Printing firms were pleased to accommodate budding authors as well as the more established ones and with no hesitation issued their works. The reasons for such printing undoubtedly were just as valid as those used by writers today whose efforts appear as "private" publications. Thus to ascribe merit or to deny it is highly dependent upon the nature of the work. There were instances in Chicago when such works came from the pens of writers whose work was also issued by recognized firms. In 1884 Robert Cartwright Givens, who used the pseudonymn Snivig C. Trebor, had his *Land Poor: A Chicago Parable* privately printed; and in 1889 Helen Van Metre Van-Anderson Gordon, whose work appeared under a variety of names, issued her *The Right to Knock: A Story* and ascribed authorship to "Nellie V. Anderson." It is significant that frequently these "privately printed" works were essentially social protests which attacked the prevailing established elites in the city or supported unpopular causes.

One of the earliest examples of a novel which was printed for the author was Mrs. Elizabeth A. Roe's *Aunt Leanna; or, Early*

Scenes in Kentucky (Chicago, 1855). It supported the anti-slavery cause; however, feelings ran high in the city. While the supporters of Abolition were vocal and active, there was also an extremely vocal minority supporting the southern cause and a functioning literary group whose members used their talents to present their opposing views. It is not surprising that Charles Palmer's *A Fool's Effort: An Echo of Civic Administration* was not only "printed for the author" but also published under a pseudonym. In 1891 as the city prepared for the World's Columbian Exposition and tried to convince the rest of the nation that Chicago had a "clean" government, a work which criticized the stupidity of the political establishment would not have been appreciated in the city.

For one reason or another, the following works which were privately printed apparently achieved a degree of popularity. Their distribution, however, seldom went beyond the city.

Armstrong, Le Roy. *An Indiana Man,* 1890
[Bone, Will, Jr.] *The "Impenetrable Mystery" of Zora Burns,* 1888
Bowers, S. Jay. *"Pleasure Promoter,"* 1888
Brown, Fred H. *One Dollars' Worth,* 1893
Clarke, Mrs. Mary G., comp. *Sunshine and Shadows Along the Pathway of Life,* 1865
Clarke, S. W. *From the Sublime to the Ridiculous,* 1875
————. *Happy Home, Woman's Rights, and Divorce,* 1875
[Denison, Thomas S.] *An Iron Crown: A Tale of the Great Republic,* 1885
————. *The Man Behind: A Novel,* 1888
Mallow, Marsh, pseud. *The Woman Did It,* 1879
[Palmer, Charles T.] *A Fool's Effort: An Echo of Civic Administration,* 1891
Paynter, Mary Moncure. *The Little Lass,* 1886
Reeves, Arthur Middleton. *Jan: A Short Story,* 1892
Roe, Mrs. Elizabeth A. *Aunt Leanna; or Early Scenes in Kentucky,* 1855
[Smith, Emery P.] *The Triple Wedding; or Secrets Revealed,* "True Story by a Clergyman," 1892

[Stowe, Mrs. H. M.] *The Elixir of Life; or Robert's Pilgrimage:* An Allegory by Elene, 1890

Tuttle, Hudson. *Clair: A Tale of Mormon Perfidy,* 1881

Weaver, Anna D. *Richard's Crown, How He Won and Wore It,* 1882

[Young, Alexander.] *Why We Live by Summerdale,* 1880

BIBLIOGRAPHICAL ESSAY

Many years have passed since Ralph Rusk's pioneer study *The Literature of the Middle Western Frontier* (2 vols. New York: Columbia University Press, 1925-26). What he recorded has not changed, but there has been an increased interest in regional materials and a greater tendency to judge such works on their own terms rather than on some absolute—albeit nebulous—scale. One of the earliest attempts to view the Middle West as a unique region with a literature peculiar to itself was also produced in 1926. Dorothy Dondore's *The Prairie and the Making of Middle America: Four Centuries of Description* (Cedar Rapids, Iowa: The Torch Press) presents a detailed study of the locale. It is also perhaps interesting to note that two of the best studies of various aspects of the literary development of Chicago were done under the auspices of Sociology. In 1906 the University of Chicago Press reprinted Herbert Fleming's papers entitled "The Literary Interests of Chicago" which had appeared in *The American Journal of Sociology* (Vols. XI and XII). The Fleming work, *Magazines of the Market-Metropolis: Being a History of the Literary Periodicals and Literary Interests of Chicago,* eventually joined that of Hugh D. Duncan whose *The Rise of Chicago as a Literary Center From 1885 to 1920* is subtitled "A Sociological Essay in American Culture." The work was a 1948 Ph.D. dissertation and was subsequently published by the Bedminster Press (Totowa, N.J.) in 1964. While there have been studies of Chicago's literature, they invariably—with few exceptions—have focused upon the Chicago Renaissance or the figures of that era, but the period up to the late 1880's has generally been ignored. *Prairie Voices: A Literary*

History of Chicago from the Frontier to 1893 is one attempt to fill that void.

Whether for good or ill, Chicago has not suffered from an absence of the "written word." Books and articles about the city are easily accessible. Much of the available material is a product of the interpretations of twentieth-century cultural historians, many of whom have produced some excellent and perceptive studies. In addition there are a number of popular works which include the inevitable "picture books." Although these differ substantially in quality, they prove that the city has an irresistible appeal for certain audiences. Perhaps the time will soon come for a critical bibliography of the plethora of materials.

I am not unmindful of the twentieth-century materials; however, for anyone interested in them, bibliographies are easily obtained. For example, I included a rather varied and full bibliography of the life and culture of Chicago in *In the City of Men: Another Story of Chicago* (Nashville, 1974) pp. 435-468. Hence, the following selected bibliography represents—for the most part —those nineteenth-century materials which provide a means for a presentation of the literary life of the city up to 1893. Reconstructing any segment of nineteenth-century Chicago is made less difficult by the rich resources of the library of the Chicago Historical Society and the Newberry Library of Chicago.

There is still much work to be done on the forays of the French into what is now the Illinois territory. Of particular help are the following works:

Albach, James R., comp. *Annals of the West: Embracing a Concise Account of the Principal Events which have occurred in the Western States and Territories, from the Discovery of the Mississippi Valley to the year Eighteen Hundred and Fifty-Six. Compiled from the most authentic sources* (1857)

Bourne, Annie N., trans. *The Voyages and Explorations of Samuel de Champlain, 1604-1616, Narrated by Himself,* 2 vols. (1922)

Cox, Isaac Joslin, ed. *The Journeys of Réné Robert Cavelier Sieur de La Salle as related by his faithful Lieutenant, Henri de Tonty et al.,* 2 vols. (1905)

Delanglez, Jean. *Some of La Salle's Journeys* (1938)

Kellogg, Louise P., ed. *Early Narratives of the Northwest, 1634-1699* (1917)

Sagard-Théodat, Gabriel. *Histoire du Canada . . .* (1636)

Thwaites, Reuben G., ed. *The Jesuit Relations and Allied Documents* (1896-1901)

The Fort Dearborn story for years was hampered by the apparent confusion which existed among the survivors. There were many discrepancies in the tales which were told, but sometimes legends are made out of distortions and confusion. This is an instance of truth being stranger than the fiction. Yet to the credit of the novelists, it must be remembered that many of them were attempting to give order and form to the events of August 15, 1812. And to some extent they have been able to find meaning as they have attempted to recreate an experience which preceded the founding of Chicago. Two major efforts have been made to correct the inaccuracies of Juliette Kinzie's work, and for anyone interested in the fiction written about the incident, the two works are indispensable:

Kirkland, Joseph. *The Chicago Massacre of 1812. A Historical and Biographical Narrative of Fort Dearborn* (1893)

Quaife, Milo Milton. *Chicago and the Old Northwest, 1673-1835: A Study of the Evolution of the Northwestern Frontier, Together with a History of Fort Dearborn* (1913)

Kirkland brings to his work his eye for romance and fiction although he notes the errors of former reports; however, Quaife presents the documents of the case and clearly explains the points at which Mrs. Kinzie changed the facts.

Of great help in re-creating the nineteenth-century were the many histories, personal narratives, and biographies. In fact references to the existence of certain journals and newspapers came from these sources. The number of histories produced in nineteenth-century Chicago and the multitude of biographical statements were partially based upon the belief that the city provided a viable model for understanding the American experience. And—as I have repeatedly said—these historians subconsciously reflected a view of history not unlike that of the New England Puritans who believed that they were as "a city on a hill." In addition, they were convinced—as they looked about the city which they were creating—that the formula for success had been effectively executed in Chicago. The pride of these early historians cannot be overlooked; however, these works tend to be extremely laudatory and few of them are either critical or selective. Yet when they are taken together, they form an interesting commentary on one facet of the writing experience about the city. Strictly speaking, of course, the authors might be called "historians" only by the broadest definition of the term.

There is a close relationship between the historical and the biographical studies. Both are predicated upon the theory that the story of Chicago is a story of the men and women who built the city. In the former, however, people are subordinated to place. And in the biographies, place is subordinated to people. But like the historical works, the autobiographies and biographies emphasize the manifest destiny of the city. As might be expected, many of them were written years after the events and necessarily viewed the early days of Chicago with a rose-tinted view which was not always justified.

The following citations represent a selected listing of those sources which are of great benefit for one interested in nineteenth-century Chicago and which proved especially helpful to me in the reconstruction of the literary life of the city prior to the World's Columbian Exposition. Since all of the following works were published in Chicago, I have dropped from each citation the name of the city and have included only the printer/publisher with the date of publication. One word of caution, however, it was not unusual for a book to be issued in the city under several different imprints. The publisher cited is the edition which I used.

Ahern, M. L. *The Political History of Chicago: 1837-1887* (Donohue and Henneberry, 1886).

Andreas, A. T. *History of Chicago: from the Earliest Period to the Present Time.* 3 vols. (A. T. Andreas, 1884-86).

Ayer, I. Winslow. *The Great North Western Conspiracy in all Its Startling Details* (Round and James, 1865).

Blanchard, Rufus. *Discovery and Conquest of the Northwest with the History of Chicago.* 2 vols. (R. Blanchard and Co., 1898-1900).

Bross, William. *History of Chicago. Historical and Commercial Statistics . . . What I Remember of Early Chicago* (Jansen, McClurg and Co., 1876).

Chamberlain, Everett. *Chicago and Its Suburbs* (T. A. Hungerford and Co., 1873).

Colbert, Elias. *Chicago: Historical and Statistical Sketch of the Garden City* (P. T. Sherlock, 1868).

Guyer, I. D. *History of Chicago: Its Commercial and Manufacturing Interests and Industry: Together with Sketches of Manufacturers and Men Who Have Most Contributed to Its Prosperity and Advancement, with Glances at Some of the Best Hotels; Also the Principal Railroads Which Center in Chicago* (Church, Goodman and Cushing, 1862).

Hurlbut, Henry H. *Chicago Antiquities: Comprising Original Items and Relations, Letters, Extracts and Notes Pertaining to Early Chicago* (Fergus Printing Co., 1881).

Kirkland, Joseph. *Story of Chicago* (Dibble Publishing Co., 1892).

Mason, Edward G., ed. *Early Chicago and Illinois* (Fergus Printing Co., 1890).

Moses, John and Joseph Kirkland. *History of Chicago.* 2 vols. (Munsell and Co., 1895).

Phillips, George S. *Chicago and Her Churches* (E. B. Myers and Chandler, 1868).

Seeger, Eugene. *Chicago, The Wonder City* (George Gregory Printing Company, 1893).

Wentworth, John. *Early Chicago. A Lecture Delivered Before the Sunday Lecture Society, at McCormick Hall, on Sunday afternoon, May 7th, 1876* (Fergus Historical Series #7), 1876
————. *Early Chicago. Fort Dearborn. An Address Delivered at the Unveiling of the Memorial Tablet to Mark the Site of the Block-House on Saturday afternoon, May 21st, 1881* (Fergus Historical Series, #16), 1881.
Wright, John S. *Chicago: Past, Present, Future* (Horton and Leonard, 1868).
————. *Investments in Chicago* (n.p., 1858).

One of the more interesting by-products of the interest of Chicagoans in their city was the production of guidebooks and handbooks. These seemed to proliferate and apparently there was a good market for them. While many of these flourished in the days just preceding the World's Columbian Exposition, the type was always prevalent from the beginning of the city's literary history. Often they appeared under the imprints of several different publishers or were issued by the authors. The following represent a selection of the more popular nineteenth-century guides and handbooks. The absence of a publisher in the citation indicates that the work was issued by the author.

Barton, Elmer. *A Business Tour of Chicago, Depicting Fifty Years of Progress,* 1887
Blanchard, Rufus. *Citizens' Guide for the City of Chicago. Companion to Blanchard's Map of Chicago,* 1866
Chicago: A Strangers' and Tourists' Guide to the City of Chicago (Religio-Philosophical Publishing Association, 1866).
Flinn, John, ed. *Chicago . . . A Guide, 1891-1893,* 1893
[Glossop, Frank]. *Glossop's Street Guide, Strangers' Directory and Hotel Manual of Chicago,* 1888
Harris, I. C., comp. *The Colored Men's Professional and Business Directory of Chicago,* 1885, 1886
[Marquis, Albert Nelson]. *Marquis' Handbook of Chicago,* 1885
Merchants and Manufacturers Illustrated Chicago Guide for 1880, 1880

[Orear, George Washington]. *Commercial and Architectural Chicago*, 1887

Schick, Louis. *Chicago and Its Environs*, 1891

Thorne, W. and Co. *Chicago in 1860: A Glance at Its Business Houses* (Thompson and Day, 1860).

Zell, T. Ellwood. *A Guide to the City of Chicago: Its Public Buildings, Places of Amusement, Commercial, Benevolent and Religious Institutions; Churches, Hotels, Railroads . . .* , 1868

Among the specialized histories within the city were those which pertained exclusively to the establishment of individual churches as well as those on specific industries. Among the most significant are:

Ackerman, William K. *Historical Sketch of the Illinois Central Railroad, together with a Brief Biographical Record of its Incorporators and some of its early officers* (Fergus Printing Co., 1890).

[Bentley, Cyrus]. *History of the First Baptist Church, Chicago, with the Articles of Faith and Covenant, and a Catalogue of its Members, December, 1889,* 4th ed. (R. R. Donnelley and Sons, 1889).

Bisbee, Lewis H. and John C. Simonds. *The Board of Trade and the Produce Exchange, Their History, Methods, and Law* (Callaghan and Co., 1884).

Bross, William. *Banking, Its History, Commercial Importance and Social and Moral Influence. A Lecture before the Mechanics' Institute, of the city of Chicago, delivered Thurs. evening, Feb. 24, 1852* (Langdon and Rounds, 1852).

Chicago: Her Commerce and Railroads [from the *Daily Democrat*] (Democrat Press Book and Job Printing Office, 1853).

[First Congregational Church of Chicago]. *The Quarter-Centennial of the First Congregational Church of Chicago, May 21st and 22nd, 1876* (Culver, Page, Hoyne and Co., 1876).

Grant, John C., ed. *The Second Presbyterian Church of Chicago, 1842-1892* (Knight and Leonard, 1892).

[Reed and Company]. *The Lumber Industry of Chicago,* 1882

Wing, Jack. *The Great Union Stock Yards of Chicago* (Religio-Philosophical Publishing Association, 1865).

The popular literature of the city included that designed to expose the seamier side of urban living. We tend to think of these works as products of the twentieth-century interest in scandal, gossip, and muck-raking; however, even in the nineteenth century there was a market for sensational studies of the city. Among the popular ones which were produced are:

Chicago's Dark Places (Woman's Temperance Publishing Association, 1891).

DeWolfe, Lyman E. *The Social Evil: Whither Are We Drifting* (Privately printed, 1870).

Quinn, John Philip. *Fools of Fortune, or Gambling and Gamblers* (The Anti-Gambling Association, 1892).

Stead, William T. *If Christ Came to Chicago! A Plea for the Union of All Who Love in the Service of All Who Suffer* (Laird and Lee, 1894).

Although many of them were published in the twentieth century, the following autobiographies and personal narratives are concerned with nineteenth-century activities in Chicago.

Addams, Jane. *Twenty Years at Hull House.* New York: Macmillan Co., 1910.

Cleaver, Charles. *Early Chicago Reminiscences* (Fergus Historical Series, #19). Chicago: Fergus Printing Company, 1882.

Cook, Frederick Francis. *Bygone Days in Chicago: Recollections of the "Garden City" of the Sixties.* Chicago: A. C. McClurg and Co., 1910.

Ericsson, Henry. *Sixty Years a Builder: The Autobiography of Henry Ericsson.* Chicago: A Kroch and Son, 1942.

Farwell, John V. *Some Recollections of John V. Farwell.* Chicago: R. R. Donnelley and Sons Co., 1911.

[Ferry, Mrs. Abby (Farwell)]. *Reminiscences of John V. Farwell By His Elder Daughter.* 2 vols. Chicago: Ralph Fletcher Seymour, 1928.

Foresman, Hugh A. *These Things I Remember.* Chicago: Scott, Foresman and Co., 1934.

[Gage, Lyman J.] *Memoirs of Lyman J. Gage.* New York: House of Field, Inc., 1937.

Gale, Edwin O. *Reminiscences of Early Chicago and Vicinity.* Chicago: Fleming H. Revell, 1902.

Gregory, Addie Hubbard. *A Great-Grandmother Remembers.* Chicago: A. Kroch and Son, 1940.

Harrison, Carter, H. *Stormy Years: The Autobiography of Carter H. Harrison: Five Times Mayor of Chicago.* Indianapolis: Bobbs-Merrill Company, 1935.

Kirkland, Caroline, ed. *Chicago Yesterdays: A Sheaf of Reminiscences.* Chicago: Daughaday and Company, 1919.

Koerner, Gustave. *Memoirs of Gustave Koerner, 1809-1896.* 2 vols. Cedar Rapids, Iowa: The Torch Press, 1909.

Read, Opie. *I Remember.* New York: Richard R. Smith, Inc., 1930.

Root, George F. *The Story of a Musical Life.* Cincinnati: The John Church Co., 1891.

Spies, August. *August Spies' Autobiography.* Chicago: Nina van Zandt, [1887].

Stephenson, Isaac. *Recollections of a Long Life, 1829-1915.* Chicago: Privately printed, 1915.

Stone, Melville E. *Fifty Years a Journalist.* Garden City, N.Y.: Doubleday, Page and Company, 1922.

Sullivan, Louis H. *The Autobiography of an Idea.* New York: Press of the American Institute of Architects, Inc., 1924.

Swing, David. *The Message of David Swing to His Generation. Addresses and Papers.* New York: Fleming H. Revell Co., 1913.

Thompson, Slason. *Way Back When: Recollections of an Octogenarian.* Chicago: A Kroch and Son, 1931.

Wentworth, John. *Congressional Reminiscences* (Fergus Historical Series, #24). Chicago: Fergus Printing Company, 1882.

Wilkie, Franc B. *Personal Reminiscences of Thirty-Five Years of Journalism.* Chicago: F. J. Schulte and Co., 1891.

The following biographical studies represent just a few of those which deal with the period from the frontier to 1893; however, they are relatively indicative of the type of work which has been produced about the leaders of Chicago.

Ander, Oscar Firtiof. *T. N. Hasselquist: The Career and Influence of a Swedish-American Clergyman, Journalist, and Educator*. Rock Island, Ill.: The Augustana Library Publications, 1931.

Arnold, Isaac N. *William B. Ogden; and Early Days in Chicago* (Fergus Historical Series #17) Chicago: Fergus Printing Company, 1882.

Biographical Sketches of the Leading Men of Chicago, Written By the Best Talent of the Northwest. Chicago: Wilson and St. Clair, 1868.

Currey, Josiah Seymour. *Chicago: Its History and Its Builders, a Century of Marvelous Growth*. 5 vols. Chicago: S. J. Clarke Publishing Co., 1912.

Fergus, Robert. *Biographical Sketch of John Dean Caton, Ex-Chief Justice of Illinois* (Fergus Historical Series, #21). Chicago: Fergus Printing Company, 1882.

Grover, Frank R. *Father Pierre Francois Pinet, S. J. and His Mission of the Guardian Angel of Chicago, A.D. 1696-1699*. Chicago: Chicago Historical Society, 1907.

McIlvaine, Mabel, ed. *Reminiscences of Chicago During the Civil War*. Chicago: R. R. Donnelley and Sons, 1914.

————. *Reminiscences of Chicago During the Forties and Fifties*. Chicago: R. R. Donnelley and Sons, 1913.

————. *Reminiscences of Early Chicago*. Chicago: R. R. Donnelley and Sons, 1912.

[Parsons, Lucy E.] *Life of Albert R. Parsons*. Chicago: Mrs. Lucy E. Parsons, Publisher and Proprietor, 1889.

Porter, Mary H. *Eliza Chappell Porter: A Memoir*. Chicago: Fleming H. Revell, 1892. [Published for the benefit of the Oberlin Missionary Home Association.]

Presbyterian Church in the U.S.A. Chicago Presbytery. *The Trial of the Rev. David Swing Before the Presbytery of Chicago . . .* Chicago: Jansen, McClurg and Co., 1874.

Scammon, Jonathan Young. *William B. Ogden* (Fergus Historical Series, #17). Chicago: Fergus Printing Co., 1882.

Starring, Mrs. Helen (Swing), comp. *David Swing: A Memorial Volume*. Chicago: F. T. Neely, 1894.

Wood, David Ward, ed. *Chicago and Its Distinguished Citizens: The Progress of Fifty Years.* Chicago: Milton George Company, 1881.

After the incorporation of the city, the two events which provoked a great deal of discussion in print were the Chicago Fire of 1871 and the Haymarket Affair of 1886. In addition to the reports of the major newspapers which are readily available, the following represent the best contemporary accounts of the two catastrophes.

Chicago Fire:

Angle, Paul M., ed. *The Great Chicago Fire Described in Seven Letters By Men and Women Who Experienced Its Horrors.* Chicago: Chicago Historical Society, 1946.

Blatchford, Mary Emily and Eliphalet Wicker. *Memories of the Chicago Fire* [Chicago:] Privately printed, 1871.

Colbert, Elias and Everett Chamberlain. *Chicago and the Great Conflagration.* Cincinnati: C. F. Vent, 1871.

Goodspeed, Reverend E. J. *History of the Great Fires in Chicago and the West.* Chicago: J. W. Goodspeed, 1871.

Loesch, Frank J. *Personal Experiences During the Chicago Fire, 1871.* Chicago: Privately printed, 1925.

McIlvaine, Mabel, ed. *Reminiscences of Chicago During the Great Fire.* Chicago: R. R. Donnelley and Sons, 1915.

Sheahan, James W. and George P. Upton. *The Great Conflagration.* Chicago: Union Publishing Co., 1872.

Haymarket Affair:

The Accused The Accusers. The Famous Speeches of the Eight Chicago Anarchists in Court. Chicago: Socialistic Publishing Society, n.d.

Altgeld, John P. *Reasons for Pardoning Fielden, Neebe, and Schwab.* [Springfield, Ill.: n.p., 1893.]

Ames, Sarah E. *An Open Letter to Judge Joseph E. Gray . . . Why the Undertone?* Chicago: n.p., 1893.

Bonney, Charles Carroll. *The Present Conflict of Labor and Capital.* Chicago: Chicago Legal News Co., 1886.

Parsons, Albert R. *Anarchism: Its Philosophy and Scientific Basis as Defined by Some of Its Apostles.* Chicago: Mrs. A. R. Parsons, Publisher, 1887.

[Parsons, Lucy E.] *Life of Albert R. Parsons.* Chicago: Mrs. Lucy E. Parsons, Publisher and Proprietor, 1889.

————. *Souvenir Edition of the Famous Speeches of Our Martyrs, Delivered in Court.* 6th ed. Chicago: Lucy E. Parsons, Publisher, [1912].

Salter, William M. *What Shall Be Done with the Anarchists? A Lecture Before the Society for Ethical Culture of Chicago.* Chicago: The Open Court Publishing Co., 1887.

Schaack, Michael J. *Anarchy and Anarchists . . . The Chicago Haymarket Conspiracy.* Chicago: F. J. Schulte and Co., 1889.

Spies, August. *August Spies' Autobiography.* Chicago: Nina van Zandt, [1887].

Zeisler, Sigmund. *Reminiscences of the Anarchist Case.* [Chicago:] Chicago Literary Club, 1927.

Much of the history and cultural life of the city during the nineteenth century can be re-told through the histories of the clubs and organizations which flourished in the developing city and were so very influential. These works are especially important today for providing an intimate picture of the concerns as well as the aspirations of the active membership of these groups. Among the most significant for a study of Chicago's literary life are:

Baird, Mrs. Lyman. *History of the Chicago Home for the Friendless, 1859-1909.* Chicago: n.p., 1909.

Beadle, Muriel. *The Fortnightly of Chicago: The City and Its Women: 1873-1973.* Chicago: Henry Regnery Company, 1973.

Blair, Edward T. *A History of the Chicago Club.* Chicago: R. R. Donnelley and Sons, 1898.

Blair, Sarah Seymour. *Early Social Life in Chicago. A Paper Read Before the Fortnightly Club of Chicago, November 9, 1905.* Chicago: Privately printed, 1916.

Brown, Edward Osgood. *The Chicago Literary Club; with a Bibliography.* Excerpts from the Papers of the Bibliographical Society of America, n.d.

The Chicago Clubs. Chicago: Lanward Publishing Company, 1888.

Frank, Henriette Greenbaum and Amalie Hofer Jerome, comps. *Annals of the Chicago Woman's Club* . . . Chicago: Chicago Woman's Club, 1916.

Freeman, William H., comp. *The Press Club of Chicago.* Chicago: The Press Club, 1894.

Gookin, Frederick William. *The Chicago Literary Club: A History of Its First Fifty Years.* Chicago: Printed for the Club, 1926.

[Lowther, Thomas D., comp.] *Memorials of the Old Chicago Library, Formerly Young Men's Association and of the New.* Chicago: John K. Scully, Printer, 1878.

[Woman's Christian Temperance Union.] *A Brief History of the Woman's Christian Temperance Union.* 3rd ed. Evanston, Ill.: The Union Signal, 1907.

The complete story of the book trade in Chicago as well as the history of journalism has yet to be told. While there have been many instances of the use of the Middle West as illustrative materials, research has continued to focus upon the firms and journals of the eastern seaboard with the tacit conclusion that "little" occurred west of the Alleghenies. Certainly many well-known firms and journals were produced in the cultural centers of the East, but this should not preclude an understanding of the efforts executed in the Middle West with Chicago as that region's cultural center. The following books might prove helpful in supplying the necessary background information for an attempt to re-create what happened in the West.

Johannsen, Albert. *The House of Beadle and Adams and Its Dime and Nickel Novels: The Story of a Vanished Literature.* 2 vols. Norman, Okla.: University of Oklahoma Press, 1950.

Kinsley, Philip. *The Chicago Tribune: Its First Hundred Years.* 2 vols. Chicago: The Chicago Tribune, 1943-45.

Kramer, Sidney. *A History of Stone and Kimball and Herbert S. Stone and Co., with a Bibliography of Their Publications, 1893-1905.* Chicago: University of Chicago Press, 1940.

Lehmann-Haupt, Hellmut, R. S. Grannis, and L. C. Wroth. *The Book in America: A History of the Making, Selling, and the Collecting of Books in the United States.* New York: R. R. Bowker Co., 1939.

Morris, Jack Cassius. *The Publishing Activities of S. C. Griggs and Co., 1848-1896; Jansen, McClurg and Company, 1872-1886; and A. C. McClurg, 1886-1900.* Unpublished M.A. Thesis, University of Illinois, 1941.

Mott, Frank, Luther. *American Journalism: A History 1690-1960.* New York: Macmillan, 1962.

————. *Golden Multitudes.* New York: R. R. Bowker Co., 1947.

Pearson, Edmund. *Dime Novels; or Following an Old Trail in Popular Literature.* Boston: Little, Brown and Co., 1929.

Scott, Franklin William. *Newspapers and Periodicals of Illinois, 1814-1879.* Springfield: Illinois State Historical Library, 1900.

Sereiko, George E. *Chicago and Its Book Trade, 1871-1893.* Unpublished Ph.D. Dissertation, Case Western University, 1973.

Sheehan, Donald. *This Was Publishing: A Chronicle of the Book Trade in the Gilded Age.* Bloomington, Ind.: Indiana University Press, 1952.

Shove, Raymond Howard. *Cheap Book Production in the United States, 1870-1891.* Urbana: University of Illinois Library, 1937.

Stafford, Marjorie. *Subscription Book Publishing in the United States, 1865-1930.* Unpublished M.S. Thesis, University of Illinois, 1943.

Stevens, Roland Elwell. *The Open Court Publishing Company, 1877-1919.* Unpublished M.A. Thesis, University of Illinois, 1943.

Sutton, Walter. *The Western Book Trade: Cincinnati as a Nineteenth-Century Publishing and Book-Trade Center.* Columbus: Ohio State University Press for the Ohio Historical Society, 1961.

Tebbel, John W. *A History of Book Publishing in the United States.* Vol. 1. *The Creation of an Industry, 1630-1865.* New York: R. R. Bowker, 1972. Vol. 2. *The Expansion of an Industry, 1865-1919.* New York: R. R. Bowker, 1975.

Walsh, Justin. *To Print the News and Raise Hell: A Biography of Wilbur Storey.* Chapel Hill: University of North Carolina Press, 1968.

INDEX

American Dream, The, xvi, 15, 68, 248, 308, 318
American Fur Company, 110–11, 113
American literary theory, fallacies of, 27
American News Company, 137
American novelists, urbanity of, 5–6
American Peeress, An, 310
American Poultry Journal, 375
American Publishing Company, 449, 465
American Push, 245, 463
American Renaissance, xvi, 30
Anderson, John, and Company, 449
Anderson, Sherwood, 25, 373
Anderson, William J., 177
Andreas, Alfred T., 79, 82, 89, 96–97, 105, 112, 115, 119, 126, 137, 165, 172, 187–90, 195–96, 207, 326, 380, 447
Andrews, A.H., and Company, 449, 465
Andrews, Shang, 311–14, 315
"Annals of Chicago, The," 97–103
Annals of the West, The, 107
anti-slavery journals, 94, 426–30 *passim.*
anti-slavery movement, 79, 82, 83, 84, 85, 90, 91, 103, 153, 469–70

Anti-Slavery Opinion Before the Year 1800, 447
Apollo Music Club, 204
Appeal, 420
architects, response of—to the commercial nature of the city, 372
architecture, xii, xiv, 20, 22, 23–24, 185–86, 356, 360, 371–73
—and literature as a result of the same forces, xiv
ambiguities of, 371
commercial, 356
flimsiness of ante-fire, 185–86
Henry B. Fuller's attitude toward, 23–24
World's Columbian Exposition, 360
"Arizona John," 232
Arkansaw Traveler, 232, 297–98
Armour, Philip, 14, 70, 71, 372
Arnold, Isaac, 118, 178–79, 447
Arnold, Matthew, 255
Arrington, Alfred W., 182
Art Institute, 18, 204, 256, 358–59, 385
art journals, 384–85
Arthur, Timothy Shay, 217, 466, 367
Arts for America, 385
Asleep and Awake, 458

Belford, Charles, 238
Belford, Robert, 238
Belford, Clarke, and Company,
238–41, 245, 414, 449,
452–55;
fiction published by, 452–54
financial difficulties of, 241
subscription series of, 452
Belford's Magazine, 195, 414
Bellow, Saul, 19, 318
Beloit College, 164
Besant, Sir Walter, 363–64
best sellers, 230, 241, 248, 462
Better Covenant, 82
Between the Gates, 341
Bierce, Ambrose, 463
Bigot, Mary Healy, 68, 223
"Bill Nye," *see* Nye, Edgar W.
*Biographical Sketches of Lead-
ing Men of Chicago,* 119
biographical studies, 119–20
examples of, 481–83
Bishop, Robert Hamilton, 321
Black, Margaret Potter, 68
Black Hawk War, The, 134–35
Black Laws of Illinois . . . ,
176–77, 419
Black Patridge, 45, 49, 56, 58,
61, 64
*Black Patridge: or the Fall of
Fort Dearborn,* 66
"Blade of Grass, A," 125
Blake, The Rev. James Vila,
447
Blakely, George E., 413

Blanchard, Rufus, 93, 137, 184
Bland, Mrs. M. Cora, 375, 439
Blaney, Dr. James Van Zant,
80
Block, Louis J., 354
Board of Lady Managers, 361
Bohemian journals, 401
Bomb, The, 366–67
Bonney, Charles C., 363
Bonney, Edward, 138–40, 441
book production in the West,
485–86
book publishers and sellers, re-
lationship between, 215
Booksellers Row, 228
book selling, 91, 228, 235–36
common practices in, 238
discount methods of, 238–39
boosterism, *see* Chicago, spirit
of
border fighting, 42
Bordland, G.W., and Company,
216
Boston, 204, 356
Boyce, W.D., 414
Boyington, W.W., 359
Bradley, Mary Hastings, 65–
66, 68
Bradwell, Mrs. Myra, 375, 389
Brashler, William, 19, 37, 367
Brautigam and Keen, 216
Brentano Brothers, publishers,
449, 465
British relationship to the

"Science of the Fire, The," 166
scientific journals, 437–38
Scott, Franklin W., 380, 440
Scott, Sir Walter, 73, 239
Scribner, Charles, 280
Scribner's Monthly, 210, 267, 280, 331
Scripps, John L., 87, 164, 378, 422
"second city," 20, 31, 218–19, 220, 280
Second Presbyterian Church, 83
secret societies, journals of, 438–39
Selected Stories (Read), 245
"Self-Reliance," 11
sentimental fiction, 232–33, 236, 460, 461, 464, 465–69
Sergel, Charles H., and Company, 468
seventeenth century, 3–41 *passim.,* 47, 69, 356
Sewell, The Rev. Alfred, 170–71, 379, 408, 409
Seymour, Horatio, 302
Shadow of Victory, The, 65, 67
"Shall I Know Her Again," 327
"Shall Illinois Be Africanized," 157
Shapiro, Dena E., 31
"Sharps and Flats," 304
Sheahan, James W., 151, 422
Sheldon, Charles, 462

Sheldon, William, 432
Shepard, Frank, and Company, 451
Sherwood, George and Company, 451
Shipman, Dr. George E., 415, 416, 434
Short Ravelings from a Long Yarn, 325
Shove, Raymond, 234
Simms, William Gilmore, 73, 455
Sinclair, Upton, 366–67
Siringo, Charles A., 232
Sister Carrie, 12
skeleton frame construction, 372
slave narratives, 177, 178
"Sleigh Ride, The," 130, 136
Sloan, Oscar, 90
Sloan, Walter B., 90, 137, 411, 422
Sloan's Garden City, 80, 90–91, 137
Smith, Alson J., 21; on the importance of the "Red Light District," 314–15
Smith, F.B., 235
Smith, Harry B., 273, 293, 414
Smith, J.A., 230
Smith, Captain John, 117
Smith, Joseph, 255
Smith, N.C., Publishing Company, 451, 468
Smith, O.J., 422

Long before the regional movement in American literature, Chicago writers had issued a call for "western literature." Until the latter part of the 1880's, however, the history of Chicago is generally dominated by the tales of the phenomenal growth of the city. Bold, innovative, frankly materialistic, Chicago stood—according to Robert Herrick at the end of the nineteenth century—as "an instance of a successful, contemptuous disregard of nature by man." The novelist continued: "In the case of Chicago man has decided to make for himself a city for his artificial necessities in defiance of every indifference displayed by nature." Certainly much of the story of Chicago has always revolved around the builders who—in the midst of the prairie—fashioned a city of their own making.

While most definitions of Chicago emphasize the materialistic nature of the city, early Chicagoans demonstrated their interest in the development of a cultural life. These migrants from the East, the South, and the West as well as from the teeming cities and by-ways of Europe realized that literature was one means by which they might establish the seriousness of their great enterprise. *Prairie Voices* is the record of the evolution of literature in the city. If it is not a history replete with such novelists as Fuller, Herrick, and Dreiser or if it is not as fascinating as the accounts of the twentieth-century Chicago Renaissance, it is nonetheless significant as it surveys the formative years of literary concern in an urban area little regarded as a bastion of culture.

Prairie Voices presents the early Chicagoans who tried to produce the city's first literature. At the same time it focuses upon several eras of the city's history. It begins by locating the beginning of Chicago's literature in the French culture which flourished on the Middle Border when Chicago was a territory and before this country became a nation. It examines the role of the Fort Dearborn Massacre in the creation of a very important legend in the city. It looks at the developments of literary interests during the Civil War and subsequently traces the effects of the Fire of 1871. From that traumatic experience to the Exposition of 1893 it summarizes the evolution of many of the publishing firms and writers.